PARENT-CHILD INTERACTION AND YOUTH REBELLION

Parent-Child Interaction and Youth Rebellion

BY
MARIANNE MARSCHAK

GARDNER PRESS, INC. NEW YORK

Distributed by the Halsted Press
Division of JOHN WILEY & SONS, INC.

New York • London • Sydney • Toronto

114231

Gardner Press, Inc.
19 Union Square West
New York 10003

Distributed solely by the Halsted Press Division
of John Wiley & Sons, Inc., New York

Library of Congress Cataloging in Publication Data

Marschak, Marianne.
Parent-child interaction and youth rebellion.

Includes index.
1. Parent and child—case studies. 2. Adoles-
cent psychology—Case studies. 3. Youth movement
—United States—Case studies. 4. Youth movement
—Germany—Case studies. 5. Youth movement—
Israel—Case studies. I. Title.
HQ755.85.M28   301.42'7   78-16157
ISBN 0-470-26476-4

Printed in the United States of America

In Memory of Jascha
who helped through questioning and clarifying,
with patience and love.
And to our children and grandchildren

Contents

PREFACE

Chapter 1   OBJECTIVE AND METHOD   1

Brief Overview   1

Two Youth Movements   2

Studies on Dissidence   8

Identification: The Role of Imitation   12

A Method of Studying the Parents' Influence on
    the Child   17

Chapter 2   OBSERVATIONS ON THE NUCLEAR FAMILY   25

Affection and Direction   25

Stephen and John   28
    The Picture of the Past   28
    Parent-Child Interactions   33
    The Picture of the Present   43

The Parents' Perception of the Child's Individuality: Paul and
    Jerry   63
    Mother with Jerry: First Interactions after Birth   64
    Paul and Jerry at Preschool Age: Parent-Child Interactions   68

Morality: General Remarks   86
    Paul and Jerry   93
    An Enlightened Alternative: Ronny   99

Some Considerations   106

Chapter 3   PATTERNS OF PARENT-CHILD INTERACTION
                  AND COUNTERCULTURE GROUPS   111

Grete—A Member of the German Youth Movement   112
    Childhood   113

Grete Joins the D.W.V.   117
Trude: The Leader   120
Exclusion   124
Issues of Identification   128

Communes and Communities   131
Commune Haven   134
Commune Pharos   146
Catherine—Another Leader   154
Issues of Identification   159
Childrearing in Communes   164

Some Characteristics of the Counterculture Person   178

Chapter 4   TWO PATTERNS OF PARENT-CHILD INTERAC-
            TION IN ISRAEL: KIBBUTZ AND URBAN
            FAMILIES   187

Childrearing in the Kibbutz   187

Studies Comparing Kibbutz and Family Care   188
Research Procedures   190
The Families   191
Parent-Child Interactions   192
Fantasy Activity: Finger Puppets   193
Organizing an Environment: Small Figures   203
Separation: The Adult Leaves the Room   210
"Take Your Child on Your Lap"   220
Modeling and Imitation   224
Stress   225

Conclusions   228

Chapter 5   SUMMARY   229

APPENDIX: THE MARSCHAK   INTERACTION   METHOD
            (MIM) Abbreviated Form   235

A. Introduction   237

B. Key of Symbols   246

C. Judging Procedure   251

D. General Lists for Describing Behaviors—All Tasks   254

E. Two Examples Illustrating the MIM Method   282

INDEX   288

Preface

We have long known that the personalities of children are influenced by the parents' behavior. The central conjecture of this book is that the interactions between parents and children from early infancy on, determine the extent to which the children pattern themselves after the parents.

Specifically it is suggested that the following characteristics of the parents' interaction with the child influence the extent to which the young adult adopts or rejects the parent's life style and values: the quality of parental affection and the quality of parental direction as well as the parent's perception of the child's individuality.

This book attempts to trace these influences in two ways. On the one hand, interviews with members of two countercultures are used to relate the lack of identification with parental values and life style to their early interactions with their parents. On the other hand, observations on parents and young children in prearranged, comparable situations are presented. They are used to study the influence of parent-child interactions on observable expressions of the child's identification.

In Chapter 1, the reader is introduced to the objective and the method of the study. Chapter 2 compares nuclear families who differ in the parent-child interactions, and the children's later identification with the parents. Chapter 3 studies representatives of two counterculture movements: the German youth movement of the first quarter of the century, and a present-day urban commune in the United States. In Chapter 4, the interaction and identification of children with parents or a parental figure in a kibbutz is compared with Israeli urban families. Chapter 5 summarizes the results.

The book concludes with an Appendix which contains a manual for setting up and evaluating the controlled interactions used.

Acknowledgments

There are a number of persons to whom I am obliged for their assistance in writing this book. Foremost among these are my daughter, Ann Jernberg, who encouraged and advised me on the project from its inception, and Theodore Hurst, who was a thorough and thoughtful critic. I also want to thank Lance Lee whose editorial help was invaluable. I am grateful further to Phyllis Booth and David Horne who read the manuscript and, as professionals in the field, made many helpful suggestions. My special thanks go to Sibylle Escalona who, in 1958, at my first try-out of the interaction method, reassured me of its definite promise; and to Justin D. Call, M.D.,who was my co-investigator at the Los Angeles study and from whose knowledge, insight, and research experience I benefited greatly.

A volume of this kind progresses from the idea to its realization only haltingly and by detours. I must therefore express my gratitude to Gardner Spungin for his forebearance and understanding which made the publication possible. Thanks also to Dr. Tony Greenberg, who prepared the index.

CHAPTER 1

Objective and Method

BRIEF OVERVIEW

Our objective is to study how the counterculture youth movements are influenced by the process of the child identifying with the parent or parent figure and how the identification is influenced by the type of interaction between parent and child.

The *counterculture* will be illustrated by the German youth movement originating at the turn of the century, and by the recent hippie and commune movements.

Identification—to identify with another person is to replicate aspects of his personality, i.e., both his observable behavior and deeper characteristics, as revealed, for example, by projective tests and in therapeutic sessions. Identification presupposes an emotional tie with the person taken as a model.

It is important to distinguish between the concepts of *imitation* and *identification*. To imitate is to replicate some observable characteristic of another person. An emotional tie with the other person need not be involved.

We shall speak of identification and of its *reversal*: a young person's tendency to develop traits which are in some sense opposite to those of the parent. We shall refer to this tendency also as *dissidence*.

The reference, in the definition of identification, to the parent's deeper characteristics is relevant in the context of this book because of our concern with the parental values and lifestyles to which the adolescent will or will not conform. When studying the effect of parent-child interaction upon identification we shall include incidents of the child's imitation of observable behavior of the parent. In addition, our method attempts to reveal the replication of deeper characteristics of the parent to whom the child is emotionally attached.

Our definitions do conform with the way Jean Piaget uses the term

1

imitation [31:81-82], and Sigmund Freud uses the term identification [10], [1] though, perhaps not our "identification reversal."

Interaction is understood as the behavior of two or more people toward each other. Mostly, it is used here in reference to the behavior of individual children with their parents and shows the reciprocal actions or influences that occur.

TWO YOUTH MOVEMENTS

The youth movements of this century originating in different countries and at different times pose a similar problem to the student of child development. They signify a deviation from the usual identification process. For many years my concern with this phenomenon was limited to the German youth movement initiated at the turn of the century. My interest stemmed from having belonged to the movement in my youth, and from trying to understand its sources three decades later with a mature and, I hope, more objective mind.

The self-styled *Wandervoegel*[2] (birds of passage) made their appearance around 1900. Their association continued throughout the Second World War. They were officially dissolved by Hitler, but some individuals met illegally. Others became Nazis. Among these, a number became leaders in the Hitler Youth Organization [14:196, 197, 246].[3]

Not unlike today's youth rebels, the Wandervoegel abandoned their parents' values and lifestyle. Then, as now, the culture of middle-class parents was threatened by new ideas hostile to the establishment.

The Wandervoegel, carrying heavy knapsacks and guitars, marched away, first on Sundays only from their homes, cities and mechanized life, and engaged in a crusade for simplicity, nature, and self-reliance in moral matters. With surprisingly sure taste, these young fundamentalists created a culture of their own complete with dress, language, tools, art, and ethics. They developed a myth that drew its roots from medieval and neomedieval poetical writings and songs whose emphasis on friendship and love replaced, to some extent, the traditional family ethics and religion.

The Wandervoegel appeared irrational to other members of society in their anti-intellectual and pro-nature stance and in their leaning toward a romantic intensity of feeling, a sublimated love for each other, a uniqueness of speech and clothing, an "all or nothing" attitude, and a high-minded seriousness. They were remarkably independent in their unconventional way of life and in their cultural innovations. Significantly, a few surviving members of the Wandervoegel, now in their seventies and eighties and spread over the continents, continue to embody this culture, leaving traces in their children and even grandchildren.

The movement was started by Hermann Hoffmann, a law student at

Berlin University, who led a group of middle-class schoolboys first on Sunday hikes outside of Berlin and later on mountain excursions through Germany.[4] He was convinced of the character-building influence of removing these youngsters from their overcontrolling or overprotective homes, their reliance on technology such as traveling by railroad instead of walking, and exposing them to the beauty and the harshness of nature. He also tried to promote a sense of comradeship among the boys by living together out of doors on vacation trips, braving the elements of nature and taking care of each other. He started what has been called a "hiking community" (*Wandergemein-schaft*) [15:43-44].

Before Hoffmann left Germany he turned over the W.V. activities to the nineteen-year-old Karl Fischer who had occasionally replaced him as group leader. Fischer added romantic and mildly rebellious ideas to the movement. He was more concerned than Hoffman with conflicts experienced by individual members in their families.

He set up "consultation hours" (*Sprechstunden*) to acquaint newcomers with their obligations and to secure their pledge of loyalty. [15:75]. He created an unconventional style of dress, began the singing of folk songs and the use of special phrases such as "Heil" instead of the bourgeois greeting "Guten Tag." He started an initiation ceremony for new members.

I used the phrase "mildly rebellious" because, although Fischer stressed the autonomy of youth ("Youth must lead Youth"), he also wooed the cooperation of more progressive parents to gain prestige and financial support for the organization. (Fischer's emphasis on the autonomy of youth must have conflicted with his own desire for unrestricted, sole leadership in the movement). In an autobiographical sketch written in 1927, Fischer traces his dedication to the problems of youth to his empathy as an adolescent with the runaways of the early 1900s.

When I was 14 to 15 years old, I was concerned with stories of runaways (Durchbrenner) then frequently reported in newspapers. Young persons left their homes and the country, to find their happiness somewhere else. These stories excited me greatly, in a way which I myself could not understand. I was partly an observer, partly inwardly reacting like them. It occurred to me that if youngsters from good families can run away like that, there must be something wrong, not with the boys but with their family relationships; and that it was wrong to prohibit that adventurous roaming to faraway places and call it foolish [15:192].

Fischer continues that he thought the motive to run away needed to be channeled and he saw in Hoffman's hiking groups a way of redirecting this drive. However, Fischer was more of a dreamer and more ambitious than Hoffmann. He visualized himself as a founder of a youth league in Germany and abroad which would counteract the oppression by the bourgeois system. His seriousness and intense concern for young people attracted a great number of them, and he was the first to form subgroups (*Ortsgruppen*) of the W.V. in other cities outside of Berlin. In time, new leaders established themselves and formed separate W.V. associations. They disputed Fischer's claim to represent the highest authority in the movement. Unable to endure the jealousies of the leaders and the rivalries among them, Fischer resigned from his W.V. duties in 1906. He followed his adventurous impulse and enlisted in a navy batallion assigned to Kiautschau, a German colony in China. Alienated and disillusioned, after fifteen years abroad he returned to Germany. Upon his arrival, he was greeted like a historical figure by a W.V. contingent. He was not motivated himself or encouraged by others to resume a role in the movement.

Even without Fischer's charismatic leadership, the movement spread throughout Germany. By 1913 it comprised about ten thousand members. Fischer had been concerned with enlisting parents' cooperation to boost the prestige of the movement; however, criticism of a materialistic and constraining elder generation became more articulated as the movement expanded. Gustav Wyneken, a progressive educator and spokesman for the movement, accused the parents of having "condemned" the young to "passivity and lifelessness" and of having "assaulted" (*vergewaltigt*) their "soul" and "conscience" [43:258].

In October 1913, two thousand W.V. hiked up the Hohe Meissner, a mountain in Southwest Germany. They were accompanied by a few intellectuals and artists, among them the sociologist Max Weber and the writer Gerhard Hauptmann. The occasion was the centenary of the battle of Leipzig in which Germany had been liberated from French domination. The W.V. youth had been excluded from the official celebration, and at their Meissner jamboree, they protested against the oppression by the system. They made speeches and sang folk songs. They proclaimed an oath pledged by all participants that they would devote themselves to a simple life and to inner truthfulness; that they would live according to their own determination and the demands of their own conscience alone (*nach eigener Bestimmung, vor eigener Verantwortung*) [42:254]. Like the early period of the flower children, in the prewar phase the German movement was apolitical and romantic. Ten years later the stark realities of the First World War, of defeat and revolution, transformed a great number of Wandervoegel into radicals of either the Marxist or fascist factions, into renewed believers in the Christian faith or in old German heathenism. Their quest for direction and their despair over the dimming of bright hopes bears an obvious similarity to recent dissident American youth. Jerry Rubin, a leader of the anti-Vietnam War movement, raging against the exploitation of the masses and the hypocrisy and selfishness of the establishment, could well have emerged from the ranks of the radical youth in postwar Germany.

I first became aware of the common features of the two youth movements when encountering the "beatniks" in San Francisco. The similarities became even more striking with the appearance of the "hippies." For in them there was the same irrationality and intensity of feeling, the same tendencies toward mysticism, and toward the natural and the primitive in art and technique as opposed to the mechanized life of their elders. It was uncanny to see how youth of a different generation, on a different continent, forty years later, improvised a form of life so similar that parallels can be found in verbal usage, natural food, simple clothing of handwoven linen, and wooden bead necklaces; in experiments in communal living; in the artistic style they preferred and in the artists they chose as idols! Herman Hesse, for example, became a cult hero in both movements.

> Each heart a different answer
> Each soul a separate name
> The images are many
> But the source remains the same.

This verse by Tennyson was painted in psychedelic letters on the wall of the Los Angeles Playhouse where *Hair* was produced. Fifty years earlier, the German youth movement had expressed a similar all-embracing feeling combined with a sense of self-assuredness:

> For in this world the noises are thousandfold
> But there is only one melody
>
> *(Denn in der Welt sind die Geraeusche tausendweise
> Doch nur eine Melodie)*

In spite of the striking similarities between German and American youth movements, there are, as one might expect of movements originating in different countries and at different periods of history, some important dissimilarities.

Each W.V. group, of about ten members, had a leader whose authority they respected and to whom they often became emotionally attached. This attachment tended to strengthen the loyalty not only to the group but to the W.V. movement as a whole. Although they became more prominent in its later commune phase, such leaders were not typical of the hippie phase of the recent movement.

The sexual freedom among hippies, furthermore, is in sharp contrast to the sexual continence adhered to by the W.V. and reinforced in its initial phase by prohibiting mixed groups.

The two movements differed in one other important respect. While the hippies believed in racial equality, two large W.V. associations, the Wandervogel E.V. (Eingetragener Verein) and the A.W.V. (Alt Wandervogel) did not admit Jews. We cannot know how many parents of the anti-Semitic ("Voelkische") Wandervoegel shared their children's fascination with the mysterious creed of the ancient Germans and with the superiority of the

Aryan race. Nor do we know whether some of these ideas and beliefs of the Voelkische W.V. developed in opposition to the Christianity of their parents. It is far easier to see the hippies' radical position on racial integration as a protest against their conventional middle-class parents' resistance to complete integration.

As to the impact of the Voelkische, or Aryan ideology, on the W.V. movement as a whole, W. R. Lacqueur, in his book on the history of the German Youth Movement, states that "there was apparently no open and organized anti-Semitism" in the movement [17:76]. He describes some W.V. associations as favoring a *numerus clausus* for Jewish members and others as avoiding a stand on the issue, thereby displaying their ambiguity toward the Jewish question. A few W.V. associations openly protested against the exclusion of Jews. Two decades later, a minority of the W.V. engaged in dangerous, anti-Nazi activities (See also p. 108, note 4 and p. 184, note 8).

In 1912, some young middle-class Berlin Jews responded to the anti-Semitic tendencies in the W.V. by forming their own W.V. called Blau-Weiss. Although the colors were those of the Zionist flag, later to become the Israeli flag, the Blau-Weiss Association was, initially, not exclusively committed to Zionism.[5] In a letter published by the Blau-Weiss journal in 1914, a soldier who had been a Blau-Weiss member writes: "The love to the Jewish people does not contradict the love to our German Fatherland" [41:206]. At this early period, the song book of the Blau-Weiss contained ninety W.V. songs and only twenty-seven Jewish or Hebrew songs. By 1918 when a new, mostly Jewish song book was published, this percentage had changed drastically. The book was soon sold out [41:210].

The Blau-Weiss W.V. resembled the other German youth movement groups in many respects. Like the others, the Blau-Weiss group protested against the "self-satisfied satiation of their bourgeois environment." The Blau-Weiss despised luxury and preferred simplicity bordering on crudeness in clothes and furniture, as shown, for example, in the style in which they furnished their "nest" (clubhouse).

Partly because of the contact between German and Polish youth movement groups of Jewish origin, the influence of Zionism on the Blau-Weiss increased during and after the war. The members of the Polish movement also imitated the German W.V. [21:46, 50]. But in contrast to the somewhat unclear objectives of the German group, the aim of the Polish youth movement was unambiguous. Having personally experienced the struggle for existence of Jews in Eastern Europe, their ultimate goal was to achieve the independence of the Polish Jews and the Jewish people in general. Their revolutionary élan seemed to have attracted young Jews from other countries to Palestine, especially since 1917 when Palestine as a home for the Jews had become a political reality.

How did the Jewish parents respond to their children's joining the W.V. movement and the Jewish youth movement in particular? Only a minority of

Jewish middle-class parents were Zionists; for the most part they were patriotic Germans and Austrians with a strong loyalty to their respective homelands, eager to pursue the burgeoning industrial and cultural opportunities of prewar Europe. Indeed, these "assimilated" Jews, relying heavily on their next generation to continue in their footsteps, were sharply disappointed if their children escaped from the industrial society into the peace of nature. There had been a strong opposition by Jewish parents against "the unsupervised hiking of their protected children" [41:205]. But the break between the two generations became evident only when the young, who embraced both the Jewish cultural past and a new Jewish nationalism, migrated to Palestine.

Here, of course, was a unique circumstance which permitted the realization of the dream of a new society and which promised to lead to the creation of a nation that is, fittingly, both new and very old.

While some of the first youthful arrivals to Israel from Europe, being ill-prepared for the harsh conditions on the land, fell seriously ill and had to leave for the cities, a small contingent founded the first kibbutz. The importance of their affiliation with the youth movement was described by one member as follows:

It was at this time that this small band of immigrants had an intense group experience that was to leave its mark on their future course, an experience which is remembered today as their "Golden Age." They were living in Nevei Gila, a spot in some then-isolated mountains and it was there that they first experienced the meaning of an important youth movement concept—a small community whose solidarity and integration are based on intimate personal relations (and on) many of the same sentiments as the Bunderlebnis of the German youth movement. . . . [39:53-54].

The present author was surprised during her first visit to a kibbutz in 1967 to find that the youth group experience of the original settlers had left distinct traces upon even the recent generation of kibbutz members. This was first conveyed to her by the style of the women's dresses and the bare, rustic furnishings of their rooms. It became even more apparent later in the members' straightforward way, in their earnestness, in the sincerity with which they related their experiences—even unfavorable ones—and in their devotion to nature, to children, and to the simple life. But it was most apparent of all in their pervasive group solidarity. Former members of the Blau-Weiss movement in Israel and of the Wandervogel in Germany have each held periodic reunions characterized by all the trappings and fervor of the original movement. The following excerpts from letters by two old D.W.V. members after their first reunion in 1954, attest to the enduring power of their youthful identifications.

Strange, strange, an hour after we met, forty years had not passed. One was young again like at that time. There was that sense of belonging together. . . .

Already on the second day, we told each other that it is unbelievable that we can be towards each other exactly as we were forty years ago. I believe from what I saw and heard that this coming together has given each of us an unheard-of lift. For a long time, maybe for the rest of our lives. And why? Because, for all of us, these same great experiences of nature, comradeship, friendship, had been the firm, all-embracing bond which has formed our character essentially and permanently, although maybe each in his or her way. . . . This feeling of happiness was so strong that it seemed impossible to talk about it with "other" persons. No one else would have understood us [36].

STUDIES ON DISSIDENCE

We have pointed, earlier, to the similarities between the previous and the present countercultures. Thus, among the motivations for joining the W.V. as well as the hippies, dissidence from parental values plays a major role. Since dissidence is crucial for our investigation, we shall report on some relevant work published on the issue.

We shall apply the general term "dissidence" to those attitudes, beliefs, and behavior in which persons deviate from the norms established by their societies. In the present framework, dissidence is understood as nonidentification of young persons with norms sanctioned by society and adhered to by their parents. When attitudes, beliefs and behaviors are acquired by members of a society through mutual contact and communication, the anthropologist R. Redfield speaks of a "culture" [32:93]. We shall refer to those attitudes, and other characteristics shared by dissident persons, but not by others, as "counterculture," a term frequently used in this context.

Dissidence in both countercultures discussed above has been described as having emerged in an increasingly competitive, materialistic, urban middle class. It has also been pointed out that the biological and psychological changes of adolescence render youth, at that stage, conflict-prone, and ready to join a movement which promises independence from adult pressures and which provides security through appreciation by the group [6:178-179]. And, finally, influenced by Freudian ideas, a number of investigators have attempted to attribute the origin of dissidence to family conflict in the individual's childhood, among them Kenneth Keniston in his study of the "uncommitted" youth [13:284-294].

A large body of literature has been written on the German youth movement.[6] The first sociological analysis of the W.V. movement was published in 1925 by Charlotte Luetkens, who had been a W.V. herself [20:23]. Luetkens sees, among the sources of dissidence, the impersonal character of the industrial society with its increase in technology and specialization, its emphasis on discipline and obedience, characteristic of the Prussian-German "State of Officials," a term coined by Max Weber [42:664 ff]. She also draws attention to ideas which the young gleaned from antibourgeois literature and socialist treatises. These publications made them more acutely aware of the national chauvinism, and of the insincerity and authoritarian demands of their parents with whom they felt no inner bond. Not only did the sons decline to emulate their fathers' professions and way of life, they even "resisted to become men" [20:12]. This characterization by Luetkens coincides with the impression of youthfulness conveyed, even in old age, by youth movement members (see below, p. 112).

Other authors corroborate Luetkens's assumption that the pressures of the industrial society played a part in the dissidence of that segment of youth which joined the W.V. In some publications, parental characteristics other than authoritarianism are assumed to have contributed to dissidence. For example, mention is made of the parents' expectations of being closely replicated by their children, of the parents' double morality, their concentration on material success, and the uninspiring, "dull," and matter-of-fact climate of the home [37:236; 31:11-12]

There are, finally, a number of autobiographies whose authors had belonged to the W.V. These individuals emphasize how important the Wandervogel experience had been in the formation of their personality. They also describe, in detail, certain parental characteristics which they consider to have been decisive for their dissidence. Some of these attitudes vary, from parent to parent, and may even be contradictory. Thus one father is described by his daughter as demanding, fear-inspiring and erratic [3:13-24]while another father is portrayed by his son as being, even as an adult, subdued by his own father and overlenient with his son [40:12-16]. These contrasting characteristics nevertheless rendered both parents equally ineffective as models for identification. Both parents created in their children the tendency to deviate from their values. The ineffectualness of such types of parents as models for their children's identification has been described in a study of "alienated" students [13].

Let us now return to the origin of the present-day dissidence. Investigators of the current counterculture frequently discuss the economic and technological advances, and the "dehumanizing" effect of the increase in industrialization. These descriptions of changes in the environment resemble some statements made by Luetkens on the "mechanizing, anti-traditional spirit of the era of the machine," and the "filing-cabinet system, where human beings become 'hands'" [20:16]. The similarity of the reasoning is not surprising since the same processes of industrialization and specialization continue at an even more rapid pace today. It is not too far-fetched to assume that the German youth movement was the first concerted protest of youth against an industrial society, a protest which expressed itself in dissidence from the values and lifestyle of that society; and that the present counterculture is a later form of this same protest.

Since we are mainly concerned here with a person's relationship with his parents as this may influence the course of his identification, we shall now examine some of the conclusions which have been reached about dissidence as originating from tensions in the parent-child relationship.

In his book, *The Conflict of Generations*, published in 1969, Lewis S. Feuer explains the dissidence of student movements in different countries and at different historical periods as arising from an unconscious struggle of sons against fathers [8]. According to this Freudian model, fear and hate of the father are generalized to all members of the older generation and to the "system," the "establishment," etc. In contrast to Luetkens's proposition that dissidence is invariably a reaction to authoritarian upbringing, Feuer assumes that a weakening of the father's power, a "de-authorization" of the father, brought on through certain critical social or political circumstances, may result in the son's dissidence. Thus the intensity of the Depression and the menace of Nazism (unopposed by the older generation) were, according to Feuer, responsible for the Marxist student movement of the 1930s in the United States. Similarly, Japan's defeat after the Second World War, for which the sons rebuked their fathers, led to the Japanese students' strikes and to the activist student movement of the Zengakuren period.

R. Flacks, on the other hand, in a questionnaire study published in 1967, compared the attitudes of activist vs. nonactivist college students and of their fathers, and arrived at still a different set of causes for dissidence [9]. He saw the activists, engaged in debates, strikes, and protest movements, as taking their fathers as models of identification. Although the sons were somewhat more radical than their fathers, they agreed on the whole with their fathers' political opinions (e.g., on civil rights issues) and with their fathers' values such as high regard for intellectual creativity [9:67].

As to their relationships with their parents, the student activists rated their parents as mild, warm, lenient and, not motivated to intervene in the decisions of their adolescent sons and daughters. Similar to Feuer's interpretation of the Japanese activist movement, Flacks explains the more radical viewpoint of the activist students (as compared with that of their fathers) by their resentment against their fathers' reluctance to act upon their convictions. It has also been suggested that the parents may be "secretly proud of their children's eagerness to implement the ideas they as parents have only given lip-service to" [13:119-120].

Let us turn now to a less active type of dissidence investigated in Kenneth Keniston's book *The Uncommitted. Alienated Youth in American Society*, which appeared in 1965 [13]. It is based on interviews with Harvard College students and on their responses to a projective test, the TAT [29]. One group of students characterized as "alienated" rejected the major values of American culture and considered any civic and political activity as futile. Although their social and educational background was similar to that of the activists in the Flacks study, they were social outsiders and rejected "success" in any form. Their outlook was described as one of "isolated individualism" [13:81].

These "alienated" students, in contrast to the nonalienated, revealed an intense and prolonged closeness with their mothers. They saw their mothers as intrusive and oversolicitious, in need of their sons' love because of the frustrations of their own lives. The "alienated" sons described their fathers as weak and distant, easily dominated by their wives, and perceiving themselves, often wrongly, as being defeated in life. Typically, the strong contrast and the conflicts between the father's and the mother's personalities had been a particularly disturbing factor in these students' development.

Keniston concludes that the "alienated" sons were unable to identify with their fathers; they could not admire and emulate the fathers as models of manhood and adulthood. The sons' identification was further impaired, according to Keniston, by their intense alliance with their mothers.

The dissidence of the hippies took neither the form of activism nor was it characterized by personal withdrawal as in the case of the "alienated" youth.[7] Instead, out of Oriental, African, and other folklores and myths, combined with images of their own fantasy, the hippies created a counter-culture which seemed to fill their emotional and spiritual needs. They adopted many ingredients of their counterculture from the "beat generation" of the 1950s, in particular from Jack Kerouac and Allen Ginsberg, bohemians and anarchists who disseminated their contempt of material values and technological progress to a receptive audience of disillusioned "dropouts." Kerouac helped to create the romantic vision of a carefree existence "on the road" (a phrase he used as the title of his most popular novel) and provided an impetus for the hazardous hitchhiking vogue among hippies. Ginsberg, who proclaimed love, peacefulness, and freedom from all oppression as the strongest unifying force in our time, has been said to be "largely responsible for the love-happy condition" of the hippies:

He has been revered by thousands of flower-wielding boys and girls as a combination of guru and paterfamilias and by a generation of students—who consider him a natural ally, if for no other reason than that he terrifies their parents with his elaborate and passionate friendliness [16:33].

The hippie custom of wearing and handing flowers to passersby giving rise to their being named "flower children" had its origin in a set of instructions Ginsberg presented to the Berkeley peace marchers in 1965. He advised them to display "masses of flowers—a visual spectacle—especially concentrated in the front line—an exemplary spectacle *outside* the war psychology" [16:38]. The use of flowers and other symbols of love and peace spread from the hippie centers in San Francisco and Berkeley to New York's East Village and to minor congregations of hippies throughout the country.

The LSD habit, sanctioned by Timothy Leary, infiltrated most hippie groups. It became a ritual and, in many cases, an addiction blinding the user to its dire consequences.

The dissidence of the hippies has been attributed frequently to their permissive, middle-class upbringing and their impersonal relationship with their parents. It has also been argued that the hippies, in their teens, were still being granted the privileges of an extended childhood and that they were therefore unable to face the discipline and regimentation demanded for job training and for military service. By 1966, a great number of these young people had "dropped out"—over ninety thousand, according to FBI reports [35:33-34].

Not all investigators have attributed the hippies' dissidence to permissiveness in their upbringing. Jay Haley, in his article "The Amiable Hippie: A New Form of Dissent" [11:102-110], considers, on the one hand, conservative families where the father had resented the stresses and drudgery of his business career and where the mother had been discontented with her social milieu as responsible for the children's protest against a career-oriented middle-class existence. On the other hand, and somewhat in contrast to Flacks' findings, Haley assumes that parents who, in their youth, had held radical political views are not readily emulated by their children because the children blamed their parents for having failed to change the system. For these children being an activist or even a social reformer meant participating in the framework of a society which they considered immoral. They believed that every person should live as he chooses, but they also needed the contact with a group of like-minded. This they found among hippies.

We have shown how the Wandervoegel and the hippies renounced similar values of their middle-class parents, and yet certain aspects of their upbringing differed. The Wandervogel became a refuge from the parental self-righteousness and the father's authoritarianism of the Wilhelminic era while the dissidence of the hippies has been related, on the contrary, to a lack of parental authority and to parental insecurity.

In spite of the diversity of parental influences on the child's later dissidence (identification reversal), there is agreement among the scholars cited above that the origin of dissidence has to be sought in the parents' childrearing atttitudes.

If we want to study the connection between attitudes toward the child and the course of the child's identification we must examine intensely the early parent-child relationship. For it is there that we may find the beginning of this process. This we shall attempt in the sections which follow.

IDENTIFICATION: THE ROLE OF IMITATION

If we contemplate childhood imitation, scenes immediately spring to mind such as a four-year-old girl dressing up like her mother, a schoolboy using phrases like his father or another defending his father's political views. And we may also remember a moment of anger when we talked to our own children with that same shrill tone of our mother's voice which, as a child, had made us wince in helplessness. But if all these are acts of imitation, could they not equally be seen as identifications?

Jean Piaget provides us with several examples of early imitation: on the night following his son's birth, the baby imitated the crying of another child [32:41]. Another of Piaget's children, two months old, imitated Piaget's movement three times when he turned his head from right to left [32:42]. Piaget has described certain normal stages of imitation he considers essential to the development of intelligence. Among others, he has shown how, by a primitive, reflex-like imitation, the child first reproduces body movements he sees and sounds he hears. He has further outlined the phases through which a child passes before he is able to reproduce another person's behavior, language, and thought consciously and intelligently.

Piaget was interested in the role of imitation for the unfolding of human intelligence, not in the feelings accompanying imitation, nor in imitation as triggered by the wish to "become like" amother person. However, Piaget conceives as an important "incentive" for imitation between the ages from two to seven the child's "estimate" of the person who becomes the model for imitation:

An adult who has personal authority or an older child who is admired will be imitated on that accord, whereas a child of the same age, and more particularly a younger child suggesting the same models will often meet with no success [32:73].

In the following passage, Piaget defines the incentive for imitation more specifically:

To our mind the dynamic link is to be found either in compulsion, authority and unilateral respect, which give rise to imitation of the superior by the subordinate, or in mutual respect and intellectual and moral equality, which are the origin of imitation between equals. [32:73].

In proposing the motives for the adult's imitation, Piaget seems to touch upon the imitation of a leader by members of a group. We shall discuss this type of imitation in a later section as a sign of identification.

Some studies on imitation have focused on parental characteristics as they may foster imitation. A few investigators have found that the parent's nurturant, warm, and rewarding attitude induces imitation of a parental behavior. In one study, one group of mothers was judged on the basis of an interview as nurturant, i.e., genuinely warm and interested in their preschool children [30:94-97]. The other group was judged nonnurturant, aloof, self-absorbed, and not much interested in their children. The mothers demonstrated a simple maze drawing of their children. The children of the nurturant mothers imitated their mothers' incidental responses ("Oh my!" "Here we go!") more often than the children of the nonnurturant mothers.

However, the two groups of children did not differ in their performance on the task. These experiments point to a spontaneous type of imitation which seems to evolve from an affectionate bond with the mother.

If by identification we mean replicating the behavior of another person with whom an emotional tie exists, we can assume that a spontaneous type of imitation accompanied by affection is an expression of identification. The following episode illustrates this type of imitation in more detail:

Emily, two, is sitting next to her mother who is writing a letter. She has, upon her request, been given a piece of paper and a crayon. She is scribbling in her usual way, "going round and round and round." Suddenly she looks at her mother's moving hand and her own production. Giving herself a command, she says dreamily, "Emily, write!" She continues writing and then hands her "letter" to her mother. Her mother acknowledges Emily's present: "That's great! Thank you, Emily!" They smile at each other [4:96].

The spontaneity of the imitation and the contented and unrestrained interaction conveyed in this episode suggest that Emily's imitation could be an expression of her identification with her mother, although we cannot be sure of such interpretation. The example points up the difficulty in distinguishing between imitation and identification in a young child. Although we will address this question later, we may here suggest that behavior observed at an early age level will become more meaningful by studying the same individuals later in life and "reaching back."

Some progress has been made in psychoanalytic work toward understanding these processes. Psychoanalysis holds that in the course of normal psychosexual development, various forms of emotional dependency lead to the child's identification with the parent as expressed in imitation, and that since the mother is the one who satisfies the infant's earliest needs and relieves his earliest frustrations, a primitive dependence on the mother leads to a rudimentary form of identification which underlies all subsequent identifications. Thus, some psychoanalytic writers have suggested that the patterns of early mother-infant interaction, especially in the feeding situation, have a crucial, lasting influence on the child's imitation and identification.

A paper entitled "Influences of Early Mother-Child Interaction on Identification Processes" describes a particular mother and her infant during feeding [34:69-70]. Usually this mother was able to adapt to the child's needs and to exert appropriate controls so that the feeding was pleasurable for both. The mother had a particular way of keeping in friendly visual contact with her child. The child subsequently developed an early interest in the human face and came to prefer toys with faces. Upon entering nursery school, she easily made contact with adults and children by glancing at their faces and smiling.

A further incident of an early imitative response to an affectionate approach was observed in an intensive study of an infant during the first three months of life [7;25::456-464]. The investigators explored the relationship between biochemical and behavioral changes in the growing infant. The following behavioral observations were made by the author:

When the infant was two weeks and three days old and was fussing soon after he was nursed, his mother picked him up and held him in her lap facing her. She was looking at him, her face relaxed. His body seemed to adjust to her body. He became quiet and looked at her, his mouth relaxed and the frown on his forehead disappeared.

The mother then talked to him in a friendly high voice. She smiled at him and he responded, very briefly, with a soft, "passive" smile.

At age seven weeks the author noted a different smile which was more distinctly an imitative response to the mother's smile:

The child had been nursed and was held upright face to face with the mother in what had become one of their established patterns. While he was in this position, the mother talked to him and smiled at him, and then that particular smile appeared on the child's face. The smile lasted for two or three seconds, and then disappeared rather abruptly. This smile was distinctly different from previous ones. It showed more active participation as if there was more tonus in the facial muscles. There was more alertness, and he was looking directly at the mother's smiling face. It was listening and smiling combined . . . it had very much the quality of an older child smiling back at the mother.

Another mother was, in contrast, tense and frightened when she handled her infant who appeared to respond with signs of similar discomfort and tenseness during the feeding period. The mother's tension and uneasiness whenever she held her baby seemed to be mirrored by the infant when in close contact with the mother and seemed to reappear as a panic-like stiffness when touched by others. The child's later bossiness in nursery school was interpreted as an attempt to ward off the fear of closeness with other human beings [34:78].

The phase which is most crucial for the development of identification (the Oedipal phase) lasts approximately from the third to the fifth year. According to the psychoanalytic model, the child experiences an intense love for the parent of the opposite sex and feelings of jealousy and hate for the parent of the same sex. The fear that his instinctual wishes for the mother and his hostilities toward the father may become punished eventually lead the boy to suppress these wishes. He strives to become like the father who, he believes, would have opposed and punished him. The girl, at the corresponding stage of her development, has become hostile toward and competitive with her mother for her father's love. In time she, too, suppresses both the sexual and aggressive impulses and seeks to become like her mother. These inner conflicts and their solutions mark the beginning of the lasting identifications with the parents' prohibitions and demands as revealed in the superego.

Up to this point the child had responded to demands made by the parents in their presence only. When the parental prohibitions become internalized, parental demands are enforced even in the parents' absence, as illustrated in the following episode:

Lisa, three years and two months old, had frequently been scolded for removing the lid from a candy dish on the coffee table. One day her mother observed her as she was standing by the door to the living room. Lisa made a few steps toward the table, stopped short, said, "No, no!" in an energetic tone, and moved away [4:96].

According to psychoanalytic theory, this incident would be seen as showing that an identification with the parent's prohibition and a sense of guilt, characteristic of the superego, have developed by renouncing Oedipal wishes.

We must remember however that, according to theory, psychic processes of fundamental importance have already laid the groundwork for the child's identification prior to the Oedipal phase. The child's wanting to "become like" a parent, for example, is believed to be influenced by a wealth of unconscious pleasurable or painful feelings toward the person who has fed him and protected him. At the same time there is always the danger that the child who is given excessive affection in infancy may later be unable to abandon his dependent needs for more mature gratifications. Such a child, it may be said, may never completely outgrow his infantile identification.

This point needs further clarification. If the source of identification is to be found in the earliest phase of childhood, we may wonder how its impact upon the child's development compares with the better known and more familiar impact of the Oedipal phase. If we say this early phase "underlies" the later, are we asserting that the later supersedes this phase, or merely that it is pervaded by it? Or is it perhaps better to say that the latter takes place within an already formed personality structure? What limits might such an early personality then impose on the personality which develops through the Oedipal phase? We will want to keep these questions in mind as we proceed to the examination of case histories. In subsequent parts we shall show how the basic and lasting patterns of the child-parent relationship originate to some extent in the earliest child-parent encounters. We shall point out how these patterns may promote likeness or divergence and, later, even rebellion.

During adolescence hormonal and other physiological changes as well as changes in social role intensify instinctual striving. The earlier conflict between Oedipal drives and the fear of punishment is replaced by a conflict between sexual drives and the restrictions of the superego. The conflict is heightened by the adolescent's uncertainty about his "real self." His emotional upheaval is characterized, on the one hand, by anxiety, moodiness, and aggressiveness and, on the other, by passionate friendships, idealism, and heightened sensitivity. He will resort to varied efforts at coping. Among them may be avoidance of intimacy with his family members and an attempt to model his behavior after another admired adult, a friend or a group of like-minded persons. Yet certain early identifications with his parents will remain essentially unchanged. Combined with later identifications, these early ones constitute the core of the adult personality. And here our questions about the development of identification and the beginning of an identification reversal take on additional importance.

To return to our initial question about the origin of youth movements: interviews with Wandervoegel and with members of the present counterculture suggest that they had given up their identification with their parents more completely than had the nonmembers. While the adolescent identifications with persons outside of the family were rather transient for the nonmembers, the identifications of youth group members with substitute models were lifelong. One of the mottos of the Wandervoegel, "To be a Wandervogel means to remain a Wandervogel all your life" is verified to a surprising degree: the surviving German group members appear unusually youthful in their old age. This phenomenon can now be understood in the light of their rejection of parental models and their identification with young group members and leaders during their adolescent years. Only the future will tell whether the persons belonging to the present counterculture will retain characteristics of the subculture in later life.

A METHOD FOR STUDYING THE PARENT'S INFLUENCE ON THE CHILD

Is it possible "scientifically" to assess the influence one person has upon another, and, in particular, the influence of a person who is in a position of authority over a younger one? In 1939 and 1940, Kurt Lewin, Ronald Lippit and Ralph K. Whyte conducted innovative experiments which were crucial in answering this question [18:271-299;19:26-49]. They studied the effects of three experimental variations of leadership on group and individual behavior. They observed adult leaders with groups of eleven-year-old children. The adults behaved either as a "laissez-faire," an authoritarian, or a democratic leader. The democratic leader encouraged group decisions, provided assistance when needed, and discussed freely the reasons for praise or criticism. It was found that expressions of irritability and aggressiveness occurred more frequently under the leadership of either an authoritarian adult or an adult who displayed a laissez-faire attitude than under the leadership of a "democratic" adult.

These experiments became well known among professionals, and an increasing number of studies were subsequently conducted on the effect of the parents' behavior upon the child, including frequencies of "authoritarian" and "democratic" attitudes. The studies were based mostly on questionnaires and interviews and on observations of child and parent in their homes. Occasionally the child was also observed in his peer group in nursery school. The Fels Research Institute, for example, in 1945 developed Parent Behavior Scales to characterize the family atmosphere and the parents' attitudes toward the child [2]. The scales included such parental dimensions as Parental Warmth, Restrictiveness, Interference, Democracy. The ratings on these behavioral dimensions were correlated with ratings of the child's behavior in nursery school as judged by nursery school teachers and observers.

In particular, the "democratic" attitude of parents was defined, in the Fels study, as generally permissive, avoiding arbitrary decisions, and engaging in a great deal of verbal contact with the child, e.g., consulting about and explaining decisions. It was found that a child brought up in such a family compared with a child whose parents are assessed as "nondemocratic" is more actively engaged and also more successful in peer-centered activities. It was found, furthermore, that he "is better able to contribute original, creative ideas to the group with which he interacts" [1:49-62].

Instead of assessing the parent's effect on the child by considering each behavioral dimension separately, some investigators have studied two or more dimensions of behavior in combination. Thus the dimension love-hostility (or warmth-hostility) has been combined with the dimension control-autonomy. Accordingly, in 1959, Earl Schaefer devised a "hypothetical circumplex of maternal behavior concepts" in which one dimension is Autonomy-Control and the other Hostility-Love [38:232]. Thus there could be on the one hand, for example, a loving mother who controls (constrains) her child by her "overprotection," or on the other hand, a hostile mother who grants the child much autonomy, her relationship with him being "detached"; there could be a hostile mother who controls the child strongly through her "authoritarian-dictatorial" attitudes, or a warm mother who allows her child autonomy.

In our own analysis we will also use combinations of parental behavior characteristics to explain the observed behavior of the child. Our particular objective, however, is to explain the development of *identification of the adolescent and the young adult* with the parent. Thus we will attempt to understand the influence of parental behavior upon the *young child*'s characteristics in his relation to his parents. We will attempt to focus upon those parental behaviors in particular which are relevant to the quality and strength of the child's later identifications.

It is likely that extreme degrees of direction and affection have an unfavorable effect on the development of the child's identification. (The meaning of the word "direction" as applied here will be discussed below.)

We will study in Chapter 2 the particular combination, "much direction, little affection" and "little direction, much affection." As special cases, these two combinations would fit into Schaefer's "hypothetical circumplex of maternal behavior concepts" (see above).

Because of the limited resources at their disposal, observers of human interaction have to choose between two alternatives. They can study a small number of cases and pay close attention to complex interpersonal processes, or they can work with large samples and concentrate on a small number of behavioral characteristics. To observe all the rich subtleties of human behavior in a large number of cases would require resources far exceeding those usually available.

It seemed appropriate for studying the identification process to concentrate intensively upon a few children and their parents. Since the author was interested in the early verbal phase of the parent-child relationship, she selected preschool children.

When observing manifestations of a complex human relationship, one cannot observe the behavior item by item—gesture by gesture, sentence by sentence—without losing the meaning of the relationship as a whole. Representative arts have always made use of the observers' abilities of introspection and empathy, and of the human mind to detect meaningful patterns in a sequence of human behavior. The researcher of human behavior can and should make full use of the same abilities. Yet for research purposes, in contrast to the arts, it is necessary to make inferences from the observed behavior.

It can be assumed that a child's daily encounters with his parents determine the nature of his identification. It would seem of value, therefore, to obtain authentic and comparable records of actual behavior and search for dimensions of the interaction which, on theoretical grounds, can be assumed to foster or hinder identification. The particular interaction situations to be observed would have to be prearranged so as to, potentially, elicit these particular dimensions. The situations would have to resemble as closely as possible those which naturally occur in the family at home. In order to compare different subjects or different groups in a given study, each parent-child pair would have to be observed in the same series of situations.

With these objectives in mind, the author devised a method of observing child and parent in a series of controlled situations. The method has subsequently been called Marschak Interaction Method (MIM)[8]. The series initially included situations ("tasks") specifically designed to elicit imitation (e.g., of the parent's arm movements, of a rhyme which the parent reads, of a block structure built by the parent, etc.), and others which were to reveal the affectionate climate of the relationship (without necessarily eliciting imitation).

The author's early experience with the interaction patterns which she saw unfolding in the controlled situations suggested that the process of the child's readiness to imitate seemed to be promoted or hindered by three parental characteristics: (1) the quality of parental affection; (2) the manner in which the parent directs the child (to be called here "direction"), and (3) the parent's perception of the child. (Chapter 2). It seemed appropriate, therefore, to examine the MIM data not only as to signs of identification, but also with regard to these parental characteristics.

The results to be presented here are based on the MIM supplemented by interviews with the parents and a questionnaire which the parents answer after the session.

Whenever possible, the initial studies were conducted in the subjects' homes. Subsequently, however, for practical reasons, the sessions had to be held in a clinic or in a schoolroom after school hours. While the familiar surroundings at home might have induced more natural behavior, the uniformity of location for all subjects was of some advantage for the comparison of behavior. In settings away from home a particular effort was made, e.g., through a warming-up period, to create conditions which would elicit, as far as possible, an interaction pattern typical of the parent and child under observation.

The records presented here have been taken from a number of interaction studies concerned with the problem of identification stretching over a fourteen-year period. The first was conducted in 1958 under the auspices of the Yale Child Study Center. It dealt with imitation and identification in four normal preschool-age children in interaction with their typically middle-class parents [22]. Stephen and John, described in Chapter 2, were included in the study. A second study carried out through the Department of Psychiatry at the University of Pittsburgh, was conducted in 1959 in conjunction with an investigation of recent Polish and Italian immigrant families. The larger study focused on the childrearing practices of working-class families in the two ethnic groups, both to some extent under siege by the culture of their adopted country. One part of this study involved identification revealed in parent-child interaction in six of these families. A third study was carried out from 1962 to 1964 through the Department of Child Psychiatry at the University of California, Los Angeles. Justin D. Call, M.D., was the co-investigator. This study focused on imitation and participation in normal as compared to emotionally disturbed preschool children interacting with their parents [29:421-427]. After a pilot study of two families in which the MIM situations and the methods of analysis were tried out, eight white, middle-class families, each with a three-year-old son, were the subjects of the investigation. Paul and Jerry, described in Chapter 2 with their parents, were included in the normal control group of this study.

In the course of the Los Angeles study it became increasingly clear that observations during the controlled interaction situations yielded far greater possibilities than was originally visualized. Different series of interaction situations were tried out and found useful for diagnostic and teaching purposes and for investigations dealing with yet other problems than those of identification. For example, even while the Los Angeles research project was being conducted, MIM interaction sessions were incorporated, as class demonstrations, into the training program for third-year medical students [27]. Other uses of the MIM adapted to specific research problems included a study carried out in 1962-63. Its focus was the development of autonomy in the child. Sponsored by the Psychosomatic and Psychiatric Institute of Michael Reese Hospital in Chicago, it investigated, in five normal, white middle-class families, changes in interaction pattern over time using regularly scheduled MIM sessions with the same mother-child teams [12]. In 1966, the Office of Economic Opportunity sponsored a study on child-parent interaction in disadvantaged black families. Three families were selected by the on-site Head Start personnel. The objective was to explore the mother's influence on the child's success or failure in early school efforts [23].

A study in Israel in 1970 based on MIM sessions reverted again to identification processes through observing interaction in fifteen families drawn both from kibbutz and from middle-class urban families [26a; 26b]. This study was made possible by the Institute for Research on Kibbutz Education, Oranim, Israel.

During the last decade the MIM has been expanded to children at different developmental stages. Seven developmental schedules, from neonate to adolescent stages, are the result. These schedules are designed so as to tap five dimensions central to the parent-child relationship: Attachment (Affection), Direction, Imitation, Alertness, Playfulness, and Stress Tolerance. The professional reader wishing to use the MIM for research, diagnostic, or teaching purposes will be interested in an abbreviated form of the MIM manual in the Appendix.

While very few families are singled our here for detailed analysis, particularly in Chapters 2 and 4 of this text, those singled out have been chosen because of their representative nature. In order to preserve the privacy of the individuals concerned, identifying details have been changed.

The author was present in each of the controlled situations to be described herein. In the preparation of this volume, the following sources of data were used:

1. Tape-recorded dialogues between parent and child;
2. The author's "log" of observations of the ongoing interaction;
3. The author's detailed summaries written after each session;
4. Interviews with each parent with regard to the past history of parent and child, the parents' childrearing attitudes, and the parents' perception of their child; and
5. Parental responses to a questionnaire given to each parent after the session eliciting mainly the parent's comments on the child's behavior

NOTES

[1] In *Group Psychology and the Analysis of the Ego*, Freud states: "identification is the original form of emotional tie with an object" [10:65].

[2] The plural, Wandervoegel, refers to two or more members of this movement. In line with German usage, we shall use the singular form, Wandervogel, or its abbreviated version, W.V., in reference to: (1) an individual member; (2) a group of members in frequent contact with each other; or (3) the movement as a whole.

[3] H. W. Koch, in his book on the Hitler Youth, reports that the majority of teachers in the Hitler Elite Schools (where future leaders were educated) had previously been Voelkische Wandervoegel. The first commander of the militantly organized Hitler Jugend Division trained for war service was a former youth movement member, Major General Witt. He has been described by his successor as having "replaced many old-fashioned principles of military training by new ones which in their final analysis had their origins in the German Youth Movement" [14:246]. Other youth movement members became, on the contrary, ardent opponents of the Nazi regime (see also Chapter 2, footnote 8 and Chapter 2, footnote 4).

[4] Hoffman remained with his group until 1900 when he finished his law studies and entered diplomatic service abroad.

[5] Another organization of Jewish W.V., the Kameraden, originated in East German cities, such as Breslau and Kattowitz, at about the same time as the Blau-Weiss. They were devoted Zionists.

[6] A printed catalogue, published by Edelmann, Hamburg, in 1960, listed 3585 books, booklets, dissertations, etc., on the German Youth Movement [17:244].

[7] Keniston's study of the "alienated" youth was begun in the late 1950s. Alienation as a form of dissidence thus preceded that of the hippies by a few years.

[8] Copyright © 1960 by M. Marschak.

[9] Among institutions which used MIM situations for research purposes are: Department of Psychiatry, UCLA, in a study on "Parent-Child Relationships, Psychological Separation and the Young Child's Conception of Space"; Department of Pediatrics, UCLA, in a study of infants with a history of premature birth compared with infants with full-term delivery; Department of Counselling Psychology, Illinois Institute of Technology, in a study of "The Reciprocal Effects of Maternal Personality and Infant Temperament." Institutions using the method for teaching purposes are: Department of Early Childhood Education, Northeastern Illinois University, Chicago; Elmhurst College Speech Department, Elmhurst, Illinois; the La Porte County Comprehensive Mental Health Center, Indiana; and the Institute for Juvenile Research and the Theraplay Institute, both of Chicago.

[10] Two additional sources of information consisted of: psychiatric interviews with each parent conducted by Catherine Kalmansohn, M.D. (Los Angeles Study, Chapter 2); and observations of Jerry as a newborn and his mother (Chapter 2), made by R. Constas, M.D., as part of the research project "Approach Behavior in the Newborn," conducted by Justin D. Call, M.D., Department of Psychiatry and Human Behavior, UCLA, in 1963.

REFERENCES

1. Baldwin, A. L. The effect of home environment on nursery school behavior. *Child Development,* **20**, 1949.
2. Baldwin, A. L., Kalhorn, J., and Breese, F. H. Parent Behavior Rating Scales. In: *Patterns of Parent Behavior.* Psychol. Monogr. **58**, (3), 1945.
3. Buber-Neumann, M. *Von Potsdam Nach Moskau.* Stuttgart: Deutsche Verlagsanstalt, 1957.
4. Buehler, Ch., and Marschak, M. Basic tendencies of human life. In Ch. Buehler and F. Masarik (Eds.), *The Course of Human Life.* New York: Springer, 1968.

5. Call, J. D. Newborn approach behavior and early ego-development. *Int. J. Psychoanal*. **45**, 1964.

6. Douvan, E. A., and Adelson, J. *The Adolescent Experience*. New York: Wiley, 1966.

7. Eiduson, S., Eiduson, B., and Geller, E. An exploratory study of the human infant from birth through the first three months: biochemical aspects; behavioral aspects. *Proc. Psychol. Assoc.*, St. Louis, Sept. 1962.

8. Feuer, L. S. *The Conflict of Generations*. New York: Basic Books, 1969.

9. Flacks, R. The liberated generation: an exploration of the roots of student protest. *J. Social Issues*, **22**, (3), 1967.

10. Freud, S. *Group Psychology and the Analysis of the Ego*. New York: Liberight Publication Corp., 1949.

11. Haley, J. The amiable hippie: a new form of dissent. *Voices*, **12**, 1968.

12. Jernberg, A. Some contributions of three preschool children to behavior changes in their mothers. Presentation to the staff of the Psychosomatic and Psychiatric Institute, Michael Reese Hospital, Chicago, 1962.

13. Keniston, K. *The Uncommitted, Alienated Youth in American Society*. New York: Dell Publishing Co., 1965.

14. Koch, H. W. *The Hitler Youth: Origins and Development 1922-1945*. London: Macdonald & Janes, 1975.

15. Korth, G. *Wandervogel, 1896-1906*. Frankfurt am Main: Dipa-Verlag, 1967.

16. Kramer, J. Profiles, Paterfamilias, I and II. *New Yorker*, August 17, 1968.

17. Laqueur, W. *Young Germany: History of the Youth Movement*. London: Routledge & Kegan Paul, 1962.

18. Lewin, K., Lippit, R., and White, R. K. Patterns of aggressive behavior in experimentally created "social climates." *J. Soc. Psychol.*, **10**, 1939.

19. Lippit, R. Field theory and experiment in social psychology: authoritarian and democratic group atmospheres. *Am. J. Sociol.*, **155**, 1939.

20. Luetkens, Ch. *Die Deutsche Jugendbewegung*. Frankfurt: Frankfurter Sozietaet Druckerei, 1925.

21. Mader, M., and Riemer, Y. *Youth Movements, Past and Present*. Tel Aviv: Ichud Haborim, 1964.

22. Marschak, M. A method for evaluating child-parent interaction under controlled conditions. *J. Genet. Psychol.*, **97**, 1960.

23. _____. *Nursery School Child-Mother Interaction*: A film on three Headstart children with their mothers. Design and narration by M. Marschak, photographed by K. and M. MacGrimmon, distributed by New York University Film Library, 1966.

24. _____. Imitation and participation in normal and disturbed young boys in interaction with their parents. *J. Clin. Psychol.*, **4**, 1967.

25. _____. The obstinate checklist. *J. Amer. Acad. Child Psychiat.*, **8** (3), 1969.

26. _____. (a) *Patterns of Parenting in Israel*; (b) *Two Climates of Childhood in Israel*: Two films on Kibbutz vs. city-reared children. Design and narration by M. Marschak, photographed by T. Rammon et al., distributed by New York University Film Library, 1970.

27. Marschak, M., and Call, J. D. Observing the disturbed child and his parent: Class demonstrations for medical students. *J. Amer. Acad. Child Psychiat.*, **5**, (4), 1966.

28. Mead, M. Some theoretical considerations on the problem of mother-child separation. *Amer. J. Orthopsychiat.*, **24**, (3), 1954.

29. Murray, H. A. *TAT. The Thematic Apperception Test Manual*. Boston: Harvard University Press, 1938.

30. Mussen, P., and Parker A. Mother nurturance and girls' incidental imitative learning. *J. Pers. Soc. Psychol.*, **2**, 1965.

31. Paetel, K. O. *Das Bild vom Menschen in der Deutschen Jugendbewegung*. Bad Godesberg: Voggenreiter Verlag, 1953.

32. Piaget, J. *Play, Dreams, and Imitation*. New York: W. W. Norton & Co., Inc., 1962.

33. Redfield, R. The Social Uses of Social Science. In M. Park-Redfield (Ed.), *The Papers of Robert Redfield*. Chicago: University of Chicago Press, 1963,

34. Ritvo, S., and Solnit, A. Influences of early mother-child interaction on identification processes. *Psychoanal. Study Child*, **13**, 1958.

35. Roszak, Th. *The Making of a Counter-culture*. Garden City, New York: Doubleday & Co., 1969.

36. Round Robin Letter of the Deutscher Wandervogel, after the first reunion in Cologne (mimeo), 1954.

37. Ruestow, A. *Ortsbestimmung der Gegenwart*, Vol. III. Erlebach, Zurich, Stuttgart: Eugen Reusch Verlag, 1951.

38. Schaefer, E. S. A circumflex model for maternal behavior. *J. Abnorm. Soc. Psychol.*, **59**, 1959.

39. Spiro, M. E. *Kibbutz, Venture in Utopia*. New York: Schocken Books, 1970.

40. Stern, K. *The Pillar of Fire*. New York: Harcourt Brace, 1951.

41. Tramer, H. Blau-Weiss: Wegbereiter fuer Zion. In *Die Jugendbewegung—Welt und Wirkung. Zur Wiederkehr des Freideutschen Jugendtages auf dem Hohen Meissner*. E. Korn, O. Suppert, and K. Vogt (Eds.), Duesseldorf-Cologne: Eugen Diederichs Verlag, 1963.

42. Weber, M. Grundriss der Sozialoekonomik, Vol. III. Tuebingen: J. C. B. Mohr, 1922.

43. Wyneken, G. Die neue Jugend. Ihr Kampf um Freiheit und Wahrheit in Schule und Elternhaus, in Religion und Erotik. In W. Kindt (Ed.), *Grundschriften der Deutschen Jugendbewegung*. Duesseldorf-Cologne: Eugen Diederichs Verlag, 1963.

CHAPTER 2

Observations on
the Nuclear Family

In this chapter, we will see how certain parental characteristics may influence the pattern of interaction in typical, nuclear, middle-class families.

In the first section, two families (John's and Stephen's) will be contrasted as to the intensity and quality of their ways of showing affection and giving direction. Comparisons will be drawn between the style and characteristics of each parent interacting with his or her son, age 3. The subsequent development of both children's identification with their parents fifteen years later will be demonstrated.

The following section will explore in-depth the parent-child interaction in one family with two sons. This family was studied several years later than the first two families and a modified version of the MIM was used. The study focuses particularly on the parent's perception of the child's individuality. This perception, influencing as it does each parent's interaction with each child, is seen to affect in turn the child's identification with the parent.

The perception held by the mother of the individuality of one of her two children will be traced to her first interaction with this infant after birth. Moreover, a controlled situation is introduced which reveals the transmission of moral values by the parent to the child. Unlike the earlier study of the families of John and Stephen, the later study unfortunately could not include a followup.

AFFECTION AND DIRECTION:
TWO "DIMENSIONS" OF PARENTAL BEHAVIOR

Loving feelings conveyed to the child (affection), and requests made, information given, knowledge transmitted (direction), are normal and beneficial ingredients of childrearing. In an atmosphere of encouragement and security both attitudes may, at times, be simultaneously expressed. For example, a father may explain to a three-year-old how a ship is propelled by steam while gently patting the child's hand.

A mother's first feeling of affection for her child may be coupled with an emotional awareness of "mine"—a sense of closeness with this human being often described as being unlike any other feeling (within conscious memory). Since it is not the same as when the infant is experienced as "part of me," possessiveness does not necessarily enter into these feelings. According to Konrad Lorenz, they can be understood as belonging to the "deepest strata of the human personality," "much older than reason," and not essentially different from the instincts of animals [27:240]. Yet, even in these primal, unreasoning, "animal" experiences, a conscious sense of "specialness" pervades the mother-child relationship.

It has been said that in modern societies similar instinctual paternal responses, biologically based on protectiveness toward the young and helpless, have been suppressed [33:480]. The tender, affectionate and competent caretaking often found in present-day fathers who, as single parents, perform all childrearing duties, presents convincing evidence that paternal instincts can be called upon when needed.

However, affection need not "come in" at the first contact with the newborn. It may be touched off later under a variety of circumstances such as when the infant is sucking or shows satisfaction after feeding or, in contrast, when he displays signs of unhappiness by fussing or crying or when he is ill.

I can remember the very moment when my affection toward my first child dispelled a certain vagueness of feeling. I had left my hospital room for a short while and, upon my return, found the baby crying violently. I picked her up for the first time without the nurse being present, held her close, and called her by a name that expressed my affection, a name which remained with the child throughout her infancy.

In early infancy, the affection between parent and child finds nonverbal expression in playful activities such as the "bunting game" (touching forehead to forehead), pushing and pulling games, games in which the parent lifts the child high up or both parents swing the child between them. Other affectionate activities take more quiet forms such as stroking, rocking, tender holding, etc.

With the child's progress in language understanding and mastery, affection will come to be expressed not only nonverbally but increasingly verbally. Provided the family climate inspires friendliness, warmth, and humor, affection may even take the form of playfully poking fun at one another and each other's weaknesses. Affection will also be expressed in a concern for each other's interests and goals and in a desire to help. In some families, parental affection may not be clearly expressed until a later phase of the child's development, sometimes not even until the child shows signs of mature intelligence, or reaches adolescence. Much later yet the child may experience a spurt in a parent's affection brought on by one of the many changes which occur in the child's or parent's personality throughout life. In some families certain nonverbal expressions of affection like a spontaneous smile, a tender tone of voice, an embrace or touch, may persist between child and parent into the child's adulthood.

The effectiveness of the earliest parental *directions* depends on certain innate reflexes of the child. The mother carries the baby, rocks him, or changes the infant's position in the crib and he calms down. The mother moves the baby's head closer to her nipple and his sucking becomes more vigorous.

Prior to verbal understanding, pitch and loudness rather than the verbal content itself may be sensed by the child as a request: upon the loud and sharp sound of "Books, no!" the little hands may be withdrawn from the bookshelf.

Somewhat later, the parents' directions may be geared toward the child's ability to reason by foresight: "If I buy you another ice cream, you'll throw up."

From school age on, the parents' efforts to guide or direct the child proceed through increasingly more complex explanations and reasoning, and through parental elaboration or revision of the knowledge and values the child has acquired outside of the family. At this stage, the effectiveness of parental guidance undergoes a crucial test, a test of the intensity of the child's identification with the parent and of the parent's ability to accept or even encourage the child's incipient identification with models outside of the family, i.e., the parent's readiness to forego, to some extent, the satisfaction of partaking in the child's molding himself according to the parental image.

The following statements on affection and direction, as two dimensions of parental behavior, are based on the preceding theoretical considerations and on the studies described earlier (in Chapter 1).

The modes and intensity of the expression of affection and the kind and frequency of directions result in a number of combinations of parental behavior along the dimensions of *Showing of Affection* and *Giving of Direction*.

A predominantly directive, fact-minded, and task-oriented atmosphere where the parents are too seriously involved in the child's intellectual achievement can stifle the child's emotional spontaneity and his natural curiosity. Since overdirecting parents do not usually encourage the child's playful fantasy activity, his need to play and his wish to imagine and explore may be repressed as well. If also marked by relatively little expression of affection, this highly intellectual approach by the parents may lead to the child's later resentment of his dependency upon his parents and even to identification reversal.

If, on the other hand, the parent relates to the child mainly through overt displays of affection, direction being less frequently provided, the child is not so apt to try to excel. For parents who are "lost" in their child and absorbed by "loving" feelings, the child's feelings and "happiness" are more important than the child's successes. They are often unwilling or unable to make the child follow their instructions and to restrict his pleasure-seeking behavior. They are unable to assist him in developing self-control. In later life such a child may show immature and irresponsible behavior. As illustrated earlier, under "Identification: The Role of Imitation," his identification with his parents may remain infantile.

There are other combinations of the two parental characteristics, *Showing of Affection* and *Giving of Direction*. For example, when the parent's behavior toward the child is marked by little show of affection and little direction, there should be weak motivation for identification with the parent. Thus the child may develop a relatively weak superego and an unsure sense of self. It would be possible that at a later age, such a child would choose a rebellious path—the origins of the rebellion lying in the parents' failure to communicate definite goals and clear values while providing inadequate affectionate support.

And, finally, appropriate expressions of affection and adequate direction should encourage the young child to explore and experiment and to develop his own unique individuality while yet being aware of and willing to abide by adult expectations and demands. This should result in a close and lasting identification with the major parental values.

While clear exposition would require that the word "affection" not be used when expression or show of affection is meant, to impose such limits would often result in awkwardness of sentence structure. Therefore, in the following pages, we will frequently use *affection* when we mean *showing* of affection and *direction* when we mean *giving* of direction.

STEPHEN AND JOHN

The Picture of the Past

The following observations were made in New Haven, Connecticut, in 1958. Both Stephen's and John's families belong to a sample of four families homogeneous in major aspects of their lives. All parents are twenty-five to thirty-five years old, Jewish, and of middle-class status. Each family has a three-year-old son. Three fathers have middle-management positions and one is a teacher. The mothers do not work outside the home. The families own their small one-story houses which are of similar value and similarly furnished.

Neither Stephen nor John has siblings. The characteristics of the only child have to be taken into account as possible influences on the interaction with the parents [13:161-260]. Stephen's mother is twenty-eight and John's mother twenty-five; the fathers are thirty-five and thirty-two, respectively.

Stephen's family lives in a small, one-story house. The living room is immaculate with a shiny, satin cover on the davenport. A spray, new on the market, makes the plants shine. Among the books are several on biology, a few on expeditions, and one with biographies of great composers. There is a bulky stack of sheet music on the piano which takes up much of the available space.

Stephen's mother is well groomed, her hair brushed away from her somewhat blank face. She is rather curt and matter-of-fact, not eager to please.

At the time of the first session, Stephen has been waiting by the window. He is pale and, except for an occasional soft, surprising smile, he has a serious look on his face. His voice has a somewhat hard and monotonous quality. Yet, every now and then, when he is excited by an activity such as drawing with colored crayons, he addresses his mother in a loud, babyish tone saying something which sounds like "Mummaeee." Sometimes he accompanies his words with a sweeping movement of his arms. Most of the time Stephen speaks sensibly, although he shouts when he wants attention. Once, when he had become tired and his mother was anxious that he should finish the MIM task, he said loudly: "You're obstinate," apparently anticipating words which had been said to him. Once in response to his mother's prodding, he asked her: "Do you like me more than you like other boys?" (She said: "Yes.") When Stephen's father was irritated at him Stephen told him: "You don't like me." These statements indicated a degree of insight, astonishing in a three-year-old, as well as an unusual ability to put these feelings into words. This is perhaps less surprising when one considers the high premium Stephen's parents place on superior verbal skill. In these remarks he also reveals some hostility toward them. The standards of behavior set for Stephen through explicit demands and prohibitions provide him with a sharp frame of reference within which to express himself for or against.

We have little information on the parents' earliest affection toward Stephen as a baby; however, we do know he had a colic-like condition for the first three months of his life. In retrospect it seems to his mother that he cried every night. Colic is more common in firstborn children and has been attributed by some investigators to the tension of the inexperienced mother [24:22]. But whether Stephen's colic was the function of an inborn disposition or brought on by his mother's tension, his parents' initial affection was partially pervaded by anxiety, fatigue and irritation. Even at age three Stephen's sleeping pattern causes concern to his parents. He awakens before six, regardless of bedtime. Possibly as a result of being prematurely toilet-trained and intellectually pressured, Stephen frequently relapses into bed-wetting.

In the interview, Stephen's mother expresses her hope that Stephen will do some kind of research and make discoveries which will benefit mankind. She mentions Dr. Jonas Salk who had just made his famous contribution to science. Her husband had majored in physics, she says, but had given up his scientific career to support his family. She herself would have liked to have gone into academic work but had not felt "capable" of doing so.

It is obvious that Stephen is expected to realize some of the goals his parents have been unable to attain. These unfulfilled goals have influenced their perception of Stephen since early in his life. Stephen adapted himself to the way his parents saw him by learning twelve words when he was one year old, by repeating words he heard, and, a year later, by literally memorizing stories that had been read to him. After telling about these accomplishments, his mother adds, "But if he could just be an ordinary child who doesn't cause any trouble, takes care of himself, is well adjusted, which is very important! and is happy in whatever he'll take up later, we'll abide by it."

Stephen's father is lanky and stiff in his movements. Even more than his wife, he seems anxious about Stephen's performance on the MIM tasks. He wavers between noninterference and giving Stephen detailed, sometimes complex directions. However, more often than in his interaction with his mother, Stephen succeeds in taking the lead. He tells his father; "You don't know how to do it, do you?" And, another time: "I show you how to do it." Occasionally father helps Stephen to accomplish a task by appealing to some authority: "Mrs. M. wants you to do it." Or "Mummy will be very angry if you don't finish." On one such occasion, Stephen says: "Get away from me. Let me go. Let me go."

In his interview, Stephen's father talks about Stephen in a somewhat detached manner: "He is a good boy," "He has a good temperament," sounding as if he were talking about someone not very close. He expresses a wish for Stephen to study physics, his own abandoned field. Father demonstrates jokingly that Stephen already knows the college he will choose. He asks Stephen: "Do you want to go to Yale, Princeton, or Harvard?" And Stephen immediately answers: "Harvard." (To enter an Ivy League college had been another of his father's unfulfilled goals.)

When asked as part of the Parent's After-Session Questionnaire in what way he and his son are similar, his father says that Stephen looks like his mother in hair and eye color and that, as is true of his mother, Stephen is above average both in fine and gross motor coordination. Stephen is similar to himself, he adds, with regard to standing height. (The author had not asked for any such detail.) An objective, physiological assessment of his son may have been the father's way of avoiding a more personal judgment.

John's family lives in a small, one-story house, just one block from Stephen's. The living room seems lived in and comfortable. The sofa is covered with flowered, washable cotton. There is a breakfront cabinet displaying china and bric-a-brac. Old and current issues of magazines, such as *Good Housekeeping* and *House and Garden*, are piled up on the coffee table. When, in the father's session, the table is moved and the journals tumble down, John's father remarks, somewhat irritably: "Why does she keep it here? I don't understand." But he adds immediately that his wife has a gift for homemaking which "not many girls have nowadays." He obviously represses his negative feelings toward his wife. Similarly, he needs to protect his son from challenges which may arouse the child's aggression as well as his own. As will presently be seen, the father affected his child's behavior by his generally protective, somewhat indulgent attitude.

John's mother is plump, has a pretty, soft face and wavy, not too carefully groomed, hair. On my get-acquainted visit to the home, the mother wears a schoolgirl-type dark dress with a white collar. John is dressed similarly in a dark jacket with a white collar. His mother is reserved at first. She seems somewhat anxious although she had easily agreed to participate in the study.

John has a handsome, round face and a charming, impish smile. When he is absorbed in an activity his lower lip protrudes and he looks like a younger infant. He is outwardly active and talkative, but he too seems affected by the presence of a stranger. He brings his Tinkertoy set and tells his mother: "Make something for me." When she tries to fit the pieces together, John tells her: "I love you," and she replies: "I love you too." He relies on his mother for relieving his tension of the moment. Their exchange of feelings has a genuine, calm quality. (His father, by contrast, has an exciting influence on John.) John helps himself to a cracker by climbing on a chair. His mother does not interfere. She tells the visitor that John usually finds something to do by himself and that he does not "trail" his mother as other children his age do. She sounds as if she approves and, at the same time, disapproves of his independence. (Years later she is to criticize herself for having worried too much about John. "I was always bothering him for something.") But even now she shows some anxiety about John's independence.

John's striving for independence coexists with a need for dependence on his mother. At this early age he combines impulsive, independent behavior with a need for maternal reinforcement, a pattern which continues into adolescence.

When asked in what way she and John are alike, John's mother says that they both have no patience, that he likes to tease and so does she, that John looks like her and also like her father, and that they both are overweight (she has tried to reduce but cannot stick to a diet). (Years later she is to report that at age twelve John began to reduce only when *she* decided to control her eating habits.) Mother obviously needs the image of a close "fit" between her and John which would reassure her feeling of "mine" which she describes having experienced toward John as a baby. That John still "needs" his bottle at age three can be party due to his mother's inability to wean him. We can assume that she feels under threat of foregoing his dependency and the early motherly feelings she derives from it.

In her interview, the mother cannot think of any wish she has for John's future other than that he should take up whatever he likes best and could do well. Besides, she has hardly given any thought, she says, to his future.

John's father is quite large. He is good looking and friendly. He has a tic in one eye when he becomes excited. He is very helpful in setting up the tables and the recorder, yet apologizes for not helping enough. He shows me with great gusto how to change the position of the microphone. He is outgoing and sometimes boisterous but clearly feels insecure. He is eager to go through the activities and to follow the instructions. However, in contrast to Stephen's parents who put the materials away neatly at the end of each task, neither John's father nor his mother replace the objects into their containers.

In the interaction with his father, John is excited but also compliant with his father's requests. For example, John names all the objects, a task which he refused to attempt in his mother's session. In contrast to his behavior in his mother's session, John completes most tasks initiated by his father. In fact, he never says "no" to any of his father's suggestions. John's father protects John by overtenderness but also helps him to master the situation by effectively guiding his steps.

In his interview, the father tells me that John knows that all his things will get fixed. "When he breaks a toy he says, 'Daddy, will fix it.' He lets me take things away from him. When I tell him it will be fixed, he knows it will be fixed. In other words, I don't believe in sneaking things away from him by telling him a story. He knows that."

When I ask the father in what way he and John are similar, he says that both like mechanical things. But John, he says, is "inconsistent" while he is not. John stays with a toy only a short time before shifting to something else. He would like John to become a technician. He wants him to learn something practical so that he can earn a decent living and, at some time, support a family. But he would comply with John's preferences: "I don't believe in badgering him into something that would only make him unhappy. The most important thing is that he'll be happy with what he does." Quite abruptly he says: "But he is almost a baby. Not much more."

John's father and John may harbor negative feelings toward each other, the father because of John's being different from him (e.g., inconsistent and self-assertive), John for not being encouraged to grow up. On the other hand, growing up probably seems to John to entail the danger of losing both affectionate support and infantile wish fulfillment.

Thus, both John's and Stephen's parents show insufficient empathy with their son's individuality. In John's case, his parents' stream of affection not only interferes with their perception of John's unique needs, but prevents their setting up standards of behavior which would strengthen his sense of responsibility. As we shall see, the abundant affection with which John's parents surround him provides no focus for his anger and does not curb the apparent impulsive behavior which will continue in later years.

Now, by means of the MIM, it will be useful to examine these family processes in their actual workings. To that end we will be observing both these families in a few revealing situations which tend to bring out expressions of affection and direction and which point to the underlying needs of the parents.

We will examine three situations in detail. First, one in which child and parent are instructed to engage in their own activity (drawing); second, a behavior-modeling situation where, in essence, the child must display his knowledge under parental stimulation (naming pictures correctly); last, one in which the task is too difficult for the child and the parent and child must cope with the resulting stress.

Parent-child Interactions

The materials consist of a suitcase containing the test objects, arranged in standard order, two folding tables, and a tape recorder. The parent is asked where she or he usually sits when playing with the child (the living room sofa is generally indicated as that place). The examiner then hands the parent the two folding tables (one for him or her, and one for the child), as well as the suitcase with the test material, telling the parent that a "guide" (placed on top of the material) describes the activities and their order. The examiner then activates the sound recorder and begins taking observational notes.

Individual Activity

Each parent is requested to copy four abstract patterns on a pad after having given an identical pad and colored crayons to the child and asking him to "draw something." This is a situation in which child and adult are both occupied with their own tasks yet in close proximity with one another. The vague suggestion to the parent that the child should draw "something" facilitates the freedom of the responses. Is the parent able to let the child proceed on his own? Does the child feel free to do what he likes? Does the child need to keep in contact with the parent? How strong is the parent's tendency to "engage" the child either by affectionate approach or by direction?

Stephen's father tells Stephen strictly to sit down on four different occasions. Stephen's mother, on the other hand, puts herself in charge of the situation right from the beginning: "I am going to give you this and I'll take that." John's parents introduce the task casually. They are often interrupted by John ("Daddy, what is it?" "Look, mommy. Mommy, look"). But John's father's repetitive use of pet names ("Yes, sweetheart. You draw something, sweetheart") reveals some uneasiness. John's mother, by comparison, is less apprehensive. She leaves it to John to carry out the task as he likes.

John: Look, mommy. Mommy, look.
Mother: Look what we have here.
John: What?
Mother: Look at that. You think you can draw something? What would you like
             to draw?

Neither of John's parents ask John about his drawing, although he provides ample information about the things he draws, especially in his father's presence. John's parents seem not much concerned with his achievement and how it might appear to the observer. Nor are they inclined to use the opportunity for instructing John. John, on the other hand, seems highly stimulated by the white sheets of paper and the crayons of many colors. He draws and talks freely while simultaneously asking for more sheets and substituting one colored crayon for another. His fantasy talk in his father's session provides an insight into his emotional state.

This is a star. I make a moon. This is red. Is this red-red? I'm in the office. I'm making a car. There are the guns. It's raining out. There are raindrops. Look, daddy, it's raining out, daddy. Now I'm making a boat. Look at all the rain. Make a big boat. Look at all that rain. There is the anchor right down there. Little, little. That's a boat. Make water . . . Rocket. See, when they go up in the air then they come down into the water, then they soak. . . .

Stephen's parents, in contrast to John's parents, are alert to whatever scribbling Stephen does. Even while working on their own assignments, both of them ask, "What are you making, Steve?" Each parent suggests a picture Stephen should draw, and Stephen's mother wants to know: "What else will you make?" Both parents do some curbing of Stephen's initiative. Father: "Take it easy." Mother: "I don't want you to take everything out please" (in a dry, suffering intonation). "Don't bear down too hard." And to the observer: "Sometimes he does things quite haphazardly. I always tell him he should do something that looks like a good job, so that he knows what's expected of him when he goes to school. He says to me, 'You think the teacher will be angry with me?' I say: 'Oh, she does like boys and girls to pay attention and do careful work, you know'." In a critical tone Stephen's mother adds: "Sometimes it's just the sheer joy of doing it. . . .

Stephen is led to believe that embarking on an unplanned, free activity for its "sheer joy" is a waste of time and an evasion of "duty." But if duty itself is only vaguely understood by Stephen, he is afraid of neglecting it. Later in life Stephen will come to recognize the constraints his parents have exercised on him. He will then want to free himself, but he will find it hard to forego his devotion to those parental rules and restrictions which he has internalized.

John, by contrast, is not constrained by his parents' demands or disapproval. He is granted the freedom he desires without any disapproval of his seeking pleasure. The unconcerned, uninterfering attitude of John's parents facilitates an impulsiveness which is rarely inhibited by internalized parental values.

Modeling and Imitation

Two identical sets of five blocks each (one set for the parent and one for the child) are used in this task, which consists of two parts. In the first part, the parent builds the structure shown on a card, but does not ask the child to copy it. The child is free to copy the parent's model or to build something on his own. In the second part, the parent repeats the building, but this time asks the child: "Can you build one like mine?"

Because of the elusive nature of psychic processes such as identification we cannot be sure that identification is, indeed, involved in a particular imitative response by the child. However, we can tentatively assume that the child who, in the first part of the task, imitates the parent's model spontaneously without being requested to do so, and the child who, in the second part of the task, is eager to try to imitate the parent and does it while smiling at, moving toward, or touching him is indicating an emotional tie and signs of early identification with the parent.

Since the block building task has been retained from the first to the most recent MIM study, we will show, in the following chapters, other variations of imitative responses, possibly relevant to identification.

Only two of the four parents, John's father and Stephen's mother, presented here succeed in having their structure reproduced.

During the first part of the task (imitation not requested), John does not forego the fun of building his own structure in order to imitate his father's. In the second part (imitation requested), John's father, as on other occasions, is able to formulate some standards of behavior. When John reaches over to his father's table for his blocks, father tells him: "No, Johnny. You build with your own blocks, O.K.?" As at other times when his father, in his mild, affectionate way, constrains an activity of John's, John obeys and almost seems to welcome the imposition. As reported earlier, John's father adheres to certain principles in his son's upbringing (he does not "badger" him into a decision; and he always honors promises).

The second part of the task is performed by John and his father as follows:

Father: All right now, sweetie. You see whether you can build one just like
              daddy's, all right? Take the big block first. No, that's too little. Use this
              here. Now the next one here. No, this one. Turn it so that it lies down,
              not up. Now the last one. That's right. What kind of a building is it?

Under his detailed guidance, John easily reproduces his father's model. This
type of imitation cannot be considered as signifying identification. On the
other hand, when John, in his fantasy talk during the drawing task, says that
he is "sitting in the office" we can assume that he identifies with his father.
John's identification with his father in early childhood, i.e., holding a job
like his father does, is of particular interest because sixteen years later, as a
young adult, John actually diverges sharply from this image of his father.

John's father shows distinct pleasure with John's perfect replication of his
block structure. Such pleasure has been observed in a number of parents
during this task. An expression of intense satisfaction appears on their faces
and is conveyed in their words and tone of voice. Curiously, the pleasure
about this achievement of a very easy task is greater than when the child
completes the much more difficult jigsaw puzzle task.

Is it possible that the satisfaction expressed by the parent is connected
less with the child's achievement as such than with the parent's desire to be
replicated by the child? There is ample evidence of such a parental
characteristic. We will call it a self-replicating tendency. This tendency can
manifest itself in various ways. It can express itself in the mother's or father's
dream of the not-yet-born baby's accomplishments as similar to those which
they themselves could or could not fulfill; in the name given to the child as
a reincarnation of a neglected side of the parent's own self; in the playgroup
associations they select for their child; in their school and college preferences
for him; in their approval or disapproval of his mate; and, finally, in their
children's own childrearing methods. Any or all of these parental characteristics can be understood as expressions of the "self-replicating" tendency.

As suggested above, this tendency may express itself in the parent's
delight in the child's imitation. It may thereby reinforce the child's imitative
behavior. It is further possible that, provided a secure emotional bond exists
between child and parent, the parent's self-replicating tendency, conveyed
to the child by subtle means, may strengthen the child's identification with
the parent.

In his session with his mother, John does not copy her model, either
voluntarily or upon request. Mother yields to John's self-appreciation: "I
know what I'll build. I'll build a tall building. I want—I can—now I make a
big one." She tries in other ways to maneuver John into compliance: "I bet
you can't build one like this!" John: "No. I can build one like that." These
words, pronounced by John in a playful, high-pitched voice similar to his
mother's, might be an indication of his identification with her, especially

since he reproduces his mother's words and intonation also in his mother's absence, in his session with his father, when he says: "Oh, what do we have there?" It is possible that this kind of imitation represents a primitive form of identification, comparable to the adaptive posture of the child to the mother during the newborn period, especially in the feeding situation as described earlier. The infant's earliest identification with the mother's body, tone of voice, etc., may be enhanced by his mother's state of "oneness" with him in which she often "knows" how he is feeling.

In the building task, Stephen's mother asserts her authority with overt demands and prohibitions: "I want you to play something else now. I'm going to give you some blocks and I'm going to build something with my blocks." Stephen then builds by himself. His slight attempt to involve his mother in his activity ("Build my house here") meets with his mother's admonition to carry out the duty at hand: "No, I can't. I have to make my own and you have to make yours." Yet when she has completed her model and is supposed to abstain from prodding Stephen to imitate, she twice whispers to Stephen to look at her model. Stephen destroys his tower and begins to copy his mother's model without an error. Unable to conceal her pride, she says, smiling and in an animated tone, "Well, we finished this one." Stephen then dreamily begins to build his own tower but is constrained by his mother from "doing it again." By way of winding up the task, Stephen's mother devises another "learning experience" (a phrase the mother proudly uses in her interview): "Give me the blocks marked one, two-five." "Now give me the ones marked with this color crayon." Although three weeks intervene between his sessions, in his session with his father Stephen does not engage in free block play at all during the first part of the task. Instead, he immediately builds his mother's block structure from memory. He angrily refuses to repeat the building after his father's model. Father: "Will you build one just like mine, Stephen?" Stephen: "No." Father: "Come on, build this." Stephen: "Oh, skip it."

Stephen's resistance to his father, his ease of compliance with his mother, and his reproduction from memory of her model, may point to the incipient state of the Oedipal conflict characterized by hostility toward the parent of the same sex and attraction toward the parent of the opposite sex which precedes the later identification with the father. Since Stephen's mother is the planner and decision maker in the household, however, one might also understand Stephen's persistent imitation of the mother as a sign of identification with the main authority figure in the family.

Some anthropologists have pointed out that in certain primitive societies the Oedipal constellation and subsequent identification relate not to the father but to the person who represents the decisive authority in the household group [28:142-143]. If it should be the position of authority and not the relationship to the mother which forms the basis of the Oedipal constellation, then a paradox presents itself when the figure of authority turns out to be the mother—a paradox and a basis for role confusion in the identification process.

The position of authority held by Stephen's mother is typical and well scrutinized in American society. Geoffrey Gorer found that the old, dominant role of the American frontier mother was still current in the 1940s [15:58-60].[1] Other authors like Erik Erikson [8:292] and Margaret Mead [35:289, 297] have continued to document this role of the American mother.

When Stephen's father, in response to Stephen's refusal to cooperate on one of the tasks, tells him, "Mommy will be very angry with you. Now come on, do it," he refers to his wife's authority in a manner reminiscent of the typical father of the 1940s quoted by Gorer as telling his son conspiratorially: "Don't let your mother catch you."

While present middle-class mothers still consider childrearing as one of their main responsibilities, their need for satisfaction through work or additional education outside the home has called for relegating some of their authority to substitute mothers. At the same time, important changes are taking place through a greater involvement of the father in child care and domestic matters and through the joint sharing of authority by mother and father. What the effect of this fusion of parental authority will be upon the child's identification, especially in the new communal forms of childrearing, will not become tangible for at least a generation.

Eliciting Knowledge

This task requires the parent to show the child fourteen cards, each with a simple pencil drawing of a shoe, cup, or leaf, etc., and to ask the child every time: "What's that?" Performance on this task demonstrates both how important the child's knowledge of words and their meanings are for the parent, and how the parent's interest in words becomes transmitted to the child.

Stephen's parents execute the task with all seriousness and concentration. They consider this situation another "learning experience," another occasion to demonstrate Stephen's precocity. John's parents do not cherish such aspirations for their son and are concerned mainly with buffering John against the possible stress inherent in the task. Regardless of his performance, they try to shelter John through their affection.

Both John's parents carefully and protectively enlist John's cooperation before asking him to name the first picture. John's father: "Now I'm going to take these cards out, sweetheart, and I'm going to ask you what they are, sweetie, and you tell me, all right?" John's mother: "Oh, look what's in here. You want to come over here and I'll show you these things and you tell me what they are?"

Stephen's parents, by contrast, present the task immediately and with only a brief introduction. Stephen's father: "Now we have to look at these cards. What's this?" Stephen's mother: "You tell me what these things are.

O.K.? What's this? Stevie?'' From then on, Stephen's mother silently holds up each card and Stephen names all the objects in a monotonous low voice so that his mother tells him: "I can't hear you. Speak up." At the end, Stephen's mother briskly replaces the cards in the envelope and, with a smug look on her face, signifies that this has been merely "kid stuff" for Stephen. Stephen, apparently attuned to his mother, shows no particular pleasure in his accomplishment.

Stephen fully meets his mother's expectation of displaying his word knowledge. He produces the words flawlessly as the cards are flashed before his eyes. By an unconscious agreement between mother and child, embellishments or additional information are omitted. That this perfectionistic performance is achieved at the price of suppressing Stephen's imagination and playfulness becomes manifest in his interaction with his father in the same situation.

In his session with his father, Stephen refers to the face of a clock drawn on a card as an "alarm clock." His father objects to Stephen's confusion of fact and fantasy: "How do you know it's an alarm clock? Do you hear it ringing?" But Stephen is not intimidated and asks, "What clock is it?" Father: "Maybe it's a plain clock." Stephen refers to an ambiguous drawing of a leaf as an "oak leaf" and an equally rough pencil sketch of a bird as "coo-coo-coo-coo." He pays little attention to his father's challenging question: "Why should this be an oak leaf?" and "Doesn't this picture look like a bluebird?" Instead he scribbles on one of the cards until reprimanded by his father. It is conceivable that in his interaction with his father he is not afraid of blundering and is able to let his fantasy go by giving names of his choice to the clock, the bird, and the leaf. However, in a formal sense, by providing additional information (albeit incorrectly), he identifies with his parents' emphasis on knowledge and on verbal skills. His reiteration of the syllable, "coo-coo," in his session with his father, compared with his drill-like uttering of words upon his mother's silent cues, suggests that the interaction with the parent who has lesser authority provides a needed outlet for the playfulness which is blocked by the more exacting and demanding parent.

We can observe a similar differentiation of roles between John's mother and father even within the affectionate pattern common to both. By showering endearing names on John, John's father appears to ward off his own anxiety about John's potential frustration should he miss an answer.

Father:	Now what's this, sweetheart?
John:	Cup.
Father:	This is a cup all right, and this is what, darling?

John, engulfed by his father's protectiveness, is given no leeway for elaborations or dawdling. He thus quite mechanically produces the names of the objects in a manner resembling Stephen's mechanical responses to his mother. Although the climate is completely different, it is equally confining. In his interaction with his mother, however, John feels free to hum, and his mother responds in a friendly tone: "Don't make funny noises." He clowns: "This—is—a—cup," mimicking his mother humorously. "And what is this?" He takes the card away from his mother and she responds pleasantly, "No, let me hold the card for you." The interchange in this task is more casual than in the father's presence and more casual than that between Stephen and either of his parents. John's mother approaches him playfully, although somewhat patronizingly: "What do we have here?" "Oh, we know what *this* is."

John's father, but not his mother, shows concern about John's performance on this task. The father conveys his relief that John had put up with the potential strain of the assignment. Obviously proud of John's knowledge, the father pats him and puts his arm around him telling the observer: "I didn't have to name too many of the pictures, did I?"

Stress

A jigsaw puzzle which is generally too hard for a three-year-old creates a situation of stress through anticipation of failure. Since the parent's attitude under threat of failure will have a decisive influence on the child's way of facing failure, the puzzle situation often reveals the child's way of dealing with stress as affected by the parent's responses to stress.

The concept of stress as used here is interchangeable with that of frustration. In recent years, in fact, writers in the field seem to have preferred the word "stress" to the word "frustration." Stress refers to a wide range of psychological and social phenomena and evokes immediate associations with discomfort through an obstructed aim or an unfulfilled need.

Freud believed that the infant experiences his first frustration when he feels hungry and nourishment is not forthcoming. From this disappointment grows the awareness of a self and not-self (mother's breast) and thus an elementary awareness of reality. Psychoanalysts have since elaborated on variations of maternal rejection as they may result in harmful frustration for the child. Thus Anna Freud distinguishes between mothers who continuously and those who intermittently reject their child and those who reject the child for accidental reasons [10:376-386]. The mother's reaction to the child's stress has been considered important in the development of his frustration tolerance:

Through all the feeding, the mother gave observers the impression of trying to gauge the optimal degree of pressure. . . . She seemed to be trying to find the right combination of gratification and frustration without harming the child [43:297].

The normal child's reactions to common situations of stress (e.g., his first confrontation with a nursery school group, stepping into a pool for the first time, visiting the dentist, being vaccinated, or having a sore throat) would seem to be influenced largely by parental and, in particular, maternal reactions in various stressful situations, past or present. Ideally the parent would be able to convey to the child sufficient empathy and confidence in his own (the child's) resources so that he can develop the inner, adaptive ways of handling stress which are best suited to him as an individual.

By directly or indirectly helping their children complete the jigsaw puzzle task, all four parents reveal restricting reactions to the child's experience of coping with stress.

John's father begins work on the puzzle himself and takes upon himself the blame for failures.

I think daddy's got this in the wrong place, that's your daddy's fault.

He almost reverts to John's age in the language he uses.

Now, let's see, sweetheart, what we got here. Oh, a little doggie. Oh boy, oh boy, oh boy. Look at the little doggie.

Then for a short while the father restrains himself, pulls his helping hand back and gives John a chance to act and to counteract his stress. As she did in the previous task, John's mother half-heartedly enlists John's help ("Shall we see whether we can put the puzzle together?") and then finishes the puzzle herself. Clearly John isn't being given much assurance by either parent: we see him shielded as if he either cannot attempt the task or cannot face the stress and possibile failure. He isn't allowed to build up his own defenses: he is, in fact, shielded from the necessity to do so. As a result his capacity to handle this particular stress is untried.

At the end of the puzzle the father shows some concern with the boy's achievement.

Now, that one goes around the doggie's head. Put it 'round his head, okay? That's right. See, now it's all finished. Very good!

These words express such marked relief at the successful conclusion of the task that one would have thought it was he himself who was being tested. In his attempt to buffer the child against stress, he limits him to safe, immature options. It is also as though he is trying to prevent failure in himself. This is even more notable in the case of John's mother who, when John refuses to complete the too difficult jigsaw puzzle, finishes it herself.

A parent's way of reacting in a situation of stress for his/her child can be assumed to affect the child's personality even under "normal" circumstances. The parent's attempts at dealing with stress become even more crucial under crippling conditions. Consider a child afflicted with a severe illness or injured in an accident: the doting, overaffectionate parent may become yet more indulgent and the afflicted child may make yet more excessive demands. It would be easy to understand that, under such stressful conditions, the parent's reactions could, in time, have a strong impact on the developing child's personality. The child may find it difficult at best to relinquish his emotional dependency upon the parent. Later we will explore some matters less susceptible of explanation, for example, the emergence of youthful counterculture rebels from seemingly "normal" home conditions, from "ordinary" families in stable circumstances. We will discuss how these ordinary parents helped—or failed to help—their children deal with both inner and outer stress.

We have seen in John's family how affectionate oversupport can foster insecurity and infantilism. Yet, we must ask: does the parent who tends toward overdirection achieve any different results? The interaction of Stephen with his parents is instructive in this regard.

We find a certain amount of defiance cropping up in Stephen with both parents. He begins by answering with an immediate "No!" to his father's request to work the puzzle. We may wonder whether he has learned to expect what will come when achievement is desired. Stephen's father pretends inadequacy to get his child going. ("Which goes first? I don't know"), a performance which pleases Stephen and evokes his active response. But as quickly as Stephen begins, he makes an error and the correction process is set into motion.

Stephen:	First it goes here, then it goes there. Then see how it goes?
Father:	I watch you. You weren't right there, Stevie.
Stephen:	There?
Father:	That's right. Go on. You were right there.
Stephen:	Here?
Father:	No, this way.

It is not surprising that the father's pose of inadequacy quickly drops away, and soon Stephen is the inadequate one. He asks "here?" or "there?" until his father (as described in the observational notes), sitting stiffly, attention directed to every move, palms pressed together, becomes more active, prodding and criticizing, though rarely handling a puzzle piece himself: "Where would this go? Where could this possibly go?" and later, "Come on, which is it?"

Stephen's mother hardly differs from his father in this situation, for although she praises Stephen's successful moves ("That's fine." "You're good!") she too becomes increasingly unfriendly as Stephen makes the inevitable errors: "That one is for a corner piece, not for a round piece. Can't you see?" She loses her capacity to be "consciously patient" (her own words) and her voice betrays irritation and hostility. It is understandable that his parents would have a stake in Stephen's correct performance, that they would try to facilitate the appropriate response. But why their obvious anxiety? Do they, like John's parents, feel that it is they themselves, rather than their child, who are really being evaluated? Why, for example, are John and Stephen neither allowed to handle the pieces for a while nor to try to fit them together themselves (an obvious desire of any child in such a situation)? The boys would soon find out for themselves that the task is too difficult and might even be able to express it in words: "Mommy (or Daddy), this is hard." Whereupon the parent, through stepping in and giving verbal hints or moving some piece, could provide just enough help to preserve the appeal of the challenge and strengthen the child's tolerance for stress.

Yet for Stephen's parents it seems to be more important that Stephen successfully solve the intellectual challenge represented by the puzzle than that they empathetically take into account both the stress and the opportunity for their child's ego enhancement in meeting the challenge at least halfway. It is not Stephen who is at stake here but his parents, and hence they disregard the fact apparent from the beginning that the task exceeds the child's present abilities to perform it. Instead of responding with affection in this threatening situation, Stephen's parents show anger and irritation about their child's failure.

John, likewise, is deprived of the satisfaction of "trying it out" for himself. His infantilization by his parents is apt to lower his self-esteem. Disregarding his need for performing in a meaningful way, they reassure him of their primitive affection, which is always available in their dealings with John but especially when he faces stress. Significantly, John's lowest moment comes when his mother goes on to complete the puzzle and John becomes passive and loses all motivation to carry out the task.

At this point we need go no further than to point out the interesting phenomenon that while both sets of parents proceed in different ways— Stephen's parents overlaying the interaction with anxiety and direction, John's with affection and near indifference to his performance—the emotional effects on the two children have a surprising amount in common. While we might rightly expect to find different lifestyles a few years hence, we would not be surprised to find certain common, underlying disabilities stemming from these early, similarly painful, yet apparently disparate, circumstances—disabilities which we will have an opportunity to review when we see these two boys again later in their lives.

The Picture of the Present

Sixteen years after the author's brief but intensive contact with the families of Stephen and John she has the opportunity to schedule their mothers for a follow-up visit. Their responses refresh her memory about them and highlight the sharp differences between them. Now, as revealed in their mothers' descriptions, certain characteristics of the children, incipient at age three, can be judged in the light of the two young adults' personalities.

The mothers' responses to questions about their sons' development from late infancy through adolescence and about their adjustment to college life revise some of the author's earlier judgments about the children and confirm or deepen others.

John's mother responds as warmly as ever to the author's call arranging the session. As far as she is concerned, she says, the meeting could take place anytime except during her office hours. Because of financial needs since the death of her husband three years earlier, John's mother is now working in a doctor's office. Her flexible, easy-going attitude is consistent with her noncontrolling, often overly lenient earlier ways with John.

The appointment with Stephen's mother, on the other hand, is changed twice since unexpected commitments have come up. She is working on a degree and needs to know exactly how long the meeting will take. Her husband is not able to participate because of his tight schedule. The author feels constrained by the mother's strong will and by the father's inability to "give," which results in a feeling of being doomed to give in, reminiscent of how the author had felt years ago and how Stephen must often have felt.

Stephen

Stephen's family still lives in the same house. The bookcase contains geographical and science magazines just as at the earlier visit. Stephen's room with his fish tank and his globe is pointed out. His mother explains that she takes good care of Stephen's cacti on the windowsill. Stephen's bed is always made up so that he will feel at home if he comes unexpectedly.

Both mothers recall the earlier sessions only vaguely. John's mother can tell nothing, while Stephen's says: "All I can recall is questions you asked me, and that you talked with Stephen and played games with him." In other words, she remembers the author as the participant in the tasks with Stephen. But she does recall one part: "You asked me what I hoped for his future and I do remember that I thought it would be wonderful if he'd be interested in doing something that would help mankind, like Jonas Salk, at that time—I thought that if he could do something in that field, it would just be marvelous to help so many people." She continues to say that all she wanted then, as now, was for Stephen to be happy at whatever he did. She adds: "Of course, Stephen is not interested in the sciences. Not at all."

That both mothers have "forgotten" their sessions with their sons is not surprising when one considers the transitory nature of those meetings. But that Stephen's mother recalls almost perfectly her vision of Stephen as a future scientist indicates the depth of her wish for Stephen. It also suggests that Stephen is likely to experience her perception of him as extremely oppressive, since a scientific career is now infinitely less likely for him than it was when he was three. When his mother says that Stephen is "of course" not interested in the sciences, she displays a resentment-clad irony. It should be remembered that when he was younger, both parents pressured Stephen beyond his intellectual limits.

Having attached the tape recorder, the author asks Stephen's mother to freely tell about the main phase of her son's development.

Preschool years. As his mother now recapitulates Stephen's intellectual development, she proudly tells of his word knowledge when he was a preschooler, and that he could read simple stories by age five. (She had conveyed the same pride when Stephen, at three, was able to instantly name each of the pictures she had shown him.) He had learned to read, she says, by following the lines when she read to him: "He was always a reader, always a reader."

Her words have a nostalgic ring. They bring out the pleasure she derives from his mental precocity. It is not too far-fetched to assume that this sentiment might have its roots in her Jewish culture, although she and her husband are not religious in a strict sense. Both Stephen's and John's mothers came from families which adhered to Jewish religion. In Jewish families, especially if the parents have not reached academic status, a rational appreciation of book learning and academic achievement goes hand in hand with the highly emotional vision of "my son the doctor—lawyer—professor." It has been reported that among Jewish refugees from Nazi Germany, when members of the older generation met on park benches in their new homelands, the talk focused in large part on their middle-aged children's past successes in college or their children's present professional careers. In previous generations the Jewish mother was given the major responsibility for the well-being of her children. The mother's feelings for them, her "emotionalism," were indissolubly mixed with her adoration of the learned and sophisticated mind—a traditional Jewish ideal to be realized by her sons. The fusion of her emotional and intellectual goals for her sons was expressed by one mother whose son had ruined his chances for an academic career: "It hurts me. I have such pity for him. I could die" [47:434].

We can assume that Stephen's and John's mothers have retained from their families' traditional culture the admiration of a learned man in the one case and the intensity of affection for the son in the other. Which attitude prevails in the rearing of one's child would depend on a great number of factors, among them the parents' personalities, and the child's abilities.

Like his mother, Stephen's father, at the author's first contact with him, had said that he derived a particular pleasure from the ease with which Stephen learned the alphabet. For him as for his wife, his child's verbal progress held the promise of his achieving a professional career. Stephen had obviously identified with his parents' ambitions and expectations throughout these years, although not without signs of resistance. (One such sign of resistance occurred at a family party where Stephen, age four and a half, was asked to recite a poem about Christopher Robin. He did not want to do it, became more and more excited as he went on and, at the last verse, lost his bladder control.)

His mother also recalls, with marked anxiety, that just before entering school, Stephen had regressed a few times to bedwetting. (It was Stephen's mother, it should be remembered, who had been instrumental in setting up the teacher as the authority figure whose "anger" when the children would not do a "good job" Stephen had already come to fear at age three.) It is likely that Stephen's regression on entering school may have been connected with the fear of separation experienced by both mother and child. Such separation anxiety (often called "school phobia") has been attributed in part to the mother's unconscious wish to keep her child at home with her. The mother's portraying Stephen's future teacher as exacting and fearful when Stephen was only three may have been related to his mother's dread, even then, of releasing some of her hold over Stephen.

School years. Once Stephen actually entered kindergarten, his mother reports, school appealed to him. Throughout his school years he was a good student, though he did not like basketball or football and only played tennis because he had to. Significantly, he also disliked mathematics. Stephen's mother believes that too much time is spent in sports and "you can get hurt in football." She thinks Stephen agrees with her point of view, and does not believe that she "had really killed a love of sports for him. Because there was none in the first place." But she had been the one who had argued, with both her husband and Stephen, that besides being dangerous, sports would distract Stephen from his studies. Her overconcern with health hazards for Stephen persists into his college years.

When Stephen was eight years old, his mother says she bought a set of Gilbert and Sullivan records. It was quite an investment then, but she thought this would be a good relaxation for her husband who was often tense when he got home from the office. Besides, she herself enjoyed the spirit and humor of the works. Unexpectedly, Stephen devoured both the words and the music. He learned the librettos just by listening. He became "addicted" to the musicals, so his parents took him to see *The Pirates of Penzance* when it was performed at the local theatre. His mother had never seen Stephen so excited. He was "red with joy." She had not suspected that she had tapped a creative spring in Stephen: "He was only a child, and he was interested in many things."

We have no knowledge of how Stephen's parents dealt with his infantile sexuality, but at around age eight, Stephen asked his mother about sex. She responded with considerable apprehension. She sent him to his father who gave the "necessary answers" and provided Stephen with books on the subject. This seemingly unemotional treatment of Stephen's questions about sexuality is consistent with the overemphasis on instruction in his upbringing.

That Stephen, at school age, repressed not only some of the information he received from his father but also his feeling about his own sexuality is suggested by the mother's conclusion that "there has been no problem as far as that is concerned." When, several months later, Stephen reported in a pedantic manner that the biology teacher had "handled the topic of human procreation quite sensibly," he gave an indication of the fact that he had learned quite readily to translate his instinctual impulses into abstract thought.

For his tenth birthday, Stephen's parents gave him a microscrope. It came with a set of plates and specimens of plant and animal cells. "It really fired him." He would spend days examining a cactus needle he had cut up. He prepared different cuts for the microscope. Then his mother looked up the literature on cactus needles in the biology library herself and found that very little had been published on the subject. Since she had some free time on her hands, she told Stephen that she could help him with abstracting articles on cactus needles. He could see what had been done by scientists and he could make real discoveries there. She told him it did not matter where one starts with doing scientific work, but that just to get the feel of it and learn something of the methods scientists use was important. He was still in school, however, and it would have been an extracurricular activity for him. By the time she gave him her abstracts, he seemed to have lost interest in working at the microscope and in cactus needles.

We may wonder, given Stephen's initial enthusiasm about his scientific endeavor, if his mother's participation dampened his zeal. Had one of the attractions of this enterprise been that he hoped he would be able to go his own way, unsupervised (although not unaccredited) by his parents? It would seem that Stephen resorted to resistance at the cost of terminating a gratifying creative effort. Through his resistance he preserved some ego autonomy. A parallel experience was reported by a former W.V. who had belonged to the W.V. group interviewed by the author (see below). He had, in his youth, passively resisted his father's domination: when he departed for his first school year away from home, his father suggested that the boy send him his reading list. The father would then read the same books as his son and they would discuss them in their letters. When the son disagreed with the father's proposition and complained of feeling "pulled back" to a childhood confinement, the first of a series of conflicts resulted, which led to estrangement and to the son's affiliation with the counterculture. Stephen, too, must have felt he was being "pulled back" to his infantile dependency on his mother. Yet he did not voice his resentment nor explain to his mother the reason for his losing interest in the cactus project. As we shall see, the loss of bladder control which accompanied the reciting of the Christopher Robin poem at four and a half, the unexpected fascination with Gilbert and Sullivan, the dislike of mathematics, and the cactus experiment, did in fact betray the presence of psychic forces of resistance which would, ultimately, lead to an assertion of individuality and even to a limited identification reversal.

In high school Stephen had a few friends, "nice kids, they still stick together." He took girls out only very rarely. "He didn't see the point in spending one's whole allowance on an evening with some girl one really didn't care for particularly. And there just wasn't anyone he cared for at that time." To judge from the mother's tone of voice and choice of words, she seems to describe her own attitude toward Stephen's dating, an attitude which he appears to have incorporated. It is possible, of course, that her discouragement increased Stephen's adolescent insecurity with girls.

College years. How does living away from home affect Stephen's personality? Does he find and follow his own calling even at the cost of the security derived from identifying with parental goals? Or is he bound into unchangeable patterns of relationship with his parents that appear to have antedated the school and Oedipal period? If Stephen should feel compelled to reject his parents' goals, how can he compensate for the lack of parental approval and rewards? To answer these questions, we must begin with Stephen's choice of college.

Stephen wanted to go to Harvard. It was "his own choice." (On this comment, the mother seems to have forgotten the game Stephen's father had played with him as a small child: Father: "What college do you want to go to?" Stephen: "Harvard.") He had held onto this desire throughout his school years, long after his parents had forgotten its origin. In a small but telling way this illuminates the ongoing bondage of child and parent, exemplified in the persistence of essentially alien expectations which are incorporated into the individual's psyche.

Stephen could get no closer to Harvard than its waiting list. The denial of the wish cherished for so long apparently resulted in Stephen's mistrusting his competence generally: "He didn't think he'd be good at anything." His mother reasoned that Stephen had failed because he had not worked hard enough. Thus the particular pattern of parent-child interaction which we observed in Stephen's infancy and which reflected the childrearing pattern to which he was exposed, was in part responsible for the first overt crisis in Stephen's life. Direction had taken precedence over affection, and the parents' expectations for the child were more important to them than his individual capacities or desires.

Heinz Kohut has made relevant observations on the role which such attitudes of the parents play in the formation of the child's self. He states that the parents, at times, "look upon the psychic organization of the child as part of their own, while at other times they respond to the child as to an independent center of his own initiative. . . ." Thus the parents can "further" or "hinder" the "cohesion" of the child's self [23:363].

We can assume that Stephen's sense of his "own initiative" was suppressed because of his intense identification with his parents' vision of his future. Under the impact of such strong identifications, the young child lacks sufficient self-awareness to question whether his goals for the future had been predetermined by his parents. When, in Stephen's case, the desired plan proved futile, not only he, but also his parents, suffered an unexpected defeat.

While Stephen submitted to his defeat with feelings of guilt, his mother did not accept what may well have been its true basis—Stephen's weakness in mathematics. Nor can she yet allow herself to empathize with him. She has to rely on a magic belief that the desired outcome had been, and still is, in some sense, within Stephen's power: "He says math is not for him, although I am convinced with some effort and self-discipline, he would get above-average grades in math." It is exactly this avoidance and distortion of a painful reality by the parents which has contributed to the protest of youth, past and present. One woman who had belonged to the German youth movement recounted how her mother had had two pet phrases when her daughter expressed concern about being overweight: first, that no one but she, herself, notices it, and second, that ten pushups each morning would remedy the condition. Similar unrealistic (and manipulative) attitudes, in place of true empathy, intensify feelings of powerlessness in the young. Parental insensitivity, in general, led some youth movement members to renounce their ties with their parents and adopt an independent lifestyle.

While Stephen must have recognized a lack of empathy in his mother's criticism, his father must have surprised him by his noncritical nonreprimanding attitude. He was mild and hardly showed any displeasure about Stephen's rejection by Harvard. In fact, he took Stephen's side with regard to his next choice of college. Stephen would have liked to apply to Columbia in order to be near the theaters. According to his mother, Stephen had become an "opera buff." Consequently, she was against Columbia. She took a stand against both Stephen and her husband in this matter and, because of her stronger voice in the family, she won. "I definitely said no, with all that we've heard about New York [she referred to the student unrest of the 1960s which still lingered and to the bohemian life]—it may be exaggerated, but nonetheless I thought Stephen had to know how we felt about it and I felt very strongly about it, but that was so wrong."

That the father was more tolerant of Stephen during this trying period was perhaps related to the fact that he himself had experienced a similar frustration when he was Stephen's age. Moreover, his recent success in his own work may have lessened his need to achieve through Stephen.

By the time Stephen was settled in a small eastern college of his mother's choice, a two-hour drive from his parents' house, Stephen had passed through a period of inner turmoil. To all outward appearances he had withstood calmly both the blow of being rejected by his most-preferred college and his mother's criticism and disappointment. During these discouraging times, Stephen must have come to accept some of his own feelings and fears and some of his attitudes in relation to his father and mother. For, according to Stephen's mother, the decisions regarding the courses in which to register had been made jointly through family discussions a few days before Stephen left home. He was to sign up for a general program combining biology and chemistry which would prepare him for a more specialized area in the future; but toward the end of the registration week, Stephen decided against his parents' plan and chose to major in play writing instead.

To change his field of study against his parents' wishes and to take the full responsibility for it, was, however one wants to interpret it, a major protest. Looking at his dissidence as originating in a particular "fit" between the personalities of parents and son, we can see the process taking form step by step until a decisive clash took place between his parents' perception of him and his perception about himself.

Looked at from a historical-social point of view, it was a protest which he shared with a segment of youth in the early 1970s. These individuals had been frightened as children by the violence and turmoil of the 1960s. They were now inclined to reexamine their own attitudes and values and to participate in personally meaningful, self-directed activities. Their goals were often at variance with their parents' strivings for status and possession—the striving of a generation which had reached maturity during the wartime and postwar periods under the pressure of planning a stable future.

When Stephen, on his weekend visit, made his resolution known to his parents, day-long negotiations followed. His mother said that she had never seen Stephen so anguished or so determined. "He was upset, I could tell, but he managed to keep his cool." Stephen's father was now less empathetic. He said that in his view classes in writing were a "waste of time and money" and that Stephen should carefully review his decision. Both parents confronted Stephen with questions. How could he be sure that he was capable of being a writer?

This time Stephen's mother was the first to make a conciliatory suggestion. As she described it, she felt pity because Stephen was frustrated once again. Besides, she concealed from both Stephen and her husband her hope that Stephen could well become a writer "and a good one," but, she added, when she told me about it: "How on earth can one make a living writing?" When the discussion had reached a stalemate and the parents were merely reiterating their points, the mother suggested that they would support Stephen for a year while he tried out his proficiency in the area of his choice. If he did not succeed, he would switch to a scientific field as originally planned.

In accordance with the pattern of interaction prevailing in Stephen's family, the conflict with his parents had been resolved, not by a release of hostile emotion or by a frank disclosure of feelings, but by a "rational" debate over alternatives. Since this pattern of interaction as well as his parents' values were still deeply ingrained in Stephen's personality, and since he was, at this time, in a state of suspension and anxiety, he accepted the compromise solution with a sense of relief. What he probably did not realize was that this solution would create in him a still greater pressure to succeed without relinquishing his dependency. This became apparent in Stephen's first attempt at writing a play.

His mother told about the first act of the play Stephen had written as a class assignment. Clearly she wanted the interviewer's opinion on the piece of work which, contrary to her own evaluation, had been strongly criticized by Stephen's professor. She condensed the content of the lengthy manuscript as follows:

The father of the main character was a wealthy, power-driven hotel owner. The son, "heir to the throne," was half-heartedly considered by his father as his successor. The son, however, plays the violin, roams the countryside and "walks on clouds" until he hears his father's employees scoffing at him behind his back. He is angry, tries to be tough, to bully them, even to fight his father. For the first time he expresses his anger.

Stephen's mother described the climax of the first act vividly, obviously admiring her son, its author:

The hotel owner and his son, by the window, argue in the plush hotel office: in front of them in the parking lot is the son's new, expensive car—a present from his father— dirty and uncared for. The first guests for a wedding at the hotel are just being seated while the ones for a silver wedding are filing into the main entrance.

The father insists that the son change his dirty shoes and put on a clean shirt before joining his family in the hotel dining room. Son: "Is that a condition?" Father: "It certainly is." The son slams the door in his father's face. The starting up of an engine can be heard outside.

When Stephen gave the finished act to his professor, he was sure that he had embarked upon a serious piece of art. He was told, instead, that the work had some merit but needed much revising, and that the best thing would be to start all over.

Stephen's mother concluded: "And Stephen thought he was going to say 'It's great! It should be produced.' You know he's read that young people have had novels published at nineteen and twenty. So I think that threw him."

Stephen's despair that his first literary attempt had not been praised can been seen as a blow to his narcissism as well as a threat to his incipient sense of self-affirmation. Since in writing about the son-father conflict, Stephen had infused his own conflict and feeling into the story, disapproval of the story (and its hero) produced a feeling of "nothingness," of rejection as a person. The teacher who criticized Stephen's work, furthermore, had had a strong influence on him. For a short time he may well have been Stephen's ego ideal. Then, through his criticism he may have activated in Stephen repressed feelings of hostility and resentment—another parent hindering him from accomplishing his goal.

Was Stephen able to endure this new discouragement by himself? Had he reached a sufficient degree of self-assurance to sustain his creative effort and begin anew? From our knowledge about Stephen's emotional dependence on his parents we can assume that he must have discussed his setback with his parents even though he could not expect affectionate support from them. Yet even the uncompromising, rational reactions, so well known to Stephen, would satisfy his need at that moment: the need to regress to infantile dependency and intimacy and to experience a sense of safety which would counteract the feelings of helplessness and utter rejection. As could be foreseen, Stephen's interchange with his parents elicited advice and instruction. They brought up library science as an appropriate field of study. They were "pushing it," his mother explained. They advised him to get a degree in this field and to find a job. He might later write again, they said, if that "makes him happy."

Stephen's mother described Stephen as being "in the dumps" during this discussion. Stephen himself, she said, felt that he had been led astray, misled by a false belief in himself. He said he had "deluded" himself. Stephen listened, seemingly indifferent, to his parents' admonition that he could never support himself as a writer even if he had moderate success. Their words must have driven home to him that whether he pursued their goal or his own, he would remain dependent on his parents for some time to come. Perhaps he also detected a punitive aspect in their suggestion that he take up library science. The handling of books in an impersonal bureaucratic fashion could have seemed to him to be the polar opposite of his goal as a creator.

Despite his parents' promptings, it was evident that Stephen did not want to go into library work. Instead he applied himself even more resolutely to the work in his chosen field. He did not seem very happy but he had overcome his recent defeat and his fear of another rejection. He had started on a part-time job as an errand boy and did odd jobs at the local theater. He had not heeded his parents' objection to his working parttime or their advice that his main purpose should now be "paying attention to his studies."

Had Stephen's confessions to his parents merely been a transient, defensive reaction brought on by his disillusion? And was he, in fact, beginning to go his own way, abandoning some of his identifications with his parents? Was he able to make friends in his present age group? Had he become attached to a girl with whom he could maintain a responsible, empathetic relationship? Stephen was invited to join a group of students who discussed issues of concern to their generation. The general topic was

"Democracy—now." The group set themselves the complex task of analyzing some of the political and philosophical principles on which the structure of American democracy had been built and on which it was now functioning. Stephen's mother was proud. She saw these meetings as an opportunity for Stephen to "sharpen his thinking" and to help him find new ways out of our "confused state of affairs." Stephen was gratified that such bright, idealistic people considered him to be intellectually on a par with them, but he soon recognized that they were primarily interested in analytical, logical debates, and unfamiliar with and not really concerned about the actual conditions within the civic institutions they proposed to analyze. Nor was Stephen able to talk to any member of the group on a personal level and form new friendships. He thought with some nostalgia of his high school pals.

He felt the need to talk to his parents about his isolation and loneliness. His mother said, "Stephen doesn't have the kinds of friends he had at home. We had quite a discussion on that. He is always very open about his troubles. I told him, and his father did too, that friends are very difficult to find. If you have one or two you count yourself very lucky. The rest should be acquaintances and you shouldn't be disheartened if you don't make the kinds of friends that you had in high school."

The interaction pattern to which Stephen was accustomed is here portrayed once more in his mother's words. It permits even painful feelings to be generalized and temporarily disposed of by intellectual discussions. This pattern is so much a part of Stephen's psyche that he has not been able to relate well with any of his male co-students except through intellectual exchange. One may speculate whether, if Stephen had been of college age a decade earlier, he would have been attracted to the hippie movement which was then at its height. The spontaneity and the individualism of these groups would indeed have appealed to someone like Stephen though the absence of controls, directions, and definite goals would probably have been difficult for him to tolerate. However, particularly for a young person of Stephen's personality and upbringing, the sense of genuinely "belonging" to a group his age can facilitate the development of intimate relationships. Whether identifications with new models could then have developed and could have supplemented the ones with his parents we cannot say, of course. Indeed, the very strength of Stephen's identification with his parents may interfere with his ability to model himself after another person.

Stephen did meet a girl whom he likes and whom his mother describes as "not pretty but very bright." The mother added, "He doesn't think of her romantically. He doesn't think of her as anyone he could be physically attracted to." It may be remembered that when he was three years old, Stephen's mother expressed the hope that Stephen's future wife would be a person who would be able to think like Stephen and would be intelligent. Stephen's girlfriend, as his mother describes her, seems to come surprisingly close to her (the mother's) early image.

Stephen's mother then complained about the "new morals" (e.g., couples living together without being married and married women refusing to go to work to enable their husbands to get their doctorates). Instead "a girl has got to be 'me'." A correspondence between this view of the mother's and Stephen's view on marriage is suggested when the mother says that Stephen is not going to get married: "He says it's just not for him, though I know he likes her and she likes him." In spite of his mother's criticism of the form of life Stephen has chosen, Stephen has been anxious for his mother to meet his girlfriend. He wanted to bring her home during a semester break but his mother repeatedly delayed answering Stephen's request, an unconscious maneuver, it would appear, by which she tried to deny Stephen's liaison even to herself. She rationalized her hesitancy by her disgust with the new morals. Moreover, the girl Stephen wants to bring home is a "political activist, although socialist more than communist." The girl had called Stephen during her semester break and they had gone to the theater together. Later, she had stayed in his room. The mother found it "extremely difficult" to invite the girl. "I am absolutely amazed that this girl would want to live with Stephen in his parents' house. That she is that kind of girl."

Stephen's own choice of his field of work and that of the people close to him throw some light on his identifications at the present phase of his life. He has moved away from his parents' wish for his future occupation and has not revised his decision under stress. He has formed a relationship with a girl who, intellectually, meets his parents' expectations but deviates decisively from his parents' political position and moral standards. We do not know whether Stephen is politically on her side, but in the closeness of their relationship he demonstrates that he is tolerant of her political beliefs. It is likely that the girl by her involvement in a political movement acts out for Stephen a protest to which he theoretically subscribes but one which he can express only in artistic form. On the one hand, he defies his parents' tradition by maintaining the relationship with his girlfriend; on the other hand, however, he does not commit himself. Nevertheless, in vital aspects of his personality, Stephen has begun to relinquish his identifications with his parents.

Why is it that Stephen is eager to confront his parents with attitudes and behavior which clearly convey his nonidentification? The answer is probably to be sought in a many-faceted, subconscious process. For the benefit of his self-approval, even when he is following his own direction, he needs to be taken seriously. He needs to be loved even while severing his infantile dependence on his parents. Moreover, the fact that Stephen openly discusses his lifestyle—a lifestyle which contrasts with that of his parents—may conceal defiance and anger about previous and present constraints. Similar sentiments are expressed by "runwaway" boys interviewed on the ABC television network in May 1975. (Running away must be seen as evidence of nonidentification with parents.) When asked why they left home, one boy said: "I was going to see whether I can make it. To show my father that I can do it." Another said: "I said to myself, I'm going to prove to them that I can do it. I couldn't stand it any more. They want one thing. I want another."

The emotional tie with parents has been assumed as basic for identifications to develop. Could it be that, in some cases, when identifications become weaker, the assurance of the original emotional tie is all the more urgently needed? This need was expressed by two other runaways in the same interview talking about their fathers: "I love him but things have to change"; "I'm sorry for the pain I caused him. I wanted to sit down with him and talk. But I never could and he wouldn't understand anyhow."

The merging of nonidentification and a strong emotional tie to the parent is documented by an extreme case of nonidentification: Rose Dagdale, a revolutionary activist in Ireland, wrote to her father from prison: "I love you, Daddy, and if there were any danger threatening you, I would stand between you and that danger. But I hate everything you stand for" [29:23].

Stephen is neither an activist nor a runaway. But he too needs his parents' emotional reassurance when his identifications with them lose their strength. We may then understand Stephen's growth in overt, emotional independence as related to his continuing need for maintaining some closeness with those from whom he intends to part. By exposing himself, through complete sincerity, to the familiar parental responses of criticism, advice, and instruction, he may derive the reassurance, however painful, that the emotional tie with his parents persists unaltered.

Being brought up with the accent on direction and a deemphasis on affection, he asks his mother, at age three: "Do you like me more than other boys?" He now requests of his mother a stronger affirmation of her affection through her willingness to accept his choice of profession and lifestyle so contrary to her own. Whether or not he subconsciously intends to evoke a confrontation, Stephen does not at the present stage of his development dare go too far his own way and thereby critically endanger the emotional bond with his parents.

John

John's mother was on her lunch hour. She insisted on inviting the author for lunch. Afterward, we talked in privacy for an hour and a half. She was carefully dressed and coiffured and did not seem hurried. As a private secretary she was able to schedule her own time. She still had her somewhat muffled voice and her half smile which now made some hard, downward lines in her face disappear. She was attentive and ready to unravel some puzzling episodes of the past. She began to cry when we touched on her husband's illnesses and death, and said that it was still very hard for her to talk about it.

John's mother, as was true of Stephen's mother, remembered nothing specific of the author's first visits to the family: she remembered them "just vaguely. It really doesn't come back."

When she replied to questions about John or made comments of her own, she tended to talk about his motivations, hang-ups, or feelings—in short, about the emotional side of his personality and about her being responsible for much of it. Stephen's mother, in contrast, had hardly ever talked about how she might have influenced Stephen's personality, although she did recall, however, that she carried over into her role as a mother what had been expected of her in her own family as the oldest of six children; that she had to take care of her young siblings while strictly supervised and disciplined by her mother. John's mother also commented on her having been manipulated by a restrictive and demanding mother who planned her education and job (as a salesgirl) and who found a husband for her through making inquiries among relatives.

When John was small, most of his mother's frustrations were caused by her interfering and critical mother who lived just a block away. She criticized John's mother for feeding him at irregular hours, "constantly" picking the baby up, and "making him nervous." John's mother believes that it was this tense relationship with her own mother and her (unreleased) hostility toward her which caused intense guilt feelings in her and made her worry so much about John. "I worried about things I shouldn't have worried about. I was overprotective. I was always bothering him for something. I think I am a lot calmer now. Maybe I'm not, but I don't let him know." His mother then added: "But then John got so much from both of us. Maybe the first child always gets that attention." She was obviously referring to the abundant affection John received from both his parents. From her further recollections and this author's earlier visits to the family it was evident that John received little incentive from his parents to develop his full ego potential and to curb his instinctual demands. He was still having his bottle at three because he did not "know" how to drink from a cup. He often had outbursts of temper when his mother did not fulfill a momentary desire of his and, in particular, when his mother left him with a babysitter. It is easy to see from the foregoing that John's mother's infantilizing behavior stemmed from her wish to give him the kind of indulgence she herself had missed and perhaps from an effort to live vicariously the "happy" childhood she had not had.

It would appear that both the mother's and father's overprotectiveness catered to unconscious wishes to preserve the closeness with John and his complete dependency as a baby. Mother in particular seemed to wish to retain this state of oneness with her child. By being absorbed by loving feelings for John and by identifying with him, she satisfied her own unfulfilled need for affection. The father's infatuation with John as a baby probably had a different origin. Since his own mother "sheltered" and "overloved" him as a child, he may have unconsciously attempted to

perpetuate this experience in his relationship with his son. John's psychological responses to his parents' affectionateness and their weakness in controlling his impulses may be partly responsible for his reluctance to move toward
greater maturity. His personality as a young adult and his pattern of
interaction with his mother (to be presently described) support this interpretation.

Preschool years. When asked about John's preschool years, his mother
said that "personality-wise" John remained pretty much the same from the
time when he was observed in the interaction session until he entered school
three years later. This statement could be understood as the mother's
"regressive pull," i.e., as her wish to prolong John's infant years. In her
memory, John's father was even more attached to John during these years:
mother often told him that he spoiled John. She did not recall that John's
father was to some extent more successful in directing and controlling John
at age three than she was. She remembered that when John was asleep as a
baby, his father sometimes stood by his crib just to watch him breathe.

School years. His mother first recalled that John got a little chubby
because he liked to eat and that he was somewhat irritated by being chubby.[2]
After school the father used to play baseball with John and other children.
John was not bothered by his father's taking part in the game as though he
was one of the boys. On the contrary, the mother thought that John was
rather proud of it. The overanxious, overprotective father of John's early
childhood changed into a "buddy" for John during his school years. Since
John had also advanced in strength and manly demeanor, the father's role as
John perceived it was that of an adult who was affectionate and intimate
with him, but who was also able to protect him by setting up and enforcing
rules. Both these images of his father remained important for the subsequent
development of John's personality.

About John's intellectual performance in school his mother makes only a
general remark: "John was good in most subjects, especially in things he
wanted to do. It's sort of hard to explain. If he liked a subject, like drawing,
he would get an A. When he didn't want to work, he got a B or even a D. It's
still the same. He does whatever he wants to do. If he doesn't want to do it,
he won't do it. He doesn't care what someone else tells him to do." Some
uneasiness was apparent in the mother's tone of voice, particularly when she
added: "I'm from the school where you go to college, you find what you
want to major in, and do it." It is in these brief intimations that one can
assess both John's deviation from his parents' values and their disappointment.

She then talked about John's social skills and his relation to his age
mates. He liked school because he liked company. "Music is not his thing
but he learned to play the tuba because he wanted to be with other kids. He
was always hanging around with his gang. And he was quite popular."
Moreover, she believed that John was a "born leader." To prove her point

she said that he was the one who thought of the pranks his gang would play, such as spreading sneezing powder during an examination or listening to a teachers' conference on grades through a crack in the wall. Even though John was brought to the principal a few times because of his behavior, his mother seemed amused and accepting when she recalled these incidents. She added: "And he still goes through little boyish pranks. He's still a little devil; he was never an angel."

Just as she had not constrained John or given him any guidance for completing a block structure at age three, it was obvious that even now John's mother did not care to instill in John an interest in school subjects, to guide him, impart her knowledge to him, or reward his achievement. And just as she had taken pleasure in John's diverting the block-building task into a humorous interchange between himself and his mother ("Can you build one like this?" "No, I can build one like that"), so his mother was still enamored of his boyish pranks today.

She could not remember that John had had "a hard time" during adolescence. He adjusted well to dating and always had girlfriends. She did not find it necessary to know any of them personally. Although concerned and proud about John's social success, one gets the impression that she tended to keep John's personal life separated from his relationship with her. She may have evolved this attitude in order to protect herself from the painful fact that John was on the way to emancipation and might one day not need her anymore. John, on the other hand, seemed concerned with asserting his masculinity. He was proud that he didn't have to ask a certain girl for a date since she herself had suggested that he take her out. When he became quite chubby he did not go swimming for fear that he looked as if he had breasts. Then he decided to lose weight. Although it was hard for him, he succeeded to some extent when his mother also went on a diet.

John's father's death. His father had his first heart attack when John was sixteen. When his mother had told John about it, he stayed in his room for hours. He then "went wild." He threw the keys of the family car down the staircase so hard that they scratched the front door. He stormed out of the house saying that he would never come back and drove off. When he came back in an hour, he screamed and kept kicking the refrigerator, shouting: "Why doesn't it happen to someone else's father?"

John behaved similarly when his father died. His mother called him to the hospital. He came and stormed out of the hospital alone, almost immediately. He didn't want to go home. When he finally came, he did the same thing he had done before. He kicked the refrigerator, shouting: "Why does it happen to me?"

By observing John as a small child with his mother and his father and hearing about his violent response to his father's death, we can speculate about John's self-image then and now. Until the time when his father became fatally ill, John probably felt that he was someone special and lovable. His parents' overprotectiveness may have contributed to forming an image of himself as safe from any grave, unalterable blow of fate. His "why does it happen to me?" expresses not only his anger but also his (magic) belief that he is to be protected from sorrow.

In a fit of rage he attacks an object as if it had punitive power. By attacking a thing which contains food he repudiates food which had previously been highly gratifying. Moreover, it is conceivable that in the symbol language of the unconscious, the refrigerator represents John's parents who until now have fulfilled most of his wishes and have supplied him with an abundance of emotional "'nourishment." He may blame his parents, subconsciously, for his first severe deprivation as well as his inability to control his rage.

Preoccupied entirely with himself, John is unable to share his distress with his mother or to realize that immediate decisions have to be made in which he could be of help. We saw that when John was small his father had to some extent been able to encourage John to deal with a situation of minor stress. Since his father is not there anymore, John is left without a vital ego support, and this is not only because of his father's affection for him but also because his father provided him with some standards of behavior. As his father had said: "When I tell him a toy will be fixed, he knows it will be fixed." His father had been able to control John so that in his father's presence he "shifted from one thing to the other" less frequently than in his mother's. As will be remembered, John completed his tasks in his father's but not in his mother's session.

The father's death occurs in John's late adolescence. Adolescence is the time when a person begins to establish his mature identity and often comes to doubt his earlier immature identification with his parents. John's despair may have been a sign of the deepening of his identification with his father often observed after a death and sometimes accompanied by the refusal of any consolation. However John does not seem to have internalized a mature image of his father. Instead he behaves like a little boy who has not been given his way. When, after the funeral, his uncle reminds John that he is now "the man in the family" and must help his mother regain her emotional balance, John resents this role saying that he is not a man yet—an attitude which puzzles the mother even years later.

College years. John's mother, unlike Stephen's parents, did not provide John any guidance regarding his choice of courses or field of study. Yet her preferences for John's career happen to be similar to those of Stephen's parents:

I still think John belongs in sciences somewhere. My husband and I always felt that this would be his area or at least that he would find a practical job with a regular income, etc. But I just have the feeling that he would be very good in science—if he takes a few courses maybe he'll catch on—he doesn't even know yet, he isn't aware—

To date John, not too different from Stephen, has not taken any science courses. Instead he took courses on Eastern Languages, Sex Roles in Today's Society, and "things like that."

In contrast to Stephen's parents, John's mother seems to avoid worrying about John's goals:

As long as he is happy and enjoying what he's doing—even if he isn't setting the world on fire—what do I want from him? Even if he goes for a year taking what he likes, he has time later to major in whatever he wants. So long as he is happy, which he is, I think, let him be happy.

She admits that she was not always so unconcerned about John's future, and that she had told him her mind a few times. It will be recalled that when John was three years old, his father had said he wouldn't "badger his son into a profession that would only make him unhappy."John's mother now recalls that she and her husband had always abstained from imposing their wishes or hopes on John. This memory seems to evoke her discomfort at John's present aimlessness. In his infancy John's inconsistent and shifting behavior did not meet with marked displeasure on the part of his parents. At that time John's mother excused this behavior saying that she herself was impatient. As frequently demonstrated through psychoanalysis, behavior and attitudes developed through identification early in life tend to persist if the bond with the parent had been close and the dependence on the parent strong. John's inability to stick to a course of action, an inability which continued into his college years, could then be traced to his early identification with his mother. And, analogous to the father's concern about John's inconsistency at age three, his mother now tries to "figure him out." She says: "Who knows what's really going on in his mind?" She is "very curious where he's going" because she cannot predict him. She may wonder whether the freedom and independence which John seems to cherish are of benefit to him or whether they cause frustrations which he cannot handle. While she seems to have a need to praise John for "doing his own thing," she also shows some resentment that she has to amend the adverse effects of John's impulsiveness:

John had lost his license plates. It didn't bother him. I sent him new ones right away.

He went sliding down a trail on a makeshift sled using a raincoat wrapped around sticks. It was John's idea. The trail was frozen and one of his friends got hurt. So I am sending packages to take to his friend. But John is very upset about it; he goes to the hospital whenever he can.

John brought a big puppy home on his vacation. A friend gave it to him. He was going to carry it in the plane under his coat, but the puppy had to be crated. So he missed the plane. But he didn't think of having me paged and letting me know about it. So I waited at the airport for hours.

John's mother concludes her story of the incident by saying:

This is the type of thing John does. He decides he will do something and he does it all the way. You cannot change his mind.

She sounded somewhat disquieted in contrast to how she sounded when she related John's pranks as a schoolboy. Yet, she is obviously able to repress whatever hostility she may harbor against him.

She then described John's social life in college:

It didn't take him long until he found friends with whom he could go out in the evening. He always makes a lot of friends wherever he goes. He says he has made some good friends. The way he describes them they are not way-out kids, just nice boys.

John has a girlfriend from high school and he has met a girl in college whom he likes. Yet his mother does not think it is "anything serious."

Let us return for a moment to the early interaction patterns in John's and Stephen's families and see how they relate to John's ease and Stephen's slowness in making friends away from home. From John's frantic reaction, as an infant, when his mother left him temporarily, one might have expected that it would be difficult for him to adjust to age mates in school and, later, in college. That John, on the contrary, is eager and finds it easy to make social contacts may stem from a desire to free himself from his overdependence, which can be linked to his parents' affectionate involvement with him. Moreover, from early infancy on, he has had constant opportunities and models for "practicing" affection, although, according to his mother's descriptions, John's affection has more often found an outlet in "having fun" than in sharing ideas and feelings with others.

For Stephen, on the other hand, friends are, in his mother's words, "not easy to find." Although Stephen had friends in school and is still in close contact with them, Stephen's main interest, reinforced by his parents, was directed toward intellectual pursuits. At the present stage of his development Stephen seems to need a friendship in which he can empathically exchange confidences and share insights and feelings. Like John, Stephen strives for greater emotional independence from family bonds by establishing new human contacts.

While Stephen's parents tried to comfort Stephen by supplying him with generalizations for his predicament, thus denying his personal need for meaningful friendships, John's mother views her son's friendships as of great importance. John's appeal to other persons and his skill in establishing relationships seem to reassure her of his worth and to dispel her occasional doubts about his future.

John's mother continues to keep aloof from John's involvement with girls, behavior which we interpreted earlier as denial. Yet a certain resignation seems implicit in her noninterference when she says about John's relationship with girls: "I wouldn't like him to live with a girl unless he was married. But I don't think you have any say over it. They know how you feel anyhow." And in the words that follow she sums up her attitude about John's nonidentification with certain of her values: "We took on the views that we were taught. If his are different, I don't think it offends me too terribly."

Conclusions

What picture can we assemble of Stephen and John in the present? Stephen seems to be reaching out to establish interpersonal relationships and to find models with whom to identify. He has not succeeded as yet, partly because of his insecurity that has its origin in his family's (and his own) continuing expectations—expectations which he cannot fulfill.

As for John, although it is quite true that, as John's mother says, "John always makes a lot of friends; he makes friends wherever he goes," his human contacts appear to be of short duration and somewhat superficial in quality. He seems now to be fleeing from intimacy, as he fled from sharing his sadness after his father's death. Does he need affirmation from many, as a substitute for the unconditional affection he received as a child? His mother says: "John is a leader." Does he try to provide for others the directions that have been withheld from him? Yet, having rarely experienced leadership, his leadership is neither adult nor responsible. He leads his friends into dangerous adventures as he led his gang into mischievous pranks in school.

John and Stephen have traveled different roads and will continue to do so, yet in their lack of a secure sense of their own selves, they seem to converge. The forms in which the two sons now deviate from the models provided by their parents' generation is, in certain respects, in line with the new youth culture. While Stephen's affiliation with the counterculture is apparent in his sexual liberation, in his unconventionnal style of life, and in the content of his writing, John displays yet other forms of dissidence. He is engaged in self-assertive, adventurous living and in searching out a multitude of experiences and a variety of human contacts. He abstains from hard intellectual work and from striving toward the kind of success which depends on affirmation by authority. John is akin, in this respect, to a number of his contemporary proponents of the new youth culture. Yet, John as well as Stephen must be considered as merely on the fringe of a youth movement. They are neither theoretically nor practically concerned with bringing about social reforms. Stephen, unlike John and unlike the new rebels, is eager to succeed in his individual effort and willing to apply himself to hard work in order to achieve his goal.

Two types have emerged from the intensive study of the early parent-child relationship in two families with reverberating implications for the children's later lives and places in society. If John is self-willed, he is so in beaten paths; he will, paradoxically, and like most of his companions, become a follower. Stephen might occasionally become overwrought by anxiety, but he may break new ground. Stephen has reversed to its opposite his parents' considerable expectations in one field of study while John, because they had no specific expectations for him, has not gravely disappointed his parents. His mother is still waiting, hoping for a purpose to emerge from John's strivings, but she is confident that as long as he is happy, that is enough. Can someone like John, lacking serious purpose, be happy for long, however? Can Stephen, burdened with purpose as he is, become happy? Could it be that the need both share for uncritical acceptance prevents them from maintaining meaningful friendships? Would their inner instability be lessened, and would they grow into mature individuals valuable to society, if they looked outside their families for deeper commitments and more meaningful identifications?

THE PARENTS' PERCEPTION OF
THE CHILD'S INDIVIDUALITY:
PAUL AND JERRY

Perception, as used here, refers to the "subjective" perception, that is the image or idea which one person forms of another by selecting, organizing, interpreting, and sometimes distorting the objective characteristics of that person. Parents' perceptions of their child frequently arise from needs which they hope the child will fulfill. Stephen's parents, for example, project a number of their own unachieved goals onto him and to some extent disregard his "real" character. A further example of subjective perception is provided by the mother of a teenage daughter observed in another study [46:418]. In situations of minor conflict, this mother perceived her daughter as her (the mother's) sister and, driven by an unconscious need to reenact an unresolved conflict with her sister and to rid herself of apprehension and anxieties, she became extremely antagonistic.

Thus, a parent's perception of the child, arising as it does from the objective characteristics of the child and from the parent's own needs, influences both the parent's and, in turn, the child's behavior. In the process, the child's feelings about himself as well as his identification with the parent are affected.

We have observed in our comparison of John and Stephen that John's parents tended to "release" John, i.e., they abstained as much as possible from directing or constraining him, while Stephen's parents tended to constrain Stephen. We saw that these modes of parental behavior were in line with the parents' perception of their children. John's mother, in large measure because of her own need for affectionate mothering, perceived John as much younger than his age and continued to infantilize him even when he had reached adulthood. Stephen's parents, on the other hand, influenced by their own unfulfilled needs to pursue academic goals, perceived Stephen, even while he was still very young, as being suited for a scientific career.

John adapted to his parents' perception of him by remaining infantile and impulsive even in later years. Stephen adapted to the perception of his parents by developing verbal proficiency and "scientific" attitudes even as a child. When, as a young adult, Stephen became aware of the discrepancy between his parents' wishes for him and his wishes for himself, he turned his efforts more and more to the fulfillment of his own goals, at the price of considerable inner stress and the danger of alienation from his parents. Figure 1 illustrates the process.

By objective characteristics of the child we mean those aspects of the child which exist without reference to the parents' needs. They include genetic endowment (favorable and unfavorable), skills, individual needs and expectations, etc., which are not directly influenced by the parents.

There are enough perspectives here to provide the starting point for a variety of studies. Not the least interesting would be an attempt to sort out social influences such as radical ideas and social reforms as they affect the day-to-day behaviors of parents to their young children. We shall touch upon these influences in the sections on communal childrearing.

With Stephen and John we saw how apparently private interactions in childhood could have made them susceptible in later years to social influences as seen in their patterns of behavior and in their insecurities typical of broad segments of society.

In the present study, we can only begin to see some of the possibilities here as we seek some of the roots of dissidence in the parent-child relationship.

In what follows we will concentrate on the early relations in the family in detail by observing in the same family interactions between the parents and their two young sons, Paul and Jerry. We will try to understand, in particular, how the parents' perception of the child influences the parent-child relationship and the child's attempts at identification or dissidence.

Mother with Jerry: First Interactions after Birth

Jerry belonged to a group of normal children who were studied as controls for a group of disturbed children [31:421-427] (see Chapter 1, p. 20). Since

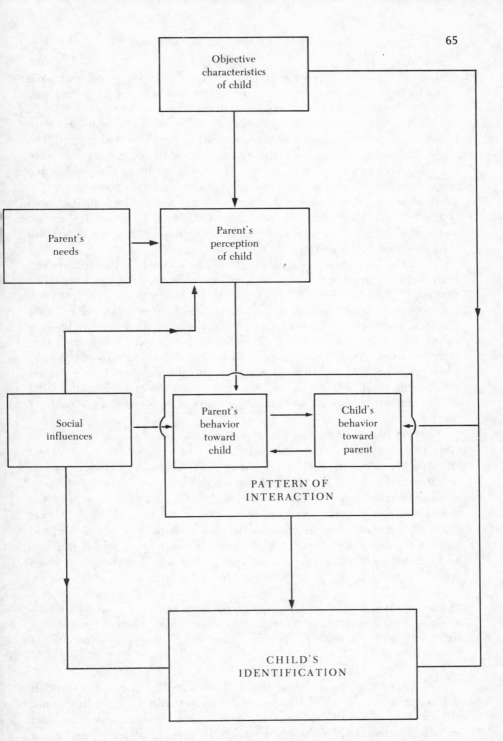

Figure 1. Determinants of Parent-Child Interaction and Child's Identification.

siblings of these children were studied whenever possible, Jerry's year-and-a-half older brother, Paul, was observed in interaction with each parent, and the parents were given the same questionnaire about each of their sons.

The parents were in their late twenties and were on the same socioeconomic level as John's and Stephen's parents. They were Protestants. The father had recently changed his place of work as an accountant, following his wife's preference, but not his own. His wife hoped that his new job in a larger firm would lead to more interesting business acquaintances than the previous one. But her husband missed the friendly contacts in the small company. Information on the earliest interactions of Jerry and his mother was available since the mother had been included in a study of mothers and their newborn babies [6:286-294].

We know from these early data that the mother decided before Jerry was born that in contrast to her previous delivery she wanted to be fully aware of her second baby from its first breath on. (When Paul was born she had been unconscious because of anaesthetics.) She refused anaesthetics even though the fetal position was unusual and she was warned that she might have strong pain without medication. According to her hospital notes, she never regretted having undergone the pain: "I really felt good in spite of the pain. I had made up my mind that if I was going to have another child, I wanted it to be the most important thing for me at the time of birth, and I felt I would miss out on this if I were under anaesthetics, even if it were just for a few minutes."

She was happy when told that it was a boy because she "wouldn't have known how to handle a girl." She later expressed repeated concern over not knowing or understanding enough about this baby. A few days later, when recalling the night of the birth, she remarked on Jerry's screwed-up face, wrinkled forehead, and large mouth, and how he had tried to expel some mucus with obvious difficulty but without crying. She then visualized him as a complacent and submissive individual easy to handle. When she nursed him for the first time, however, she revised her earlier perception of Jerry. The following observation by a research assistant describes the first interaction of the nursing couple on the second day after birth:

The infant was brought to the breast quickly before he had a chance to reach for the nipple with his lips. Sucking was intermittent, eyes closed. The mother said:"Oh, you're not holding on. You're just playing." She added, disappointed, "No, you don't have the idea at all."[3]

The mother apparently began this first feeding with her initial perception of Jerry as an "easy baby" who would follow her wishes. When he did not live up to her expectations, she saw him as apathetic and uncooperative, and was disappointed. Then she changed her perception of Jerry once again during the same feeding when he surprised her by the vigor of his sucking.

"That's the boy. Now you've got it." He took about six good sucks. "Gee, he's got a much better sucking than Paul [addressed to her husband]. Paul didn't have it that good until a few days."

Like all mothers who have more than one child, her perception of the newborn was formed in part through comparison with his sibling. During the next day or two, the baby appeared to the mother as more strong-willed than his brother. Jerry's liveliness and impatience were unfamiliar qualities to her. Bent on "knowing" and "understanding" Jerry's individuality, she tried, at times, to "test" his reaction. The following pattern of interaction between Jerry and his mother was observed while they were still in the hospital:

In the nursing position, the mother would sometimes lift the infant slowly to the level of the breast "so that there was a lag between the time the infant was brought to the feeding position and when the breast was actually available" [6:288]. On one such occasion, the mother explained her slowness by saying that she was interested in finding out how he would reach for the nipple. The infant's reaction consisted of turning his head from side to side, a movement which sometimes persisted even while the mother tried to insert the nipple and which suggested to the observer the baby's frustration.

When Jerry was one and a half years old, his mother thought that her relationship with Jerry had become "more secure" because she had "begun to understand his behavior." When Jerry was two and a half, however, she said, "Coming here together and being given certain tasks has been an interesting experience because I am never sure how he will react." At that age, the mother's perception of Jerry was that he was unlike her. Both mother and father saw him as independent, standing up for himself, and unpredictable. The father described Jerry as "different" and "unique."

Paul, four at the time, was seen by both parents as cooperative, friendly with people, and "easy." The mother was quite articulate when she compared Paul with herself. She felt he resembled her in various ways: like her, for example, he enjoyed looking at pictures and dancing. He also "sounded" like her when he expressed anger. She said that, unlike Jerry, Paul frequently imitated her movements and tone of voice.

The mother's perception of both her children appeared to be related to her need for security—a need which could have originated in having suffered rejection and insecurity in her own childhood. Her perception of Paul as similar to herself seemed to alleviate her need for security, while her perception of Jerry as unpredictable and independent did not. Instead, her early insecurity may have been revived with Jerry. Her discomfort about the dissimilarity between her and Jerry, suggestive of a self-replicating tendency (see page 36), may explain her wish for knowing who Jerry really was and how he could be expected to behave.

Paul and Jerry at Preschool Age: Parent-Child Interactions

The interaction sessions were conducted in an observation room in the UCLA Department of Child Psychiatry. The dialogue of child and parent as well as a running record of the interaction (observed from behind a one-way vision screen), were tape-recorded.

The following tasks were used with Paul and Jerry: individual activity, modeling and imitation, stress, choice making, separation, and morality.

Individual Activity

Instead of copying three abstract patterns as in the previous study, the parent was to draw a house, a tree, and a person. The child was asked by the parent to "draw something." Colored pencils were provided. The parent's assignment was taken from the widely used "House-Tree-Person" test [5]. In the present study, the house, tree, and person to be drawn by the parent were used to provide meaningful topics of conversation between parent and child as well as drawings which might tell something about the parent's perception of the child.

At first Jerry is told by his mother that "you're going to do this all by yourself." She is unable to tolerate his independent activity for long, however, and soon asks him, "Can you draw Mummie a pretty picture?" And "What are you drawing for me?" To Jerry's evasive reply that he is drawing "a scribble," she responds by saying:"You're drawing a scribble for me." Jerry: "Yeah, I like scribble." After her unsuccessful attempt at making Jerry copy her house, an assignment too hard for a child Jerry's age, she becomes involved in her own work. She ignores Jerry's request to look at his picture and, instead, tells him, "Mummie is not a good artist." Then she asks a question he cannot and is not expected to answer: "Are you a good artist?" "When she shows him the "silly man" she made, however, Jerry responds in a surprisingly mature fashion: "No, it's fine."

He can answer his mother's again-too-difficult questions, "Why don't you use pink?" and "Why don't you use more olive?" only with "cause""" and "Because I do." Jerry refuses to put a chimney on his mother's house or ears on her cowboy. His feeling of frustration and hostility about not being accepted on his own level and being restrained from a fun activity ("I like scribble") is expressed in his wish to mess up his mother's picture. His mother seems impervious to the reason for Jerry's destructive mood. "You want to mess it all up after Mummy worked so hard on it?"—a question obviously designed to arouse his guilt.

His mother's constraint is reminiscent of her early interaction with Jerry as a baby when she delayed the actual feeding briefly to "find out more" about his behavior. Her attempts at involving Jerry in her own work, even beyond his capacity, can be understood as arising from her wish to overcome the separateness between her and Jerry which is such a disquieting part of her perception of him. Yet she does this in such a manner as to provoke his resistance and to foster his insecurity, prompting his passive compliance rather than overt cooperation in the task.

During the drawing task mother and Paul communicate almost on an equal level. Paul succeeds in getting mother involved in his spider-like drawing of a "man" and of a dog. He elaborates on the dog's figure: "This is the body. Here's the face. Here's the eyes. All dogs have fur, don't they?" Paul's fluid talk about his drawings shows both his ease and his self-assertion in his mother's presence. When she criticizes her drawing of a person as she did in Jerry's session, Paul, like Jerry, comforts her: "But you made him all right. That's the way they look." Both children appear to be responsive to the mother's need for recognition and reassurance.

The mother's drawing of a person, completed by Paul upon her suggestion, points to her perception of Paul as "fused" with her. By involving Paul in her drawing, she paradoxically constrains him to some extent, while at the same time boosting his self-confidence. Thus her perception of Paul's intrinsic similarity and oneness with her can present a threat to his growth toward independence and may make it more difficult for him to relinquish his early identification with his mother. On the other hand, Paul seems to possess resources which counteract his dependency need. When his mother tells him that he cannot take his drawings home because they are kept at the clinic, he reveals a sense of self-accomplishment by asking her: "Cause I'm such a good artist?" He also seems to need to set himself apart from mother by implicitly claiming his superiority: "But, Mummie, you are not a very good artist."

Jerry shows less infantile behavior and more initiative in his session with his father than with his mother. Without hesitation he says that he is going to "draw a house" (not a scribble). He easily succeeds in engaging his father's attention ("Watch this!" Father: "O.K. Let's see what you're drawing.") Jerry seems to enjoy his scribbling during the minutes of silence while his father draws. Jerry also invents a different use of the pencils by holding a bunch of them in one hand going over the paper in round strokes and zigzag lines. He pays no attention to father's suggestion to "pick up one at a time," but is eager for father to acknowledge his accomplishment: "This one, I colored this one. Now you can see all the colors." Father gives it a side glance and, perhaps because Jerry's unusual activity fits in with father's perception of Jerry as "unique," does not pressure him any more.

Paul, in his session with father, asserts himself as he did with mother. He does not praise his own accomplishment but competes with his father's.

Paul:	Daddy, not that way.
Father:	Why?
Paul:	Cause you have to make a circle.

Paul:	Daddy, is that the way you draw a man?
Father:	That's the way I'm drawing him, yeah.

Paul: That's not the way—the way you draw a real man.
Father: It isn't? How do you draw a real man?
Paul: There. See?

Paul transforms father's tree into an apple tree and, next to it, draws "a little boy picking the apples with his mother." Psychoanalytically interpreted, Paul's competitive strivings as well as his feelings of rivalry with his father over his mother's love are indicated by the little boy who, together with the mother, picks apples from the father's tree. Paul's struggle for superiority over his father is, indeed, conveyed in various other situations. Father responds to Paul's role of superiority with a tongue-in-cheek seriousness which seems to disguise his amusement. And in his answer to the question of how he felt about the session with his son, he writes, "I got a kick out of the way he showed me what to do." Yet in his interview father reveals how he dislikes his own passivity, a passivity which he attributes to his reaction to his dominant, aggressive mother and to his identification with his placid, ineffective, and "never ruffled" father. As a parent in everyday situations, Paul's father has to assert himself to some extent. However, in the game-like climate of the drawing situation, he can use or forego his authority as he chooses. He may feel a need to reexperience his early submissive relationship with his mother, if for no other reason than to be able to abandon it.

How Paul reacts in various other situations to the immature model his father personifies for him will be illustrated below. In the meantime it should be noted that father's preference for a passive role not only originates from his (the father's) individual childhood experiences, but is also conditioned by cultural processes which make the father's unquestioned authority obsolete. These changes will be discussed in more detail later.

The content and style of the parent's drawings in the presence of each of the two children warrant a closer look. In his session with Paul, father produces a realistic drawing of a man. In his session with Jerry, he draws a handless muscleman wearing a top hat. While mother draws the "person" as a cowboy in her session with Jerry, her person drawing in Paul's session, like the father's drawing in his session with Paul, is a general representation of a man. It is possible that both parents withdraw more easily into fantasy in Jerry's presence than in Paul's. No doubt Jerry's younger age relieves them in part of the obligation to take their task too seriously. Moreover, their perception of Jerry as unique and different may give freer scope to their imagination. It is not easy to find an explanation for mother's cowboy drawing except perhaps as an effort to gain Jerry's interest and appreciation which might stem from her insecurity with him.

The father's muscleman may be *his* male ideal for Jerry. That this ideal is unrealizable for either himself or Jerry might be signified by the lack of hands which expresses a sense of thwartedness.

Choice Making

The parent is required to present the child a book of nine rectangular pages, with three abstract, colored patterns on each page. The parent is to choose the pattern which appeals to him/her the most ("I like this one") and then ask the child for his/her own choice ("Which do you like?").

Most parents show some anxiety over whether the child's choice coincides or diverges from their own. Althought we might expect the parental attitude to have some influence on the child's decision, the majority of children tested disagree with their parents' choices. (The strength of a child's disagreement could further be judged, by the position on the page of the pattern he chose—by whether it was adjacent to, or removed by one pattern from, that chosen by the parent.)

Regardless of whether the interaction prior to this task has been agreeable or not, the children obviously welcome the chance to express their deviation from their parents' choices. Could it be that a motivation for later dissidence stems from a primitive wish to differ from the parent and thereby to shed the infantile dependency? This tendency would then originate, in part, during a period long before the age when rational, aesthetic, or moral judgments lead to youthful attempts at emancipation.

Both Jerry and Paul disagree with all but one of their mother's choices: they seem to make use of this opportunity to differentiate themselves from their mother. Jerry's dependence is still noticeable in the way he always picks a pattern adjacent to his mother's, while Paul tries to soften his deviation from mother by suggesting a reason for it. Mother: "I think I like this one, it's awfully pretty." Paul: "I also like this [other] one because it's pretty too."

The mother tries to constrain both Jerry's and Paul's choice making by extolling the pattern she chooses. She challenges Jerry's choice by saying, "You don't like the blue and purple [her own choice]?" Jerry sulkily tells her, "No." Yet in her questionnaire about the session with Jerry she enters choice making as her favorite task. Perhaps this shows the pleasure she feels in having her perception of Jerry's individuality (as being different from hers) confirmed.

Paul is, as usual, treated as an equal by his mother. She asks him why he chose a particular pattern, and when he cannot give a reason she provides it for him, enumerating the "pretty" colors on his pattern. Another time Paul and mother argue about his choice. Paul: "It's more colorful." Mother: "But this one [her choice] is even more colorful."

As can be expected, mother does not check choice making as the most enjoyed task in Paul's session. Paul's divergence from her choices must be disappointing to her since she probably expects him to conform to her taste. This interpretation is supported by her attempt to constrain Paul by telling him: "So you don't like the ones Mummie likes."

Jerry's divergent choices are accepted good humoredly by his father—

although not without some attempt to influence him ("You really like that one?"). The interaction is animated and the task ends in a game initiated by the father: he waves his hand over all the patterns on the last page and says, "I like them all," an act which is imitated by Jerry. Jerry also mirrors father's diction and tone of voice. Jerry's mirroring has the quality of a spontaneous game. His father responds with humor ("Doncha like mine?"). He accepts Jerry's agreement in a similar joking mood ("Well, we agree for once").

One may question whether a parent's jesting and regressing to the child's level contributes to his or her effectiveness as a model for identification. Does a similarity of humor which one sometimes encounters in a parent and a child originate in the young child's mirroring the parent's jesting during spontaneous games? And does identification with the model's style of humor facilitate identification with the other, more serious, characteristics of the model? Humor is a way of escaping from the reality of a stressful situation. Are Jerry's and Paul's divergent choices as threatening to the father as they are to the mother and could humor be the father's way of mitigating his anxiety?

With Paul, father again conducts the task in an animated fashion. But Paul, unlike Jerry, frequently tries to outwit father, e.g., by choosing first or by choosing simultaneously, or by directing or correcting him, or by making use of his knowledge of the game acquired in his session with mother. Paul, in fact, struggles throughout the task for superiority over father, and tends to choose patterns most distantly located from father's.

Father willingly, and with a certain gusto, follows Paul's lead. His comment in the postsession questionnaire (cited above) vouches for the gratification he derives from his "submissive" role. It was suggested earlier that father in fact has some need to see Paul as superior to himself. On the other hand, Paul's response to one of his father's choices—"Mummie likes this. You must like another"—suggests the wish for a less submissive father as well as the wish that his two parents be clearly differentiated.

According to Margaret Mead, we have just entered an epoch in which adults learn from their children, a period in which the young are claiming a "new authority" and the parental generation is tempted to join youth uncritically [34:57-64]. By attire, verbal expressions, and even ideologies, parents may fashion themselves after the model of their children. Yet the young, seeking adult models they can respect or admire, tend to reject these "ever-young" parents as models. Paul's and his father's exchange during the choice-making task shows how a child may go about modifying a parent's modeling behavior according to his own needs; and we observe how (within limits) the parent's behavior as a model may, in fact, become adapted to how he or she is perceived and desired by the child.

However, the attempt to drastically modify the parent's behavior will of course be futile. If at some later point Paul should complain of what he did not receive from his father, he would be making a complaint typical of today's youth. Yet what hope could he have in asking for modeling behavior such as determination and assertiveness from someone who, by his very nature, is incapable of being such a model? The complaint (you should have been what you weren't), as in childhood, would stem from a wishful fantasy.

Modeling and Imitation

It is in the carrying out of this block-building task that mother is seen to exert considerable effort in making Jerry conform to herself. At the same time, she seems to acknowledge his divergence with some satisfaction. Her ambivalence about directing (constraining) Jerry, on the one hand and fostering his independence (releasing him), on the other, becomes particularly tangible during this task. Yet it is quite evident that Jerry derives more pleasure from proceeding on his own than from following his mother's moves. In fact he even succeeds in reversing their roles ("Let's make steps.") Mother, behaving like a child ("Shall I knock mine down?"), readily agrees and makes steps. But when she starts her structure again, she becomes irritated with Jerry's noncompliance: "You're not even looking at what Mummie is making." She tries once more to direct him: "First you go like that, then like that." But Jerry only builds "some more steps" while mother—by laughing and chuckling—covertly encourages his divergence.

She does not try to guide Paul. Instead, both she and Paul express some interest in each other's doings. Paul: "Are you making a tower?" Mother (about Paul's building): "Sometimes it's hard to stack them up just right."

Mother does not show any concern about Paul's noncompliance. She is probably relying on her overall perception of him as close and similar to her. She does not feel as uneasy about his occasional resistance or divergence in this particular task as she seemed to feel about his deviation from her more personal "choices". The latter seems to have more painful meaning for her than Paul's noncompliance with the prescribed impersonal procedure of the block building.

The interaction of father and Paul during this task suggests that father may sense Paul's need for a stronger, more determined model and that this may influence father's behavior in a situation where he has to provide the lead. Before asking Paul to imitate his structure, father allows him to savor his (Paul's) superiority ("Daddy, these are the ones you're not supposed to play with," "Now you're supposed to have the same as I have," "Now, hand me this thing, daddy"). When he has completed his model, father challenges Paul: "Look at my building and see whether you can build the same thing." The seriousness and decisive tone of father's few, brief instructions seems to induce Paul to begin without delay and proceed without error. Once Paul has finished, father reacts to Paul's correct imitation with that extreme glee which has been observed previously in other parent-child pairs upon the child's completion of this simple task (see pp. 36, 67).

With Jerry, on the other hand, father does not insist on Jerry's trying to imitate. Perhaps he takes into consideration Jerry's young age. Father tries to enlist Jerry's attention. But Jerry does not once look at his father's structure. Instead, he says he is building a castle. He says he is going to knock father's building down (though he pushes against it only slightly). Father wants him to sit on his lap but Jerry wants to remain on his chair and to continue building. He builds, smiling, and again makes a castle. Jerry does not regress as in mother's session, and his father does not constrain him to the point of frustration.

Stress

Parents can help a child cope with stress through strengthening his inner resources. A parent's perception of a child's potential for tolerating stress will determine the kind of assistance he or she gives the child under stress. How early a parent forms a perception of the child's stress tolerance is shown in Jerry's mother's report that as early as immediately after birth he attempted to expel mucus from his mouth but did not cry: his reaction to his discomfort made her perceive him then as particularly calm under stress.

When his mother places the puzzle before Jerry, he calls out "Puzzle," sounding interested. Giving him only vague suggestions, such as: "Look at that," and "I wonder where this goes," she lets him try to work the pieces by himself. Jerry becomes whiny and passive. He surprises his mother by getting up, going to the door, and preparing to open it. Mother rushes after him and carries him back over her shoulder as she might have carried him as a baby. She says, "You're getting kind of hungry, aren't you?" (She has, in fact, provided food for Jerry to pacify him if necessary.)

The mother tries again to make Jerry attend to the puzzle and makes a suggestion. Jerry is unwilling and the game has lost its attraction for him. He coughs; almost cries; jumps in his seat a little. She asks him: "Want Mummie to work it?" He does not answer. The mother then works the puzzle herself. Jerry seems relieved, his face becomes "more friendly."

In contrast to the mother's earliest wishful, perception of Jerry as a child of an easy, compliant disposition able to withstand frustration, her later perception of him as unpredictable is apt to arouse her anxiety in a situation of stress. Quite possibly mother's prolonged withholding of adequate help leading as it does to his frustration, regression, and subsequent need for protection, is a subconscious attempt on her part to assure herself that he depends on her as a source of security.

Paul, when confronted with the puzzle in his mother's presence, refers to it as if it were a task to be solved jointly with mother. ("Now, what do *we* have to do? Shall *we* turn it around?") Although mother responds with a similar assumption about the assignment ("We have to put the puzzle together"), neither of them considers mother as the leader. However, when Paul, proceeding unaided, says, "We can turn it this way," his use of "we" seems to substitute for mother's help. Mother never handles a piece of the puzzle herself. Instead, she tells Paul upon his request for help—"You try," "You work it," "You figure it out." One is reminded of birds teaching their fledglings to fly by pushing them from the nest. When we consider how mother reacts to Paul's increasing frustration, this analogy becomes even more convincing.

Paul:	So why don't this go?
Mother:	Well, what are you gonna do about the top?
Paul:	Well, I don't know—what are we—[almost crying] it won't go! This does not go in there!
Mother:	Well, of course, it doesn't. They don't fit in the top, do they?
Paul [exasperated]:	Well, where *do* they fit?
Mother:	Does it look like the pieces that go on the top?
Paul:	Nooooo!
Mother:	Well, then fix it.

Even at the risk of exposing him to frustration, mother is able to release Paul. When he does become frustrated she sees no need for assisting him. Whatever motivation underlies her attitude toward Paul, it does not interfere with his sense of security. In interaction with her, as compared with father, Paul does not feel an urge to assert himself. When she fails to show anxiety about his potential frustration, she may rely on her perception of him as an equal, and as basically competent to carry out the task at hand. Paul does, in fact, complete the puzzle by himself. Thus the interaction between this mother and each of her children suggests that a parent's perception of the child's individuality influences how and to what extent the parent can reinforce the child's tolerance for stress.

Let us compare, in more detail, the mother's perception of Jerry and of Paul and how it may have affected each child's ability to tolerate stress. As discussed before, this mother was puzzled in her relationship with Jerry almost from the moment of Jerry's birth, by her insufficient knowledge of his "inner" self. Her quest for "understanding" her children is, to some extent, typical of a great number of those present-day parents who search for professional advice about "efficient" childrearing. It is possible that Jerry's mother attempted too early to gain intellectual understanding of Jerry's personality, and that she formed a perception of him before she had fully used her capacity to "attune" or "orient" to him.

In the study of an infant described earlier (p. 15), the author observed how the mother carried her infant, on the second day after birth, slowly up and down the dim hallway. It appeared that she was engaged in a most important act, cautiously and carefully feeling her way to the body and rhythm of her child. By the time the infant was two months old, his mother had formed an adequate perception of him and of his tolerance for stress. In assisting him in a stressful situation, she did not become anxious but let him use his own resources for overcoming stress.

The lack of early rapport between mother and Jerry may be related to the mother's strained search for a fuller understanding of him. The lack of rapport could account for her inconsistent behavior toward him, for her anxiety about Jerry's behavior under stress and for her indecision about exposing him to stress. The mother's insecurity is likely to have brought on, in turn, Jerry's insecurity and uneasiness about what to expect from her. Under imminent stress as in the puzzle task, these behaviors of mother and of child will tend to become intensified. Left without either emotional support or clear guidance, Jerry withdraws from what could have been a tempting challenge.

Although we cannot know with certainty what motivates Jerry to walk away from the puzzle, the most likely motive is that of "flight" from frustration. Humans as well as subhumans have the option to withdraw from the source of stress. This withdrawal can occur very early in life. Small babies "will turn [their] face or body away from the threatening stimulus, shut [their] eyes to shut out such a threat, curl into [themselves] and so forth." [36:78-80]. The author who made this statement remarks on the possibility that, in later stages, the withdrawing may signify an appeal for "reinstatement of love." Such an appeal could be inherent in Jerry's withdrawal. Considering the complicated nature of his relation with his mother, in the course of their relationship not only his mother but Jerry, too, may have developed a defensive rapport, quite apart from their ususal, day-by-day rapport. Regression as a defense carries the reward of being nurtured again. By his regression, Jerry unconsciously so provokes his mother's insecurity that she does the task for him and thus, as indicated by his friendliness at the end, relieves his stress.

In contrast to Jerry, Paul is no enigma to his mother. She believes that she understands him and can predict his behavior. Paul's regression does not, therefore, prevent his mother from treating him with respect and thereby reaffirming his self-respect. She appears to rely on her perception of him as mature for his age.

His father shows his regard for Jerry by presenting him with the alternatives: "D'you want daddy to help you with it? You want to try to work it by yourself?" Jerry rejects father's help and his father does not insist. He does not seem uneasy about Jerry's struggle. When Jerry whines at a difficult part of the task, father does not step in immediately, but assures himself of Jerry's approval before putting in some pieces.

Father tries to buttress Jerry's independence by asking him: "How can you fit it in?" "You think it goes there?" At another time, Jerry easily follows father's careful directions:

You almost got it. Turn it a little—turn it—there! Now put it in! That's a boy! Hey, twist it a little bit—no, down this way! That's it!

His father occasionally praises Jerry for a right move and, at the end, further boosts Jerry's self-respect: "'Ray for Jerry! O.K.! There! You put the doggie together!" Upon these words by father, Jerry wants to do the puzzle over again. His father obliges without hesitation.

In Paul's session the dialogue between father and son contains elements by now recognizable as characteristic of the interaction in this father-son pair. Paul displays self-assertion and competitiveness: "It's a hard puzzle, but I can do it." "This is not the way! This is the way it's supposed to be." The Oedipal implication of Paul's competing with father for his mother's love is again suggested by his rebuke of father: "No, that's wrong. That's not the way Mummie and me played it. Mummie played it with me not like that." As in other situations, father plays the subordinate, submissive role with some pleasure: "You must show me how to work it." Father provides verbal help only when Paul has exhausted his own moves. Father rarely handles a piece himself. (Very likely he takes Paul's age into account and his previous experience with the puzzle in the mother's session.) He does not elaborate on Paul's achievement as he did on Jerry's success. Only at the completion of the task does he say: "Yeah. O.K. Good, Paul." Nor does there occur the lengthy, happy dialogue that takes place between mother and Paul at the end of the task. At the completion Paul moves his puzzle to father's side as if asking for recognition of achievement ("You see, I did it") or as a sign of his affection ("I did it for you"). We shall discuss the possibility of other meanings of this gesture in a later section.

During the puzzle task both with Jerry and with Paul, father shows that he meets a potential stress for the child by continuing his usual, seemingly unanxious behavior. The child's failure does not make him feel compelled to take over the task himself but rather he is able to foresee and forestall the child's frustration. In short, in this as in other situations, father is less intensely involved with the child's reactions than is mother.

In general, the mother's behavior toward Jerry differs distinctly from her behavior toward Paul while the father's behavior toward both of his sons shows strong similarities.

In the interactions in Jerry and Paul's family which we have studied to this point, we have focused on the parent's perception of each child. This perception, while of course being decisively affected by the child's objective characteristics, may also have been influenced by certain needs within the parent. How the child "lives up" to the parent's perception of him, or how he defends himself against being inappropriately perceived, is suggested in some of Jerry's and Paul's responses.

Paul's mother may well have perceived him from the beginning as someone from whom she could receive the affection, approval, and security which her own parents failed to provide. In addition, as Paul grows older she perceives him as very much like herself, a perception probably based at least in part upon some of his objective characteristics. The result is the development of an unusually strong bond between the two.

While Paul is generally cooperative with his mother, he also shows that he is beginning to ward off his restricting dependency upon her. He diverges from his mother's preferences (choice making) but feels the need to rationalize his divergence. He does not imitate his mother's model (block building) while he does imitate his father's.

As we shall show subsequently, Paul identifies closely with his mother's moral values.

By the time Jerry was born, mother may have recognized that Paul would not fully satisfy her need for emotional security she had hoped to derive from his dependency and from caring for him. This may have been one reason why she desired an uninhibited closeness with Jerry (as indicated by her refusal to be anaesthetized during his birth). She felt it was necessary to know and understand her newborn child completely so that an intimate and close relationship could develop. Her initial perception of Jerry as "easy" and adaptable seemed to have satisfied these expectations. Yet she changed her perception of him when she became aware that he was, in fact, strong-willed and independent.

Observing her with Jerry at age two and a half, we see that her hope to understand him as fully as she wished has been disappointed—thus the ambivalence on her part which we have described above. Her uneasiness in her relation to him, coupled with the intensity of her involvement with him, may create in Jerry a wish to free himself (seen in his resistance and negativism). By physically removing himself from the frustrating situation (puzzle) he may also be "testing" the extent of mother's concern for him.

Jerry's father is friendly, patient, and easily amused; he is not challenging. He perceives his children sometimes as playmates and sometimes as needing his protection against impending frustration. He consistently adapts himself to their particular ages. He perceives Jerry as "different" and "independent" and, at times, as "puzzling." Yet, in contrast to his wife, he does not seem motivated to "know all about" his children. His lack of deep involvement with them and his joking approach toward them discussed earlier may have had its origin in his early need to protect himself from closeness with his mother and in his developing a somewhat detached attitude toward her.

As indicated in the preceding figure, not all parental perceptions and behaviors stem from the parents' individual needs. A mother's intense involvement with and intrinsic domination of her sons and a father's somewhat passive and protective behavior in interaction with his sons may also be culturally and historically determined. In the 1940s, Margaret Mead described how the educated, middle-class mother, anxious to prove to herself what a good mother and good wife she was, poured all her energy into managing her house, her husband, and her children [35:289, 297]. Mead and others saw that, for middle-class mothers, the world of work held attractions not easily found in the day-to-day rearing of children. The issue of home versus career has become both more open and more crucial today. Thus, in the three mothers we have studied, the wish for closeness with their sons and the wish for their son's prolonged dependency can be understood not only from the mothers' individual needs but also from their social situations. None of the mothers is working although all admire working women. Preoccupation with their children and the feeling of being needed by them may substitute for the imagined gratification of outside work.

The behavior of the three fathers toward their sons can also be seen in social-historical perspective. The American father was described in the 1940s as a "pal" to his children rather than an authority figure—a role that developed as generations of immigrant children rejected their parents' old-world views. When the subsequent American-born generation of fathers are described as "confidants" and "friends" to their own sons, we are reminded of Jerry's and John's fathers; and when we read of fathers who protect their sons from their mothers' domination, we are reminded of Stephen's father telling Stephen to do his task so that his mother will not be angry with him.

The impact of social influences on behaviors of fathers toward their children is becoming even more evident in the present. While comic strips of the 1940s depict the father as inefficient, incompetent, and entirely subdued by his energetic, efficient wife, such characterization seems less appropriate today. Present-day fathers competently assume a variety of parental roles, some of them previously reserved for mothers. However, a basic question is repeatedly asked: Can fathers care for the young child as effectively and as beneficially as mothers? In line with the tendency to equalize parental sex roles it has been suggested that in order to make society more "human" fathers would have to develop their more feminine, nurturing qualities, while women would have to become more masculine (ambitious, striving, and asserting leadership).

In our present framework, we would want to pose the question: How will such transformation of the traditional male and female roles affect the child's identification with the parents? It would seem that the change toward a more nurturing father which is already taking place in certain present-day families is unlikely to impede the boy's identification with the father (see, for instance the case of Ronny, pp. 99-106). On the other hand, the mother's strivings for achievement and leadership, perhaps part of her struggle for women's social equality, could interfere with her personifying to her children an image of motherliness in the traditional and valued sense, with which the daughter can identify. (An extreme example of a mother fostering the nontraditional image in her child is Betsy, described in Chapter 3.) The transformation of the parents' male and female attitudes discussed here must also be seen as subconsciously in conflict with contrasting attitudes, derived from identification with their own parents. How well the new male and female images will become integrated into the parents' personalities and thus into the child's identification, will depend largely on the strength of their marriage. It will depend on the maturity of their love for each other, the ability of each to relish the partner's development, and their skill in integrating individual self-fulfillment into the framework of their relationship.

Separation

In the MIM, a separation situation is designed in which the parent is asked to leave the room for three minutes without the child. The interruption of the emotional contact calls out a variety of affective responses in both parent and child. Since the ongoing emotional relationship with the parent is basic to the child's identification, the separation task can provide further insight into the identification process.

It has been shown that a child separated from the mothering person even for a short time may experience a trauma, sometimes called "separation anxiety." Three classical studies show that the mother's extended absence has a deleterious effect upon the young child: Goldfarb found that children placed in an emotionally depriving institution at age four displayed what appeared to be irreversible intellectual impairment as adolescents [14:109]. Spitz reported gross mental and physical retardation in children placed in institutional care for a prolonged time [45:53-74]; and Bowlby, who studied a group of fifteen- to thirty-month-old children separated from their mothers and removed from their usual environment for several weeks, detected three phases of the child's reaction to the separation: an active protest accompanied by anxiety (restlessness, crying, calling for mother, etc.); distress (an apathetic, seemingly depressed state in which the child avoids contact with persons and toys); and the last phase in which the child is resigned to the separation albeit to only a limited extent. [3].

In a more recent study the effect of mother-deprivation in institutionalized children as described by Spitz was reexamined and described in more detail. It was found that from the fourth month on, retardation in motor, intellectual (especially verbal), and emotional development was conspicuous [40].

Bowlby states that, for his mental health, the young child needs a "warm, intimate, and continuous relationship with his mother (or permanent mother-substitute—one person who steadily mothers him)." The effect of limited maternal care and of lack of certain qualities of mothering, especially with regard to young children, has come under scrutiny with the increase in maternal employment and substitute care. Achievement-seeking, frustrated mothers who stay at home, for example, provide less adequate mothering than mothers who are satisfied with their full-time maternal role [37:78]. Moreover, it is commonly agreed that, under certain circumstances, substitute mothers of the latter personality type can be more beneficial for the child than natural mothers of the former.

The first study of the effect of mother separation under controlled conditions was made on young animals with the aim of relating the findings to the human infant. Harlow, a psychologist studying animal behavior, published his observations on "The Nature of Love" in 1958 [17]. He particularly wanted to examine the psychoanalytic hypothesis that the "oral-erotic" satisfaction which the mother provides for the infant through nursing him is of crucial importance to the development of attachment.

Harlow found that laboratory-raised infant monkeys clung to a "cloth mother," whether this mother surrogate was equipped with a milk supply or not. When fear-inducing objects were introduced, the monkeys clutched the mother surrogate and used her as "a source of security, a base of operations" [17:679]. Upon separation from the mother surrogate the monkeys showed signs of fear and distress, and maladaptive and anxiety-like behavior. Upon reunion with the surrogate mother, attachment behavior became intensified.

Harlow concludes that, for the monkey infant, consistent and frequent physical contact with the mother is a more important "basic affectionate love variable" than the variable of nursing.

As a practical application of his findings, Harlow suggested that, because of the increase in the number of working mothers, maternal care can be adequately provided for by trained females or males—an issue which, twenty years later, is still a crucial topic for discussion.

The most thorough work on experimentally induced separation of human infants from their mothers was done by Ainsworth [1]. Like Harlow, she found that the one-year-old infant uses his mother "as a secure base from which to explore the world or as a haven of safety from which he can face an external threat without panic." Ainsworth also reported that the one-year-old infant is actively involved in the forming of "attachment." He takes the initiative by reaching for or moving toward his mother, by smiling and vocalizing. According to Ainsworth, a sign of "healthy" attachment at this early stage of development is the infant's willingness to explore, in the presence of his mother. Instead of the word "attachment," which generally implies affection, one may use "emotional dependence." It is evident that the separation experience may evoke emotions such as affection, fear, anger and anxiety in the child. Yet in one way or another these emotional responses all seem to express dependence on the parent.

We know that Jerry's mother still strives toward emotional closeness with Jerry through "understanding" him more fully. How has her involvement with Jerry affected his emotional dependence on her? How easy is it for his mother to separate herself from Jerry "never knowing how he will react?"

At the moment when Mother reads the instruction to leave the room, Jerry is standing on the sink, having just explored the faucets. Immediately upon reading the card, Mother says: "Jerry, Mummy's going to be right back. I have to go to the potty. I'll be right back." Mother leaves Jerry standing on the counter of the sink.

Jerry climbs down, stops in the middle of the room, gazing at the door. A minute later he follows Mother out of the room.

She brings him back telling him: "Go in and close the door. You wait for me. I'll be right back." Jerry stands briefly by the door. He looks tense and flushed and makes whining sounds. He then goes out and returns with Mother.

Mother handles her first exit abruptly, letting Jerry stand in a precarious position. She does not prepare him sufficiently, giving him an excuse which he may have sensed was false and providing him with no incentive to engage in an activity by himself. She is equally inefficient in influencing Jerry to stay the second time, since it was unlikely that her request (to close the door and wait for her) would be heeded by Jerry in his now upset state.

His mother may have behaved the way she did because of her perception of Jerry as independent and able to occupy himself in her absence. Thus we see how a seemingly simple interaction reveals a complex relationship, and, moreover, with what ease a particular perception (that Jerry is independent) leads to an unspoken assumption ("I need to do little to reassure him, i.e., I can take his self-sufficiency for granted"), which, when acted out (her abrupt exit), creates the contrary of the expected behavior. Yet Jerry's behavior, may, on the other hand, have been triggered by his mother's unconscious motivation to affirm her child's dependence on her since she is, in fact, uncomfortable with her child's independence.

Since this early incident of separation brings out the complexity of the parent-child relationship (pointing to the parent's overinvolvement and the child's pseudo-autonomy), we may ask whether some traces of the early conflict may remain if the child later separates himself from the parents' values and style of life. We may further ask to what extent this later dissidence springs from a protest against objective social reality and to what extent it is a final attempt at liberation from parental intrusion and demands for dependency.

Let us look at Jerry more closely. He has shown during the puzzle situation that, under stress, he regresses to early infantile dependence. When, in the present situation, his mother is not available to ease his distress, he remains in the state of the year-old baby described by Ainsworth who needs his mother in order to be able to "face an external threat without panic."

The separation incident brings into focus the strength of the child's emotional dependence on the parent as well as the parent's perception of the child's dependence. The following conversation takes place before mother separates from Paul:

Mother:	Paul, will you wait for just a minute, honey? Will you wait in here for Mummy for just a minute?
Paul [*whining and crying*]:	ˑI wanna go with you.

Mother:	Well, honey, I'd appreciate it if you'd wait in here because I wann—I wanna run down the hall. And I'll be right back. Okay?
Paul:	I wanna go with you.
Mother:	Well, why don't you stay in here, and you can find something to do in here, because I'll just be a minute. Okay?
Paul [*wailing, protesting*]:	Wanna go with you.

That Paul regresses to a babyish state is in sharp contrast to his facility in mastering the demands made on him in each of the previous tasks. He seems to feel "let down" by his mother, his self-esteem being depleted by the brevity of her announcement and the lack of intimacy which must seem unfamiliar to him. Thus when she appeals to Paul's affection ("Please? For Mummy!") he seems angry about being manipulated and unable to muster empathy with his mother's wish. His renewed reply: "I wanna go with you!" now sounds irritated and obstinate.

Only when his mother changes her attitude and tries to convince Paul that they both are under the same obligation and have to obey the same rule is he able to regain his self-respect.

Mother:	The card says that Mummy has to go down the hall by herself for just a minute. Okay?
Paul:	Okay.
Mother:	Thank you.

Here the mother reverts to relating to Paul as an adult. She reassures him that it is not that she is rejecting him, it is that "the card says" to do it. And that seems to make her departure acceptable to him. Thus Paul's behavior, too, is controlled by a (false) perception: that he is Mummy's equal.

When Paul is alone in the room he is able to entertain himself by gesturing to the mirror, grimacing, and playing with his fingers. When mother returns she wants to know what he did and Paul shows her some of his behavior. She wants to hear "what else" he did, and he recalls all his antics.

As in her interaction with Jerry during this situation, the mother has overtaxed Paul's independence by inadequately preparing him for the experience ahead.

Like Jerry, Paul regresses under the stress of separation from the mother. Yet she does not treat Paul as a baby. She does not appear to derive the same satisfaction from his dependence as she did from Jerry's. Since she knows more about Paul than about Jerry, she is sure of his closeness with her. She rightly expects that Paul's ego will recover strength when she approaches him as an adult. One may ask whether a congruence between the parent's perception of the child and his objective characteristics, as in the case of

Paul and his mother, is apt to prepare the ground for a strong identification with parental values and a generally conforming personality later in life.

The separation task in father's session with Jerry begins on a completely different, lighter tone than in the session with mother. Father: "Come here, Jerry. [Child laughs, teasingly.] Hey! [Jerry opens the door even before father talks about leaving the room.] You are a character! Okay, okay—now, wait a minute! Wait a minute! [Child laughing, "Ouch."]"

Father tells Jerry to sit down and that he will tell him something. He then explains carefully and slowly that he will go out in the hall and that Jerry can do anything he likes, but that he must stay in the room until he comes back. Before leaving, father says, "You have some fun!"

Child sits immobile while father leaves, looks at father leaving. Child gets up, stands by the wall, looks around, comes back to the table, makes faces in the mirror. Goes to the toy box, moves the drawer out and back again. Handles the lid. Pulls the drawer out. Tries to take out one envelope. Now he has it out. Handles the envelope, tries to open it. Says "block," takes one block out. Again, "block," puts it back, puts the envelope on the table, gets up on the chair, stands on the chair. Shakes the envelope against the table to get the blocks out. Doesn't quite open the envelope but gets all the blocks out. Immediately builds a tower; one block falls on the floor. He doesn't pick it up. Builds a tower, higher and higher, a very precarious building— well balanced. Tower falls. Now he picks up the block he dropped. He gets up and stands on his chair, walks over from his chair to father's chair, stands on one foot, supports himself on the table, back to father's chair, sits down on father's chair.

Father enters and Jerry smiles at him right away. Father asks: "Did you find any toys?" "No, because I was playing with the blocks." Father wants him to put all the blocks away, but Jerry wants to keep five out; he does not want to give the last two blocks away. Father does not insist.

Unlike mother's session, Jerry explores and engages in a constructive activity. Before father leaves he strengthens Jerry's tolerance for separation by giving him a slow, realistic explanation for his absence and by encouraging his freedom to occupy himself. Father neither invites nor is threatened by Jerry's unpredictable behavior.

The father's perception of Jerry as "unique" and "independent" does not seem to influence his handling of the situation. He seems intent on preventing Jerry from becoming frustrated, bored or restless. His careful way of introducing the task to Jerry, as compared with his much briefer, matter-of-fact introduction to Paul, suggests that he allows for the difference in their ages, Jerry being more vulnerable to the separation experience than Paul.

We should distinguish between the perception an individual claims he holds of another and that which his behavior portrays. Thus father may believe that he shares mother's view of Jerry, but in fact he acts towards Jerry *as if* Jerry is only what he is: a little boy needing reassurance. As we have noticed, the fathers in our studies appear to be more easy-going than the mothers. We have raised questions about the negative effect of this easy-going attitude and criticized it, to a certain extent, in the preceding pages, but we should call attention here to the beneficial side of this behavior, which may enable the father to shed his authority and adapt to the needs and feeling state of the child. If we grant this, we do so with caution, as this attitude, if coupled with only few demands and expectations, can be, as we have seen, as harmful as overexpectation.

Father's first question to Jerry when he returns is: "Hi, did you find some toys?" Jerry answers, "No," which is puzzling even to father, because all the blocks are still out on the table. But children often answer in terms of their own line of thought rather than switching to the adult's. Jerry may be reacting to the prohibition he remembers from other occasions against removing an intriguing object from a closed container. We can assume that even while Jerry is working on the building in father's absence, he is experiencing some vague uneasiness and anticipation of punishment. Although his father has given him leeway to explore and find toys, Jerry still abstains from freely having fun, i.e., from getting other toys out of the box.

What is it in his father's behavior that accounts for Jerry's curbing his actions in the father's absence—what is the internalized parental prohibition, the parental value with which he identifies? Later in this chapter we shall return to this question when we discuss the issue of Jerry's morality.

Attachment to father is suggested in that game of Jerry's which ends in Jerry's taking his father's place. We may wonder whether this game is an effort at relieving tension through "magical" thinking, presumably characteristic of the young child. Jerry's activity may serve to substitute for father's absence or to bring father back. The games frequently encountered in response to this MIM item strongly suggest an effort to achieve mastery over a painful situation. Similarly motivated play incidents in situations of stress have been reported from other sources. [32:198].

Paul does not respond with pleading and whining to father's announcement that he will leave as he does in mother's session. Paul's apparent ease in accepting the separation may have something to do both with father's expectations that he be his chum and with the unanxious yet decisive way in which father presents the task.

Father: That's what we're going to do next—I'm going to get up and go in the
           hall, and I want you to stay in here for a while, okay?
Paul: Okay.

When separating from father, Paul reminisces about his experience with mother in this situation ("That's what Mummy did"). In fact, it appears that he may have, in fantasy, retreated again to proximity with his mother as a source of security. When his father has left, Paul repeats the same sequence of behavior that he displayed during separation from his mother. He then engages in freer and more inventive activities.

He says, "pee-pee, pooh-pooh," touches nose; rubs, picks his nose. Shooting gestures; lets out Indian war sounds; alternately stands and crouches in his chair. When father returns he says, dreamily, "Mummy," then "Daddy."

Paul's release of repressed infantile tendencies and the freedom of his fantasy can perhaps be linked to his calm attitude when father leaves. Compared with his resistance to the separation from mother, Paul's behavior when father separates suggests that Paul's emotional dependence on his father is less strong than is his emotional dependence upon his mother.

Jerry, too, in this situation more than in others, shows his infantile dependence on his mother, especially compared to the independent activities he conducts in the absence of the father.

Although Jerry's independence which we occasionally observe and to which both his mother and father attest, may be, to some extent, an objective characteristic of his, it may also have become intensified by his mother's subjective perception of Jerry as independent.

I would like to suggest that certain identifications of the child originate in his wish to behave like the parents' perception of him, rather than in an attempt to emulate their behavior. If the parent's perceptions are incongruous with the child's objective characteristics, as in Stephen's case, his identification with the parent's perceptions is apt to fail. As a protection against the pain of failure, defensive behavior, such as regression, may set in, as displayed by Jerry. Or, in later years, the incongruence between parental perceptions and the child's perception of himself may facilitate the abandonment of identification with certain parental values, as revealed by Stephen. As will be seen in the following chapter, the life histories of youth rebels abound with incidents of clashes between the parents' perceptions of the young person and the young person's concept of himself.

In some respects Paul and Jerry have come to behave according to their parents' perceptions of them. Some of these perceptions seem to be based on objective characteristics of each child such as age; others seem influenced by the parents' needs and expectations. If, much later, the child's wish to be "true to himself" comes to the fore, it is likely that his sense of self will retain traces of how his parents perceived him in childhood and how they currently perceive him.

MORALITY: GENERAL REMARKS

Let us return to the roots of identification or nonidentification. Whatever the outward trappings of the various dissident youth movements of this century, the adherents were alike in their rejection of some basic parental values and in their attempts to adhere to a different set of values which fulfilled their individual needs. In the preceding pages we have observed, also, how the pattern of a personal interaction may tell us more than its ostensible purpose. In addition, we have seen that a relatively consistent pattern of interaction can be observed very early in a parent-child pair. It is clear from the families we have studied that even while the process of identification is going on, the child's covert, subtle struggle for individual self-affirmation is also present and may portend later partial reversals in identification.

We will keep in mind both Stephen's private rebellion and his continuing compliance with his parents' expectations of high intellectual achievement; and we will remember how John's formlessness continued to prevent him from pursuing definitive adult goals. We will remember the manner in which Jerry learned to defend his independence against any threat to it, as well as Paul's relative release from constraint which resulted in more conforming behavior. In all these instances we could detect that the manner of interaction played a very great role in shaping the individual's earliest modes of dealing with his reality, including dealing with his parent's expectations—both those attuned to his own potentialities and those which he might have to work against. In view of the crucial role of values in youth rebellion, let us consider how the identification with parental values may be influenced not only by the particular values emphasized by the parent but by the way in which they are transmitted as part of the interaction of parent and child.

The child's imitation in the situations discussed so far suggested identification with some parental ego functions, since the activities which were imitated involved dealing with and adjusting to the environment, e.g., imitating the parent's block structure. The discussion of a moral issue is apt to bring out the identification of the child with the parents' superego i.e., their conscious, or, in many situations, unconscious notion of what is good or bad.

We have mentioned earlier how, according to psychoanalytic theory, the superego develops through the child's repression of hostile instinctual wishes toward the parent and through internalization of parental demands and prohibitions. The early superego tends to correspond closely to that of the parent. If the parents are overstrict, the superego may be severe. Later, when a sense of guilt and self-criticism has developed, the superego may begin to lose some of its dependence on the parent's values. In school, and particularly during adolescence, the internalized parental values tend to become supplemented by values adopted from persons or ideas outside the family.

Piaget has investigated the child's moral development in relation to his progress in reasoning [37]. By eliciting children's judgments on offenses varying in severity, he adduces two developmental stages of moral judgment: in the earliest stage the child follows parental demands indiscriminately and automatically. Good or bad is, at that stage, whatever the parents designate as good or bad. Piaget calls this stage "moral realism" or "adult constraint." When asked why an act is bad, the child considers the damage the act caused as an estimate of its badness and not the intention which led to the act. Consequently, breaking two cups by accident is, to a child at the phase of "moral realism," worse than breaking one cup intentionally.

The phase of moral realism is followed by a "morality of subjective responsibility" where the child takes into account not only the amount of damage caused by the act, but also the intention or motive of the one who committed it.

In an intensive study of his own three children, Piaget observed that moral realism can be found as early as age two and a half, and that at age three the child can distinguish between a wrong act committed intentionally and one committed without intention. However, from his study of moral judgment in six- to twelve-year-old children, Piaget concluded that moral realism was not uncommon, in the younger children at that level. It alternated with subjective responsibility which became predominant from age ten on.

More recently, Kohlberg applied a research design similar to that of Piaget and arrived at a more detailed scheme of stages of moral development [21:11-33]. He elicited from groups of four- to sixteen-year-old children their solutions to a moral conflict situation: for example, whether or not to steal a drug to save a sick person. At the lowest "premoral" stage the child's judgments of right or wrong were guided by the fear of impending punishment, by obedience to learned rules, or by a naive desire to obtain favors in return: "hedonism." At the intermediate level, "morality of conventional conformity," the children's judgment were based on a desire to maintain good relationships, to get the approval of others ("good boy morality"), or to follow an authority who sets the rules for moral behavior. At a more mature level, "morality of self-accepted moral principles," the young person's moral judgments were based on the ideas of contract, or individual rights, and of democratically accepted laws. At the final stage, moral behavior was found to be guided largely by individual principles of conscience.

Although stage theories of moral (superego) development differ in their theoretical orientation, they agree on some basic assumptions:

1. Morality arises from an instinct-dominated stage through fear of punishment or expectation of reward, and proceeds to stages where it becomes increasingly determined by an inner sense of right and wrong as well as by a sense of responsibility.
2. The stages of moral development overlap. The precepts of each stage are only gradually abandoned. The child may oscillate between a less and a more advanced stage.

3. Under severe stress, the child's morality may become arrested at a particular stage or may regress to an earlier stage.
4. Among the experiences which influence the child's moral progress, the nature of the child's relationship with the parents is of major importance.

Piaget's work on the moral judgment of the child provided an incentive to study the development of morality in American children. It was found that in American as in Swiss children, judgment based on moral realism decreased between the ages of six and thirteen [25; 26:249-269]. One study showed that judging the severity of an offense according to the intention rather than according to the consequences of an offense is more prominent in middle-class than in working-class parents [22].

In recent years a number of studies have focused on the child's reaction to his own transgression as a function of the parent's method of dealing with it. These studies were conducted on preschool and school-age children and on college students. The children's moral judgments were elicited at early age levels by doll play, sentence completion tests, and observation of the child in a moral conflict situation, and at later age levels by questionnaires. The parents' reactions to the children's offenses were derived from questionnaires and interviews.

The reviews of these studies by Paul H. Mussen et al. [38] and by Martin L. Hoffman [18] suggest that certain ways in which children react to their offense are related to a particular type of parental response. Some children confess their transgression, seek to correct the bad effect of their act, manifest guilt and awareness of their responsibility, and, in general, behave as if they were motivated by a moral sense. The parents of these children express their disapproval strongly while still conveying their basic affection. They tend to insist that the child who has not repaired the damage must do so, if repair is possible. They encourage the child to explain how he sees his motivation for the act. They assume that the child's reasoning and self-understanding may prevent a similar act in the face of temptation. The same parents tend to express their affection consistently in various situations. They tend to praise the child, but rarely do they punish him. They abstain, in general, from taking advantage of their power position.

Other children tend to hide the evidence of their offense. They tend to deny or lie about it. These children manifest fear of detection and punishment. They perceive their parents and other adults as authoritarian and in some cases as threatening. They consider their offense as wrong because of its immediate consequence and not because of the motivation that led to it. Feelings of remorse or guilt or readiness to amend the damage are conspicuously absent. The parents of these children react to the child's offense by emphasizing the external consequences of the act, by intimidating the child or asserting their power in other ways. They use verbal aggression (shouting, yelling, etc.) and may reiterate the child's past sins. Most of these parents are not adverse to the use of corporal punishment.

There is another group of parents who represent models of self-restraint and strong self-control to their children while at the same time repressing their hostile impulses. Yet, these impulses become subconsciously communicated to the child. The child's anxiety and guilt may then increase unreasonably, and the self-restrained parents may have an equally threatening and intimidating influence on their child as the punitive parents.

It will be noted that the two contrasting types of childhood morality resemble the lowest and highest stages of moral development as described by Piaget and others. Since each type of morality seems to correspond to a particular type of parental reaction to the child's transgressions at certain ages, the child's progression from one stage of morality to the next may be influenced by the particular way in which the parent deals with the child's offense. We can then assume that acceptance or rejection of parental values in later life may stem from the parental reactions to the child's good or bad behavior, e.g., praising Jerry's obedience (to be described below), reinforcing John's indulgence, rewarding Stephen's pursuit of certain parental goals, etc.

The studies reported above tell us how the parents through their response to the child's offense can influence the child's morality. We shall consider, more specifically, how the parents' reactions may reflect their perception of the child's individuality.

A particular MIM situation was designed to tap the child's moral judgement as elicited by the parent. This situation was applied to the normal control group in the study at UCLA (p. 20), and to the study of Headstart mothers with their sons (p. 21).

Two instruction cards were given to the parent to indicate his or her interaction with the child.

Think of something "good" the child recently did and talk a little about it.

Think of something "bad" the child recently did and talk a little about it.

The task was designed to elicit a dialogue between parent and child which would bring out both the child's and the adult's conception of what constitutes a child's "good" or "bad" behavior and would demonstrate the parents' ways of transmitting and defending their values in discussion with the child. It was also hoped that the child's responses would reflect his progress in moral development: e.g., his fear of external threat and his inclination to deny wrongdoing or, on a higher level of morality, his feeling of guilt and his tendency to admit his offense.

Before examining how Jerry and Paul and their parents responded to the assignment, we shall first summarize the responses of a sample of eight mothers and eight fathers and their three-year-old sons.

The example of children's behavior judged by the parents as good or bad acts and the parents' attitudes toward the child when discussing the acts will be grouped into certain types or tendencies. It must be noted that sometimes parents gave examples or expressed attitudes belonging to more than one type.

Praising the child for "*not* screaming to get (his) will" or for "*not* running away in the store" illustrates that the parent addresses the child on the earliest level of moral development where, according to stage theories, behavior is controlled mainly by fear of punishment or expectation of reward ("I told you you'd get a lollipop, remember?"). The parent who praises the child for being helpful in the household or to a particular member of the family appeals to the child on a more advanced level of morality. Typically, fathers praised their sons for carrying out the trash can, helping to water the lawn or wash the car. Mothers commended their sons for helping to dust, set the table, water the flower pots, or clean away baby's mess. Among praiseworthy acts which showed more concern for a parent than for the household were looking for keys mother had lost, making a birthday present for father, showing empathy for mother's headache.

Parents who exaggerated, in tone or words, a good act of the child evoked, occasionally, the child's rejection, contradiction, or even a primitive, negative response such as whining, sighing, or grumbling. The discomfort of the child who is overpraised might be attributed to the stressful implication that he has to do as well or even better next time.

Most acts which the parents mentioned as examples of "bad" behavior were relapses to quite primitive levels. Among these primitive, impulse-dominated acts were screaming, throwing toys around, and other attempts at releasing anger.

Aggressive acts against family members, e.g., "pushed baby with your feet," "took baby's spoon away," "hit father," can originate as release of pent-up, largely unconscious anger; or, such an act, if previously uncurbed, may arise from an unconscious wish to be punished by the parent.

The parents also recalled bad acts against nonfamily members ("took mail out of the neighbor's mailbox and scattered it around," "hit a girl on the street"). These acts, like the ones against family members stemming probably from pent-up hostility, may have been responses to interpersonal experiences in the family, projected onto other persons.

Damage to a variety of household objects belongs, in a sense, with the category of offenses just mentioned: "smeared lipstick all over the wall," "broke the salad spoon," "took stuffing out of the easy chair," "spilled water (flour, soap flakes) all over the carpet." But some of these acts are probably the result of mere clumsiness, described so perceptively by Piaget as "an enormously important part in a child's life, as he comes into conflict with his adult surroundings. At every moment, the child arouses the anger of those around him by breaking, soiling, or spoiling some object or other." [39:121]. (Piaget also points to the effect which the adults' reactions have on the child's moral progress, viz. the adult who is angrier over fifteen broken cups than over one, independently of the child's intention, perpetuates the child's "moral realism"; see p. 88.)

Some parents brought up acts which resulted or could have resulted in physical harm to the child himself or to other persons: "A car could have run over you." "Everybody was slipping on the kitchen floor." These warnings were aimed at the child's reasoning or empathy and appealed to a somewhat higher level of morality than the preceding responses by parents. A still more mature level of the child's morality was presumed by parents who appealed to his desire to be approved by his peers ("Didn't you look kind of silly when you went out into the yard with only one shoe on?" "If you yell at them they won't want to play with you anymore").

One father asked the child, cautiously, for his reason for committing the act. He conveyed a genuine desire to help the child understand his need, uncover the frustration that led to the offense, and help him recognize his wrong:

You pulled things out of the drawers because you were waiting for Mummy and Daddy to get up and you didn't have anything to do because your toys were packed away to make room for the tenants' little boy's things. And maybe you were angry that a little boy would live in your room you hadn't met yet. So you got bored and got mad. Am I right?

The father went on discussing preventive measures with his son:

Was there anything we could have done to stop you from getting into the drawers? Should we have left a toy out for you to play with? Or something to eat or something else?

The child's response: "A Tinkertoy."

It is of interest that this father's approach differed from that of his wife when she reacted not to the same but a similar offense of the child. The mother considered briefly and merely rhetorically a preventive measure, "What do you think I could have done?" She then resorted to a coercive approach:

Mother: You mustn't go into my room and mess up things, you understand? Listen! This is important. You are not going to do that again!
Child: Can I go to the elevator now?
Mother: To the elevator? Why try that now? Why change the subject?

This mother obviously perceived her son as morally less mature than did his father. Their child's behavior reflected some aspect of each parent's perception of him and each parent's approach to his offense. He showed some initiative in his discussion with his father, while with his mother he tried to withdraw from the situation altogether.

This example suggests that the parent's perception of the child may determine his or her reaction to the child's offense. But it also poses some questions: How can the method by which the parent tries to reinforce the child's morality influence the child's moral progress? Since moral progress depends on identification with parental values, is the child apt to identify more closely with the parent's values if the parent is inclined to help the child understand the motives of his transgression than if the parent tends to emphasize the consequences of the bad act while asserting his or her authority? We shall return to these and similar questions when we examine, in detail, how the children's offenses were handled in two families, and when we subsequently report on some childhood experiences of individuals who strongly rejected or inhibited their identification with parental values.

Paul and Jerry

We shall now consider how moral issues were discussed in Paul and Jerry's family. Since we are acquainted with the parents' perception of each of the children, we will have a deeper understanding of the parents' part of the formation of their children's values.

In response to the "good card" in the session with Jerry, his mother immediately mentions that Jerry sat very still and quietly in the puppet show. This behavior of Jerry is in sharp contrast to his usual active, unpredictable, and independent demeanor. But it is in line with his mother's desire for Jerry's dependence on her.

Do you remember what a good boy you were in the puppet show and how you sat on Mummy's lap? Very still and quietly and on Daddy's lap and you were just quiet like a little kitten? Do you think you could always be a good boy and sit quietly when we take you to a show or somewhere?

Sitting quietly on mother's lap carries for mother, as well as for Jerry, the meaning of being a well-behaved small infant. No wonder that Jerry cannot easily agree to the merit of sitting "very still and quietly" on mummy's and daddy's laps. He interrupts his mother and reminds her of what to him seems "good" behavior, namely that he went "all the way downstairs" all by himself in the theater on the way to the bathroom—an actual or imaginary feat of self-sufficiency. Yet the mother reiterates what she considers commendable: "You stayed right with Mummy." She tries to enforce in Jerry the earliest morality as described by Piaget, where the child believes in the adult's omniscience and conforms without question to the adult's judgment. She asks Jerry, in conclusion, "Why is it important to do what Mummy says when Mummy tells you to do something?" and she answers herself: "It is important so that we can go to other shows together." Here she appeals more specifically to the stage of "moral realism" or "moral constraint" where an act is judged by its consequences and moral behavior is prompted by constraints from adults.

The value which the mother emphasizes when recalling this incident corresponds to her perception of Jerry as an infant who is physically and emotionally dependent on her. Jerry's discomfort with and rejection of his mother's praise point to his incipient inclination to resist identification with those parental values which result in a constriction of personality. We have raised the question earlier whether a tendency toward nonidentification may be "built in" at a young age. Jerry seems to express such a tendency. This tendency may later motivate the young adult to reassess parental values which he has adopted and which may block his need to assert himself.

Jerry's response to his mother's praise opens a perspective on the early role of the child's self-perception as it may influence his identification process. I refer to the concepts Erikson has introduced into developmental psychology, viz., identity and identity confusion. He describes identity as a sense of inner sameness and continuity [8:261-262]. Adolescence and youth are considered as the developmental period in which a person searches for and forms his identity and where identity crises are apt to occur. Erikson believes that identity is rooted in childhood. The manifestations of early identification and nonidentification with the parent, which we have noticed throughout our study, would then be building blocks for the person's identity.

It is not surprising that in her session with Paul, his mother lets him decide which of his good behaviors they should discuss. It will be remembered that, in various other situations, the mother perceived Paul as her equal. When Paul suggests, however, an impersonal accomplishment, his mother brings up an incident where he was of special help to her:

Mother: Remember when Mummy was asleep and you and Jerry were getting
             something to eat in the kitchen. And you came running down the hall
             and said, "Mommy, Mommy, come quick! Jerry's making a mess!"?
Paul: Yeah.
Mother: And is that something you—you should always do when Mommy isn't
             awake—or in case Mommy doesn't know?

Tattling on someone would probably not always be considered morally good by the outside world. To be informed about Jerry's mischief and preventing the mess in the kitchen is of some benefit to the household and to mother who is anxious to "know all about" Jerry. On the other hand, Paul's role of informer undercuts his brother's confidence. This role may weaken whatever affectionate tie has been formed between the two brothers, while at the same time providing an outlet for any sibling rivalry Paul may entertain toward Jerry. Doubtless the mother's request also leaves an uneasy feeling in Paul at his age where a sense of loyalty to peers is emerging.

Paul's telling on Jerry is important for the mother because it helps her to relieve her fear of Jerry's independence and her uncertainty about Jerry's attachment to her.

Being drawn into an inner conflict of his mother, Paul's identification with her may become intensified, and this at a phase in his development where some of a boy's identifications with the mother usually begin to give way to the ones with his father. Paradoxically then, functioning as his mother's "eye" elevates Paul to a level of quasi-adult morality, while fulfilling the mother's demands uncritically puts him back on an earlier level of moral development, where he is not expected to judge the motives of his acts by himself. We may wonder whether this two-sided role the mother assigns to Paul is not analogous to the role which her husband fulfills for her. There is evidence from the interview that at times the mother looked to her husband for care, in a dependent way, while at other times she subtly dominated him, e.g., in his job decisions.

His father cites an instance of Jerry's self-sufficiency as the first example of Jerry's good behavior: Jerry carried a big bag with groceries up to the house all by himself. Father then mentions, as did mother, that Jerry was quiet in a situation that must have aroused his desire to run around: "You were quiet and well behaved just now outside in the waiting room." As father recalled it, he himself had been instrumental in Jerry's good behavior, before the session, by playing with him and telling him stories.

We have seen earlier that the father tends to protect Jerry against frustration. It was pointed out that Jerry's impulsive behavior when frustrated may be threatening to the father who had, since early childhood, repressed his own feelings of frustration. The father himself described his difficulty when compelled to assume a dominant, aggressive role.

The mother's handling of the "good card" assignment in Paul's session and the father's reaction to it in Jerry's session suggest how the parents' own needs may enter into their transmission of values to the child. Here, we see either dependence or independence strengthened, according to the parent's need.

As another example of Jerry's good behavior, the father recalls that Jerry volunteered to help water the flowers:

Father: That was sure a good boy. Why did you want to do it?
Jerry: Just did it.
Father: You just did it, heh?
Jerry: Sure.

A little later the father himself suggests two reasons for Jerry's good act: "Do you like to help daddy by doing this? Is it fun to water the plants nicely?"

Jerry, at his age, would hardly be able to tell about his motivation to help. But the question itself may "spark" Jerry's wondering why one thing he does is good and another bad. By talking with the child about a moral issue and engaging his reasoning about basic moral values, the parent may help the child to progress from judging an act merely by its outcome to judging it also by its intent, as suggested by Piaget.

Yet the quality of the parent's praise, whether adequate or exaggerated, seems to affect the child's interest in the moral issue. Jerry first accepts father's repeated praise with "yeahs," but terminates the discussion rather abruptly, suggesting: "Let's go out."

In his session with Paul, the father praises Paul for being cooperative this morning on their trip to the clinic. He then mentions how helpful Paul was the other day to a little girl: ". . . when you were riding your trike and you got down and showed her how to ride hers, remember?" As with Jerry, father suggests a motive for Paul's good act: "You like to take care of other people, don't you?" Paul disregards father's question, probably because a painful incident comes to his mind that had happened right afterward: "But the others throwed dirt at me—I go told Mommy." The father's response is: "Oh, you don't fight them?" Thus the father mentions fighting as an alternative to tattling. He may unconsciously wish that Paul would fulfill his (the father's) own need to fight back and defend himself. He characterized himself as having been dominated by his mother and hating himself for it.

It is of interest that at the time of the incident Paul did what he assumed would meet with his mother's approval—he "told" her and did not attempt to fight back.

As response to the "bad card," the mother reminds Jerry that he "got into the aspirin this morning." Prompted for a reason why this was bad, Jerry answers: "Because you shouldn't." Pressed for more details of the offense, Jerry states: "It makes us dead."

Upon the mother's urgent request that Jerry promise that he won't do it again, without being prodded further, Jerry adds his own reason for refraining from the forbidden act: "Cause it—it makes Mommy mad!" Jerry's reasoning takes the mother by surprise: "It what?"

Jerry:	Makes Mommy mad.
Mother:	Makes Mommy mad? It's not so much that it makes Mommy mad as it makes Mommy worried. Because Mommy doesn't want your tummy to get sick.
Jerry:	No.
Mother:	No.
Jerry:	Mummy, I like you [sentimental tone].
Mother:	Aw, I like you, too.

When Jerry explains that the act was bad "because you shouldn't," his judgment is typical of "moral realism," the earliest stage of morality where the child "follows parental commands automatically." Although in his next statement Jerry takes account of the consequence of his act, which is assumed to be a slightly more advanced judgment, he obviously reproduces a phrase told him by adults: he could not fully understand the meaning of "dead." When Jerry spontaneously offers a third reason for the badness of his act, that it made his mother mad, he shows an awareness that his goodness and badness may touch off his parents' giving or withholding affection.

The development of the child's conscience or superego has been related to the threat of losing the parent's affection. Jerry's guilty conscience seems similarly connected with his need for parental affection: he considers his act as bad because it brought on his mother's anger and possible withdrawal of affection. When the mother tells him that he was not mad, but worried, Jerry unexpectedly responds by saying, "Mommy, I like you." The mother's assurance of her affection despite his offense seems to have relieved Jerry of his feelings of guilt which then gave way to feelings of love. We may remember that John said the same words to his mother in a situation of mild stress (see Chapter 2). Such statements by young children can be understood as affectionate reassurance to themselves that the parent represents a "haven of safety from which [the child] can face an external threat without panic" [2:49-67]. Jerry's statement, however, seemed to have originated in a threat "from within," in his guilt feelings.

The need for reassurance of her mother's affection under threat of separation was expressed similarly by a two-year-old girl:

The separation act in the morning runs a somewhat peculiar course. Emily stands by the door. When her mother takes out her coat, Emily . . . approaches her with "Good-bye, Mummie," repeating the words till they take on a half-crying tone. She draws closer to the door which the mother slowly opens. Instead of crying, Emily now says in a sad tone: "Mummie, I like you very much" [32:195].

In her session with Paul, the mother chose as a "bad" act that Paul wrote with crayons on the wall. To Paul, whom she perceives as her equal, she can admit, retrospectively, her negative feelings: "Mommy was pretty upset, you remember?" In her discussion with Jerry, in contrast, she has to appear self-controlled and protective; she denies having been mad at Jerry. But before his mother begins to discuss Paul's offense, Paul himself condemns his act: "That was a bad one, wasn't it?" And to the mother's question on how to prevent a recurrence, Paul suggests that he himself will put the crayons high up: "I'm gonna put 'em high up where nobody can get 'em unless they want—write on paper," a solution which the mother herself may have proposed earlier.

When the mother asks Paul why the act was bad, Paul tells her, obviously replicating the mother's complaint word for word: "Then you have to work and work and work." In these reactions Paul displays an early form of the superego described by Anna Freud, where the child "introjects the qualities of those responsible for his upbringing" [12:116], and where the internalized criticism is not yet transformed into self-criticism.

In Piaget's terminology, Paul's reasoning shows signs of both the earliest morality of constraint and of the subsequent stage where the child evaluates an act by its consequences.

If one compares Paul's and Jerry's reactions to their transgression, Jerry shows some independence of observation and reasoning when he comments on the mother's upset state, whereas Paul accepts his mother's reasoning without qualification. The difference between the children may be due to "objective" personality characteristics; but the difference may also stem from their unconsciously complying with the mother's perception of them, since she views Jerry as more independent and Paul as more conforming. And we have seen to what extent Jerry's mother both creates Jerry's independence in accordance with her perception of him, and then acts to constrain it by emphasizing qualities of dependence—which have the paradoxical effect of augmenting Jerry's own need to be independent.

In his session, Jerry's father brings up a "bad thing" Jerry did: that Jerry climbed on father's desk and "messed it all up." His question, "Didn't you know you weren't supposed to do that?" elicits first Jerry's denial, then an evasive reply: "Last time I didn't." His father merely restates that Jerry knew that this was a bad thing to do and that he had been reprimanded for it before.

His father then poses questions to which there is no easy answer: "Where are you supposed to be? What should you do instead of getting on the desk?" Jerry finally provides a real or imaginary reason for his offense: he had climbed on the desk to turn on the light. His father does not accept this reason as an excuse: "Why didn't you ask daddy to turn on the light? Why didn't you do that?" Thus, in this case his father interprets Jerry's offense merely as an act of disobedience against parental demands, without discussing the reason or consequence of the act. He appeals to Jerry's morality on its earliest level.

Although previously the father had shown understanding of, and patience with, Jerry's unpredictable behavior, in the above situation, the father is brusque and rather negative. He seems threatened by the task which may seem to him to require an authoritative stance in his relation with Jerry. As we have seen, this assertion of authority is difficult for Jerry's father. He has been seen most at ease with Jerry in "fun situations," where he could relate to Jerry as a pal and where Jerry's "uniqueness" was animating rather than threatening to him. The father's behavior in the above task would seem to be connected with both his own conflict and his perception of Jerry's individuality, and is reminiscent of John's father, among other parents.

When his father discusses a bad thing that Paul did, he criticizes Paul for having hit another boy (although Paul did it in retaliation). As will be remembered, the father had previously mentioned fighting to Paul as an alternative to withdrawing and telling his mother. Paul is thus given three contrasting moral judgments, one by his mother and two by his father.

His father's reason why fighting is bad—"Because Mummy and daddy don't want you to do it"—corresponds to a primitive stage of morality. Paul first meekly agrees, but then provides his own reason for not fighting: "Because they just hit you back." Although father sides with Paul's reason, "Yes, that's right, they'll hit you back," Paul seems to sense the lack of moral direction, and asserts more strongly his right to fight back. "But Danny and Margie, they throw dirt and hit and push and point—and point guns at people." Since the father withholds his opinion, Paul, excited and eager for the father to share his indignation, formulates a self-discovered rule: "And g-g-guns aren't—are not good to point—to point at people."

For the father who has a lifelong conflict about being dominated and who perceives Paul as self-assertive, it may not be easy to show Paul how to stand up to an attacker firmly but not provocatively. It would seem equally difficult for the father to convince Paul that, in some situations, e.g., when the fight persists or where someone might get hurt, it is not cowardly but sensible to resort to an authority, or to withdraw.

An Enlightened Alternative: Ronnie

Unlike most of the parental attitudes summarized above and unlike the attitudes of Jerry and Paul's parents, at least one pair of parents showed an "enlightened" approach toward discussing a moral issue with their son and toward childraising in general.

Ronny was three years and two months old. Ronny's father was a high school teacher with some training in sociology. He had had a close relationship with his own father whom he remembers as dependable and affectionate. His mother was sensitive, but immature and self-involved. When he was ten his parents were divorced. His mother later remarried. At seventeen, when he could support himself, he moved away from his mother. He described himself as always self-sufficient and independent. He sent himself through school. He kept in close contact with his father and stayed with him during his terminal illness.

Ronny's mother described her own mother as warm, giving, loving, but as too weak to defend herself and her daughter against her dominating, harsh, and vindictive husband. The father demanded of his daughter high intellectual performance which she could not achieve. She attributes her lack of self-confidence to her father's criticisms when she was a child. His fault-finding and cutting remarks hurt her even now. Her mother, on the other hand, has remained close to her without ever intruding into her life.

Ronny's parents had some conflicts in adapting to married life; certain difficulties in the sexual area still persist. They had, at some time, considered obtaining professional help, but they now believe that they can overcome their conflicts themselves by complete sincerity.

Ronny has one younger brother, age two. Both pregnancies were planned.

About Ronny's birth and neonatal history, the mother gave the following report: Ronny was delivered by "natural birth" (a statement made with a certain pride); no drugs of any kind were used. Her labor lasted twelve hours, and was without complications. Ronny weighed almost seven pounds. He was breast-fed and was a vigorous sucker. He was weaned at ten months. The mother regrets that she then weaned him to the bottle, instead of a cup, which he could have managed without difficulty. As a result he still occasionally requests a bottle at night. He was given regular food at six to eight months. He ate readily with fingers and progressed to spoon-feeding by himself. He was somewhat precocious in sitting up, walking, etc. He was toilet trained by age two and a half, mostly self-trained. He sleeps fairly well, but occasionally walks into the parents' bedroom at night when he needs comfort. When Ronny was thirteen months old his brother was born. Ronny reacted with strong envy to the brother. He tried to attack him physically on several occasions. He became aggressive toward other young-sters as well. Now, however, Ronny and his brother get along very well.

The parents' entries in their aftersession questionnaire provide some insight into their relationship with Ronny:

Could you comment on how you felt about the hour you've spent here with the child?

Father: It's been interesting for me focusing my own attention on his activities and responses. In general, he's a pretty interesting guy to interact with. His own interest was infectious.

Mother: Interested, warm, happy. Ronny was so cooperative.

If you were to rank how similar you and your child are, on a scale from 1 to 4, "one" being very much alike and "four" not at all alike, how alike would you say you and your child are? (Please comment if you wish.)

Father: Two.

Mother: One. I do feel kinship with Ronny. He is the child and I'm "supposed" to be the adult, so in some ways we differ.

When Ronny was small his mother did not entrust anyone with the responsibility for him. Now she leaves the boys occasionally with a babysit-ter. His mother feels that she is not firm enough with Ronny and does not set limits for fear of making him "feel neglected."

In his interview after the session the father claimed disinterest in Ronny's performance. On the other hand, he made it clear that Ronny had not been up to his intellectual level that day because of a cold and having gotten up so early, and he mentioned Ronny's high IQ. He was eager to talk about Ronny's "well-rounded personality" and said about Ronny: "He has never disappointed me."

These data from the interviews with Ronny's parents and from their questionnaires show that, in spite of grave childhood experiences, his father and mother each had had a satisfactory relationship with one parent, whom they trusted and loved, and with whom they could identify. Although their own marital difficulties had not been resolved, the supportive, ego-strengthening relations which they experienced in childhood seemed to have enabled them to form a stable, affectionate relationship with Ronny.

The parents' answer to the aftersession questionnaire suggest the influence each parent's personality may have on Ronny. The father accentuates Ronny's independence, calling him a "pretty interesting guy," and describing their interaction rather objectively. As we shall see, the father's interaction with Ronny is characterized by an adult-type of exchange and the almost complete absence of playful or silly behavior. The mother, in contrast, remembers her and Ronny's warm and happy feelings during the session. By ranking Ronny as most similar to her and by her interpretation of her judgment, she did not seem to refer to an objective likeness between herself and Ronny but to a deep sense of partnership and closeness with him, and to a possibly unconscious rejection of having to be an adult in her relation to Ronny. As can be expected, her interaction with Ronny is interspersed with humorous and playful exchanges.

The following dialogue between father and Ronny occurs during the "bad card" assignment:

Father:	Remember yesterday when we went to the supermarket, you with dad, you and I?
Ronny:	Yeah.
Father:	And what did you do?
Ronny:	I started to be a naughty boy!
Father:	Yeah. Why was that?
Ronny:	Wanted some bubble gum!
Father:	Oh? and gee—what happened?
Ronny:	Daddy—you had to spank my hand.
Father:	Yeah, I had to spank your hand. Wasn't that—what do you think about that?
Ronny [Pause]:	Yeah!
Father:	What do you think we ought to do about that?
Ronny:	I dunno.
Father:	Hm? What—how should we do that next time?
Ronny [Pause]:	Maybe tomorrow.

Father:	Yeah—[Pause] what tomorrow, Ronny?
Ronny:	Do something else.
Father:	Oh. Do you think that, er—were you a naughty boy, or was I naughty, or who was naughty? I got a little naughty too, didn't I? Do you know why?
Ronny:	Why?
Father:	'Cause I lost my temper a little bit, didn't I?
Ronny:	Why did you?
Father:	Because I was angry with you, remember?
Ronny:	Oh—
Father:	Remember that?
Ronny:	Yes—okay, I know it.

Instead of denying the act, blaming someone else or defending himself, Ronny immediately admits his bad behavior: "I started to be a naughty boy."

The father truthfully concedes his own impulsiveness: "I got a little naughty too—I lost my temper a little bit." He thereby opens up the incident to a mutual appraisal by father and son. Having laid his own imperfect behavior open to scrutiny, he encourages his son to think about reasons for *his* bad action.

When discussing the good thing Ronny did, namely helping his father to put back the records into the shelves, the father again admits to Ronny his own wrong behavior—that he had left records scattered on the floor: "Why did daddy do that, I wonder? Was he angry or what?" Not surprisingly, Ronny has no answer to these questions, and his father does not insist: "Well, you don't feel like talking about it, huh? Not now. O.K."

Such statements would seem to affect the relationship of the father to his son in two ways: they create a climate of frankness between parent and child and they help to dissipate the aura of infallibility and of unquestioned parental authority. At the same time, the child may begin to view his own impulsive behavior with a certain detachment. An example is a statement by Ronny to his mother: when Ronny remembers that his father had scolded him for hitting a child he says: "Daddy got real angry. And I cried and I got real angry [loudly] at him, at daddy!"

When later in the session with mother Ronny recalls an outing with his father, a minicar ride and ice cream his father had bought him, he asks his mother: "Why did daddy do it?" She tells him: "Because he loves you." Ronny's question points to his budding interest in what underlies people's good or bad behavior. The mother's answer indicates the mutually supportive and affectionate roles of Ronny's parents.

The following situation shows Ronny's identification with his father's reasoning. The jigsaw puzzle is presented as it was to John and Stephen. The puzzle consists of a dog running after a ball. Half of the ball is covered by the dog's ear. Looking at the completed puzzle, in the mother's session,

Ronny asks: "Where's the rest of the ball?" (a question which rarely occurs during this task). When in the father's session the puzzle is completed, the father asks Ronny the same question Ronny had asked his mother: "Where is the rest of the ball? Why can't we see the rest of the ball?" The incident suggests that Ronny has internalized some of his father's ways of thinking.

In the imitation tasks Ronny shows a definite tendency to imitate his father's behavior. One example is Ronny's frequent imitation of his father's choices in the choice-making task where he replicates seven out of nine of father's choices (see the discussion of this task on pages 71-74). When Ronny imitates the father he seems to be enjoying himself, to judge from his smiles and happy tone of voice.

Yet, whenever possible, his father encourages Ronny's initiative and self-sufficiency. On the choice-making task he emphasizes that Ronny could choose his own pattern: "You can like something quite different from daddy's." In the drawing task where the child is given no directions, his father tells Ronny: "You draw whatever you like to draw" and "You can draw some more. It's up to you."

Yet, occasionally Ronny relies too readily on father's emphasis on his independence. When he gets bored with one of the tasks he asks his father: "Can I finish the game whenever I want to?" The father then reminds Ronny of the commitment at hand: "No, not until you get through with this one."

When Ronny works on the puzzle Father seems more tense than he does in other situations. He rarely provides a suggestion but praises Ronny for his right moves. At the end his father comments warmly on Ronny's "tenacity."

Ronny's mother is less involved with Ronny's achievement on the puzzle task than is his father. Although for the most part she lets him work the puzzle alone, she gives him more frequent verbal hints. After completion she smiles and strokes Ronny's head and praises him abundantly: "This was a very good puzzle. Gee, this was good!" Ronny hands her the puzzle—an affectionate gesture occasionally observed in other children after completion of the building or puzzle. (We have called this the "dedication gesture.")

Ronny's mother is quite articulate and definite in giving instructions when needed. Prodding is at a minimum. Sometimes when Ronny calls for his mother's assistance but receives no help, just calling her name seems to give him the support he needs. Occasionally he gets impatient and in the middle of an activity asks for "more games." It then becomes difficult for his mother to redirect his urgent request.

In the block-building task she guides Ronny by *doing* more than by talking. Instead of describing the task in detail as many parents do, she builds her structure and says merely, "See?" He imitates her structure readily. In the choice-making task Ronny deviates from most of his mother's choices: yet she does not seem to mind. He complies with her emphasis on replacing each object in its container at the end of a task.

While his mother calls him "honey," her tone is more matter-of-fact than tender. She fosters her child's autonomy, but is not always able to limit his impulsive behavior.

In response to the "bad card," mother first reprimands Ronny for having hit a child. She appeals to his understanding of the reason why the act was bad:

Mother: What did mama tell you, remember? Why you mustn't hit a child?
Ronny: 'Cause, 'cause they won't like you.
Mother: Sure, mommy told you that children don't want to play with you when you hit them.
Ronny: And daddy yelled at me.

Mother's reason for the badness of the act is characteristic of a more advanced stage of morality than the one given by Paul and his father: "They just hit you back."

As another offense, his mother brings up Ronny's having taken a toy away from his brother, again sharpening Ronny's understanding of why he must abstain from such an act: "You know why it was wrong that you took Jimmy's fire engine from him, don't you? Because you mustn't take something that belongs to someone else." Ronny's response: "Yeah, I took it. No one comed." To which his mother replies: "It doesn't matter whether someone is around. It's bad anyway, see?"

It is evident that here the mother teaches an important moral axiom to Ronny although he will not fully understand why good behavior in the absence of the parent is particularly good. From the studies of parental influences on the child's moral development mentioned earlier, it has been concluded that attempts to change the child's behavior "in the context of an affectionate parent-child relationship appear to foster the development of an internalized moral orientation at least with respect to one's reactions following the violation of a moral standard" [18:233]. His parents' affectionate and dependable attitudes may enable him to remember and respond to his mother's admonition when in a situation similar to that described above.

The affection which characterizes the relationship between Ronny and his parents is genuine, although not always unconditional. Except for the father's emphasis on Ronny's intellectual performance and the mother's concern with orderliness, the parents do not confine Ronny's behavior by giving unneeded directions.

Two things are remarkable in Ronny's family: the frankness between child and parent is evident when they discuss their own wrongdoings— apparently free of fear or apprehension; and their respect for Ronny as a person, seen when they enlist Ronny's reasoning, encourage his attempts at accomplishing a task, and discuss his misdemeanor.

Some readers may feel that the extent of Ronnie's autonomy is indicative of the kind of permissive upbringing nowadays blamed for the ills of our youth. And, indeed, Ronny's father seemed occasionally too lenient and abstained from suggesting alternative behavior in place of Ronny's naughtiness. A few times he asked Ronny questions without providing him guidance toward a solution. And mother at times gave free rein to Ronny's self-willed behavior. It is not intended that the reader be left with the impression that these parents are exceptional. Though not as clearly or consistently, other parents in the study tried to instill these same basic values in their children, values which are typical of their common cultural background. In Western cultures as in most others, not hurting another person ranks high on the scale of values. Respect for another's property, protecting one's own possessions, and striving for individual achievement are also highly valued in our Western culture—more so than in cultures based on collective ownership.

Clearly, Ronny's father's expectation that his child will fully understand his wrongdoing, as well as his emphasis on Ronny's intelligence, sets up expectations which may be beyond the boy's capacity. Ronny's difficulty in controlling his frustration in his parents' presence resembles that of John's interaction with his parents. Yet the relationship of Ronny's parents with their son seems in many ways more apt to promote his growth than that of John's parents and of several others we have examined heretofore. What seems to be crucial in Ronny's family is the mutuality of concern for each other unmixed with deep-seated insecurity or disappointment—a relationship in which values are transmitted clearly and flexibly.

We have presented Ronny's family in detail because Ronny's parents seem to practice two of the major utopian goals of dissident youth, past and present: first, frankness between parent and child—that is, an open, fearless discussion of areas of conflict; and second, parental approval of their children's autonomy, extolled by the dissidents as the freedom to "live [their] lives according to [their] own conscience and with inner truthfulness" mentioned earlier (see p. 4).

This question then arises: Do children who, like Ronny, grow up with a high degree of mutual frankness between parent and child, and with respect for their strivings for autonomy—within reasonable limits—feel the same need to break away from their parents' values and lifestyle in adolescence as do those children whose parents were insincere or dominating or whose interactions were affected by their personal needs and insecurities (to mention only some qualities for which the youth movement members blamed their parents).

Yet, whether children raised with parental attitudes similar to those of Ronny's parents will become attracted to a youth movement will depend on the totality of their early experiences within the family and on their reactions to the emotional and bodily changes typical of adolescence. The confidence and frankness which Ronny experiences in childhood may, for instance, unexpectedly give way to a need to isolate himself, to be noncommunicative at times, and to avoid, temporarily, identifications with his parents' way of life. Although it may not be easy for them, his parents, given their earlier support of his autonomy, may be able to respect his privacy and not seek signs of his previous intimacy with them, thus assisting him to achieve what Freud has described, with reference to adolescence, as "one of the most important as well as one of the most painful psychic accomplishments—the breaking away from parental authority, through which alone is formed the opposition between the new and the old generation which is so important for cultural progress" [12:607, 618].

SOME CONSIDERATIONS

In a recent psychoanalytic paper, Eugene Pumpian-Mindlin proposes that the present youth rebellion is a manifestation of the adolescent's omnipotent fantasies and feelings [41]. According to this view, feelings of omnipotence are present in earliest infancy. With developing brain functions, feelings of impotence and helplessness are experienced. These feelings are intensified in the Oedipal phase, when a sense of weakness and anxiety accompanies the child's attempts to ward off aggressive impulses toward the very persons whose love he so requires. Beginning with puberty and early adolescence, the pressure of id impulses increases and infantile feelings of omnipotence reemerge. Yet by now the ego's resistance against these instincts will have become stronger. The testing of the "omnipotential" fantasies against the limits set by reality will enable the youth to become committed to definite tasks and values.

Pumpian-Mindlin refers to adolescent omnipotence as "creative omni-potentiality." By omnipotentiality is meant the variety of directions into which the omnipotent "energy" can become channeled. For example, some adolescents will accomplish constructive and ingenious feats: they will adapt and contribute to the parental society. The author attributes such "healthy omnipotentiality" to "some degree of successful identification" [41:17]. Other adolescents, reinforced in their infantile, aggressive feelings against their parents, may rebel against them and their entire generation.[4] We have seen how basic personality characteristics can appear much before the Oedipal phase and we have become aware of the extent to which these characteristics are susceptible to patterns of parental perception. We have seen how parental perceptions themselves are conditioned, at least in part, by inner insecurities, and how these can influence the growth of the child. In countless normal, commonplace ways, even the picture of normalcy which we have examined often shows a disrespect of the parent for the child.

Although we may be justified in stating that individual youthful protest may be rooted in certain typical parent-child relationships of the kind we have observed, it goes without saying that the formation of an actual movement depends not only on these psychological features, but on a country's historical moment. The historical situation itself may, in fact, intensify youth's urge to break away from the family and form or join a movement.

It is interesting to contrast the psychological view quoted above with the sociological-historical perspective of Karl Mannheim. In his book *Diagnosis of Our Time*, written in 1943 in England, he attributes the adolescents' inclination to join a youth movement to their social position as "marginal individuals" [30:36], i.e., persons who live on the margin of society and may not be given the same rights as others.[5] Mannheim relates both the adolescents' protest against the dominant society and the "dynamic potentialities" of youth to the outside position of these young individuals. He sees youth, in fact, as representing "one of the most latent spiritual resources for the revitalization of our [English] society" [30:46-47].[6]

Implied in both Pumpian-Mindlin's and Mannheim's statements is the likelihood that movements depend for their existence on the joint effect of psychological and social conditions.

Yet, as Mannheim also states, the actual development of a youth movement is further influenced by a country's historical situation. He attributes the absence of a spontaneous youth movement in the England of the 1930s to the strength of tradition in English society and to the high prestige accorded the experience of the old generation. In contrast, he attributes the formation of the Wandervogel to the historical situation in Germany at the turn of the century, viz., among other factors, to the general breakdown of tradition caused by the increased power of the new bourgeoisie [30:43].

While Freud in the above comment on the adolescent period recognizes the vital and, from a historical viewpoint, adaptive role of the adolescent plight and rebellion, his formulation does not account for the organized movements of youthful rebellion which we have witnessed. Pumpian-Mindlin's psychological view is provocative, but leaves one wondering what role historical factors may play. The converse is true of Mannheim. Pumpian-Mindlin's tribute to the "vast strength" of youth and Mannheim's "dynamic potentialities" both do hardly more than refer to a psychic energy in youth with which we are all familiar. Their explanations must remain part answers.

In the preceding sections we have been concerned with psychological influences on the young child's identification with his parent. In the following we shall consider some social influences on the identification process. First we will describe how three particular persons (one in the past and two in the present) became motivated to join a counterculture movement, the ways in which these movements differ from and resemble each other, and how each fulfills certain needs of the individual.

In the final chapter, we will look at the psychological and social aspects of the Israeli child's identification in the kibbutz, for in the kibbutz, the effects of multiple mothering, early peer group ties, and economic independence from the parents should all favor what has been called a "dilution of the Oedipal conflict." The adolescent in the kibbutz, not being a marginal individual and having neither psychological nor social motives to rebel, should be expected to find no need for joining a rebellious youth movement.

NOTES

[1] Gorer has also outlined how the children of immigrants were taught the value of equality in their lessons and textbooks and how these beliefs led to a questioning of authority in general and, in particular, to the rejection of the father's authority [14:58-60].

[2] John's tendency to overeat and his chubbiness appear to be of the kind found in obese children who were overprotected by their mothers. These children also were manipulative of their mothers [4:467-474].

[3] From the notes by Dr. Constas, then one of the medical students who assisted Dr. Justin D. Call in his study on "Newborn Approach Behavior and Early Ego Development," performed at UCLA in 1963 [6].

[4] The strikingly different, even opposite, beliefs and actions among rebelling youth as outlined by Pumpian-Mindlin can be clearly documented in youth movement members of both epochs. For example, a number of hippies were known to have undertaken spontaneous relief actions such as snow shoveling, volunteering as fire fighters, or "providing free meals for impoverished young people in the community" [16:10]. Other hippies, in contrast, became engaged in militant, destructive actions as members of the radical student movement of the 1960s [9:480].

A divergency of convictions also existed among previous youth movement members during the Nazi era. In contrast to the large segment of W.V. who became ardent Nazis [20:197], certain members of the "Buendische Jugend" (a name adopted by groups of older W.V.) engaged in anti-Nazi activities, occasionally endangering their lives [7:26-27]. The fate of Hans Scholl is an extreme example of such heroic actions. Scholl was the chief instigator of the Munich student revolt in 1943. He, his sister, and three of his friends were executed. They had belonged to a group described as "the last remnants of the dispersed buendische Jugend" [44:16-17]. (See also Chapter 3, footnote 8.)

It is relevant here that Scholl's protest and ultimate sacrifice did not originate in an opposition to parental values. On the contrary, the strength of his conviction which made him attempt the impossible must be attributed, in part, to his identification with his father's (anti-Nazi) beliefs [44:16-17].

[5] The concept of social marginality was invented by Robert E. Park, a sociologist (1864-1944). It is now understood to apply to persons "who make creative adjustments more often than they relapse into old orthodoxies. . . . They may be more prone than others to succumb to anomie and thus to become carriers of trends leading toward social disorganization rather than to creative innovations" [19:427-428].

[6] It will be noted that Mannheim's concept of "dynamic potentialities" inherent in youth resembles that of omnipotentiality proposed by Pumpian-Mindlin. The latter also pays tribute to the "vast strength" of the "truly omnipotential youth" through whom "the failure of the past may be transcended." With a similar expectation Mannheim advocated the support of a nationwide youth movement as part of the war effort against Hitler [42:33-34; 30:52].

REFERENCES

1. Ainsworth, M. D. The development of infant-mother interaction among the Ganda. In B. M. Foss (Ed.), *Determinants of Infant Behavior*, Vol. 2. New York: Wiley, 1963.
2. Ainsworth, M. D., and Bell, S. M. Attachment and exploratory behavior of one-year-olds in a strange situation. *Child Development*, **41**, 1970.
3. Bowlby, J. *Child Care and the Growth of Love*. Baltimore: Pelican Books, Inc., 1953.
4. Bruch, H. Obesity in childhood and personality development. *Amer. J. Orthopsychiat.*, **11**, 1941.
5. Buck, J. N. The H.T.P. technique. *J. Clin. Psychol.* Monograph Supplement, No. 5, 1948.
6. Call, J. D. Newborn approach behavior and early ego-development. *Int. J. Psychoanal.*, **45**, 1964.
7. Ebeling, H. *The German Youth Movement: Its Past and its Present*. London: The New Europe Publishing Co., 1945.
8. Erickson, E. H. *Childhood and Society*. New York: W. W. Norton, 1963.
9. Feuer, L. S. *The Conflict of Generations*. New York: Basic Books, 1969.
10. Freud, A. *The Ego and the Mechanism of Defense*. New York: International Universities Press, 1970.
11. _____. The concept of the rejecting mother. In E. J. Anthony and Th. Benedek (Eds.), *Parenthood: Its Psychology and Psychotherapy*. Boston: Little, Brown, & Co., 1970.
12. Freud, S. The transformation of puberty; contributions to the theory of sex. In *The Basic Writings of Sigmund Freud*. New York: Random House, 1938.
13. Gewirtz, J. L., and Gewirtz, H. B. Stimulus conditions, infant behaviors, and social learning in four Israeli child-rearing environments: A preliminary report illustrating differences in environment and behavior between the "only" and the "youngest." In B. M. Foss (Ed.), *Determinants of Infant Behavior*, Vol. 3. New York: John Wiley, 1965.
14. Goldfarb, W. Emotional and intellectual consequences of psychologic deprivation in infancy: A re-evaluation. In P. Hoch and J. Zubin (Eds.), *Psychopathology of Childhood*. New York: Grune and Stratton, 1955.
15. Gorer, G. *The American People*. New York: W. W. Norton, 1948.
16. Haley, J. The amiable hippie: A new form of dissent. *Voices*, **12**, 1968.
17. Harlow, F. The nature of love. *Amer. Psychologist*, **13** (12), 1958.
18. Hoffman, M. L. Childrearing practices and moral development: Generalizations from empirical research. In G. R. Medinnus (Ed.), *Readings in the Psychology of Parent-Child Relations*. New York: Wiley, 1965.
19. Hoselitz, B. Economic growth: Noneconomic aspects. In *International Encyclopedia of the Social Sciences*, Vol. 4. New York: MacMillan and Free Press, 1968.
20. Koch, H. W. *The Hitler Youth: Origins and Development 1922-1945*. London: MacDonald and Janes, 1975.
21. Kohlberg, L. The development of children's orientations toward a moral order: Sequence in the development of moral thought. *Vita Humana*, **6**, 1963.
22. Kohn, M. L. Social class and parent-child relationships: An interpretation. In G. R. Medinnus (Ed.), *Readings in the Psychology of Parent-Child Relations*. New York: Wiley, 1965.
23. Kohut, H. *The Analysis of the Self*. New York: International Universities Press, 1971.
24. Lakin, M. Personality factors in mothers of excessively crying (colicky) infants. In *Monogr. Soc. Res. Child Develop.*, **64**, 1957.
25. Lerner, E. *Constraint Areas and Moral Judgment of Children*. Menasha, Wis.: Banta, 1937.
26. _____. The problem of perspective in moral reasoning. *Amer. J. Sociol.*, **43**, 1937.
27. Lorenz, K. *On Aggression*. New York: Bantam Books, 1966.
28. Malinowski, B. *Sex and Repression in Savage Society*. New York: Harcourt, 1953.
29. Mangold, T. The case of Dr. Rose Dugdale. *Encounter*, **56** (2), 1975.

30. Mannheim, K. *Diagnosis of Our Time*. London: Kegan Paul, Trench, Trubner, & Co., 1943.
31. Marschak, M. Imitation and participation in normal and disturbed young boys in interaction with their parents. *J. Clin. Psychol.*, 4, 1967.
32. _____. A puzzling episode. *Psychiatry*, 31, 1968.
33. Mead, M. Some theoretical considerations on the problem of mother-child separation. *Amer. J. Orthopsychiat.*, 24 (3), 1954.
34. _____. *Culture and Commitment: A Study of the Generation Gap*. New York: The Natural History Press, 1969.
35. _____. *Male and Female: A Study of the Sexes in a Changing World*. New York: Dell, 1973.
36. Murphy, L. B. The problem of defense and the concept of coping. In E. J. Antony and C. Koupernik (Eds.), *The Child and His Family*. New York: Wiley-Interscience, 1970.
37. Murray, A. D. Maternal employment. *Amer. J. Orthopsychiat.*, 45 (5), 1975.
38. Mussen, P. H., Conger, J. J., and Kagan, J. *Child Development and Personality*. New York: Harper and Row, 1969.
39. Piaget, J. *The Moral Judgment of the Child*. New York: The Free Press, 1965.
40. Provence, S., and Lipton, R. C. *Infants in Institutions*. New York: International Universities Press, 1962.
41. Pumpian-Mindlin, E. Omnipotentiality, youth and commitment. *J. Amer. Academy Child Psychiat.*, 4 (1), 1965.
42. _____. Omnipotence, omnipotentiality, conformity and rebellion. (Mimeo). Presented at the 12th Annual Sandor Rado lectures, Columbia University, Psychoanalytic Clinic for Training and Research, April 26, 1968.
43. Ritvo, S., and Solnit, A. The relationship of early ego identifications to superego formation. *Int. J. Psychoanal.*, 151 (4-5), 1960.
44. Scholl, I. *Die Weisse Rose*. Frankfurt: Verlag der Frankfurter Hefte, 1955.
45. Spitz, R. A. Hospitalism: An inquiry into the genesis of psychiatric conditions in early childhood. *Psychoanal. Study Child*, 1, 1945.
46. Sprince, M. P. The development of a preoedipal partnership between an adolescent girl and her mother. *Psychoanal. Study Child*, 17, 1962.
47. Wolfenstein, M. Two types of Jewish mothers. In *Childhood in Contemporary Culture*. Chicago: The University of Chicago Press, 1955.

CHAPTER 3

Patterns of Parent-Child Interaction and Counterculture Groups

In this chapter we will trace the connections between childhood identifications with parents and later identifications with members or the leader in two counterculture groups. We will document these processes through the life stories of three women: a German woman who joined the Wandervogel in Berlin in 1913, and two American women who joined an urban commune in 1974 and 1975.[1]

While the original hippie movement has faded out, many present commune members were previously hippies or have adopted significant values and aspects of the hippie lifestyle. They consider the hippies as their predecessors and trailblazers.

In Chapter 2 we studied the identification process through observing the patterns of interaction between children and parents in conventional middle-class families. The adults to be presently introduced were not observed as children. But the interviews with them were conducted so as to evoke a picture of their early relationships with their parents. Naturally, their recollections included their impressions, feelings, and subjective interpretations. This "subjective reality," or the reality as preceived by them, although it may have been distorted at times by the interviewees, was nevertheless pertinent to our inquiry. For we must assume that this subjective reality contributed heavily to the course of their identification with their parents.

One advantage of interviewing the two commune members was that both were mothers of young children. Since they had abandoned their identification with their parents to varying degrees, it is relevant to our topic to explore their roles as models for their children. Will they want their children to replicate them closely? Will they, in contrast to their parents, intentionally restrict the traditional role of setting standards for their children?

111

GRETE—A MEMBER OF THE
GERMAN YOUTH MOVEMENT

The Wandervogel association studied was the Deutscher Wandervogel (D.W.V.) mentioned earlier as one of the associations which included Jews. The author herself belonged to this Wandervogel association in her early teens. The D.W.V. was founded in 1908 by a Jewish student, Walter Bergmann, and existed until 1918.[2] It was limited to Berlin and its suburbs. The D.W.V. was liberal both as to religious affiliation and social class status. Working-class youth were encouraged to join. However, as in other W.V. associations, the membership of the D.W.V. remained almost entirely of middle-class and upper middle-class background, which must have been sensed economically and educationally as a barrier by lower-class youth.

In 1952 the author began to contact a few previous D.W.V. members who had, as adults, emigrated to America during the Nazi regime. Through them she was able to trace others. Altogether, a total of eleven D.W.V. members—six women and five men—were interviewed. Ten additional individuals were interviewed—five women and five men who had not belonged to a W.V. Being of the same (middle-class) background and of the same age group as the previous W.V., they provided an informal "control" group. All but two of the interviewees were either Jewish or half-Jewish or married to a Jew or half-Jew.

The interview guide focused on the interviewees' relationship with their parents from early childhood on, their vocational choice, their choice of a marriage partner, their marital relations, their adaptation to America, etc. The previous members were asked about their motivation for joining the movement and their parents' reactions to the W.V.[3] The nonmembers were asked about their attitudes to the W.V. Parents among the interviewees were asked about their own childrearing attitudes and practices.

In contrast to the nonmembers, whose appearance, behavior, and style of life seemed quite age appropriate, former Wandervoegel often seemed surprisingly youthful in their facial expressions, gestures, way of talking, and leisure-time activities. Some previous members had chosen unconventional jobs. One former youth group leader who will be described in more detail later, for example, at age forty improvised her own outdoor therapy for emotionally disturbed children. Long before it became commonplace, another member sought to introduce a more "beautiful" style into traditional school architecture and school interiors. Yet another one introduced an innovation into a prosaic profession by inventing a means of reusing metal from the city garbage dump.

Former W.V. members, more frequently than the nonmembers, recalled dissatisfactions and frustrations in their early relationships in the family, such as considerable tension with or fear of a dominating parent. Some remembered an inclination toward fantasy and daydreaming.

The nonmembers admitted having at times been attracted to the unrestrained, enthusiastic hordes of Wandervoegel they met on their family outings. Yet they never seriously considered joining them. In contrast, most W.V. were drawn toward the W.V. upon their first encounter with a W.V. group. In different ways and with different emphases, members expressed the feeling that their "real life" had begun only after they joined the W.V. and that it was the movement which formed their personalities. They reiterated, in their personal wording, what had been one of the credos of the Wandervogel: "To be a Wandervogel means to remain a Wandervogel all your life."

Grete's life history has been selected as representing that of other youth movement members for two reasons: (1) the inadequacies of parental affection and direction in her childhood show certain similarities with those reported by other W.V. interviewed; and (2) since Grete became affected by the reshuffling of W.V. groups in wartime, her reaction to separation from her original W.V. group provides an insight into the intensity of identification which seems to characterize members of a counterculture group.

The author interviewed Grete in Chicago in 1955. Grete was then fifty-three years old. She had come from Germany to visit friends, refugees from Hitler, among them two previous Wandervogel members. This undertaking marked her first visit to America.

Grete is Protestant. She had stayed in Germany through the Hitler years and had helped her Jewish friends whenever possible. She had, on occasion, harbored some of them in her apartment, endangering herself. She had, in fact, been temporarily dismissed from her job because some anti-Nazi remarks of hers had been overheard. She was fortunate that no further attention was paid to her.

Childhood

Grete had one sibling, a brother three and a half years older than she. Her mother was soft, submissive, and childlike, her personality formed under the influence of her own strong-willed, dominating mother. Her maternal grandmother complained to Grete about a woman's "torture to get small children over the worst," such as, for example, toilet training, and had told her that she disliked children, "until they made sense." Grete believed that her mother had spent a lonely childhood, helplessly dependent on her mother's attention and whims. Grete's mother was already fifteen years old when she bought herself a large doll "to keep her company." She was obviously seeking a substitute for emotional gratification denied to her.

Grete's childhood was different from that of her mother. Her mother appears to have intensely enjoyed Grete as a baby. Grete recounted how her mother had described her as cuddly, placid, and easily comforted. At Grete's toddler stage, her mother found the handling of her child more difficult. Grete has a vague memory of an anxious mother who restricted her from running and exploring. Grete appears to have been active and self-assertive at that age while her mother seemed unable to tolerate Grete's strong feelings or obstinate behavior. Grete recalls one incident, either from her memory or from what she had been told: Grete and her mother had spent these years exclusively in each other's presence, a factor which could not help but heighten the tension between them. Each morning her mother took Grete to the same bench in the park, while the afternoons were spent mostly in the house with mother and child close together. (Nursery schools were rare and expensive at that time.) Once, on a trip to the park, Grete asked her mother to shake one of the big trees so that the chestnuts would fall down. Her mother could neither make Grete understand her refusal nor calm or distract her. In tears herself, she looked on, until Grete's temper tantrum had taken its course.

Grete remembered one girl her age with whom she played in the park and whom she liked. Grete suffered her first serious disappointment when her father did not let her go to the school which this girl was to enter. He had chosen another school for Grete, with emphasis on German nationalism in line with his own.

In her first years in school Grete was shy and afraid of getting bad grades. Years later, she could still hear her teacher yell at her "Speak up!" and "I can't hear you!" She had two school friends but was hesitant to confide in them.

Some of her inadequate feelings in school found an outlet in her angry reactions to her mother. It angered her, for example, when her mother responded to a frustrating experience of Grete's in school by repeating to her, "My poor baby!" Grete was repulsed by this phrase and her mother's plaintive tone. Even in later years her mother retained much of the manner with which she had behaved toward her in infancy. Her mother still refrained whenever possible from expressing irritation and from making her demands known. Instead of asking her to drink milk, for example, she would observe only, "Milk is good for you." Once Grete told her mother that she had received the worst possible grade for a paper in school. She had thought it would be "bad" and "cowardly" to conceal this "disgrace" which had not happened to her before. Besides, she needed to get rid of her anger and her guilt feeling. Her mother's response was, "Don't ever tell me about such things again. Erwin [Grete's brother] never comes to me with such rubbish [quatsch]." Her mother could not deal with upsetting experiences from any quarter. From then on Grete did not share with her mother any of the unpleasant things that happened to her. Sometimes she had to make a conscious effort not to show her sadness or anxiety to her mother. Yet the question that weighed heaviest on her mind was how she could endure it when her mother died. The thought of her mother's death was so frightening that she contemplated ways to end her own life upon her mother's death.

Grete has a memory of summer afternoons when she was doing her homework at the dining table while her mother was lying on the sofa sighing about the content of a *kitschig* (trashy) novel she was reading. The mother had an aversion to reading a serious book.

Grete's father was a traveling salesman, selling men's ties. The glamorous fabrics and variety of the ties which he himself wore to call on his customers fascinated Grete as a child. She remembered them in later years as phony and pitifully incongruous with his worn clothes.

Grete's father was on the road for days or sometimes weeks at a time. When he returned he took immediate command of the household, not too different from the Wilhelminic father described by Erik Erikson as fear-inspiring to both his children and his wife [6:331]. Before her father returned home, the maid had to polish doorknobs and stove doors while the mother anxiously finished darning his socks or pressing his clothes.

Grete's paternal grandfather had been a military man. He had worked his way up from private to sergeant. Having been commissioned to instruct recruits in the use of a new type of gun, he was assigned to supervise the building of an artillery range. Because of his efficiency and his untiring military zest, he was decorated and promoted to officer's rank.

Although a military career appealed to Grete's father in his boyhood, he lacked his own father's drive and self-discipline, qualities required for the rigorous military training. After an ill-fated attempt at admission to the service, he gave up his hope of becoming a professional soldier. Yet in spite of his disillusionment, his father's military feats retained a self-aggrandizing influence on him, his fascination with the German army, and his strictness with his children. His insistence on obedience was relentless. But it seemed to Grete that her father was even more demanding and sterner to her than he was to her brother. She says of her father, "I could not stand him. More than anything, I hated his commanding sergeant's tone."

While her father was occasionally chummy with his son and involved him in a hobby such as constructing a primitive camera, he paid little attention to Grete. At one time she thought that the reason for her father's indifference was her thin, straight hair. But although for a time she rolled her hair in curls every night, this did not change her father's behavior toward her. Only when she collected "kaiser photos" did she succeed in engaging him briefly in a joint activity. He supervised her pasting the postcards of the imperial princes and princesses into her album in order of seniority. Grete has kept this album until the present time and still experiences a slight feeling of "sacredness" when looking at the photos. This feeling she described as not entirely unlike the one which sometimes got hold of her in church at Sunday service with her family.

When Grete's brother volunteered for the army in the First World War, her father was elated about his son's taking part in Germany's assured victory. At about that time her father decided that Grete should become a gymnastics teacher after she had finished the school he had chosen for her.

As a gymnastics teacher Grete would contribute to the physical fitness of girls—future German mothers.

When Germany's defeat became likely and the news arrived that the kaiser had fled the country, Grete's father astounded her by becoming withdrawn and listless, completely contrary to his usual, self-assured manner. His vicarious participation in the emperor's world had come to an end.

Grete's father's punishments were severe and frequently uncalled for. She considered one such incident her most painful childhood experience. She was about nine years old when, having visited a school friend one afternoon, she came in for supper an hour and a half late. Her father opened the door and did not let her in. She had to sit outside on the dark stairs until midnight. Neither on that occasion nor on others did her father discuss her misdemeanor with her. She was given the impression that she was not "big" enough to be engaged in a serious exchange about "right" and "wrong." Besides, she knew that her father was not willing or not patient enough to listen to what he called her "silly excuses."

As to the values her parents transmitted to Grete and the methods they used, Grete remembered one incident which showed how her father expected total compliance with his demands, even if they were immoral. Although she needed an adult ticket for her streetcar fare to go to school when she was ten years old, her father gave her only enough for a ticket for a child under ten. He paid no attention to her request for the proper fare, nor to her tears. It was obvious that he meant for her to lie about her age. Every morning from then on she was beset with guilt and fear on her ride to school. She was so troubled by her father's attitude that she asked her school friend whether her father always did what was right or whether he sometimes did something wrong. When the friend told her her father always did what was right, Grete was afraid to tell the girl what bothered her about her father. She still remembered how it hurt to keep her anxious feelings bottled up.

At a later time, Grete herself behaved in a similarly dishonest way: she withheld her weekly contribution required from each Wandervogel for the upkeep of the city apartment where the group met. Since the coins were deposited anonymously, Grete could retain hers without being noticed. When recalling this transgression, Grete excused herself by adding: "There was never enough money in our house." But she also expressed her dismay and unhappiness about her father's amoral influence, when she said, "I was just like my father. Can you imagine?"

Until Grete joined the W.V., her relationship with Erwin, her brother, was frustrating to her. Like her father, her brother did not want to spend time with her. She thinks that both males in the family considered her unattractive and awkward and her conversation boring. She remembers that she wanted to be taken seriously by them and that when she addressed them she was afraid of their criticism. She envied her brother for being older, for being a boy, and for appearing at times on an equal footing with her father.

Erwin became a Wandervogel and, later, a group leader. Her father had no objection to Erwin's joining the movement. He favored the adventurous Wandervogel spirit and the self-discipline which he erroneously likened to that in the army. The mother missed her son on Sunday family outings and did not see the merits of his unconventional and, to her, somewhat bewildering way of spending Sundays. But as in other matters, it was the father's opinion which decided the issue. When Erwin suggested that Grete, too, should join the movement, Erwin, who had gained a voice in family matters, did not meet with opposition from his parents.

Grete Joins the D.W.V.

Grete remembered, in detail, not only her first hike with the Wandervogel, but also the evening of that day after she and her brother had returned from their separate hikes. At supper, as usual, the father was the first one handed the main course. It consisted of meat with a kind of warmed-up vegetable which Grete particularly liked. Usually after the father had helped himself there was not much vegetable left. This time Erwin "came with a big spoon and dished out two extra-large servings" onto her plate. She was deeply grateful to him. Since they both now belonged to the youth movement, a new relationship had begun between them. From then on he became her comrade and protector.

Grete was twelve when she joined the Wandervogel. She remembered her long walk (in order to save the streetcar fare) to the railway station with her brother. Her mother had cut Grete's hair but it fell again in straggly strands. Grete was afraid she might not be dressed right and was unhappy about her looks in general. Carrying her own rucksack and keeping pace with her brother was some comfort.

At the station, Grete's brother introduced her to a young woman whom he greeted with an energetic handshake and "Heil, Trude!" Trude was the leader of Grete's group of *kueken* (chicks, the youngest Wandervoegel). Erwin then went to join the group of boys in his charge.

Grete remembers Trude's bright smile and "motherly" face, and that, for fun, she was carrying one *kueken* piggyback and holding another by the hand. In the train, Grete got to know the other members of her group. Someone suggested: "She is a *kueken* and Erwin's sister. Let's call her ER-KUE." Grete felt good about being given a new name, but she was still very shy.

When they began their hike, an exhilarated feeling came over her. She remembered how she ran up and down a hill several times, and how the others shouted to her: "You'll get tired long before rest time." Many years later, Grete could still recapture both her extreme joy and the feeling of relief about "not hearing or seeing anything from back home." At the same time she felt protected by the group in an entirely new way. (Similar exultant feelings are reported by members of the present counterculture upon their first contact with their group; see below.)

She remembered that later the same day they sat in a meadow and sang songs she did not know, to guitar music, and that the others made her join in the refrain. Being unmusical, she had always kept silent in the choir at school. But at that occasion, she was able to carry the tune of a folksong whose mood seemed to match that of the landscape, arousing strange, somewhat sad feelings in her. The appeal of folk songs Grete now attributes to the inclination toward romanticism, a characteristic feature of the W.V. Folk songs about peasants and medieval noblemen affected Grete, as they affected the others, by conjuring up images of old-German, rural ancestors and scenes.

One other experience fascinated Grete that day. Nature, which had meant no more than part of a disagreeable Sunday outing with her family, took on a beautiful quality, became "festive." It seemed to her that she saw clouds and trees for the first time. These sense impressions, as they were shared with this particular group of people, became an intense human experience. Grete summed up her recollections of that day by saying "it had given a meaning to [her] life."

As did most members of the movement, Grete proudly adopted the W.V. garb and even wore it to school. She cut her dresses into overblouses, adorned them with wooden beads around the neckline, and wore them over a full skirt. In the city she wore sandals on bare feet or, occasionally, her heavy hiking boots. She wore no hat. Needless to say these were not the customs for schoolgirls at that time.

This anticonventional German youth culture has been interpreted by Margarete Buber-Neumann, herself a former Wandervogel, as "forms of fight [*kampf-formen*]" through which "one mainly attempted to distinguish oneself, in behavior, language, looks, from all other people. Of course, one addressed each other, with *Du* [the intimate form of addressing relatives and close friends] at the first casual meeting. One shook hands with such force that wrists cracked, and looked deeply into each other's eyes. One abandoned, whenever possible, all bourgeois forms of politeness. One tramped, singing loudly, through the streets, danced (folk dances) on town squares, slept in barns, talked one's own jargon. . . ." [4:25].

Interestingly, at that time Grete did not see her anticonventional behavior as a fight against bourgeois society in general but as an aggressive, self-affirmative reaction against her family. She recalled, with a certain glee, the recurrent hints by her mother about her "peculiar" and "unbecoming" self-styled outfit. Although her mother was not given to outright criticism or demands, she referred to the Wandervogel girls who shunned the corset, worn by most young women at that time, as "corsetless rabble."

Grete found it not always easy to bear her difference from her classmates, in style and behavior. Occasionally she caught herself envying girls who appeared in modish, young-lady outfits, or listening with interest to their tales of flirtations and secret talk about boys. On the other hand, being different gave her a sense of superiority, of belonging to a "better-than-they" group.[4] Her happiest weekday moments were when, after school, she met a few girls from other classes whom she had recognized as W.V. from other associations. She greeted them with a loud "Heil!" and they, in turn, responded with "Heil!" The lack of femininity was somewhat compensated for by this newly found sense of belonging to a special group.

However, at that time Grete still felt unsure about being fully accepted by the W.V. She had heard of the "blue letter" which some newcomers had received asking them not to participate any more. They had been judged, in a leaders' meeting as "not *Wandervogel-maessig*" (not a Wandervogel type). The threat of being rejected preoccupied Grete a great deal. Yet, at the interview twenty years later, it seemed to her that she had then not yet even been "touched" by the spirit of the movement. What attracted her mostly at that time was being away from home, in close contact with people her age and guided by a young adult who made minimal demands on her and for whom she felt some affection.

Grete experienced the deep, mystical attachment to the movement, not unlike a religious conversion, a year later at the first solstice celebration which she attended in the autumn of 1914. The girls had collected autumn leaves and had made the wreaths they wore. Toward the evening, all boys' and girls' groups of the D.W.V. met. They collected firewood and lit a fire on the highest hill.

One of the oldest leaders gave the speech. He linked the freedom of the W.V. to that of the soldier, and quoted a verse by Schiller about the soldier going "into battle, into freedom."[5] He ended by addressing those W.V. of military age, of whom the fatherland now demanded the ultimate sacrifice for the German land, the land which they "have made their own through numerous hikes [*erwandert*]." His words brought home to Grete what she had suppressed in recounting the events of that day: that her brother had enlisted as a volunteer and could be called into service any time.[6] She remembered that she was overcome by fear and sadness but that suddenly the song "Rise, flame, rise, from the hills by the Rhine" burst forth. Her hands were grasped and she moved with the others in a big circle around the fire, singing and partaking of the exalted mood.

After the celebration, each group assembled for the return hike. Grete heard different voices calling her name. When she found her group they seemed seriously concerned about her and genuinely friendly. That night, walking through the dark woods, Grete felt more sure of herself and more able to accept and return the friendship offered to her. In retrospect, she believed that the events of that evening had created in her a heretofore altogether unknown "We" experience.

The W.V. *fahrten* (hikes) and the weekly meetings in the city "nest" became the center of Grete's life. She felt more and more secure in her relationship with the others and with Trude, the leader. She enjoyed listening to stories by the romantic, mystical, or lyrical writers favored in the W.V., in particular those of Hermann Hesse. At some of the meetings warm socks were knitted for W.V. soldiers. In one meeting, the question was raised as to whether friendship or comradeship should predominate in the Wandervogel. But discussions like this one were rare in Grete's group. "Brooding and philosophizing" or concern for political issues were, in general, considered youth-alien (*unjugendlich*) in the early phase of the movement. During the later war years this view gave way to an interest in the political and social situation (see below, p. 125) perhaps in protest against the bourgeois indifference and indulgence. But Grete's antiintellectual bias remained unaffected.

Grete found in the W.V. the safety her family had not given her. Her feelings of being inferior and of being unappreciated were replaced by a sense of belonging and specialness. Yet this girl who felt so insecure about herself was still far from achieving true individuality. The gains she did make were all at the cost of subsuming her own identity within a communal one. True, a prohibitive family had been replaced by a permissive one. Yet, though there can be no doubt of the great personal benefit Grete derived from the change, the basic inadequacy the former (family) caused her to feel was not so easily removed by the latter.

During the first two and a half years in the W.V., a period Grete considers the most fruitful one of her life, Trude had a crucial influence on Grete.

Trude: The Leader

At a reunion of the D.W.V. in 1954, one member told how lastingly the leader of her W.V. group had influenced her values [32:6]. Even many years later she was able to recall the precise moral precepts which this leader had set forth at a solstice celebration:

Do not ever forget that you, as Wandervoegel, must not only think decently and honestly but that you must also act that way, never mind that it may be disagreeable or even dangerous.

She then illustrated how this maxim still guides her:

For example, when, not long ago, I stopped a man who was beating his dog in anger and grasped the man's arm and was bitten by the dog, or when I tried hard to wake a drunkard who had fallen asleep in the snow, or when I interfered when two boys were hitting each other badly—the old Wandervogel in me makes me do all these things—frankly, it often is unpleasant and I have to struggle with the "bad me" which tells me "keep out of it." And yet I do it because it was, at that time and still is, the "right thing" to do.

This woman's statement throws some light on the identification of the youth group members. They readily internalized those values to which the leader was most strongly committed.

The German youth group leaders were of various personality types. Even the two initiators of the movement described earlier were of almost opposite dispositions. Hermann Hoffmann, later a consul-general in Turkey, was a systematic, careful organizer of the first weekly hikes which were undertaken under his guidance. He was eager to reassure the parents of his young charges who feared the ill effects of their sons' overnight camping. Karl Fischer, on the other hand, introducer of the guitar as well as of the name "Wandervogel," was romantic and impulsive. He instilled the spirit of adventure and discovery and the sense of their specialness into his followers. One of his visions was to convert the Chinese youth to the W.V. idea.

Yet, certain characteristics did seem to typify the leader personality. These characteristics are described in a study of rural commune-type settlements founded by previous W.V. in Germany in the 1920s [5:67]. (Unfortunately, the author Georg Becker, does not deal with the identification process through which group members mold themselves in their leader's image.) Leaders of these settlements are characterized in the study as persons clearly "born to lead," to whose charisma the group is highly susceptible. Although outside of the group the leaders are not successful, within it they perform unique functions. They do so primarily through their intellectual or educational superiority, but in some instances through particular abilities or work skills. The group appreciates the leader's uniqueness but does not want to be dominated by him. Nor does the leader want to dominate. The leader remains first among equals. Those who flock around him are insecure and unable to find their bearing in the wider society. They sense that the leader may be able to assist them in mobilizing their own resources.

Our observations of Grete take on a pointed relevance in this connection. Under Trude's leadership Grete became more alive and less self-conscious. She developed an affectionate relationship to Trude and Trude became for her, as she did for other members of her group, a model for identification.

Grete described Trude as enthusiastic and as able to share the enthusiasm of even the youngest *kueken*. She was loving, courageous, gentle, yet resolute if necessary. As an example of Trude's courage, Grete told how, on an overnight trip, Trude had faced a bunch of hoodlums who beleaguered a barn where her group was sleeping, and how she had been able to talk the gang into leaving. Trude was the first person older than herself whom Grete completely trusted. When Grete menstruated for the first time she was bewildered and upset. No one had prepared her for this occurrence. The only person in whom she could confide that she had what she believed was an illness was Trude. Trude gave her a complete biological rundown of the menstrual cycle, and did it in a way that made Grete feel more mature and more "whole" as a person. Grete was even able to confess to Trude her dishonest withholding of her monthly dues for the rent of the W.V. nest. Trude's reaction was to provide Grete with small sewing jobs so that Grete was able to pay her contribution. (Grete's description of Trude matched the impression Trude made on this author when she interviewed her in Los Angeles in 1957.)

Trude had been introduced to the W.V. by her brother who is five years older than she. Both siblings were first members and later leaders in the D.W.V. Trude maintains that much of her idealism and vigor stems from molding herself after her brother, although, similar to Grete, she had difficulties in her relationship with her brother until he made her join the Wandervogel. Her brother had retained the W.V. attitudes all his life, and, when seventy, wrote: "The dreamland of my youth became the guiding star of my life."[7]

Trude's father was Protestant and her mother Jewish. The children were brought up as Protestants. Her father wanted to be a doctor but his family could not afford it. He became a railway official instead. He was interested in various fields such as astronomy and folk medicine. Like Grete's father, he was a "monarchist": Kaiser-and-Bismarck portraits adorned their walls.

The education which Trude and her brother received was "Prussian": strict and puritan. There was always a prayer before meals. Yet one day Trude's father told his family: "If I were not a Prussian official I would have left the church long ago." Meanwhile, the children kept attending Sunday school where the minister impressed on them: "Believing, believing, believing—that is the most important thing in life."

Her father was convinced of the healthy force of the sun's rays. When Trude had a bad skin rash he made her expose her skin to the sun for hours at a time until her condition became so grave she had to be treated in a clinic. In spite of her father's confusing and odd directions, both children were attached to him. They sensed his affection and his concern for them. Their mother was lenient, mostly unassertive, and self-sacrificing in her motherly and domestic duties.

As a nature lover the father was in favor of his son's hikes with the W.V. and had hardly any objection to his daughter's joining the movement. Trude's mother, on the other hand, was critical and anxious about Trude's taking part in the adventurous, "unsafe" W.V. trips. There were recurrent quarrels about this issue between Trude and her mother. When Trude became a leader, however, she gained some esteem in her mother's eyes. Ironically, this was a period when Trude had to withhold a number of actions from her mother. As a leader she occasionally helped children to participate illegally in activities prohibited by their parents—activities such as a night hike in December with a swim in the icy water—which, in Trude's view, were in line with the W.V. spirit of challenge and adventure. Trude also acted as a counselor to overanxious parents. She recalls in a letter written when she was sixty how zealously she was engaged in freeing certain youngsters in her group from their overcautious parents. The letter was addressed to a friend of hers in New York, the mother of a teenager. This woman had bombarded Trude with advice about what Trude should let the daughter do and not do when she came to visit Trude in California. After the girl's visit, Trude wrote this to the girl's mother:

Your last telegram: "Avoid exertion!" was the last straw. It reminded me vividly of all the over-anxious Wandervogel-parents and their guilt feelings who spoiled our fahrten, our nest evenings, our meetings, with their trying to restrict their children and to interfere. How much some youngsters had to lie, how they hated their parents! But they did manage to climb up the chimney secretly if this was the only way to join the rest of us for something that we did together that was real and good and enjoyable.

I believe that you somewhat spoiled B's and my getting-together, which could have been fruitful. I believe that with so much fearfulness the parent makes the young person insecure, un-self-sufficient, and maybe even anxious. . . .

Interviewed in California, Trude described how she now tries to help emotionally disturbed children by relating to them in a way similar to the way in which she had related to the young Wandervoegel in her charge in Germany. She was gentle toward them, not manipulative. She was natural and deeply trustful. She would wander either with one child or with a group of children in the Hollywood Hills, at times taking her guitar along and singing with or to the children while they walked. If a child was overrestrained or overmanipulated at home, she tried to foster a sense of freedom and self-sufficiency in him. For some, she had discovered, there was benefit in silence in the company of an adult; for others it was beneficial to be allowed to urinate outdoors. She let the ones with eating difficulties choose the ingredients for the meal which they would prepare together on an open fire or in her small cottage. The author's interview with her had to be interrupted once because she had to visit one of her children in the hospital. The boy had been operated on the previous day and she had been with him before and after the operation. Her intense caring for this child was obvious.

Trude now lives with her husband in a low-income housing area in a Swiss city; they have no children of their own. But children from the neighborhood whose mothers have little time for them congregate in her kitchen where they are fed when hungry and sometimes put up for the night in a room reserved for this purpose.

Exclusion

The longer Grete felt appreciated as part of the youth group, the more self-confident she became. She was now able to stand up for what she felt was right. Her girls' school was one of the most nationalistic ones in Berlin. The pupils' parents belonged predominantly to the Deutsch-Nationale (German National) party and were devoted to the imperial house and Germany's military power. At each victory over the Allies the classes were summoned to the auditorium for a celebration. At one such occasion, a teacher, addressing the assembly, appealed to the girls' pride as future mothers of German heroes. He impressed upon his listeners their "most glorious task," to instill in their children the desire for conquest, and the hate for "our enemies." At the speaker's words, "We rejoice in our hearts when we see little children loading their toy cannons and blasting their English toy army to smithereen," Grete felt so disgusted and angry that she got up and ostentatiously left the auditorium. When she was summoned to the school's director later and told that a child must never disagree with a teacher, especially not on one of Germany's glorious days, Grete was able to defend her antiwar feelings. Another time, Grete spoke up against the formation of a "Schul-Wandervogel" to be formed under the auspices of the school and under the leadership of teachers. The aim of the administration was to counteract the rebellious, autonomous youth movement. Grete told the audience of teachers and pupils that such a plan was doomed from the start because, in the "real" Wandervogel, youth is led by youth. At these occasions, Grete now was no longer shy and defenseless, as she had been, but determined and ready to be counted on. Buber-Neumann has described how the communal ties strengthened the individual's self-reliance: "While previously every clash with my father had oppressed me, I now felt my own personality affirmed through the arguments with him" [9:27].

Grete believed that her change of attitude did not occur through thinking about and clarifying the issues to herself, but that she derived an inner strength from the bond with the leader and the members of her group. As she put it, the group continued to be her "backbone."

Grete experienced her "highest" moment when she received the W.V. pin, a flying bird on a white background. Members became eligible for the pin after their fourteenth birthday, and the event can be compared with an initiation rite. It was eagerly awaited by each *kueken* and by far outshone the enjoyment of family celebrations. Trude wore her pin under her velvet dress at her confirmation. "The pin had to be with me in church." Some Wandervoegel wore the pin at their church or temple wedding. Trude described the act of receiving the pin as deeply moving (*erschuetternd*). She said that she still experiences some similar feeling when she thinks of this day. When asked what could have accounted for the intensity of the experience, she said: "It was the confirmation that one was a decent person, that there were people who completely trusted you." The emotions released in the initiated, and, to some extent, in the participants too, must have resembled those aroused in the solstice celebration described above. Such cult-like events, nowadays encountered in communes, have been understood as enhancing the closeness of the group.

As part of the ceremony, Trude read to Grete and two other girls the text of a document attesting their worthiness to wear the pin. The document extolled self-sufficiency, responsibility, truthfulness, and a sense of communion with the other members and with nature.

Only a few months later occurred what Grete has described as "the catastrophe of my life." It was the third year of the war. Most male members of the Wandervogel of military age had been drafted. Some girl leaders, among them Trude, had taken up nurses' training work in lazarets. Others became social service workers to assist poor families, in particular families of service men.

Because of the shortage of W.V. leaders, a reshuffling and recombining of groups took place in the D.W.V. Grete's previous group was dissolved and Grete was assigned to a group she hardly knew.

From the beginning Grete felt ill at ease in this group. Three or four of the girls and the leader herself were enrolled in a sophisticated school in which the emphasis was on Greek and Latin. Grete was baffled by the scope of their intellectual knowledge and interest which greatly exceeded her own. Moreover, in a great number of W.V. associations, certain changes in ideology had occurred as a consequence of the political and social events. Margarete Buber-Neumann describes these changes in her autobiography, as follows:

The ideals changed. In 1915 one still emphasized that one wanted to have nothing, absolutely nothing to do with politics. In 1917 and '18 it was very different. In 1915 one did not fight for political and social reforms. The watchword was then "truthfulness." In the last year of the war, politics had entered the Wandervogel [9:25].[8]

A D.W.V. member described in his interview his experience during the summer solstice celebration in 1918. The group had gathered around the fire and was singing the solstice song, "Flame arise!" which contained references to Germany's greatness. A W.V. in a shabby uniform, home on leave, entered the circle, interrupted the ritual, and scolded the participants for still singing this nationalistic song. He decried them as being superficial and thoughtless while thousands of young men were being driven to their death in a senseless war which caused enormous waste and general misery. He accused the bourgeoisie, to which they all belonged, of taking advantage of the black market while the workers starved and froze in their unheated apartments. His words found open ears among his listeners. He inspired them to begin to acquaint themselves with socialist and Marxist writings. The activities at the "nest" evenings, which previously consisted of folk dancing, singing, and the reading of romantic-mystical writers, or Oriental poetry, were now supplemented by discussions on present-day issues such as nationalism versus world government, and "progressive sex morality."

This change occurred in the group to which Grete was assigned when her original group had been dissolved. Grete remembered one evening in particular when the necessity and ultimate purpose of war was debated and whether the fate of Germany was more important than that of mankind. Since Grete's brother was still at the front, she had intense personal feelings about this question, but she did not take part in the discussion. Nor did she participate in other group debates on political or social issues. Although Grete, too, suffered from the scarcity of food and coal, she did not voice her concern about her own or the general circumstances. The possibility that a new social order could do away with shortages and suffering was, at that time, less pressing for Grete than were her feelings of insecurity and her frustrated needs for friendship and intimacy.

Considering the importance of identification for the adolescent, Grete's tension and helplessness at this phase of her life can be attributed to the disruption of her affectionate ties with her previous group and the separation from the leader with whom she could so readily identify. On the other hand, she wished to be approved in her new group and appreciated as a person with her own merit. Although no group member was unfriendly or discouraging toward Grete, she felt that she was excluded from the intimate relationship which existed among the others. The more attention Grete paid to any evidence that she was being excluded, the more disappointed and resentful she became. At times, while on a hike, she did not talk to anyone for hours.

In spite of the change in their ideology, however, this Wandervogel group, as most of the others, still adhered, to some extent, to their original lifestyle and activities. They sang their folk songs, cooked their meals on an open fire, and slept in the woods or in a barn on overnight trips. Such emotionally and romantically tinged undertakings and the soothing effect of nature created in Grete, at times, the illusion that she had been accepted as part of the group and that she shared their ideals and feelings. What Grete did not realize, or suppressed, was that her resistance and somewhat aloof attitude had a dampening effect on the others. In retrospect, Grete fully recognized that her behavior worried the leader, since it threatened the cohesion and spontaneity of the group. Yet, at the time, it was most painful and unexpected for Grete when, one day on a hike, the leader told her that it might be better for her to try to join another group or even another W.V. association. Grete said that she felt as if she was about to faint: "Something went to pieces inside me."

When she came home that night, since she was unable to keep it to herself, she briefly told her mother what had happened to her. She made her mother promise not to ask her any questions and not to pity her: being treated by her mother once again as a small child would have been intolerable. Grete described her emotional state after the thwarting experience in these words: "Whatever was hurting me, I was able to discipline myself to a degree that I could force myself to laugh when I felt desperate." She was ashamed about what had happened and blamed herself for her misfortune. When recalling the incident, she said: "I'm surprised how it upsets me even now when I talk about it."

Grete could not recollect whether her despondent state lasted half a year or longer. She did remember that she lost interest in her schoolwork and did not mind that her grades dropped to an unprecedented low. Apparently she automatically performed the minimum of what was requested of her. And the selfconfidence she had acquired earlier gave way once more to restraint and shyness.

When Grete's brother returned from military service and found Grete changed, he talked to her empathetically, trying to understand her listlessness. But he could not help her recognize how deeply her depressed feelings were connected with losing the affectionate support of her earlier group and being rejected by the other group which could have compensated for the loss.

In later life Grete guarded herself against intense relationships and thus against rejection and loss of love. In her late twenties she had a sexual relationship with a man who helped to dispel some of her fear of abandonment. After a year or so, however, Grete decided that she could not commit herself permanently to her boyfriend. Feeling they had too little in common, she broke off the relationship. Later, she realized that it was not this which was important but rather her fear that their mutual attraction would not last.

Although Grete differed decisively from Trude in character and temperament, it seems to her now that some of Trude's intensity and compassion, especially for the plight of young persons, has "rubbed off" on her. She attributes her vocational choice of child welfare work partly to her own childhood experiences and partly to Trude's influence. In her approach to children who are intimidated or mistreated at home, Grete senses that she often behaves like Trude. Trude's example, she believes, enabled her to empathize and work effectively with the uprooted *Halb-starken* (half-strong), as the German counterparts of the hippies were called. She also sees some likeness with Trude in her courage to provide temporary shelter for persons persecuted by Hitler.

In later years Grete joined the anthroposophic society based on Rudolf Steiner's somewhat metaphysical, nature-dedicated philosophy. The role of nature in anthroposophy closely resembles the worship of nature which played a dominant role in the overall Wandervogel movement.

Issues of Identification

How did it happen that the Wandervogel experience decisively influenced Grete's personality? How did her change in identifications occur?

Let us consider, in particular, those parental characteristics which have been assumed here to influence the course of the child's identification—the parent's perception of the child; parental affection and direction; parental values and the ways in which they are transmitted to the child.

Her mother's perception of Grete, which hardly changed throughout Grete's growing-up years, was that of a light-hearted, joyful little girl, obstinate at times, but without marked inner conflict. Her father, well into her teens, perceived Grete as a docile, submissive child, with only a limited ability to reason and act on her own.

If, by identification, we mean the tendency to take on characteristics of another person (Chapter 1, p. 1), or "the act or process of becoming like something or someone in one or several aspects of thought or behavior" [8:44], identification could also involve the adoption of another person's perception of oneself. We have suggested earlier that, in their tendency to identify with their parents, children also identify with the parents' perceptions of them. If a parent's perception of the child contrasts markedly with the child's perception of himself, any meaningful interaction between parent and child may be blocked and may hinder the process of identification. We have seen, for example, how Grete progressively abstained from sharing negative experiences with her mother as she became less and less able to "fit" her mother's perception of her. It is conceivable that Grete's identification with her mother became further weakened as a result.

The kind of affection which Grete received from her mother, even in adolescence, had the quality of early protective mothering. Since it provided her with a sense of security, this primitive maternal affection may have been beneficial for Grete as an infant. Later on, however, in a crisis, Grete had to protect herself against her mother's way of showing her affection which Grete feared would oppress her.

Grete's irritation with her father's inattention shows how she suffered from her father's lack of affection.

Her unquestioned submission to his requests and her tolerance for being humiliated by him can be understood as unconscious attempts at eliciting his love.

Grete's mother, shy and dependent on her husband for all family decisions, did not, on her own, provide Grete with firm and consistent directions. She rarely rebuked Grete for a misdemeanor, or openly discussed with her, causes of, and alternatives for, her wrongdoings. To induce Grete to comply with her wishes, she made indirect statements of the kind described earlier.

It will be remembered how John's parents were unable to deal with

John's strong feelings and assertive behavior in ways other than by showing him their unlimited affection. They rarely clarified their directions by assigning limits or providing goals. Here we see how Grete's mother, through a similar inability to provide clear directions, inhibits her daughter's ability to cope with strong and troublesome feelings.

Grete's father, in contrast, was stern and uncompromising in his directions. Either because she feared his anger and punishment, or, as suggested above, out of eagerness to please him, Grete usually followed his directions literally and without dispute.

Both parents transmitted to Grete their middle-class values, including respect for parents, cleanliness, punctuality, and thriftiness. We must not fail to note, however, the stability of the early-internalized parental values even if these are consciously rejected. We saw, for example, how Stephen had rejected his parents' goals for himself, yet continued to strive for high achievement: he kept the "high goal" but altered its content. In the same way, Grete's resistance against the intellectual climate in her second youth group may reveal her continuing identification with her mother's antiintellectual bias, reinforced, perhaps, by Trude's nonintellectual inclination. In Grete's immoral act of withholding the dues for the Wandervogel nest, one may see an identification with her father, who approved of Grete's lie about her age to save money on the streetcar fare.

Although she rejected her parents' religion, Grete remained susceptible to other forms of religion. She changed her belief from scripture to nature, to anthroposophy. Moreover, the values of her parental culture were evident in her consciously felt envy of more feminine girls. Her insecurity in herself as a woman was assuaged by the W.V. ideal of women as nonflirtatious and as primarily "comrades" of men.

Grete's first W.V. group filled her vital need for reassurance and for a model for identification. The role which the W.V. played in replacing her family ties is typical of the personality development of youth movement members.

Otto Paetel, a previous Wandervogel who has written what to this author is a sensitive and, at the same time, historically competent analysis of the movement in its various stages, had this to say about the impact of the early Wandervogel group upon the individual member:

In quiet hours with each other, when singing an old folk song together, in the silent circle around a dying down fire, in other assemblies of the "independent" youth, one was aware that one was partaking of a new tranquility and security, that one found one's support where one never before had searched for it, in the circle of age mates, in their love, in the love for a young leader and through following him or her, in the self-sufficiency, the rebellious flight from a civilization emptied of meaning [30:11-12].

The affection which developed between group members is accurately described in a contemporary diary of one member: "On this fahrt [hike] we realized that we had become one community [Gemeinschaft], and we loved each other" [32]. Subsequently, we will encounter a similar group sentiment in members of the present counterculture.

As to directions to be followed by group members, the Wandervogel had announced at their Meissner mass meeting, in 1913, only one year before Grete joined the movement:

Our strength is that we have no program, that we limit ourselves to one aim, to make the young persons flexible for all that life demands, [to make them] free of prejudices and one-sidedness; the aim being for the time merely to help them to form their character and their personality [30:15].

By adapting to the group one did, of course, follow certain, mostly unspoken, directions, e.g., to keep together on walks, to share duties, to take only limited rest periods. In contrast to the directions Grete was used to receiving at home, these directions were given without regard to hierarchical positions. They were followed by the leader as well as by the youngest member of the group. In a climate of mutual affection with minimal explicit direction, a young person, especially in adolescence, would seem easily inclined to adopt the values adhered to by the group. In particular, these values consisted of "genuineness, spontaneity, proving oneself in the every-day, primitive life together, ability for brotherly fellow-feeling, for friend-ship, for devotion to the chosen and approved leader—and for inner truthfulness" [30:14]. To free and develop one's genuine and unique self (*Selbsterloesung*) was of further importance [30:18,21]. A parallel between the self-discovery value of this early counterculture and the "consciousness raising" tendency and the search for identity of the present counterculture is obvious.

Grete's relative isolation during her early childhood in her family, and her sensitivity, her unfulfilled need for affectionate reassurance, and for being understood and guided with understanding, can well explain her fascination with the affectionate rapport between members of the W.V. group. It made her urgently desire to be accepted by the other members and to partake in their affective bond with the leader. For Grete, Trude seemed to have assumed the role of a security-giving mother and the group members seemed to have fulfilled the psychological roles of loving siblings in a closely knit "good" family. It was natural therefore that Grete took the group leader as her model for identification. She adopted the youth movement's values by identifying with Trude who "lived" these values. Her reversal of identifica-tion with parental values was enhanced by the romantic and occasionally mystical atmosphere, the fascination with nature, the remoteness from the ordinary city life, and even the silences shared with the rest of the group.

Grete's ultimate exclusion from the W.V. seemed to have stirred up her inner pain about the separation from her first group. Although both groups were W.V. groups, it was the first group alone which met her needs. This group helped her to overcome the feelings of isolation from which she had suffered within her family. Her identifications with group members and with the leader in particular enabled her to abandon certain ideas and prohibitions instilled in her childhood.

It would appear that similar to the one of the present counterculture, the lifestyle of the W.V. satisfies youth-specific inclinations—e.g., romance, idealism, and even omnipotence—which deviate assertively from those of their parents. The lifestyle of the counterculture often attracts young persons who through the emotional constellation in their family became isolated or who are, for other reasons, in a critical phase of their lives. It would seem likely that such persons tend to attach themselves to individual members and/or the leader of the counterculture group whom they experience as ideal parental figures. Their identifications with these individuals come more and more to substitute for the early identifications with the parents.

The psychic situation is analogous to the one described by Anna Freud as typical of adolescence [18:167]. She sees the "passionate" attachments of the adolescent to age mates or to an older person, and the modeling of their behavior, philosophy, and religion after these individuals as substituting for the attachment to and identification with parents.

COMMUNITIES AND COMMUNES

A commune has been defined as an intimate group of three or more persons, not related by blood or legal ties, living together and sharing certain unconventional values and assuming certain financial and caretaking responsibilities toward each other.

The communal experiments in America go back to the early nineteenth century. The members of the small cooperative communities supported themselves mainly through manufacturing or farming. Religious sects were the first to form such settlements. In 1817 the Quakers founded a "village" at Niskeyma, New York, where they produced furniture and art objects. In the same year another community, Harmony, was established in Indiana under the leadership of Father George Rapp, the founder of a second-adventist sect, the Rappites, who had emigrated from South Germany and subsisted mostly on agriculture. Many of the contemporary and later communities harbored the chiliastic hope, adhered to by the Rappites, that "from the lives of brotherly harmony to the Kingdom of Christ would be an easy transition" [7:6].

Somewhat later two socialist reformers, Fourier in France and Owen in England, arrived, independently of each other, at the idea of small self-sufficient communities as an alternative to the competitive system of industrial enterprises. In these communes, based on principles of common property, shared income, and social equality, an effort was made to combine manufacturing with agricultural labor. Education was to be provided for children as well as for grownups. Fourier came from a wealthy merchant family, while Owen's cotton mills in Lenark, Scotland, had become famous through his liberal and successful management. Both Fourier and Owen had therefore direct experiences with the hardships of laborers. Both were also aware that the capitalist's profit depended to a large degree on the workers' happiness.

Owen purchased the Rappite village in Indiana in 1824, and transformed the premises into a cotton-manufacturing and farming community in accordance with his program for social reform. At about the same time, Fourier's writings stimulated the founding or reorganization of some communal enterprises in America. In Brook Farm, as one example, a huge unitary structure was begun at great financial sacrifice, according to Fourier's scheme and his theory of group life. (It burned down just before completion.) Brook Farm has become famous because its membership consisted largely of intellectuals; among them were the writer Nathaniel Hawthorne and the Reverend John S. Dwight. (Dwight was a young liberal in the Unitarian ministry and an admirer of Ralph Waldo Emerson. He was highly successful in gaining converts for community life in his immediate family, and converted his parents and his two sisters to join him in Brook Farm) [35:152-164]. Some letters and comments by members of Brook Farm attest to the struggle of people with a conventional past who attempt to change to a minority lifestyle. The change seemed to have been difficult. Mothers, for example, resented leaving their young children in the nursery all day in order to fulfill their domestic tasks. A cause for further anguish for some members was the prospect of a "universal family" into which the nuclear family was to blend. One participant-observer discussed the point of dissent in an article published in the community's journal:

The maternal instinct, as hitherto educated, has declared itself so strongly in favor of the separate fire-side, that association, which appears so beautiful to the young and unattached soul, has yet accomplished little in the affections of that important section of the human race—the mothers. With fathers, the feeling in favor of the separate family is certainly less strong; but there is an undefinable tie, a sort of magnetic rapport, an invisible, inseverable, umbilical cord between the mother and child, which in most cases circumscribes her desires and ambitions to her own immediate family. . . . If, as we have been popularly led to believe, the individual or separate family is in the true order of Providence, then the associative [community] life is a false effort. If the associative life is true then is the separate family a false effort [26:91].

Similar difficulties in adjusting to communal living were encountered by a present-day family who moved into a commune, as described by a sociologist who was a temporary member:

The Pennicks quickly found that the commune's values conflicted with their traditional sex roles. They often withdrew into their room with their children, forming a nuclear family within the commune [1:6].

Brook Farm existed for only six years while New Harmony lasted but three. Yet in spite of the short duration of such endeavors, and despite the constraints imposed on the members in adapting to the new culture, the communal experience seemed to lead to a broadening of personality in a number of individuals. One member of New Harmony described the benefits he derived from communal living in these words:

I have become a Harmonite and mean to spend the remainder of my days in this abode of peace and quietness. I have experienced no disappointment. I did not expect to find everything regular, systematic, convenient—nor have I found them so. I did expect to find myself relieved from a most disagreeable state of life, and be able to mix with my fellow citizens without fear of imposition—without being subject to ill humor and unjust censures and suspicions—and this expectation has been realized. I am at length free—my body is at my own command, and I enjoy mental liberty, after having long been deprived of it [7:167].

Nathaniel Hawthorne, who joined Brook Farm in his young years, had this to say about communal life:

In the interval of my seclusion, there had been a number of recruits to our little army of saints and martyrs. They were mostly individuals who had gone through such an experience as to disgust them with ordinary pursuits. On comparing their minds one with another they often discovered that this idea of a Community had been growing up, in silent and unknown sympathy, for years. . . .

On the whole, it was a society such as has seldom met together; nor, perhaps, could it reasonably be expected to hold together long. Persons of marked individuality—crooked sticks as some of us might be called—are not exactly the easiest to bind into a fagot. . . .

Our bond, it seems to me, was not affirmative, but negative. We had, individually, found one thing or another to quarrel with in our past life, and were pretty well agreed as to the inexpediency of lumbering along with the old system any longer [26:212-213].

Similar grievances and search for a new existence were noticed by the sociologist abovementioned in members of a recent commune:

The commune has changed nearly all aspects of family life-household structure, sex roles, childrearing, openness about conflict and feelings, work vs. home life, community involvement, values and friendships—for the people who live there.

While there has been stress, conflict and the breakup of couples, these have taken place in a context of adults struggling to grow and change the way they live [1:7].

Rosabeth Kanter, who has studied both the American communities of the nineteenth century and the American communes during 1960-1970, has found the following similarities between both communal movements:

Similar dissatisfactions with capitalism were expressed. . . . In both periods there have been anarchists resisting any kind of structure as well as spiritualists totally obedient to their messiah. Concern with life style and nutrition as integral parts of their spiritual growth. . . . Large numbers of people wandered from commune to commune then just as others are doing today. A concern with individual fulfilment can often be found . . . in both periods [19:169].

Kanter notes, however, that in the present commune there is a lack of faith in the traditional religion and a lack of concern with social reforms and utopian visions based on a belief in progress. She mentions Twin Oaks, a commune in Virginia, as an exception because of its utopian belief in a network, across the country, of socially concerned communes.[9]

The concern with individual fulfillment common to communities then and communes now has taken on a particular urgency in our time among individuals adhering both to traditional and to nontraditional norms. Moreover, among those who join a counterculture, there are many who clearly suffer from feelings of loneliness and abandonment. They who search for sympathy and reassurance, in short, for a "giving" parent. Their need is reflected in advertisements in commune newsletters. One such advertisement tried to attract new members by promising them "emotional and mental healing" through "[catering] to the human urge to belong, to feel needed and appreciated" [27:19]. In a group of individuals similarly alienated, where a friendly climate prevails, and especially where an empathetic leader is present, a new member may be able to form affectionate ties and develop new identifications.

Commune Haven

Estimates about the number of American communes in the early 1970s vary from a figure of over two thousand for both urban and rural communes [16:4] to that of twenty-five thousand for urban communes alone [19:18]. It is difficult to arrive at the actual number of communes because the census does not yet provide information as to how many people are married or blood-related in a household and how many are not. Yet the number of urban communes is said to be growing.

Communes differ with respect to features other than their rural or urban location. Some communes are committed to a political or a religious creed. Some support themselves almost entirely by farming and gardening,[10] or by producing goods or running a business for outside customers. A "craft commune" with a workshop for ceramics or leather work exemplifies the latter. A commune in Maryland (Heathcote) supports itself by publishing a newspaper, *The Green Revolution*, and by conducting workshops on communal living, homesteading, etc. The underpinning common to most communes, however, is the attempt to provide emotional support through intimate, interpersonal relations. The fact that many commune members move easily from one commune to another vouches for the similarity of interpersonal attitudes which have evolved in communal living.

As mentioned earlier, commune Haven—a fictitious name, as usual—was selected by the author because it furnished the opportunity to pursue her interest in the childrearing attitudes of commune mothers. Additionally, Haven had been recommended by a colleague who knew one Haven member and who described the commune as having retained the hippie culture in a relatively "pure" form. Some of the deviations from the hippie movement in the present-day commune life will become evident. A group of Haven members had moved to Haven from Pharos, another commune located in a different state and varying from Haven with respect to certain arrangements. The interviews with three Pharos members and two Haven members provided insight into the two somewhat different communes.

Commune Haven was established in a western city in 1968 by a group involved in the hippie movement who later became members of Students for a Democratic Society. The house, first only rented, has recently been bought in the names of four of the present members. I talked to George, who is one of the owners and an original founder. George wears an Indian band over his long, straggly hair. He is a competent plumber, electrician, and carpenter. He applies these skills in the house, but also uses them intermittently to earn money outside. Because of his outgoing and friendly nature and easy humor he is sought out by members who need help with various problems. He was instrumental in setting up certain rules of behavior for Haven members, which have evolved over the years. The present rules are less confining than the original ones. George quotes three rules: "Hang loose but don't fall apart," which he considers basic; "Share the bills"; and "Keep the house clean." George is not as inspiring a leader by nature as, for example, Catherine, the leader in Pharos (see below). George's predecessor was more charismatic, but he created conflicts because he became "too much 'God.'" He left and now lives with his wife and child on the land.

At present, of the twelve adults and five children living at Haven, five adults and three children had lived at Pharos and consider Haven as a way station. Members have occasional and sometimes relatively stable outside jobs. Unemployment checks pay for their needs between jobs and are the main support for mothers with children. Jobs include carpentry, furniture moving, music, sandal making, and auto repair. Members keep their earnings. Expenses for food and housing are shared. Evening meals are sometimes, but not regularly, eaten jointly. Most members are vegetarians. Each member has a room on the upper floor of the house. Mothers share theirs with their children. To avoid the danger of a child's falling from a bed, mattresses placed on the floors are used for sleeping by all inhabitants. Children are free to walk through all the rooms. The neighborhood immediately adjoining the house is inhabited by blacks, Orientals, Mexicans, and a few whites; most of them are lower middle or lower class, and all are "very nice," according to George.

As we examine two present-day commune members—for whom the identification with the values of this counterculture group has come to replace the identification with parental values—we will again ask the question: Which early experiences in the parent-child relationship might have been responsible for their identification reversal later in life?

Betsy

Betsy was twenty-four years old at the time of her interview at Haven. She had a nine-month-old son, Zephyr.[11] She had lived with Zephyr's father, Eli, "on and off" in a "stormy" relationship, unmarried. She left Eli, taking the baby with her, and joined the Pharos commune. Together with the small group from Pharos she had recently moved to Haven. After six months of commune living, she is convinced that "couple living" is humiliating, oppressive, and "death dealing," while commune living "makes you free of a lot of your hang-ups."

Although Betsy finds it hard to lose contact with members of Pharos, and especially with Catherine, whom she describes as the "guru," she sees an advantage in "moving on." At Pharos people knew one another too intimately:

You know what the other is going to say. You speak the same vocabulary. You want to lose yourself, start all over.

The feelings of confinement and restlessness expressed in these words seem to have motivated Betsy to leave Haven. She will leave together with two other women from Pharos, each with an infant:

We're going to hit the road. Just get in the car. What we have in mind right now is: with three babies just get all the diapers and all that stuff together. Get in the car when we're feeling calm. And we all want to start anew. . . .

Some are drawn here, others are drawn there. We'll leave each other plenty of space so that we don't have to live together. We like each other and we might like to live in the same situation, but it might not work. . . .

We're going to pull out the driveway and go to a river, sit down out of this environment we feel we should leave and into a neutral environment and decide what we feel like doing, go North or South or East or West or any city that anybody likes. We don't know.

(After three weeks, a card from New Mexico where the three women had decided to stay "for a while" suggested they had no plans to separate.)

Childhood and young adulthood. Betsy grew up in a mideastern city as the first daughter and the second child of a lower middle-class family. Her father had grown up during the Depression and his family had no means for his education. He began as an unskilled mechanic and later became a supervisor in a chemical plant. Betsy's mother came from a "poor background." The mother was eighteen when she married and 20 when she had her first child. Within three years she had three children. Betsy has a brother, two years older than she, and one younger sister.

Betsy described her mother as sensitive and "not a forceful woman," and her relationship with her mother as "really strange and touchy." Betsy also said about her mother:

It was easy for me to see her as the enemy. I don't think she ever put me on her lap. My memory of her is that she was no fun. She was not "heavy." But she was busy setting limits on my behavior. I constantly felt that I wasn't doing right by her. She sighed and I got the message very early that she suffered and sacrificed herself for us and it made me very nervous. Later on, we all bought the most extravagant Christmas gifts for mother. Mummie got the best because we felt she had worked all year. We got that vibration although she didn't say it.

Her mother had "explosions" because "she bottled it up a lot," but she rarely hit any of the children. Yet Betyy felt that her mother's punishments were psychologically more destructive than spanking might have been. One incident when she was five aroused feelings of intense hate for her mother: a new family had moved in down the street. Betsy's mother had forbidden Betsy to watch the moving van being unloaded. The mother was afraid, Betsy thinks, that the neighbors would "rap" about her children being nosey. But Betsy could not restrain her curiosity and stood by the van until her mother dragged her away. With a long leash which was used to prevent Betsy's baby sister from running away, the mother tied Betsy to a tree, leaving her there, visible to all the kids in the street, for about an hour. Betsy believes that her later feelings of being confined and her hostility against whoever tried to govern her life stemmed from that humiliation.

From her childhood on Betsy's mother told her that she was sure Betsy would marry a wealthy man who could afford a house in the suburbs and a cleaning woman. This wish of the mother became "rounded out" in Betsy's fantasies by glamorous movie and newspaper stories.

Betsy felt differently toward her father. She was "a Daddy's girl and into tomboyish things." It seemed that Betsy's dependence on the father and her affection for him was somewhat stronger than the typical daughter-father attachment: she would become utterly despondent whenever her father was angry with her. She remembered one time in particular when, together with her brother and his gang, she had taken part in throwing rocks from an overpass onto the cars passing below. The gang was picked up by a police car and their parents were notified. While Betsy's brother was only scolded by the father and forbidden to go to a ball game, she herself received a hard spanking. She thinks her father was more angry with her than with her brother because he was more ambitious for his daughter. Because of her good grades and for emotional reasons which she did not understand, her father had singled Betsy out among his children for a career which he himself could not afford—a manager in, or executive of, a big firm. To achieve that goal, Betsy was to get an advanced degree in a business school. She was to earn part of the tuition through scholarships; any necessary additional money her father was prepared to pay from the meager family savings.

Betsy's mother avoided discussing with Betsy the contradiction between her own vision of Betsy's future and her husband's and Betsy did not dare to disclose to her father how little she was interested in becoming a business-woman. Since her siblings had reason to resent Betsy's preferred position in the family, her good relationship with them suffered. Although Betsy felt alienated from almost everyone in her family, she was anxious to please her father, and thus began to earn money as soon as she was legally permitted to work. She felt exhilarated when she could buy her own clothes and shampoo. Although she remained aloof from the subject matter, she took courses in economics and business administration at college.

At a church event which she attended with her family, she met a boy her age, a "real nice guy," to whom she got engaged after a few weeks of a superficial relationship. This is how Betsy described her thoughts and feelings before her engagement:

Basically, I had given up the control of my life to my parents. I would be a business executive so that my father could be happy. I would be a housewife so that my mother would be pleased. My father had been so enthusiastic about my career and I was at such a loss as to what I wanted to do, that it came to a point that I wanted to break loose, rush off. I was under a lot of pressure.

About the status of being married and its advantages, she said:

It was that idea of getting a ring on my finger and everyone thinks you're legitimate, you're grownup and you get all these rights and stuff. I figured I didn't have to pass college anymore. I figured I wouldn't have to do anything. You know what a housewife does [with an angry tone of voice], she sits at home and cooks.

The engagement lasted only a few weeks. It was dissolved because "he wasn't up to it, and his family wasn't." Betsy's parents tried to help her get over her disappointment. But listening to her mother's "old wives' advice" that "time heals everything" made her feel worse. For the first time, she also got "really uptight" with her father who kept suggesting, as a remedy, that

Betsy should now concentrate more than before on her coursework. Betsy instead became apathetic, exhausted, and markedly depressed. She said:

My life was knocked out. I couldn't think of any reason to get up in the morning. I just screwed around. I'd drive out to college and sleep all day in my car and come home at the end of the day.

Break with family. One day when Betsy was lying curled up in her car, a man who looked like a hippie stood by her window and wanted to know what was wrong with her. He said he had seen her lying in her car a few times and from her face he could tell that she was unhappy, and was clinging to whatever irked her. He said: "Why don't you do something from within yourself to get yourself out of that rut?" He was the first person Betsy had met who seemed able to understand her hopelessness. His name was Eli. He was older than Betsy and looked "flashy." He seemed sure of himself and he looked like someone to be relied on. They met often from then on. Betsy said about Eli: "He gave me the words I needed. He said, 'You don't have to please your parents, you need to be content deep inside yourself. No one but you can help you to find yourself,' and so on."

Eli had previously lived in a hippie commune. He had, later, joined the leftist student movement and subsequently, had been drawn to Zen Buddhism.

Betsy began to live with Eli, having told her parents that she would move in with a girlfriend who lived close to college.

With Eli, Betsy had her first sexual experience: "I had held onto my virginity until then. I gave it up gladly and had fun doing it." When she became pregnant, Eli wanted Betsy to decide for herself whether she wanted to have an abortion. He did not want her to feel deprived of her freedom by having to care for a child. Although Betsy felt relieved when she decided for an abortion, she was also disappointed that Eli did not try to convince her to have the child.

Betsy's parents discovered that Betsy had lied to them, and that she had had an abortion. They found out where she lived and "kidnapped" her. They took her home and threatened to blackmail her and Eli if she should return to him. But Betsy went back to Eli the next day. To escape further harassment, they drove to Oregon where Eli had friends. These friends helped them find a place to live and a temporary job for Eli as a gas station attendant. Later he became employed in a health food store.

At that time, Betsy's life, in her own words, "got real neat." She thought she "got what [she] wanted—to keep alive, well fed and with money, set up housekeeping, and be free from [her] parents." She telephoned her parents once every few months to tell them that she was "alive and well," but did not disclose to them where she lived.

Eli was pleased with his job, which combined selling in the health food store and waiting at tables in the adjoining luncheon room, a meeting place for people from the counterculture. Here Betsy met the woman who later introduced her to the commune.

Life with Eli. Betsy and Eli's lifestyle in Oregon reflected Eli's hippie background and his Buddhist views. He ate only vegetarian meals, not more than twice a day, and they furnished their household sparsely. Eli succeeded in convincing Betsy that marriage would deprive each of them of further growth, but that they should have sex relations only with each other. This kind of monogamy, he told her, was best suited to attaining "insight into one's inner being," and to "becoming whole." Later Betsy could not understand how she willingly agreed to Eli's demands.

Yet, she did get some satisfaction in complying with the limitations Eli imposed on their life, through his thriftiness, for example. On her own initiative she saved on her grocery bill by shopping at bargain stores. She kept a ledger for all her expenses the way her father had done. She said that she was, in many ways, a "proper middle-class housewife." Her class consciousness was most evident in her refusal to have a child without being married: "I couldn't handle the stigma of an illegitimate child."

Although Betsy was "not wildly in love" with Eli, he gave her the security she needed. Moreover, for some time, they were sexually adjusted to each other. She said: "Sex was fine for a while. Then it wasn't fine anymore." Alone for hours while Eli was at work, she became irritated with him, "for no reason at all." She took part-time jobs—in an ice cream parlor, a shoeshine place, a service station—but after a short time she would become uptight at her place of work, "for some silly reason," and quit. At home by herself again, she was, at times, overcome with self-pity.

She felt that Eli's friends, especially one couple, did not fully accept her. They and Eli often played a game in which Betsy could not participate—one person would say a word, and the others would respond, in brief sentences, with associations to their common past in the hippie commune. On these, and other occasions, Betsy felt that she was treated like a child, and she hated herself for not openly telling them her grievances. Only when they all smoked pot did Betsy feel friendly toward them.

Because of the relaxing effect of marijuana, Betsy did not object too strongly when, on another occasion, Eli and his friends persuaded her to take LSD with them. To be excluded from the group seemed worse than risking the ill effects of the drug. Moreover, Eli assured Betsy that the small dose which she would get could not be harmful. Yet what Betsy experienced that night was utterly terrifying. Except for enjoying some beautiful recurring visual images, Betsy remained in an agitated state for hours, so that the others, who had all taken the drug before, worried that she would not "pull out of it." She became aggressive against each person in the room, especially Eli. She was later told she had yelled at Eli's friends, accusing them of conspiring against her by using a secret code. She accused Eli of being indifferent to how she felt, of ignoring her intellect, and of being concerned only with his "Buddhist stuff." She denounced him as vain and a show-off, as exploiting her day and night. At one moment the others had to restrain Betsy from attacking Eli physically, and, at another, from packing her belongings and leaving "for good."

After this episode, Eli's attitude toward Betsy changed. He felt guilty about not having prevented Betsy's "bad trip." He was anxious to show her his affection, and fearful that she would seriously want to leave him. He now suggested they get married. Although earlier this had been Betsy's wish, Betsy now recognized feelings that had "simmered in her" for some time: "I felt that a lot of my discomfort came from being what Eli wanted me to be, just as I had accepted what my parents wanted me to be and what the world wanted me to be. How I looked at myself came entirely from how other people looked at me."

Zephyr's birth. When Betsy became pregnant for the second time, Eli advised her to have an abortion. He was now convinced that Betsy would resent being tied down with a child. But in spite of Eli's fear, and disregarding her previous objection against having an illegitimate child, Betsy decided to go through with the pregnancy. She thought that giving birth held the promise of creating someone close and dependable who would provide her "a solid ground to stand on." At the same time, Betsy was determined not to "let the baby interfere with [my] freedom." She recalled her thoughts and feelings when the baby was born:

When he was born, my immediate reaction when I was seeing him coming out was, I knew he was a male. The next thing was, I made an immediate separation from him but a very fine one. I am not talking about bad separation. I felt we've shared bodies now. You are you and I am me. Just because you came out of my womb, does not mean that we shall be friends. You may like me and I may like you, or maybe not, and I didn't want to get into being very hopeful and therefore very disappointed. I wanted to enjoy whatever there is to enjoy. There was one thing I hadn't anticipated. I was expecting a baby coming out of my womb to look like me. But it looked like every picture of every newborn baby. I found this was a very important message.

Betsy's hope that the baby would resemble her seems to illustrate the "self-replication tendency" of the parent, i.e., the parent's desire to be replicated by the child, which we have discussed earlier as entering into the identification process. It will be remembered that Jerry's mother was disappointed that Jerry, as a newborn, did "not look like anyone in the family," that she saw in Jerry's uniqueness a threat to their relationship and tried in other ways to foster his dependency on her.

Betsy's response when she found that the baby did not resemble her shows a similar disappointment. Her hope that the child would resemble her can be understood as her wish for closeness with her child. On the other hand, her thought of "an immediate separation" from the child seems to indicate an unusual lack of maternal feelings. But it is also possible that any close relationship is likely to be feared by Betsy, since her mother had failed to provide closeness and affectionate support for her. This would explain the meaning of the "important message" which Betsy gave herself—to avert a symbiotic relationship with her infant.

When Betsy began to breast feed the baby, she seemed to derive an intense gratification from the physical closeness with the child. She nursed him every two hours for six weeks. As an "excuse" for her indulging the child, she told herself that he was "a very hungry baby." Betsy said about this period: "I really felt great for a while."

Once the baby had been weaned, she became restless and lonely. Her apprehension about Eli returned. She was irritated by his picking the child up too often or being "all sweetness" with the baby. It appears that Betsy feared that too close a relationship might develop between Eli and the child.

Not unlike other women today, she was ambivalent about her maternal role and her role as a housewife. She did not follow Eli's suggestion to resume her part-time job and to entrust the infant for a few hours to a babysitter; she told herself that the baby still needed her around. At the same time she resented being tied to the house, having to clean, cook, and wash diapers, and having to get up from her sleep when the baby cried while Eli took his needed sleep because he had to go to work in the morning. Although she did not have any alternative plan for herself, she felt that Eli was exploiting her by holding her back from a life of her own. She now believes that, without her being aware of it, the women's movement had "gotten under [her] skin."

However, Betsy's ambivalent behavior toward her infant as well as toward Eli may reflect her approach-avoidance need. When she first met Eli she had been drawn to him by the affectionate support he gave her. However, this very closeness to him became more difficult for her to bear as time went on. Her inner conflict, originating in unfulfilled needs in her childhood, may have become intensified in watching Eli's budding relationship with the child.

One incident occurred during her interview which indicated that Betsy still tends to avoid affectionate commitments. A young man, a member of commune Haven, passed by and made an intimate, humorous remark to Betsy. She answered him in a similar fashion. When asked by the interviewer whether he was going to leave Haven with her, she said in a determined tone: "No, he is not. I'm sleeping with him now. He was one of the people who were here when I came. But he's going to stay here and continue his life."

Betsy joins the Pharos commune. One day, Betsy took the baby and visited a woman whom she had met in Eli's health food store who lived in Commune Pharos. The woman had earlier suggested showing Betsy the communal setup and introducing her to her friends. Betsy said that that day she felt more depressed than usual and needed to get out. At the time she did not think of the commune as a place where she wanted to live.

There were a few women and men in the house at Pharos that day. Betsy thought one of them, half asleep, was "freaked out, probably from drugs." They asked Betsy no questions. They were friendly, played with the baby and showed him to the kids playing in the backyard. She talked with Catherine, the "head guru," only briefly. As will be seen, Catherine's leadership was, indeed, all-important for the Pharos group. After this first visit to the commune Betsy felt more at ease than she had felt for a long time. Since they seemed to improve her peace of mind, Eli did not object to Betsy's subsequent visits to Pharos. In a long, open conversation, Betsy told Catherine about her break with her family and her frustrations in her present life. She found Catherine remarkably understanding and empathetic. At one of her next visits, Betsy was able to tell Catherine that she would like to live in the commune, that she "liked the people" and "wanted to link [her] life with them." Catherine was agreeable to the idea. A group consensus was not needed for admitting a new member. So at Betsy's next visit she was asked to join. Yet Betsy waited from one day to the next to tell Eli about her decision. She seemed to experience again the painful conflict between her need for separation and her need for closeness. Even after she had told Eli that she would join the commune, she tried to overcome her "initial heartbreak" by inviting Eli to come whenever he wanted to and by assuring him that the separation would only be temporary. This promise was not altogether hypocritical since she did have some doubt at the last moment as to whether she could adjust to Pharos's lifestyle, particularly its lack of privacy and sharing of all possessions.

Paula

Paula was one of the five women who had lived in Pharos and had moved together to Gates. Unlike the other four, Paula's decision was to stay at Gates for an uncertain period. Her one-year-and-three-month-old daughter, Souza, is with her. At the time of the interview at Haven, Paula was twenty-five years old. She had been married briefly once. She had then tried twice, unsuccessfully, to live with a boyfriend. The last one was Don, Souza's father. Feeling irrevocably wronged, she left him shortly before Souza was born. Like Betsy, Paula found protection and a respite from her conflicts in Pharos.

Childhood. Paula's family lives in a middle-sized city in the Midwest. Her father owns a plumbing firm which has been in the family for two generations. She has a sister three years older who was born out of wedlock and had lived with her mother three years before her parents got married. Paula believes that her sister envies her because of her legitimate birth, and that this was the reason why the two sisters were never on good terms.

Paula remembers her mother as frail, kind, and also "explosive." She speaks of her nostalgically with great feeling, and, paradoxically, at times with no marked effect. She recalls vividly and affectionately how her mother had wanted her to have the best of everything, whether that was the prettiest doll or the best fudge ice cream—Paula's favorite dessert.

Paula describes her relationship with her father as rather impersonal. "I did not really have a relation with my father." She remembers one occasion in particular: she had finally succeeded in making her father play a game of checkers with her when, in the middle of the game, he hurried downstairs to his shop to finish some work. This incident convinced her that he "had not much use" for her. Later, when the question of Paula's foster placement came up, it seemed to her that he was too willing to part with her.

Mother's death—Paula in foster care. When Paula was five years old her mother became ill with TB. As her illness progressed, she spent increasing periods of time in a hospital. Paula's mother died when Paula was seven years old. She remembers her anxiety and distress over her mother's death as a piercing pain which stayed with her for a long time. Repeatedly she tried to spot her mother's face in a crowd.

For a time Paula lived alone with her father, her sister boarding with relatives. Her father gave Paula his attention, in her words, "as well as he could." She was listless, however, and kept to herself. She blamed her father for her mother's illness and death. When he remarried, her relationship with him grew worse. Paula reacted with stubbornness and hostility to attempts by her stepmother to gain her confidence. After a particularly bad quarrel with her stepmother, Paula ran away and, suitcase in hand, arrived at the door of the relatives with whom her sister was living.

Soon afterward, Paula was placed in the care of the foster mother, who turned out to be a warm, competent, and motherly person whom Paula still calls, affectionately, "mama." She describes her foster mother as calm and patient. Unlike her mother, who would have had a "fit" if Paula broke a dish, Paula's foster mother did not become upset. Paula sees her foster mother as someone who rescued her from her worst tragedy—her mother's death. While her foster mother has stood by her during her irregular life, Paula's father became repulsed by Paula's unconventional lifestyle. Despite his being the father of an illegitimate child himself, he considers Paula's having an illegitimate child a disgrace. According to Paula, her father still believes that "one of these days [Paula] will turn around and marry a nice doctor and have a dishwasher and a regular way of life."

Young adulthood. Paula attended college despite the turmoil in her past. There, like so many other young women too bright to remain uneducated and too unsettled to make any concrete choices of career, she found herself drawn to English literature. She did, however, as is often done, use her education to earn a teaching credential.

She fell in love with a co-student while at college and married him only a few weeks after they'd met. Referring to her relationship with men, Paula says, "I have been heavily married three times, but only the first marriage involved a paper." She explains her hasty decision to get legally married the first time with a tragically typical remark: "I thought then that this was the thing to do—get married and live happily ever after." Her sentiments were similar to Betsy's. Divorced soon thereafter, she has not again sought a legal husband.

In each of her relationships there were "very happy moments." Yet the "usual marital trouble" set in each time—"jealousy, possessiveness, pain." Alone at home, she always wondered "where he was, what he was doing, why he wasn't with me."

With Don, the father of her child Souza, Paula made one last attempt at "couple living." After a trial period, both partners agreed to stay together without a formal marriage, and did not change that decision when Paula became pregnant. Don was older than Paula's previous lovers. His attention and understanding enhanced her self-respect. One day, when she was in her sixth month of pregnancy, however, Paula discovered that Don had recently had an affair with a young girl, an employee at his place of work. Although Don had terminated this relationship himself, fully understanding Paula's wounded feelings, and was eager to amend his fault, Paula's resentment did not subside. She describes her thwarted feelings in these words:

He had been very good to me during the first months of pregnancy, very helpful and considerate. But when I learned about his relationship I went through the typical marriage thing. We didn't have rings and we didn't believe in marriage, but I still had the same awful hang-up, you know. I was the wife and I was outraged.

Paula refused all Don's attempts at reconciliation and she separated from him before her baby's birth.

Paula describes the months that followed as a "long, painful stretch of days." Although she could not "get herself together," and felt very low at times, she never considered having an abortion. It was during this time that she saw an ad that read:

If, for some reason, you need very badly to change the way you live and hope you can, we are willing to help you find out.

Paula went to the house whose address was given in the ad; it was the address of the Pharos commune.

Paula joins the Pharos commune

At Pharos, Paula was told that some members were looking for additional participants in a series of group therapy sessions which were being tried out in the commune. Paula met Catherine and seemed to have been captivated immediately by her personality and by Catherine's warm interest in her. Paula's reaction to the people and to the lifestyle at Pharos resembled that of Betsy at her first visit.

A similar first experience with a hippie group was described by a woman who later became a radical activist in the Weather Underground:

I joined the group on the meadow. They began singing a freedom song and without thinking about it I sang with them. . . . Without any effort, without knowing who I was or wasn't, this casual group of people had made me happy. I felt like I belonged. For the first time in my life, I felt I belonged somewhere [34:4].

These reactions are markedly like Grete's first enthusiasm when joining the Wandervogel.

Margarete Buber-Neumann also described her immediate fascination with a group of Wandervoegel at her first encounter with the movement. She met them at a street corner assembling for a night hike:

They talked loudly and behaved as if they owned the street and as if they were different and better than other people. Although I somehow felt ashamed for their behavior on their behalf, they fascinated me so much that I went to one of the girls and asked her what all this was about. She said something about a winter solstice celebration and that I could join them, but it would get very late before I would get home. Without letting my family know, without even thinking of it, a few minutes later I marched with them through the dark Potsdam forest to the tune of a song unknown to me [9:31].

It is conceivable that these "conversions" are due to the impact which a group of people with a lifestyle created by youth itself and exhibited with enthusiasm and conviction has on a young outsider, an impact which is apt to be particularly strong if the outsider is in a state of inner imbalance.

Paula became increasingly attracted to the commune. Soon she was to go there early in the morning, remain until 1 A.M., go home, and be back a few hours later. When Catherine finally suggested that Paula should join Pharos, she felt relieved as if from "an inner burden." Betsy's relief when asked to live at Pharos was similar. Parallels can be multiplied: Grete's feelings of bliss when she received the badge of her youth association, the radical activist's sense of exaltation when asked to join the Weathermen and move into their collective house. ("Feeling reassured, I waited a second longer and then, tears in my eyes, I said, 'Yes, yes I will'" [34:152]).

Commune Pharos

Some comments on the types of contemporary communes will help to understand the character of the Pharos commune.

As we have seen above, communes vary as to beliefs, leadership, standards, admission requirements, rules of behavior, etc. Yet there are common features shared by most of them. The members are predominantly white and middle class, ranging in age between eighteen and thirty. Most communes have a bias against status, bureaucracy, and regimentation. They are opposed to capitalism and technology, and are antiintellectual. A charismatic leader is unconditionally accepted as authority, by most members. They adopt his philosophical guidelines and emulate his way of life. Sexual freedom is often approved of, and generally takes the form of time-limited, monogamous living, long-lasting attachments being discouraged as endangering group cohesion. The care of children is shared by all members. The mother's special responsibilities for the care of her own child vary greatly from commune to commune.

Among the values stressed by commune members are self-sufficiency and resourcefulness. Further valued are the ability to understand and relate to others and the concern with one's own "growth" or self-development.

Sociologists have attempted to classify communes according to their relative emphasis on some of the above characteristics and their deemphasis on others. Rosabeth Kanter has introduced a classification which is fruitful for our inquiry because it helps us understand why a person is attracted to a particular type of commune [20:191-212]. Kanter distinguishes between "service" communes and "retreat" communes. The two types are not understood as mutually exclusive, but as overlapping. "Service" communes, calling themselves "helpers" of the society, tend to interact with the wider world. These communes are exclusive and strict. They have specific membership rules and adhere to definite norms of appropriate behavior and to specific schedules of events. Service communes usually exist four to five years longer than do retreat communes. An example is Twin Oaks, the commune in Virginia mentioned earlier. It is known for its stability and successful organization, and has a long survival record [2:8]. Kanter attributes the longer duration of service, as compared to retreat communes, to such features as firm organization, definition of roles, rules initiated by group consensus, and a common goal.

While the service communes are large, the largest, The Farm (see Note 10), comprising eight hundred members, retreat communes average between eight and fifteen persons, and none has more than thirty. As the term implies, retreat communes tend to separate themselves from society. They have no formal requirements for membership and they admit visitors who may stay for days or for longer. They refrain from strict rules and from setting goals. Making minimal demands on their members, most decisions are left to the individual. Matters of concern to the wider society, e.g., politics and community events, tend to be ignored. The abnegation of American and Western society as a whole, including organized medicine and the judicial system, seems to strengthen the sense of dependency on the group. Because they reject all official authority, retreat communes have been said to be "anarchistic." Of great concern in retreat communes is the closeness of the affectionate bond between group members, the choice of sexual partners, and the intensity of a sexual relationship. Other major issues to which much attention is paid by each member are self-examination, self-criticism, and self-development.

According to the above typology, both Pharos and Haven are, to some extent, retreat communes. In fact, "Hang loose, but don't fall apart," the guideline posted on a wall in Haven, corresponds to Kanter's comment about retreat communes: "Plans seem unnecessary, while to 'hang loose' is a positive value" [20:184].

Charles, brother of the leader Catherine, was interviewed. He describes how admissions were handled in Pharos: "If you felt comfortable, that meant that people liked you and wanted you to stay. Then you stayed." Kanter quotes the following advertisement by a retreat commune looking for new members: "Come see whether you like us and we like you" [20:182]. Haven is somewhat more organized than was Pharos. George, who manages Haven, explains that in his commune, new members are admitted only on a group consensus. He considers an ideal admission procedure, a prospective member's living in the neighborhood for about half a year and visiting the commune regularly before being accepted as a member. Both Betsy and Paula disapprove of the more organized life at Haven where meals and certain chores are planned—irregularly as that may be—and where some members occasionally lock their doors.

Pharos admitted and Haven admits nonmembers for various periods. Pharos was overflowing with visitors at times, on their ways to and from places west. Commenting on the visitors at Pharos, Charles says that "people came and went. It looked like a good place to be, especially because of Catherine. She gathered a lot of people around her."

Pharos members did not think of Pharos as a permanent institution though, nor did they openly admit any dismay about its possible dissolution. Paula says, "We are all transients. We never plan to stay in one commune very long. There is no guarantee that I may stay here for another week or another day or for any particular time." Betsy puts it this way: "I dug the commune. It fitted my life *at the time*." However, as we shall see, the dissolution of Pharos had an unsettling effect on Betsy. While Pharos closed down after four years, Haven has existed for several more years, having undergone a number of organizational changes. It changed from a retreat to a service commune. Recently it has tended to become a retreat kind of commune again.

The rejection of American and Western society, referred to earlier, was conspicuously present in Pharos. Newspapers were rare and news reports as well as political commentaries were deeply mistrusted. At the time of Paula's interview, the Harris trial was in its last stage.[12] Paula did not read the proceedings because the reports were "so colored" that one could "not know what really happened." The Harrises, she maintains, "could never be tried by a court, for what they stood for, for their convictions as revolutionaries."

Paula thinks they were right in their cause but they were wrong in using violence.

In Pharos, as in other retreat communes, the rejection of society included a prejudice against accredited medical practices. Folk medicine was held in high esteem. Babies were delivered in the commune with the assistance of members self-taught in midwifery. A certified midwife was called in only in an emergency. As we shall see from Paula's description of the birth of her child, this event became a profound group experience.

The reverence for pregnancy and for childbirth seems to contradict the belief in impermanence prevailing in retreat communes. It also seems to contradict the "apocalyptic" view—a view which has been said to "recur in one form or another in countless conversations" in countercultqre groups [38:471]. Appocalyptic threats also haunted the historical commune members and were a strong motive for their flight into isolation and for their attempts to prepare themselves for the end of the world by creating a "purified, spiritual society based on fundamental biblical truths" [7:15]. Contemporary communes are seldom set up to actively deal with what are seen as imminent, life-threatening events of a divine plan. Yet, perhaps as a function of insecurity, frustration, and isolation, members of the counterculture often come to have an essentially apocalyptic view not only of the threat to Western society but to "our world," "our planet," "the universe." To be sure, present-day apocalyptic notions are based in part upon the realistic dangers of atomic war, overpopulation, and air pollution. In a climate of helplessness and threatened existence, the experience of a woman giving birth may be felt by all to be a new beginning. Temporarily dispelling gloom about man's future, it may give way to a worship of creating.

Betsy and Paula at Commune Pharos: Personality Changes

What prompted Betsy and Paula to join Commune Pharos? How did Pharos fulfill their needs at the time?

Various motives have been proposed for individuals joining a commune. Among its inducements are: "a strong inner search for the meaning of one's own life, an openness and willingness to communicate and encounter, coupled with a compelling desire for personal growth and development" [29:9]. A founder of Twin Oaks, the commune mentioned earlier, believes that the reasons which most frequently attract people to a commune are: "The dream of no longer being lonely, the hope of finding a compatible mate or a close, warm group of friends" [20:2], and that the love he receives is the main reason for a person's being content with the commune. A member of the commune Findhorn, in Scotland, which expects its members to participate in hard construction work, makes a similar statement: "The group is what holds you steady. Loving is the most important thing. I am in a group of people who love me more than I love myself" [17].

There is no question that, for both Betsy and Paula, the interpersonal relations at Pharos played a major role in their wish to join this commune, and in their becoming attached to it. About her relationship to the Pharos members, Betsy says,

I loved them. I felt loved. I *feel* loved. I consider them my friends, my family. I felt they were really interested in me and wanted to know me. I became one of them.

About the two women with whom Betsy was going to leave Haven, she says: "I consider them my sisters more than anyone else."

Both Betsy and Paula compare their previous pair relationships with the varied relationships in the commune. Betsy: "I felt different kinds of love because different people satisfied different needs in me." And Paula says:

The commune is an ideal spot because there are lots of people to give and share love. But if I did not want to, I did not need to have sex relations with any of them. I knew and I know sex is always available to me, and that takes care of chasing after somebody, takes care of the whole courtship deal and everything. It's no problem. Also, I don't have the great need for it, I thought, before, I had.

However, both Betsy and Paula admit that they sometimes lapse into their "old thinking" and become jealous, competitive, and possessive. Paula describes it in these words:

When you try to abolish being jealous, it's hard in the beginning. Needs lots of work, but can be done. Two women sleeping with the same man could create difficulty but we worked it out. Sincerity played a role. Also, most things were happening in the open. Living that close together, you don't have many secrets.

Each commune develops its own group character just as did the two youth movement groups described before. We will see that even within the homogeneous environment of one relatively small kibbutz, the climate of one Children's House may differ from that of another one nearby (see Chapter 4, Note 1).

Among the values stressed at Pharos, complete sincerity was of ultimate importance. Betsy: "You had to tell the truth, even if it hurt." Paula: "Being sincere to each other was most important." Both women mention abstaining from judging a person as a crucial value. Betsy: "One of the things we were not into was judgment. We tried not to see things as good or bad in each other, as right or wrong." There was, finally, an understanding that one did not "expect" anything from one another. Betsy: "Because I had no expectation of them they could not disappoint me, dissatisfy me. And they did not expect anything from me. They let me be." Paula, describing her behavior toward other members, and especially her attitude toward her child (see below), shows that she too adheres to both of these precepts.

As will be seen later, the values sanctioned at Pharos originated largely in

Catherine's view of the world and of mankind. The renunciation of private property was, for Catherine, *the* criterion of a member's definitive change from society's to the commune's values. As Catherine expressed it: "As long as you can say 'my' room there is possessiveness." Other Pharos members interviewed willingly accepted Catherine's principles. All property, e.g., clothing, previous possessions and earnings, present earnings in outside jobs, was pooled. Moreover, as Paula describes, privacy was at a minimum:

No one "owned" a room. There was no definite sleeping arrangement. There were bedrooms with mattresses on the floor for a maximum of 20 people. People went to bed at different times. Whoever wanted to sleep found a room and a bed. One could sleep each night in a different room.

Some of the values the two women had incorporated at Pharos still guide their behavior at Haven where life is more organized and where privacy is respected, at least to some extent. Both Paula and Betsy criticize these regulations at Haven. When called for her appointment, it took Paula a long time to come to the telephone. She then explained in a self-affirmative tone that no one could find her because she was asleep, "curled up in some corner," probably a habit carried over from her Pharos period.

In Pharos, as in other retreat communes, the desire to maintain the close, intimate bond between members went hand in hand with a strong need to grow and to develop one's unique inner resources. Lawrence R. Veysey in *The Communal Experience* has drawn attention to the similarity between Rousseau's emphasis on individualism as well as community living, and the double concern in present communes, "doing your own thing" combined with collective living [38:424-425]. The members of Brook Farm had not aspired to self-development, self-transformation, or growth in the present-day sense. Instead, they emphasized "self-improvement," by which they meant, among other things, a greater appreciation of the "fine arts" or philosophy.

Although even as early as Brook Farm some members hoped to solve "individual problems" through an "associative life,"[13] attempts at examining and modifying an individual's inner self within a group setting have become general only in present-day society. No doubt this relatively new use of the face-to-face group has taken on such importance not only because of our contemporary pressures and the psychological advances of the twentieth century, but also because methods of dealing with inner conflicts, which sufficed earlier, have become rare today: traditional religious assemblies, for example, romantic solitude (often in rural settings), friend-to-friend relationships of a special, intimate kind, and of long duration, all seem to be losing their significant role in meeting present psychological needs.

We have seen, as illustrated by Grete's increased ability to stand up for herself, how an individual can be changed through group experience. At the reunion of Grete's W.V. association forty-five years later, the participants agreed that the group experience had decisively formed their personalities and that this had happened through "jointly searching, more or less consciously, for self-realization [*selbstverwirklichung*]" [32].

In present-day communes, the concern with the group's influence upon the individual has moved to the fore. It has been said that even those communes which began with somewhat formal, work-oriented communication sooner or later tended to become concerned with relationships, "family feeling," and "personal growth" [20:167]. We have seen the same tendencies expressed by Pharos members. On the other hand, Betsy also appreciated that at Pharos she was given "plenty of space." She did not feel bound to or confined by the other members. "We would be apart if we felt like being apart. I was quite free to freak out" (through occasionally smoking pot).

In the vocabulary and thinking of the present counterculture, the desire to discover one's inner self is linked with the wish for "space." "Space" means both the physical expanse apprehended with one's senses and affecting one's feelings, and an inner freedom, often depending on well-intentioned others—thus the expression: "loving space" (p. 170).

Dissolution of Pharos

Yet it was this very need for "space" which was, according to Betsy, a major reason for the dissolution of Pharos:

We decided that we all wanted to move on and get into different things. We loved each other and had our riffs worked out together. And the things we hadn't worked out we ironed out then. And then it was time for something new.

When asked why the Pharos members decided to move on even though given "plenty of space," Betsy said:

You get closed-minded. You know each other too well, knowing each other's past and present. It got so I knew what someone was thinking. You need to get to know other people. You need to grow.

Paula gives a surprisingly similar answer to the same question:

Basically because of my own growth. If it doesn't feel good anymore, if you are getting too hung up with the group, if you feel you want to go to another place where you can flourish, you move on.

We have pointed out before that Betsy longs for closeness while, at the same time, guarding herself against an intense relationship. In her statements above, Betsy criticizes the familiarity between members as oppressive, although earlier she had extolled the very closeness of these relationships. It is likely that the dissolution of the commune came at a time when, without being consciously aware of it, Betsy still needed the emotional security provided by the Pharos group. That she is not ready to detach herself completely from this group is indicated by her decision to stay with two of its members. She may also have sensed the dissolution of Pharos as a personal failure. This may explain, to some extent, her urgent desire to change herself at this time in her life:

I feel I'm retaining a whole bunch of old characteristics of myself and of insecurities. It comes from wanting to be Betsy L. I know I come from this father and this mother and this background and I have this education. I'm this person. But I want to just melt into the universe and be anybody. The more I am Betsy L., the more limit I put on what this particular person can do or be and how I define myself. I want to undefine myself, so that I can go on. I keep moving.

She added after a nervous laugh and a pause:

Just lose yourself. Shed what you were and get into what you are going to be or what you sometimes are when you are by yourself.

Betsy's wish to "un-define" herself in order to "go on" suggests her puzzlement, her disappointment, and her loss of self-love. Her old fear that she will be left without sympathy and affection seems to have gotten hold of her once again, arousing fantasies of "melting into the universe," and "being anybody," which also means to be nobody.

It is of poignant interest to note how, in her depressed and empty state, images occur to Betsy which appear in the writings of medieval mystics when expressing similar feelings. In moments of despair they yearned for oneness with the cosmos, for "leaving one's self" (in German, *sich ent-fahren*) and achieving a state of "not-being" (*"ent-sein"*). Not unlike these writers, Betsy expects that a state of nothingness will be followed by a rebirth. Her hope that contacts with new people will help her to become a different person would seem illusory. Since she avoids deep commitments these contacts will not aid her to develop or change.

Kanter quite succinctly describes the predicament of commune members who reject strong and lasting commitments:

There is still much to be learned about the personal consequences of having a series of temporary relationships and a constant turnover in one's social network. Does it add variety and richness and enhance the ability to relate meaningfully to many different people, or does it eliminate the depth and sharing that comes from *mutual commitment*? Does it promote strength or insecurity? [20:215].

On the basis of the present impasse in Betsy's life we can venture an answer to the last question. For Betsy, who had formed a strong identification with the group at Pharos, its dissolution has left her insecure about her needs and her commitment to the group. On the other hand, she blames herself for still being identified with her parents' lifestyle.

Betsy's conflict raises an important and difficult question: How deeply ingrained are the identifications with exponents of the counterculture? Although we shall not be able to answer this question with any certainty, we may begin to see that there are more facets to the process of identification reversal than was apparent when we first set out to explore the development of identifications.

The earlier parts of this investigation showed children who were hindered in perceptible ways from expressing their individual interests, character, or potentialities. To varying degrees, they were induced to identify with parental perceptions. We saw two children in whom, indeed, the parental expectations could be seen to create the expected behavior at least to some degree. (Often brief segments of the interaction conveyed these parental influences.) We noticed how, later in life, Stephen struggled to assert some lifestyle and interest of his own—short of overt rebellious behavior or the joining of a youth movement. We noticed how John suffered from an inability to do so. Not only in these two individuals were issues of childhood identification rigidly preserved, but, judging from certain statements by Grete, Betsy, and Paula, their later identifications, also, did not completely break either the magic cycle of their childhood identifications nor the emotional relationships with their parents. Their early unmet need for and fear of love and intimacy became infused into subsequent relationships and affected the forming of new identifications.

Since from these observations we can conclude that members of a youth movement, or those on the fringe of such a movement, cannot wholly shed their identification with parental models, we may want to ask: Which parental attitudes or values are more powerful than others in strengthening identification and which are more likely to undergo identification reversal? This question, obviously important to our investigation, eludes, as yet, any specific answer.

We may, however, be able to gather fresh insights into the adults' influences on the child's identification when we investigate the childrearing practices and theory which operate within Pharos and Haven, especially those adopted by Betsy and Paula. First, however, we will need to consider Catherine, who was to Betsy and Paula the "good mother" Trude was to Grete—with some crucial differences. We will return to individuals who function as "alternate parents" again later when we meet some unexpected solutions in the role of the metapelet in the Israeli kibbutz.

Catherine—Another Leader

Catherine's resourcefulness, her theoretical knowledge, and her sureness about "cosmic" and social events, as well as her empathy with troubled persons, draw others close to her. These same characteristics motivate members like Betsy and Paula to talk and think like Catherine and to adopt her values.

At the time she was interviewed, Catherine was fifty-seven years old. Her brother, Charles, was two years younger than she, and lived in the Haven commune (see above). Catherine grew up in the Bronx. When she was four years old, her father left the family to live with another woman. Two years later her mother married a man who became a kind and conscientious father substitute to the children. While Catherine retained ambivalent (love-hate) feelings for her biological father, she also recalls the intense sadness, sustained by her mother's sadness, which lasted in her for years.

Catherine's mother was a warm, sincere, giving person, liberal in her views. Charles recalls that the mother wanted him to spend the money he got for his birthday not on anything practical, but on a "fun thing." When Catherine started secretly smoking cigarettes and her mother discovered it, she reassured her that she was not doing something morally wrong and told her: "I'd rather not have you smoke behind my back." It seemed to Catherine that the unspoken rule in the family was "make each other feel good," and that there was very little in the way of "playing tricks on each other."

Catherine turned out to be "more of a thinker" than anyone else in her family. She searched for reasons to explain what she saw happening around her: the misfortune of her mother; the maid's having to wash the floors while her mother did her needlepoint. Gradually she discovered that there were "more questions in the world than answers." She "read a lot and thought a lot."

In the late 1930s Catherine became a student at City College in New York, majoring in English literature. As a member of the radical student movement, she embraced orthodox Marxism. The belief in the inevitable abolition of the class structure and of the poverty in evidence during the Depression made communism particularly appealing to Catherine. Moreover, together with other radical students, she was determined to work against fascism.

Catherine met Ernest, her future husband, at a debate on the future of communism. A young college instructor in physics, he was a member of the same radical movement. They were married in 1940 and had three boys and one daughter. In line with their idea that "you owed to your endowment of high intelligence a large progeny," they had planned for two more children.

Ernest became a well-known professor in his field. They lived in a midwestern university town. For the first years of their marriage they traveled a lot to other universities in the U.S. and abroad where Ernest was a guest professor, gave lecture tours, etc. Catherine did not find it too difficult to bring up her children under these circumstances. She thinks she managed to travel with small children remarkably well. However, she became increasingly more dissatisfied with her life. She talked to wives of other professors who felt as she did. Yet she could not talk to Ernest.

Continuous arguments ensued. She had what she called "depressive streaks," especially in the afternoons. When things got worse over the years, she thought it must be either his fault or hers. "I felt if I had another man who would be better, more devoted, more outgoing, handsomer, or if I were smarter, prettier, etc., everything would be all right." But gradually she came to realize that there was nothing wrong with either of them, that she and Ernest still loved each other, but that it was the relationship, prescribed by society, i.e., the conventional marriage, that needed to be changed.

At a time (the 1960s) when alternatives to family life were being widely discussed, they were divorced after thirty years.

Catherine moved to Berkeley—at that time the center of the politics of the New Left. The antibourgeois and antiestablishment zeal had a nostalgic appeal for Catherine, so she planned to participate in the Free Speech or the anti war movement.

After she had found a place to live, however, she preferred spending a lot of time by herself. She had not expected that leaving the security of her home would be so severe a shock. Only gradually did she become interested in outside happenings. In a course on yogic principles at the Free University of Berkeley (set up by graduate students as an alternative to those offered by the "Educational Establishment"), she met a young unmarried couple to whom she felt immediately attracted. The couple lived some distance north of San Francisco. They became friends and Catherine offered them her apartment as an occasional place to stay. They made use of the offer and after a while they all agreed that they should move in with Catherine. There was still room in her apartment, and, somewhat later, two friends of the couple joined the three. At that time communes were springing up throughout the states. Without realizing it, Catherine had initiated a commune.

Two years later, Catherine and her group moved to Portland, Oregon. There they found a house large enough for two more members who had liked the Berkeley setup but could not be accommodated there. Since it was to guide persons in need, the Portland commune was called Pharos (lighthouse). It existed for four years.

Catherine said about her role in Pharos: "When I left the straight society I did not want to depend on anyone or have others depend on me. I did not want power." She obviously did not know then, but certainly must now, that at Pharos she did have the authority of a leader endowed with charisma.

Max Weber, introducing the concept of charismatic leadership into sociology, describes such a leader as endowed with a particular "gift of grace (charisma)" through which he inspires "enthusiasm, hope and a very personal devotion" in those "in need" [39:141] (see also p. 121). The authority of the charismatic leader is irrational and lacking in rules (regelfremd). He is apt to reverse the past and, thus, is revolutionary. This characterization applies also to Catherine in her role at Pharos.

Rosabeth Kanter gives examples of charismatic leaders in historical communities: Father Rapp, the founder of Harmony Society, and John Humphrey Noyes, the founder of the Oneida community.[14] Father Rapp was described by a member of his group as a man who "knew everything—how to do it, what was the best way" [20:117]. John Humphrey Noyes was characterized by a contemporary as a man who "has mastered the art of so controlling his disciples that they think they are carrying out their own ideas when they are really executing his designs." [20:117]. Demandingness and control over others have also been attributed to some charismatic leaders of present-day communes. Laurence A. Veysey gives a vivid picture of this type of leader when he writes about the domination of the members by the leader of commune New Age in New Mexico [38:292-294].[15]

Catherine's charisma is reflected in statements by Paula, Betsy, and George. Paula says: "Catherine makes you feel high," and Betsy: "We all felt high around her. She has some magnetic power." Charles calls Catherine the "prime energy source," and "an intensely exciting person."

The tendency of Noyes's followers to "appropriate" his feelings and opinions as if they were their own is also evident in those who think of Catherine as their leader. Betsy says Catherine "looks at people and things the way [Betsy] has considered things." Paula remarks that Catherine likes the same things she does and that Catherine's ideas about marriage are like her own.

In these examples we see how, in their fantasy, the followers come to adopt the abilities of the charismatic leader. We have previously suggested that because the early mother-child closeness was insufficient in Betsy's, and disrupted in Paula's, case, both developed a proclivity for forming symbiotic relationships. Their fantasy about thinking Catherine's thoughts and sharing her biases, then, would arise from their need for a mother-infant union. In her psychoanalytical interpretation of emotional disturbances, Helene Deutsch has drawn attention to a clinical type which she calls "as-if" [11:262- 281]. These personalities are adults who show an inclination to temporarily merge with the psyche of another person in order to overcome their feelings of nothingness. Anna Freud has applied this concept to the adolescent who adapts his handwriting, or his way of speaking or dressing, to that person who "at the moment occupies the central place in his affection" [18:169]. The two authors emphasize that the "as-if" manifestations are of short duration since the models for identification are frequently changed. But, we may ask, are identifications in the counterculture as easily changeable? We have seen a lasting impact of her leader upon Grete's personality. Catherine's influence on Pharos's members suggests a certain stability, although we cannot know its long-range effect, as pointed out above. Perhaps, by molding themselves after a leader, these individuals incorporate not only the characteristics of the leader's personality, but the characteristics of the leader's culture as well. This may explain the impact of the leaders on their followers in counterculture groups.

Catherine's world view, which so influenced Betsy and Paula, was an amalgam of Darwin's theory of the survival of the fittest; of Wilhelm Reich's proposition that the authoritarian society and the authoritarian family cause sex suppression and thereby damage the child's personality; and of Marx's unalterable laws of history by which the capitalist system will perish whether the individual wills it or not.

In the interview, Catherine talks hastily, with a highstrung urgency in her voice. She expresses a Darwinian principle in these words:

Each species has to adapt to changes of environment. Since our planet has changed, through pollution of air, of water, invention of atomic energy, etc., our survival as a species depends on how we adapt to the new environment.

At times it is difficult to follow Catherine's somewhat rambling monologue and to understand how she connects changes in the physical environment with those in the social arena. Some of her ideas apparently are influenced by her personal experience:

The fact is that the nuclear family is not viable anymore because it imposes a sexual restraint on the child that is irreparable. Since the women's movement has gained momentum, marriage has been recognized as false, unnatural, and a hindrance to progress.

In an oversimplified version of Marxist thought, Catherine links her proposition to the history of mankind:

History itself has shown how the human species has been a victim of the power struggle, how the truth about what men are and can be has become obliterated. Man's ancestors lived in a society which fulfilled the "natural" needs of men—to live with each other in peace and be free and creative. Peace and freedom can't be reached until classes are abolished and people can live again naturally and harmoniously with each other.

For Catherine, the commune is a step toward this "natural" society. In line with Reichian ideas, she approves of varied sexual relationships instead of a lifelong monogamy. She believes that, since in a communal setting it is not difficult to find another suitable partner, the sexual freedom practiced in Pharos reduced both jealousy and the fear of losing a partner. Catherine also believes that sexual freedom reduces the intensity of the infantile ties to father and mother and that the child's naturally developing sexuality is less likely to be damaged in the communal group than in the nuclear family.

These ideas in themselves are not remarkable (they are expressed in other communes as well), but what is surprising is the extent to which individuals like Paula, Betsy, and Grete internalize an entire subculture from the individual viewpoint of one leader. Persons who form identifications of such a precarious nature may need continued reaffirmation of their affectionate bond with the leader and with the group. This may create the feelings of emptiness, as in Betsy's case, should the contact with these individuals be prematurely broken. By the same token, it may create feelings of euphoria should there be an unexpected reestablishment of the contact after a long separation. Such reaffirmation of affectionate bonds may well account for the high level of excitement observed at the D.W.V. reunion described earlier.

Issues of Identification

Let us go back over our study of identification. We have explored patterns of interaction in a few families, paying particular attention to parental expressions of affection and direction giving and to the parent's perception of the child. Although a number of other parental characteristics and a variety of experiences outside of the family can be assumed to enter into the identification process, as suggested in Figure 1, the above parental characteristics seem to have a decisive influence on the child's identification with the parent. In Chapter 2 the weakening of identification in young adulthood was seen to relate to the particular "blend" of parental affection and direction in infancy. In Chapter 3 we caught a glimpse of the process by which, in the same family, the parent's differing perceptions of each child influence each child's identification with the parent.

We shall now reexamine Betsy's and Paula's life histories and consider their identification reversals as these may be related to the kinds of affection and direction which each received from her parents.

Betsy's mother failed to provide her with affectionate closeness and emotional security. Betsy says that at an early age it was "easy for [her] to see [her] mother as an enemy." Nor did Betsy's father seem to have been any more fulfilling of her need for emotional support. Whether explicitly given or implicitly conveyed, his directions were strict and merely work oriented. Parental punishment for noncompliance was occasionally harsh and irrational, and led to Betsy's lying and to her feeling that she "betrayed them all the time."

My mother expected that I was destined to marry a respectable, well-off man and live close to the family into which I was born. My father scared me by what he expected me to accomplish. So I came into a lot of pressure. But I did what I wanted to do and I lied and betrayed them all the time.

This lying and betraying were probably among the earliest signs of her nonidentification with parental values. She became aware of departing from her parents' values and lifestyle more definitely when she began to live with Eli. But even then, she retained some traces of her identification with her parents: she transferred to Eli the authority she had feared in her father and kept house as properly and thriftily as her father would have wanted her to. Her bias against having an illegitimate child is another case in point. However, when she subsequently abandoned this bias and especially when she refused to legalize the birth by marriage, she abandoned her identification with important parental values more drastically. Compared with her previous, somewhat random attempts to free herself from parental values and prohibitions, her move into the commune can be seen as her final step toward a reversal of identification.

How did Betsy herself experience her identification reversal? She felt that her contact with the Pharos group had fulfilled her need for "ideas and love." By ideas Betsy obviously referred not so much to exchange of thoughts as to the group's values.

Among the values adhered to at Pharos, freedom in sexual relationships and abolishment of private property contrasted strongly with the moral precepts by which she had been raised. Betsy describes how she sees her dissidence:

I realized that most of my unhappiness and confusion came from feeling that I needed to live in a couple or live alone. I became convinced that I would not have lost anything if Eli had had sex with another woman, and that I was not gaining anything by being married.

Betsy acknowledges in a firm tone of voice the value of shared ownership adhered to at Pharos:

We weren't holding on to anything. We shared bread, life, money, rooms, everything.

She then contrasts the sincerity prevailing between commune members with the insincerity which permeated her relationship with her parents.

Paula had an affectionate relationship with her mother and her foster mother. Since she describes her mother as being "devoted" to her and "spoiling" her, we can assume that even if she had later exaggerated her mother's qualities, as a child she did have the benefit of an affectionate relationship with her. No doubt her mother's presence compensated for the insufficient expression of love and approval from her father. After the disastrous shock of losing her mother, Paula missed all the more the signs of her father's affectionate support. His remarriage was "proof" for Paula that he rejected her. Yet Paula's need for affection was satisfied to some extent by the warm relationship with her foster mother.

As to the directions given to Paula by the three adults close to her, she recalled no inhibiting or oppressive controls or demands from any of them. Her natural mother was lenient and undemanding. Her father did not provide firm directions or impose his expectations upon Paula. Nor did her foster mother reinforce in her her own conventional values. However,

Paula did internalize the major middle-class values of the significant adults in her childhood. She aspired to become as good a housekeeper and seamstress as her foster mother. As a student she adopted her father's belief in achievement through hard work. She insisted that her first sexual relationship shoulb be a legal one. Paula's fear of closeness, probably rooted in her early bereavement, led to conflict in this and other relationships. Because of the failure in her marriage, Paula later sustained sexual relationships without being married. If she thereby reversed the middle-class sanction placed on marriage, her refusal to marry her child's father could also be viewed as identification with the unconventional aspect of her father's personality.

Only after Paula's need for closeness had been frustrated by her lover's infidelity did she definitively abandon her identification with the wider parental culture by joining the commune. Yet when Paula became a mother, her identification with her natural mother reemerged. Her intrinsic wish was that her child should replicate her own mother (see below).

Betsy's and Paula's recollections of their early relationships with their parents suggest that they suffer from certain deficiencies in affection and direction in their parents' relationships to them; and that, if the parents lack these qualities it is likely that the children will seek them in other identification models.

We have drawn attention to Paula and Betsy's search for a person to whom they could attach themselves and we have seen their failure to sustain an affectionate bond when they found such a person. However, both women were able to form such a bond with Catherine because she fulfilled their wish for unconditional affection. Free love as practiced at Pharos met their need for a sexual relationship while avoiding the commitment of more intimate and exclusive affectional ties which they feared.

Betsy says of Catherine's affection toward individual members, "Being loving was natural to her," and Paula believes that Catherine's warm interest in people was the "glue that held everyone together." About Catherine's empathy and emotional participation Betsy and Paula have this to say: "She listened and she understood what irked you. . . . She had a way to smooth out hurt feelings and emotions so the hurts were not as painful anymore and one could live with them."

To the question of how conflicts could arise in such a protective atmosphere, Betsy gave this answer: "Of course, we got uptight with each other at times. Sure, we had explosions. But Catherine made us understand what we were trying to get from each other. And this was so important that we tried to live in peace. But, of course, it didn't always work."

The emotional bond with Catherine was so intense that it had a mystical quality. Mystical or irrational contacts with an idealized leader have been found to emerge under conditions of grave uncertainty [28:137]. Betsy said about her being "connected" with Catherine:

I don't feel isolated when I am not with her and I don't feel disconnected either. I know she is somewhere in the world but she is still with me.

Paula described the bond similarly:

Catherine is either there or not there. If she is physically present she's totally there. If she's not, you don't have to explain to her what is going on. She knows it anyhow.

What kind of directions did Catherine give her "followers"? What was the set of values which she transmitted to them? As revealed in her own statements, as well as in Betsy's and Paula's, her main rules of conduct were: "Don't use power and don't submit to power! Avoid possessiveness! Don't judge another person! Obey the golden rule: 'Don't do to others what you don't want others to do to you!' Preserve your independence!"

We have seen that both Betsy and Paula readily adopted these rules, casually communicated as they were. Paula says: "When she [Catherine] wanted us to do something or when she wanted something changed, she put it in a way that one understood her point. She never made it sound like a rule." And Betsy says:

Catherine gave us plenty of space. So there wasn't built up that resentment to a teacher who makes you do things his way.

Both Paula and Betsy stress their independence from Catherine's guidance emphatically. In Betsy's words:

Catherine just happens to be a very bright light, but not blinding. I could see some value in my own thinking and doing. I felt I had a life of my own.

A similar motivation makes Betsy emphasize her freedom at Pharos:

They were not attached to living with me or not living with me. I knew that I could go when I wanted; that they enjoyed living with me but that it would be O.K. if we felt like being apart.

Even if one allows for a certain idealization of Catherine by Betsy and Paula, it is evident that Catherine became for them the kind of parent who did not constrain or threaten them with her directions, yet made her directions clearly known and her affectionate support distinctly felt. Catherine's philosophy, defying of the dominant society, provided a rationale for their joining the commune and for more safely relinquishing their former identifications.

Thus Catherine's apparently nonauthoritarian, permissive, radically unconventional lifestyle fulfilled the needs of her followers. Understandably, she became for Betsy and Paula, and probably for other Pharos members as well, their model for identification. It is likely that the members themselves, and in particular those who had joined the commune earlier, acted to further strengthen the identification reversal of newcomers. Betsy says of them: "They lived their ideas and I fitted right in." She is aware of the group's influence on her identification reversal when she says: "They had a way of thinking that changed my life." Thus if Catherine fulfilled the role of a parent, the existing group was, for the newcomer, what older siblings are to a younger child when they transmit to him or her family values and culture and a "we" feeling. In fact, terms such as "father," "sister," "brother," and "family" were in use by members of early communities in referring to one another, as they are in some present communes.

It was then unavoidable that when Betsy and Paula were threatened with the loss of Catherine's love and guidance and the group's affection and approval, they experienced a sense of emptiness and dejection. They tried to rid themselves of these feelings by escaping from their present existence, Betsy by "hitting the road," Paula by moving to a far-away place (at least in fantasy; see below). Betsy, more than Paula, suffered from an inner turmoil and, under the strain of her current insecurity, questioned the completeness of her counterculture identifications ("I feel I'm retaining a whole bunch of old characteristics of myself".) In her bag she still carries her "heels" (her high-heeled conventional shoes), although she knows she will never wear them, "these sons o' bitches." She needs not only to withdraw geographically but also to change from being her present self.

Betsy's greater insecurity and helplessness (compared with Paula) at losing the affectionate relationships with Catherine and with the Pharos group may be due, among other reasons, to the fact that Paula, in her childhood, had the ego-strengthening experience of being loved by her mother and her foster mother. These kinds of experiences were denied to Betsy.

During her interview, Catherine is observed interacting with adults and children in the yard. The picture she presents is generally consistent with Paula's and Betsy's descriptions of her. She seems to give her undivided attention to each adult or child with whom she comes in contact. She relates in a similarly intense manner toward the interviewer. Yet, albeit subtly, she made her disapproval known. Her tone of voice and her silences conveyed her criticism if there was disagreement with her view of the world. She challenged the interviewer to defend her conventional life as wife and mother in a nuclear family. It could be concluded from these observations that, in spite of the "space" she provided for Pharos members, Catherine did impose certain directions in a subtle way.

Permeating Catherine's philosophy, as it does that of other commune leaders, is a sense of doom or hopelessness. The "state of harmony" of which Catherine talks is merely a utopian vision for her. She sees man as an instrument of either social or environmental forces. Personal strivings and attempts at social betterment are, in reality, of no avail.

By comparing both Catherine and Trude, a charismatic quality can be perceived in each of them. Yet there is a great difference between Trude's "joie de vivre" and Catherine's somber outlook. This difference between the two leaders corresponds to the difference in climate of the W.V. in its prewar phase and that of the American counterculture in the 1970s.

The prevailing mood in the W.V. before the outbreak of the war was described as "spontaneous, unintentionally natural, not loud, not boisterous, not showing-off, not committed to any political party or reform movement," and as reflecting the "joy of being together and of breathing freely" [37:315].

The change from the elated mood of the "amiable" flower children to the mood of gloom characterizing the counterculture of the 1970s has been attributed to the failure in resisting the Vietnam War, the persistence of racial injustice, the threatening changes in the environment, and the menace of atomic weapons. This mood of gloom, however, must not be understood as replacing the hedonistic mood of the earlier period altogether, but as merging with it. Only for certain persons and for spiritual leaders such as Catherine does the discontent with the times remain a dominant trend in their personalities. Correspondingly, a great deal of the buoyant, enthusiastic mood of the youth movement of Trude's time remained with Trude into her old age.

Childrearing in Communes

In this section we will first describe the roles adults play in communal childrearing as well as some characteristics of children reared in communes. We will then deal with Betsy's and Paula's beliefs about childrearing and their perceptions of their own maternal roles.

In most communes the duties of childcare are shared by all adults. This practice seems to have developed for two reasons. The traditional upbringing of children by one or two parents is seen by commune members as inhibiting the optimum development and as potentially damaging to the child. Moreover, the parents' concentration on, and full responsibility for, their child is believed to limit the parents' freedom and growth, and to hinder their involvement in the group. However, there has always been great leeway in the degree to which commune parents participate in the care of their own child.

In one commune, mothers were meant to forego the closeness with their infants by placing them in the communal nursery (one parent finally left with her child) [23:144]. In other communes, it was agreed that mothers would care for their children during infancy. From then on other adults would share the caretaking with the mother. [10:23].

An extreme attempt at weakening the mutual bond between the child and his natural parents was reported in the description of an early, radical commune. In this commune the women were expected to have intercourse with each male member so that the identity of a child's father would remain unknown. Thus a fantasy was created about the child being born by the whole commune. Some evidence for the same kind of fantasy was noticeable at the birth of Paula's baby, in the role assumed by her group.

The anxiety middle-class parents experience in relation to their child's upbringing has been claimed to be minimized in the commune by including children in almost all facets of the adults' life. Bennet M. Berger, in his report on the "decline of age grading" in hippie and posthippie rural communes, considers the "equalitarian" attitude toward commune children as the major difference between commune and conventional family upbringing [6:165]. The commune children play near the place where the adults work. They are encouraged to participate in or experiment with certain adult chores. They are exposed to sexual activity between adults and to the use of psychedelic drugs. In Berger's study, children were observed to use drugs under adult supervision at certain ritualized occasions. Prepubertal children occasionally engaged in sexual intercourse. The adults reacted with "mixed feelings." After considerable self-scrutiny, they came to the conclusion that there was no reason for their initial negative response since "sexual behavior seems to do no visible harm" to children. From the mental health and medical perspective, however, we must be greatly concerned about the trauma of age-inappropriate sex experiences as well as about the not visible, adverse, and possibly long-term effects of drugs upon the children.

As suggested in the above report, it is plausible that by granting a high degree of autonomy to children, hippie commune members attempt to compensate for the lack of autonomy and for the restraint from adult authority they felt they themselves had suffered in their childhood and their youth.

From his contacts with hippies, the author of the same report inferred that in the 1960s they, together with other students protesters, had demanded the "right to participate in the decisions that shape [their]lives" but had been told that they were "too young," "too inexperienced," and "too incompetent" to be consulted on such matters (e.g., the curricula of universities or the evaluation of professors). As members of the commune, they sought to satisfy their previously frustrated wishes for autonomy. By allowing to excess for their children's natural desires for autonomy and equality they vicariously gratified those needs of their own which remained unsatisfied in childhood.

It is no coincidence that this right to autonomy demanded by the student movement and put into practice by the communes bears a resemblance to the demand of the early youth movement "to live [their]lives by [their] own decisions and [their] own responsibility." Nor is it surprising that the grievances of the earlier movement, "to be excluded from the public life of the nation, to be confined to the passive role of learners and to be nothing but an appendage of the old generation" [41:8]resemble the grievances of the present one. However, there is a difference in the extent to which the former and the present counterculture groups achieve autonomy, i.e., in the extent of their identification reversal or dissidence. The members of the German youth movement, more often than members of the recent movement, retained their ties to their families. In spite of the conflict with their parents and with bourgeois society in general, German youth movement members shared certain values with their elders such as patriotism, love of nature, and an enthusiasm for great literary figures like Goethe. Their moderate stance can be partly attributed to their younger age level (mostly twelve to eighteen), their economic dependence upon their parents, and the strength of authority and persuasive self-righteousness of German parents at the beginning of the century. Moreover, a protest movement against a subordination of youth, a redefintion of youth as a group, and a formulation of the "rights" of youth had no precedent prior to 1900. These facts explain to some extent the inexperience and tentativeness of members of the German youth movement in its early phase, and their refraining from political and from other actions.

The autonomy practiced by the present counterculture, in contrast, is much more extreme and is buttressed by other liberation movements (e.g., the ones against racism and sexism). Furthermore, although commune members would be reluctant to admit it, their emphasis on their children's equality has been influenced by the permissive childrearing philosophy widely accepted by middle-class parents during the last thirty years. More recently, the issue of equality and autonomy of children has been subjected to a critical and constructive examination by professionals. In 1977, the *Harvard Educational Review* published a symposium on "The Rights of Children" in which scholars and policy makers discussed issues such as whether children are best served by extending all adult rights to them; whether adults can be trusted to act in children's best interests and whether parents should have the right to choose their child's education. This effort points not only to the timeliness of the children's liberation movement, but also to its complexities. It brings to our attention the somewhat naive, experimental way in which hippie communes grant near-complete autonomy to their children.

Certain similarities of behavior have been observed in commune children regardless of the ideology of a particular commune. These similarities arise partly because members of most communes reject traditional childrearing attitudes and the conventional "training" of middle-class parents, and partly because all communes have the task of preparing their children for the communal values and lifestyle. Thus, competition and possessiveness, which are acceptable, if not encouraged, in the wider society, tend to be discouraged in the commune. The traits often described as typical of commune-reared children include: independence, self-reliance, freedom from emotional disturbance and common "behavior problems" such as "nail biting, thumb sucking, skirt clutching, and couch hiding" [21:59]. The children are said to be unafraid of strangers. Aggressive behavior toward each other, on the other hand, was described as occurring as frequently in commune as in conventionally reared children. Commune children were observed to "fight over toys, T.V. and apple pie" [21:59]. As a rule, however, commune adults allow the children to settle their own disputes. Since children are treated like adults, in many respects, adults tend to abstain from protecting and supervising [6:169].[16] Since "sincerity" is of major value among adults, the adults deal with children of all ages in a frank, straightforward manner. Thus adults have been said to lose their temper toward a child without apparent anxiety or signs of guilt [6:170].

The following behavior of children was observed in what were apparently retreat-type communes:

He throws temper tantrums while his mother calms him with rhetoric but refuses to discipline him [21:59].

The children of Yea God, a spiritual commune of 40 members, may wander for hours around the large grounds, swim in the pond, or sit in the sand pile. They do not read books, listen to music, or watch T.V. [2:6].

An 8-year-old in an urban commune spends most of his time on a junk heap near the house, idling, alone [2:8].

In communes where more constraint is placed upon the individual, children perform household and community chores at an early age. They take an active part in group decisions, including decisions which concern themselves.

In The Farm, small children are "free to play." From their sixth year on, they are occupied with certain chores, most of the day having been assigned to one of the working crews. A girl of 13 shoes horses and gives riding lessons. A 16-year-old girl delivers mail on horseback. . . . In an urban commune, a 5-year-old boy and a 6-year-old girl set their own time for doing the dishes and limit their play time on their own account. Both children "can cook complete meals and shop with ease in any store" [2:8].

One recurring criticism of commune-raised children is that, intellectually, they are inadequately prepared to enter public schools and to become part of the American society if they should choose to do so. Certainly, commune adults do not prepare their children for entrance into college. Their stated aim is to make their children "feel good." In communal thought and jargon: "The goal of emotional goodness replaces the self-centered drive that leads to personal achievement." The main, oft-cited assets of communal upbringing are the children's self-sufficiency, their self-confidence, and their ability to relate intimately to a number of persons of varying ages and personalities.

One commune member who has lived in several communes criticized the following specific aspects of communal upbringing: the lack of privacy, the lack of quiet, and the lack of an environment conducive to developing a sense of order [16:200]. These conditions, together with a lack of individual attention, tend to make the child feel "lost and confused." According to the same author, ignored and unhappy feelings of commune children are occasionally released in crying spells or in destructive acts. He points out that children cannot acquire a sense of security in a commune whose status is unpredictable, where "people are forever splitting for Montreal or San Francisco or wherever every couple of weeks." The author ends with a warning note for commune members:

Be very careful not to lay your trips on the child or expect the child to necessarily get off on your trips. A sensitive, excitable young child will not benefit from being taken to a long, loud rock concert, no matter how much his or her parents dig it [16:200].

This "insider," an individual who considers commune upbringing as potentially the best for children, recognizes the danger when self-centered adults do not concede that their children need affectionate attention from caretakers who are consistently available. He sees the children suffering from a confusing and overstimulating human environment.

Interviews with commune members and observations at Haven of adults interacting with young children reveal some of the childrearing attitudes described in the above studies. Betsy and Paula consider the sharing of caretaking as beneficial for the child and as highly preferable—for child and parent—to caretaking in the nuclear family. Catherine has her opinions also:

Raising children is a hard job, especially for women. Women in the commune are likely to think their happiness depends on who gets up at 2 A.M. and heats a bottle when they hear a baby cry. There isn't a right answer. But there are three possible ways of thinking: "I'm not going. Someone else will." "I'm lazy if I don't go. I better go or someone else will think I'm bad." Or "Why should I go. Someone else can who has no children."

Catherine's comments raise these questions: If children cannot expect to be cared for—especially to be fed—by the same person each time, how does this affect their sense of security? How does the alternating of caretakers, and how do their nondirecting attitudes affect the child's formation of social habits? How are commune values transmitted?

At lunch one day, Catherine and this interviewer join a few adults and children in the yard. Catherine has fixed a plate with toast, watercress, and sliced tomatoes. A naked (as were the other children) one-year-and-nine-month-old girl comes and silently takes some watercress and tomatoes from Catherine's plate and pulls a piece off Catherine's toast. A boy, about the girl's age, follows her example. The girl then samples the green and red heaps on the visitor's plate and tears a piece off her toast. Following Catherine's lead, she (the visitor) lets it happen and, off and on, they continue their lunch. Obviously the adults provide the children no incentives for the acquisition of traditional social habits. On the other hand, perhaps the adults are trying to transmit the value of communal sharing to the children and not the values of a traditional lifestyle. Catherine may have a similar thought. Moreover, the naked children, unrestrained, following their natural drive, are readily accepted into this group of adults who are so disdainful of the unnaturalness of the outside world. This motivation explains another incident. While with the group in the yard, the girl described above defecates. Since she is naked, a change of clothes is not required. The girl herself does not pay notice to what has happened. Catherine, perhaps slightly embarrassed by the presence of an outsider, motions to the girl's mother who, without making the child aware of a more social way of relieving herself, removes the stool. A boy urinating in the yard meets with the same inattention.

Their chosen method of childrearing thus is that of allowing the young child optimal "space" without much concern for developing his inner controls. To what extent this is an advantage, and to what extent one problem only substitutes for another, does not seem to worry the adults. They feel that the children's behavior is natural and that they will outgrow it.

Betsy's Maternal Role

When Zephyr was nine months old, even more than at Zephyr's birth, Betsy was convinced that she and her child should not be emotionally bound to one another. She is in favor of all commune members, men and women, sharing child-care duties. "I don't want to be Zephyr's mother and I don't want anybody to be his father." However, Betsy adds that Zephyr has her last name and that he belongs to her. Like other commune mothers, Betsy values her child's independence. But she is also aware that she prevents his dependence for her own sake. Even before he was born, she feared she would lose some of her freedom. "I was attached to my freedom. And when I described my freedom to myself, and how I saw childrearing, a baby would not interfere." By a magical, omnipotent thought, she assures herself that the baby will suffer no harm even if she is not available. "A child is beautiful and cuddly. That's part of their survival mechanism. That's why people want to nurture them and care for them." That subconsciously Betsy values her baby's attachment is indicated in her disappointment that the newborn did not look like her. Her desire for her child's dependence is implicit when she describes Zephyr, at the age of nine months, as less mature than is evident from his behavior. She says that Zephyr has only now begun to crawl and rarely tries to stand; that he does not understand a "no," and that this is the reason why she does not try to inhibit him. But this statement contrasts noticeably with the general impression Zephyr creates. The observer can see that he successfully pulls himself up, and that he is intelligent and capable of understanding a negative. It would seem then that Betsy derives some gratification from her child's babyish helplessness and from preserving his early dependence on her. Her reluctance to prohibit and direct him may stem from her anxiety lest Zephyr become a person of his own. She may also wish to prevent any negative reaction of his for fear that her own anger may erupt and endanger the affectionate closeness between them which she seems to need.

Betsy's fear of her child's negativism may have become transferred to her anguish about another commune child, a two-year-old boy who has the habit of biting. If he bites in Betsy's presence, she leaves the room. She explains her behavior in these words:

I could pick him up and move him where I want. But who am I to say "I'm not violent, so don't you be." So I try to give him space. When I stay and tell him "No" it would come out of hatred or aggression, not out of a loving space.

Betsy's handling of this situation, similar to her reluctance to restrain Zephyr, suggests that a child's negative behavior tends to scare her. Perhaps even a "no" threatens to turn into aggression on her part and thus to endanger her relationship with the child. Paradoxically, her wish for closeness with him makes her withdraw from him and, in doing so, she is concerned with forgoing the mutual bond which was denied to her in her childhood.

Betsy's concerns with sharing both the child's affection for her and his independence while neither interfering in his negative behavior nor encouraging his mental progress are in line with the permissive philosophy in Pharos and in other communes. However, these attitudes do not help the child cope with his anger or help him develop a sense of what he may or may not do.

Zephyr appears surprisingly self-sufficient for a nine-month-old. The following account describes his observed behavior:

Zephyr was the first commune member whom I met when I visited Haven. I had opened the door slowly, heeding a sign by the door which warns the visitor that children may be crawling inside nearby the door. Since I was early for my appointment I waited in the hall. Zephyr was sitting in a corner of the large room, occupied with some object. There was no one else in the entrance hall. After a while he started to crawl toward the winding staircase. Having arrived there, he reached out toward the railing and tried to pull himself up. He did not succeed, lowered himself, and after a few moments tried again. A young man, a Haven member, entered, and while we talked about my reason for visiting Haven, Zephyr continued his effort and succeeded once or twice in pulling himself up momentarily.

The young man fetched a walker and, with an easy smile, lifted Zephyr into it. At once Zephyr began "walking" across the hall. When he discovered me he took a direct course toward me and stood still in his walker near where I sat. He looked at me with open eyes, not smiling, yet unafraid and interested. He moved away and, after a while, came back and repeated his behavior. I found it hard to believe that the child was only nine months old.

The second time that I observed Zephyr, I "discovered" him crawling near Betsy's chair. I say "discovered," because he had silently crawled into the room obviously looking for his mother. She had not interrupted her talk and did not acknowledged his presence except by lightly stroking his head; that was when I noticed him.

An encounter of a mother and a baby, even while the mother was otherwise engaged, would ordinarily lead to a different, affectionate response from the mother. On the other hand, this child's behavior impressed the observer by the unusual degree of self-sufficiency in a child so young, and by his initiative in "searching" for his mother.

The observer was eager to know how Zephyr had spent the five hours since she first met him at ten o'clock in the morning. Betsy told her that Zephyr had been fed by whoever was feeding the children around noon and later had found a mattress to sleep on or had been helped to find one. (At Haven, as at Pharos, mattresses placed on the floor were used instead of beds to protect children from falling.) By the time Zephyr appeared in his mother's presence, he must have explored other rooms searching for her. He found her in an unusual location, i.e., in a somewhat remote room.

Zephyr's behavior may have developed as a result of mother's alternately restraining her affection and reassuring herself of his closeness with her. Zephyr's self-sufficiency may also have been reinforced by the behavior of others toward him, and by the examples of the other commune children.

The personality characteristics observed in Zephyr could then be attributed both to his mother's individual influence and to the influence of communal rearing. A brief encounter with Zephyr suggests that up to now the lack of consistent, affectionate maternal care has not had the detrimental effect on his development which one might have expected. It will be remembered that, except for a brief period when she was nursing him, Betsy had been depressed and emotionally unavailable to Zephyr as a baby. It must therefore have been of decisive benefit for him subsequently to be cared for by a group of adults who became attached to him and gave him a sense of security. (One small example was the friendly attention Zephyr received from the young man who placed him in the walker.) As was suggested by a commune member, (p. 300), commune rearing can make up for some of the mistakes made by parents in the nuclear family, because, in the commune, the child can have secure relationships with a number of persons.

Paula's Maternal Role

Souza's birth. A birth is the peak event in the life of the commune. It is as though a child born in a commune gives its members the sense of reality which is often missing in a tentative existence they build up from beliefs, visions, and experimentation. A newborn child is indisputable, however. By sharing the responsibility for the baby's growing up and well-being, and by partaking in his care at the time of delivery, the hopes of all are raised. These phenomena may account for the widespread desire for children in the commune, and for the shared emotions surrounding pregnancy and birth. Twin Oaks suffered because young children who had briefly lived with their mothers in the commune departed at a young age. The commune then made a decision not to accept any more children until a pregnant woman decides to give birth in the commune and have her child raised there. This, the members felt, would fulfill an important purpose of the commune. A children's house was therefore built at Twin Oaks in preparation for the event. With the same anticipation, while all members were still living in tepees and temporary structures, Yeah God erected a concrete building as a nursery for newborns before any pregnancy had yet occurred. Members of Brook Farm also hailed, as a highly important event, the birth of three babies in one year [13:36-37]. It is also significant that a certain elation was felt about the first death at Brook Farm.[17] Both birth and death seemed to affirm, to its members, the relevance of Brook Farm as a human group with a history of its own.

Like the other Pharos mothers, Paula did not want her child to be born in a hospital. In fact, for her one of the attractions of Pharos was that two babies had recently been born there. Paula shows slides of these deliveries. In various closeups, all phases of the birth process are documented, beginning with the first contractions through the head emerging and the cutting of the cord. All persons present at the two deliveries are shown in their positions of assisting the woman. When Paula explains the slides, recalling her own delivery, her mood is unmistakeably "high" and differs from her often low-spirited tone as she recounts other memories. This is how Paula describes the preparation for her delivery (note the emphasis on "we"):

We prepared ourselves heavily before the birth. We read up on it [she shows the large book with anatomical tabloids of the positions of the fetus], did breathing exercises, prepared ourselves with gloves, a thread and everything. The cord you tie in two places and cut in between. Sterilization, that's a concept that works more contrary than for it. But we did keep the scissors sterilized. We boiled them and put them on sterile cloth. 96% of all births are totally normal, take care of themselves.

For the delivering woman, the birth process (as inherent in Paula's description) fulfills various needs such as the need for self-assertion and even the need for power—needs which cannot be met in the day-to-day life in the commune. The need for self-assertion is evident, for example, in Paula's choosing those members who should and should not be present during the birth:

The birthing woman was in charge. If I didn't like something, it would stop. For instance, I was having contractions when some people arrived, very nice people. And I said I don't want them, and they went away. On the other hand, when preparing for the birth I was dependent on some people to be there. One woman was going to another city at that time. I said: "No, you can't." Then I realized that I can give birth by myself. I don't need certain people though it would be nice and I really, really wanted this woman to be around.

The participation of particular members may be important for the birthing woman as a proof of their affection for her. She may also wish for certain members to be present at the first breath of the child as a way to secure their emotional involvement with the newborn. For it is on all commune members that the child's well-being will largely depend. Catherine, two women who had recently given birth at Pharos, two other women, and three men were present at Souza's birth. Paula sighs happily when she tells how she had felt the baby sliding out, and, seeing it was a girl, had thought: "How neat."

A few weeks later the commune "baptized" the baby in a self-styled ceremony. Paula gave her the name Souza because she liked the sound of it. After a festive meal in the yard at which, sitting at one long table, all commune members participated, the baby was handed from one member to the next. Each member pronounced the child's name and added a personal wish for her life. When Paula held the baby, she made her wish silently.

Self-fashioned rituals such as the one just described have frequently been reported of other communes, especially those of the retreat type. Daily rituals such as holding hands in silence before meals, meditation at a particular time, celebration at the completion of a building or after bringing in the harvest have been considered powerful vehicles for the heightening of group consciousness [20:47-49, 99-102].

Souza at age one year and three months. The following observations of Souza and her mother were jotted down immediately after Paula's interview:

Souza is in the room most of the time of the interview. She sits with her mother on the mattress which is on the floor; the mattress has no cover and serves as a bed for child and mother. There is one small table for writing and one small chest of drawers for the child's underwear. There is a walk-in closet, open, with clothes hanging, a small bookshelf. All are in disarray, including the very few playthings or parts of them on the floor.

Souza is naked (warm weather). When beside her mother, her mother pats her, puts her arm around her, calls her "sweetie." Her mother is naturally affectionate with the child. Yells at her when upset, but not angrily. At other times she moves aimlessly around the room, spills the box of animal crackers I had brought, plays with the crackers—to which her mother objects ("I don't want her to play with food"). Mother interferes only once, then lets her play with the crackers. Souza has a bowel movement which her mother silently wipes away. When Souza first sees the two reels on the tape recorder turning, she begins to dance, her hands on her hips, very rhythmically, obviously thinking there was a tune on the tape—something apparently familiar to her. When her mother leaves the room briefly, Souza goes to her chest and calls to me: "Open! Open!" While I hesitate, her mother returns and opens a drawer for the child. While the interview continues, Souza puts one garment after another on herself and opens all the drawers herself. She struggles with a sweater she cannot put on; her mother helps her.

When she wants something her mother cannot give her, she cries loudly and her mother cannot calm her. Bob, a young man, comes by and looks at Souza crying. Her mother explains Souza's "eskimo" outfit. Bob offers to take her away, picks her up, and carries her over his shoulder down to the yard to play. She quiets immediately when picked up.

Souza returns one half hour later. When crying begins again, her mother goes and gets a bottle and holds Souza in her arms, gently. Souza sucks from the bottle, half asleep, while the interview continues. Souza sleeps on the mattress. She wakes up later, and when her mother eats the pastrami sandwich which someone brings her from the eating place where some commune people had their supper, Souza grabs it and gets bits of it put in her mouth. (It was probably Souza's supper.)

Paula is asked about the difference between Betsy and herself in their relating to children. (Paula appears softer, more feminine, and more affectionate with Souza than Betsy does with Zephyr.) Her answer: "Basically, Betsy and I have the same approach. We don't force the children to eat when they don't want to eat. I tend to play more with the children. Betsy has a more factual approach like, 'O.K., you need this and you need that,' and I get them to eat by playing the food into their mouth rather than saying 'You want it? Open your mouth. Now come!' "

Judging from Paula's recollections of her first encounter with her newborn, she expressed genuine maternal feeling. Her present-day interaction with Souza shows a similar affectionate responsiveness to her child. It seems unlikely that Paula ever considered an "immediate separation" from Souza as did Betsy. Paula describes her relationship to Souza in these words:

I am most attached to her of all persons. It is not a biological tie. I had prepared myself for nine months. I wanted to be with that person growing in me. I love that person.

In a surprising afterthought, however, Paula does not perceive Souza as a person in her own right:

I have carefully planned her genes, have selected her looks and intelligence which I like. And if she does not get to know her father, that's fine. I wanted the genes. It came out just right.

Paula's idea of Souza's personality as being completely under her (Paula's) control suggests a sense of omnipotence. She denies her previous affectionate bond with Souza's father and depersonalizes him. Her omnipotent thinking apparently relieves some of the anxiety embedded in her complex relationship to Souza. While she showers Souza with affection, she also desires Souza's independence. She wants Souza to address her by her first name. When Souza calls her "mummy," Paula tells her: "I'm not mummy, I'm Paula." Betsy's remark, "I don't want to be Zephyr's mother," shows a similar tendency. Yet in her caretaking, Paula clearly backs away from her child's growing capacity for independence and from helping her to develop the control which would be necessary if she were to achieve that independence. While this was clear when observing mother and child, various statements by Paula seem to contradict her behavior. For example, "To believe that 'Be a good mother and you have good children' is an illusion." "Much loving and touching is counterproductive for the child." (Betsy expresses similar ideas but Paula expands them more freely.)

As with Betsy, Paula's emphasis on her child's independence conflicts with her need for closeness with the child. By not expecting anything of her, she delays Souza's independence. She even quotes an "expert's" opinion in support of her permissiveness:

Some expert has said that any person who lives with a child and has expectations will be disappointed. The children will under-achieve in what their parents expect of them. Souza walked when she was eleven months, talked very early [the observer's impression, however, was that she talked very little, and was babyish for her age], communicated early, is very coordinated [observed to be so].

I have no expectations for Souza. I don't know when she will go to potty by herself. I'll show her that that's a desirable thing. I don't know when she will talk. I don't expect her to keep her room clean. I don't expect her to wash her bath by herself. I'll show her that's a desirable thing. But you see [pointing to the cluttered-up floor] I'm not particularly tidy myself. So who am I to expect it from her? She's doing what she feels like doing. And I let her. I have no set expectation outside of her feeling good.

Not unlike Betsy, who conjures up an inborn survival mechanism of the baby which makes adults cuddle and protect a child, Paula speculates upon the independence of children at three or four years of age and bestows on them the capacity to survive on their own.

We could have a Children's House where children from three years on live together who have economic independence. There is a certain stage where children need help of older people, not necessarily adults. Until age three they need someone to survive.

By age three or four they can survive themselves if you give them economic independence to buy food, prepare food and take care of their clothes, select clothes. Set the children up with washing machines and stuff. I'm positive a four-year-old *can* take care of himself if he is given economic independence and means to do it. Fifteen children, age four, can get their "trip" together, wash their clothes, prepare their food, clean up after themselves. What they need is some way of being supplied with the food and I am sure they could perform some form of service in exchange for food and clothing they get. It could be tried. It would be easier if this was a mixture of four to ten-year-olds. Four-year-olds might have too many conflicting interests to get a trip together. I don't know. Would be a trial-and-error situation to see what the optimum mix is.

Paula's fantasy about children's self-sufficiency could perhaps be traced to her fear of depending on human relationships, having been abandoned by her mother and now threatened by the separation from Catherine; having been rejected by her father and, later, by Souza's father. The impact of these happenings on Paula, due partly to her own personality characteristics, may underlie her fantasy of granting immature children almost complete independence, thus avoiding, at an early age, the painful consequences of dependency.

Yet, the emotional tone and choice of words in which Paula argues her point makes one wonder about the part played by her own defensive denial of her passive, dependent longings which she harbors deep within herself.

One can also see Paula's statement as originating in the communal credo of not only racial and religious equality but also of equality between adults and children (to whom Charles refers as "big and little people"). Even the extreme self-sufficiency Paula grants to young children, in her fantasy, may be in line with the utopian belief, not unusual in a commune, that human nature can be molded so as to fit the ideals of a new society (young children caring for themselves would, in fact, be an asset to society).

One can, finally, detect in Paula's utopia Catherine's influence. She has adopted Catherine's views on the ills of society, her belief in complete equality, and her opposition to all forms of power and manipulation by the bureaucratic system.

Paula shows her belief in sexual equality when she takes pain in trying to inhibit in Souza a conventional sense of femininity.

I'm against dolls for children. All dolls are females. Lots of other things are better to play with. Boy dolls would be fine. But teddy bears, rabbits would still be better. If there's a choice between dolls and animals, I shall always choose animals. There isn't much you can do with a doll outside of housewife and cleaning. Sew their clothes, wash clothes, put them on, comb them, feed them. I don't want her to be programmed to be a housewife. What she needs to be a housewife is two hands and two feet that reach down to the floor to walk. That is not sex determined. In order to cook a meal you don't need a vagina. I don't want her to think that women cook and men put their feet on the table. It certainly doesn't happen in our house [commune], but certainly it is a struggle at times.

Paula will also use her influence with Souza to oppose official schooling. Bolstering her position, she points to the nonconformity of other commune parents:

I don't ever want to send her to school. I'm a qualified teacher. I can teach her myself. I don't know for sure but that's most likely what I'll do. I don't know. If she decides school is fun that's what she'll most likely do. Some mothers here have removed themselves to an area where no school can get them. One mother moved north with her son. She didn't want him to go to school here. She's living on a piece of land far away from things where they can't force her. Basically, parents in other communes are doing the same thing.

Although it can be assumed that Paula, more or less subtly, transmits to Souza her antischool and antiestablishment bias, she tells herself that she would not mind if Souza were to enter the straight society:

If she wants to be bourgeois, that's her thing. I'll love her for whatever she chooses to do. That's partly difficult, partly easy.

From what we know about Paula's need for closeness with her child, we must wonder how Paula would be able to handle her despair and her anger if Souza were to deviate considerably from Paula's own lifestyle. But, then, if Souza herself were to undergo an identification reversal, where could she turn if not to conventional society?

Pointing out the strong similarity between them, Paula shows me her mother's photograph side by side with one of Souza. Her intense joy about the similarity suggests that, in her fantasy, she has substituted Souza for her mother. Later, with signs of satisfaction, Paula comments how alike she and Souza are in the color of their hair and eyes. This incident illustrates that the self-replicating tendency (the wish to be replicated by one's child), exists in the communal parent-child pair as it does in that of the conventional family.

Paula and Betsy, in their need to maintain their closeness with their children, expect nothing from them and stress the importance of not interfering and of giving them "space." It is well-nigh impossible to foresee how these children will fare once their own, age-appropriate struggle for autonomy sets in. Who will set limits then? make demands? take responsibility? and prepare them for the future?

It is with a view to Souza's future that Paula wrote a poem for her. Characteristically, each sentence begins with the words "You will not fear. . . ." Of particular significance are these lines:

You will not fear solitude for you will never be
friendless.

[*Note Paula's longing for dependency and fear of abandonment
mentioned earlier*].

You will not fear your child for no enemy can be
born of love.
You will not fear to grow up for the years will show
you new horizons
You will not fear to grow old for in each horizon you
will find further wisdom.

We have previously proposed that the parents' needs determine their perception of the child, and that frequently children are "appointed" to achieve goals the parents could not reach. It may also be possible that the parents perceive their children as better able than they are to cope with fears and anxieties from which they themselves suffer. The fear of solitude and of growing old, for example, and, in particular, the fear of "your child" being "your enemy," thus may well be Paula's own fears.

SOME CHARACTERISTICS OF
THE COUNTERCULTURE PERSON

The portrayal of a few members of past and present counterculture groups suggests a basic question: Which are the behaviors and attitudes which evolve as a result of group upbringing? And a corollary question: How permanent can these behaviors and attitudes be? The answers can be only speculative, of course.

In a previous section we have presented findings on some characteristics of commune-reared children. Among these characteristics most observers noted independence. Some observed tolerance, cooperation, and a de-emphasis on competition and material possessions. Independence is one feature which would seem to be influenced by the adults' behavior, since it is likely to be fostered by "inattention" (an attitude typical of adult commune members toward children). According to one observer, commune adults view "all children" as "intrinsically worthy of love and respect, but not necessarily of attention." [6:175]. Both Betsy and Paula show "inattention" toward their children to some extent. It has been argued that the inattention shown by noninterference in children's quarrels, for example, is "benign" in comparison with the "arbitrary" and "self-serving" restrictions imposed upon middle-class children [6:175-176].

It is too early to know what the long-range effect of communal childrearing will be. Not enough commune-raised children have reached adolescence and none has attained parenthood. Nor can we predict how Zephyr, who is surprisingly mature at nine months, will tolerate the impending separations from familiar persons, the move from one temporary house to another, and the ever-new groups of adults involved in his caretaking. However, some predictions have been made of the personality development of commune children.

Berger foresees that the equality between adults and children fostered in communes, "minimizing the extent and duration of authority" [6:182], will help the children to grow up faster and will bring the generations closer together. Since the young persons have been participating members from childhood on, he further foresees a decline of "adolescents" as a "distinctive category of persons."

There is some evidence that after a period of communal living, adults identify with each other to the extent that they develop common behavior characteristics. Members of Rockridge, a small rural commune in New Mexico, have been described as slow moving and slow speaking, their speech sounding like a "tentative drawl" [36:200]. It appeared to Veysey that this particular rhythm, having possibly originated in protest against the demanding pace of the industrial society, had become internalized by all members of the group. In another (religious) commune, both the leaders and the members speak so softly that they can hardly be understood [4:4]. That the children in this commune speak in a whisper suggests their identification with adults.

Commune members have been said to be receptive to each other's experiences. Betsy's description of her intimate knowledge of the members' responses and even thoughts, and Paula's mention of the "internal language" shared by her and Catherine, are relevant here.

The behaviors reported as characterizing other commune groups range from those presumably enhancing cohesion (such as outgoingness, openness, lovingness, and honesty between members) to those impeding cohesion (e.g., self-righteousness, withholding, apathy, valuelessness). George, who is in charge of the Haven commune, lists a number of types who would not "fit" with Haven members and who would not "make it" at Haven. Among these are male chauvinists, heavy drug abusers, liars, cheaters, persons who are not "open," those difficult to get along with, old-fashioned Catholics, religious zealots of any kind, persons tied to one thing, and persons who cannot handle children.

Some of the characteristics encountered in members of present communes had been observed, in dissident youth, fifteen years earlier. Kenneth Keniston, in his book, *The Uncommitted: Alienated Youth in American Society*, published in 1964, describes a segment of the young college generation as reluctant to emulate their parents [22]. Keniston argues that the rapid social changes had rendered these parents ineffective as models for identification [22:231-234]. Their sons and daughters lack concern with society's problems. They do not strive for any goal beyond short-range fulfillment of personal desires and fantasies. In sexual, as in other relationships, they seek intimacy while at the same time being threatened by it:

In all their encounters, they retain the same agonizing combination of desire for closeness and fear of it; and the way they deal with this ambivalence—the way they choose their potential intimates and the way they deal with those to whom they might be close—often merely serves to confirm their view that intimacy is the prelude to disappointment and disillusion [22:99].

As we have seen, similar attitudes are characteristic of commune dwellers today. Although communal relationships can provide sympathy and affectionate support for a certain time, commune members, like the "uncommitted" youth, abstain from too-intimate ties for fear of being hurt. This fear seems to lead to a group characteristic which could be called *impermanence of affection*. Pharos members paradoxically considered this characteristic to be as vital for group cohesion as were sincerity, avoidance of judgment, and avoidance of expectations. It is possible that, especially in retreat communes, impermanence of affection has developed as an adaptation to the nomadic existence. It is also possible that attachments of short duration which can be easily abandoned and quickly forgotten are a regression to adolescent tendencies, mobilized through the precarious life of the communes. Anna Freud has discussed contradictory attitudes as coexisting in adolescence, i.e., "empathy and outrageous lack of consideration to those nearest to [them]," as well as a "lofty view of love and of the obligations of a lover" [18:160].

We have seen evidence of impermanence of affection in Betsy's account of the dissolution of Pharos, in her behavior to her lover at the Haven commune, and even in her attitudes toward her child. Paula expresses the same tendency even more assertively:

We are all transients. We never stay in one group very long. I came here for two weeks, but after three months I am still here. However, I might leave tomorrow or another day. You move if it doesn't feel good anymore. If you get too dependent on being with another person, you leave. It's wrong to get hung-up too much on someone else. This is what I have found in people in communes: if someone tells me on December 6, let's do this and this, even if December 6 is only one day away I don't depend on it. The same with me. I say, "I'll go there," but when the time comes I might go somewhere else. I have some attachment to people here, but I wouldn't mind if they left tomorrow.

Although impermanence of affection as well as a changeable way of life appear to Paula most desirable, she does not feel compelled to "move on" as do Betsy and other Pharos members. At present her wish for leaving Gates takes place in her fantasy and not in her action. She indulges herself in a nostalgic dream of childhood existence without commitments or demands:

I have been thinking of going to Hawaii for a while. There is one particular little canyon I really like. With a lot of fruit trees, and Souza can pick fruit all day long and we can go to the beach—wonderful, white beach. And all the people are so friendly as if they knew you all your life. If I get there I might stay for a while. But eventually I'll find another commune to join.

Paula's tranquil fantasy differs from Betsy's anxious search for a new place where she will find a new group of people who will help her in her inner struggle for self-awareness and "growth." Both women, however, are convinced that they will always want to live in communes. They consider communal living as the only sound substitute for "couple living" or the loneliness of solitary life.

Similar beliefs are common among other commune dwellers. George Hurd, a philosopher at a retreat commune, who considered the commune as an extension of a new religion, envisioned a chain of communes strung across the country like Howard Johnsons. These communes would be "temporary way stations in an increasingly mobile society" and retreats from its pressures [20:189].

How long the characteristics of commune members described above will endure as part of the members' personalities cannot be foreseen. The influence of the German youth movement, however, has lasted throughout the life of many of its members. From the author's contacts through the years with members of the early counterculture and investigative reading about the movement, she can recognize group characteristics which have remained resistant to the aging process (e.g., straightforwardness, exemplified in Trude's letter to a friend), simplicity of taste, devotion to nature, a certain irrationality, and a sense of superiority over those in the dominant society, labeled "bourgeois" or *buergerlich* then, and "square" or "straight" now. There is still, among the survivors, as expressed in their newsletters, the same romantic overevaluation of the German land and character which made a number of them susceptible to Hitler's call for self-sacrifice for the German fatherland [14:231].

In 1976, Ruedeger Dilloo, a reporter for the West German weekly, the *Zeit*, visited a previous Wandervogel, Klara Haas, age eighty-two [12:10]. He hoped to write an article for his magazine on the occasion of the seventy-fifth anniversary of the founding of the Wandervogel. What he found was a strong correspondence between his interviewee's present personality and those of other original members of the movement, as described in the literature. A photo of Klara Haas as a young girl with sandals, "hippie" dress, and flowers in her hair shows her kinship to present-day commune dwellers in Germany and in the U.S. Klara Haas still lives a simple and self-sufficient life, without "poisonous" food as she calls it. She weaves the linen for her skirts, bakes her own bread, and grows all the vegetables she needs. Until ten years ago she was in charge of a children's home. She says that she could never have lived the life of an employee; she was "too revolutionary" and she needed her spiritual independence.

This report illustrates once more the personality-forming influence of the youth movement. Klara Haas has remained, in old age, antibureaucratic and individualistic. But, like other youth movement members, she entered the mainstream of society, holding a conventional job and remaining "revolutionary" in a private sense only, although the job she selected and the way she carried it out may well be connected with youth movement ideals.

A tendency to compromise between early counterculture ideals and society's demands is also seen in the present commune movement. Certain communes have become more moderate, e.g., allowing private ownership and respecting the privacy of individuals or families (see the remark on a family in an urban commune, p. 133). Urban communes are regarded increasingly not only as a refuge from family conflicts and/or loneliness, but one of the available options for a life style, and filling certain needs of society. Alvin Toffler, the author of *Future Shock*, goes even further [36]. He anticipates that, in the "superindustrial society" with its increased mobility and accelerated way of life, communal living will completely replace the nuclear family. However, he argues strongly against the "hang loose" tendency and the irrational, mystical, and emotional inclinations of the counterculture, and propounds, instead, rational planning and linking of social, economic, cultural, and psychological forces. But, not unlike commune members, he sees a necessity for short-lived relationships to replace the long-term commitments of the past. He foresees the social recognition of temporary marriages and, as a consequence, a drastic change in the responsibilities of parenthood.

One may argue against this view. One may point out the value of the nuclear family. Especially in the urban, industrial society the family can provide intimate contact and care, often unavailable from other persons, and support in situations of stress. These essential functions were fulfilled in preindustrial families dominated by the father's authority, protected by law. They are still being fulfilled in those modern families where wife and husband have equal rights and share in providing financial support. This would seem to point to a certain "capacity" of the family to adapt to social, cultural, and historical changes, thus suggesting its survival.

Moreover, are there not intrinsic satisfactions in family life which serve to perpetuate it as a human institution? I am thinking of the security and deep joy of continuing love and friendship which parents and children can provide each other. Children growing up in such a familial climate will, through identification, become similar models to their own children and thereby tend to preserve the nuclear family. Its value might even be more apparent if it becomes regarded as one way of living to be chosen from a number of equally respectable alternatives.

We have explored how incomplete identification, rooted in unhappy childhood relationships, can lead to affiliation with a counterculture group and to reversal of identification. We have tried to show this phenomenon during two historical periods, separated by half a century and occurring on two continents. We have also drawn attention to those similarities in the two dominant societies (i.e., the competitive, materialistic, "dehumanizing" aspects of these societies) which provided the "fuel" for both incidents of youth revolt.

The discussion of kibbutz living which follows will widen the view on communal childrearing. Among other basic differences between the kibbutz and the commune described above, it will be shown that the family plays an important role in the present kibbutz society.

NOTES

[1] One might also have studied those Wandervoegel who, after World War I, founded or joined rural settlements (*Siedlunngen*) either with a socialist-religious orientation or based on the Aryan ideology (the former were subsequently dissolved by the Nazis and the latter were coordinated—(*gleichgeschaltet*)—with the agricultural planning of the Nazi regime). Members of one of these settlements could have been compared with members of present-day rural communes. (For a personality description of their leaders, see p. 121). Such a study would, however, have exceeded the scope and resources of the present investigation.

[2] The first *fahrt* (hike) was attended by thirty-five boys. During the same year, the membership increased so much that several local groups (*ortsgruppen*) were formed. The first girls' group was founded in 1909. Although the boys' and girls' groups hiked separately, they attended the occasional jamboree-type meetings and the biannual solstice celebrations jointly.

[3] The parents' attitudes to the Wandervogel ranged from antagonism to indifference to approval of the healthy aspects of the outdoor activities. Some interviewees believed that their fathers who openly criticized the movement secretly desired to participate in the hikes. There were a few intellectual parents, similar to the adults who took part in the Meissner gathering, who actively supported the movement. Among them were the painter Koethe Kollwitz and the physician Dubois Reymond. But from the interviews and from personal memories, it is not wrong to assume that the Meissner vow in which youth took a stand against the adult world did not "register" with the majority of parents. It is not known how many parents of hippies reacted with similar indifference when their children handed flowers to passersby.

[4] The desire to differentiate oneself from the mass of youth was still characteristic of the later postwar phase of the movement. In a description of previous Wandervoegel who formed rural communes, one reads about the "emphasis on being different" (*Betonung des Anderssein*) and the illusion of being able to "stand on the apex of the creation pyramid" [5:73].

[5] The founder of the D.W.V. was also present at this meeting and shared the enthusiasm of the speaker. But forty years later, in the Round Robin Letter to the reunion members in 1954, he wrote: "If before and during the First World War some of us were convinced that we as youth and as members of our particular movement were capable to fulfill a historical mission, we were misled."

The contrast between the Wandervogel patriotism and the stark realities of the battle was described fifty years later by the well-known German author Karl Zuckmayer, who had belonged to the youth movement as a youngster: "Being a soldier, that meant freedom, freedom from bourgeois narrowness and pettiness—from all the things we had felt consciously or unconsciously as affluence [saturiertheit], suffocation [stickluft], torpidity [erstarrung] of our world against which we had rebelled in the Wandervogel" [42:168].

⁶ The brother was drafted two months later. He was wounded once; recuperated, he resumed his military duties. He returned from the war gravely disillusioned.

⁷ I interviewed Trude's brother in Germany in 1961. He had belonged to the first D.W.V. group which was formed in 1905. At the age of sixty-five he initiated the reunion of former members (see pp. 7-8, 120-121). It took him two years to trace their addresses, correspond, and make plans. He sent an autobiographical report to his former comrades, who had written him on his seventieth birthday. In it he attributed his inner strength and resiliency as a soldier in the First World War and on his flight from the Russian occupation of East Germany in 1945 to the character education he received as a youth group member. He told, as another act of courage, how he transported four members of his family, individually, across the River Elbe and how, in a primitive self-constructed raft, they reached the U.S. side of the river. At my visit, he proudly showed me a gas mantle factory which he had set up at age fifty-seven with the help of American credit, and where he incorporated an invention of his own. Adhering to the ideals of the youth movement, the factory was run on profit-sharing principles with special workers' benefits. He communicates with each worker on a personal basis and strongly refuses to convey an image of an authoritarian director. In the basement of his factory he keeps mementoes of his escape, e.g., a two-wheel potato cart.

⁸ It must have seemed to members of the youth movement as if their ineffectual protest against oppression, inequality, and injustice had now reached a worldwide scope. The prewar youth movement had advocated both social equality and the supremacy of the German people and land; toward the end of the war the members differed as to these goals. Certain groups extolled the international, social revolution while others condemned it. The latter maintained their nationalistic stance and, in spite of military setbacks, the belief in a German victory. Members of both controversial orientations became later attracted to the Nazi youth organizations, influenced by the party's dual claim of fostering nationalism and socialism [24:196-197, 246]. At that time, the Communist and Socialist parties, as well as the Catholic Center party and various other religious factions, had founded their own youth organizations ₈(14:17-19]. Some of these organizations and some older youth movement groups, although opposed to National Socialism, were able to persist for the first five months of the Nazi regime. In 1933 the government officially dissolved all youth organizations [14:5]. Illegal contact between members continued to some extent in the so-called "Wilde Buende" and in the organization "Edelweiss," whose activities led to persecution and severe penalties [33:9; 14:28] see also Chapter 2, footnote 4).

⁹ Twin Oaks was founded in 1966 and is, as of this date, still in existence. It was based on B.F. Skinner's behavioral psychology, which emphasizes "positive reinforcement." Its founders were inspired by Skinner's utopian novel *Walden Two*, published in 1948.

¹⁰ The Farm, run by Stephen Gaskin, occupies 1800 acres. It has increased its soybean earnings to a $1.5-million per year enterprise with a trucking company to deliver its produce throughout the country; a citizen's band radio and a publishing company which has issued a vegetarian cookbook, books on midwifery and of sayings by Gaskin. The commune is strictly service and work oriented. Work begins before sunrise. Gaskin preaches to the commune members his own version of Christianity with elements of Buddhism in it. He supervises the rigid soybean diet of the members.

¹¹ Betsy's son was given a conventional name at birth. At Pharos, Betsy renamed him Zephyr. In this and other communes, children are often named after plants, events of nature, or mythological figures. The names are explained to the outsider with a certain pride and aesthetic enjoyment of the match between the word's meaning and the personality of the child. Similar types of names are also given to kibbutz children, and a similar emphasis on the names can be noticed in kibbutz parents.

[12] The Harris couple, with Patricia Hearst, were accused of acts of violence as members of the radical band which called themselves the Symbionese Liberation Army.

[13] Marianne Dwight, the sister of John C. Dwight (see p. 132), and a member of Brook Farm, wrote to a friend, in 1845:"When one is working for humanity, it is true that individual trials are lightened and lost sight of... but here would be my trouble. I am ever seeking sympathy. When I find it it makes all difficulties naught, all work a healthful pleasure. But unless the sympathies of my nature are answered, I am paralyzed—I can do nothing.... I never knew happiness and joy before; and this is not a transient, momentary feeling, but a deep, solemn joy that has taken possession of my soul, from the consciousness that there is something worth living for. In the hopes and views that the associative life has disclosed to me, I feel that I have a treasure that nothing can deprive me of" [12:81,97].

[14] The Oneida community, based on principles of the primitive Christian church, consisted of two hundred members who supported themselves by farming and industry. They shared most of their possessions and provided communal childrearing. Pair relationships were structured according to a principle called "complex marriage," by which sex relations were regulated by the central committee which decided about mate selection and duration of the relationship.

[15] The commune New Age is occupied with farming, building, artwork, and theater productions. Veysey describes, in detail, Ezra's, the leader's, influence on the commune members. The members are unconsciously wishing for his approval in everything they do. Assaults and "confrontations," launched by Ezra, are considered by him as part of the self-development of a person. Although the relations between members are lacking in warmth and sociability, affective bonds to the leader develop through his charisma.

[16] Bennet Berger reports that in over two years of field work in hippie communes, only rarely were adults seen to settle the not-infrequent quarrels, fights, or disputes between children [6:169].

[17] Marianne Dwight writes to a friend about the "beautiful grove of cypress trees" selected for the grave of a member of the community and ends her comment about the "universal sympathy by the group" with the words: "Here is one of the pleasantest blessings of Association" [13:55].

REFERENCES

1. Alam, S. E. Middle-class comune. A case study. *J. Cooperative Living*, **20**, 1975.
2. Barclay, D. Communes losing flower child image. *Los Angeles Times*, Part VI, Nov. 10, 1976.
3. ———. Commune children evaluated. *Los Angeles Times*, Part IB, Nov. 25, 1976.
4. ———. Religious commune—hymns and huts. *Los Angeles Times*, Part VI, Dec. 25, 1976.
5. Becker, G. Die Siedlung der Deutschen Jugendbewegung. Eine Soziologische Untersuchung. Inaugural Dissertation, Cologne University, 1929.
6. Berger, B. M. On the decline of age grading in rural hippie communes. *J. Social Issues*, **30** (2), 1974.
7. Bestor, A. E. *Backwoods Utopias: The Sectarian and Owenite Phases of Communitarian Socialism in America: 1663-1829*. Philadelphia: University of Pennsylvania Press, 1950.
8. Brenner, C. *An Elementary Textbook of Psychoanalysis*. New York: Doubleday, 1957.
9. Buber-Neumann, M. *Von Potsdam Nach Moskau*. Stuttgart: Deutsche Verlagsanstalt, 1957.
10. Constantine, L. L., and Constantine, J. M. *Treasures of the Island*. Beverly Hills, Calif.: Sage Research Papers in the Social Sciences, Series No. 90-038, Vol. 5, 1976.
11. Deutsch, H. Some forms of emotional disturbances and their relationship to schizophrenia. In *Neuroses and Character Types: Clinical Psychoanalytic Studies*. New York: International Universities Press, 1965.

12. Dilloo, R. Sie nannten sich Wandervoegel. Wer sind heute ihre Erben? *Zeitmagazin*, Oct. 29, 1976.
13. Dwight, M. *Letters from Brook Farm, 1844-1847*. Amy L. Reed (Ed.). Poughkeepsie, N.Y.: Vassar College, 1928.
14. Ebeling, H. *The German Youth Movement: Its Past and Future*. London: The New Europe Publishing Co., 1945.
15. Erikson, E. H. *Childhood and Society*. New York: W. W. Norton, 1950.
16. Fairfield, R. (Ed.) Utopia, U.S.A. San Francisco: Alternatives Foundation, 1970 (mimeo).
17. "Findhorn," quotation from interview in documentary film on Findhorn, religious commune in Scotland, produced by R. Johnson and V. Mudd, aired on Public Broadcasting System, January 1979.
18. Freud, A. *The Ego and the Mechanism of Defense*. New York: International Universities Press, 1970.
19. Jerome, J. *Families of Eden*. New York: the Seabury Press, 1974.
20. Kanter, R. M. *Commitment and Community*. Cambridge, Mass.: Harvard University Press, 1974.
21. Kellogg, M. A. Counter-culture kids. *Newsweek*, March 29, 1976.
22. Keniston, K. *The Uncommitted: Alienated .Youth in American Society*. New York: Dell Publishing Corp., 1964.
23. Kinkade, K. *Walden Two Experiment*. New York: William Morrow & Co., 1973.
24. Koch, H. W. *The Hitler Youth: Origins and Development, 1922-1945*. London: MacDonald and James, 1975.
25. Kohut, H. *The Analysis of the Self*. New York: International Universities Press, 1971.
26. Lane, Ch. *Autobiography of Brook Farm. A Book of Primary Source Materials*. Henry W. Sams (Ed.). Englewood Cliffs, N.J.: Prentice-Hall, 1958.
27. *Newsletter*, Center for Alternatives in Urban Living. Commune Forming Section, 1971.
28. O'Dea, T. F. Sects and cults. In *International Encyclopedia of the Social Sciences*, Vol. 14. New York: MacMillan and Free Press, 1968.
29. Otto, H. A. The communal alternative. In R. Fairfield (Ed.), Utopia, U.S.A. San Francisco: Alternatives Foundation, 1970 (mimeo).
30. Paetel, K. O. *Das Bild vom Menschen in der Deutschen Jugendbewegung*. Bad Godesborg: Voggenreiter Verlag, 1953.
31. Pumpian-Mindlin, E. Omnipotentiality, youth and commitment. *Acad. Child Psychiat.*, 4 (1), 1965.
32. Round Robin Letter of the Deutscher Wandervogel after the First Reunion in Cologne, 1954 (mimeo).
33. Scholl, I. *Die Weisse Rose*. Frankfurt-am-Main: Verlag der Frankfurter Hefte, 1955.
34. Stern, S. *With the Weathermen. The Personal Journey of a Revolutionary Woman*. New York: Doubleday, 1975.
35. Swift, J. S. *Brook Farm*. Secaucus, N.J.: Citadel Press, 1973.
36. Toffler, A. *Future Shock*. New York: Random House, 1970.
37. Traub, G. Auf dem hohen Meissner. In *Der Fahrende Schueler. Monatsschrift fuer die Deutschen Wandervogelbestrebungen*, 3, Nov. 1913.
38. Veysey, L. R. *The Communal Experience*. New York: Harper & Row, 1973.
39. Weber, M. *Grundriss der Sozialoekonomik*, Vol. 3. Tuebingen: J. C. B. Mohr, 1922.
40. Wolf, S., and Rothchild, J. *The Children of the Counter Culture*. New York: Doubleday, 1976.
41. Wyneken, G. Die neue Jugend. Ihr Kampf um Freiheit und Wahrheit in Schule und Elternhaus, in Religion und Erotik. In W. Kindt (Ed.), *Grandschriften der Deutschen Jugendbewegung*. Duesseldorf-Cologne: Eugen Diedrichs Verlag, 1963.
42. Zuckmayer, C. *Als Waer's Ein Stueck von Mir*. Frankfurt-am-Main: Fischer Buecherel, 1969.

CHAPTER 4

Two Patterns of
Parent-Child Interaction in Israel:
Kibbutz and Urban Families

CHILDREARING IN THE KIBBUTZ[1]

The kibbutz is a voluntary, predominantly agricultural, Israeli settlement with a typical population of one hundred to four hundred members. The first kibbutz was founded in 1909. There are now two hundred thirty kibbutzim in Israel comprising about slightly less than 4 percent of the Israeli population, about ninety thousand people. In the kibbutz property is owned in common.

In 95 percent of the kibbutzim, infants live in the "nursery" in groups of five from soon after birth to the age of eighteen months. They are cared for by the metapelet (caretaker). During the first two months the mother spends ample time with her baby, feeding him (breast-feeding, if possible), carrying him around, and playing with him, while the metapelet assists the mother in performing the routine duties of the nursery. Both parents spend time with the baby after work hours.

After two months, the mother returns to work, first for four hours a day, then for the full seven-hour workday. In most cases, the metapelet herself is a mother, her own children growing up in other housing units in the kibbutz. The metapelet takes over the mother's caretaking functions only gradually. The mother is involved in most of the feeding during the first six months and in half the feeding and caretaking during the second half. By the child's second year the metapelet handles all caretaking routines. The child visits his parents each day.

The infant remains in the "nursery" until he is eighteen months of age, at which time he is moved to the "Toddler House" where he is one of a group of four to six similar-aged children. In some kibbutzim a child remains in the Toddler House until he is four to six years of age; in others, a child transfers to a "Children's House" at three to four years of age. A child in the Toddler House is under the care of another metapelet.

Metaplot, (the plural for metapelet), are professional educators who receive one year of basic training in the Oranim Kibbutz Teachers' College. (Kindergarten teachers receive two to three years of basic training.) In addition, a future metapelet assists in the care of children on a part-time basis.

The metapelet for a particular housing unit is selected by an education committee which represents the kibbutz community and thus the parents also. The chosen metapelet consults with and gives advice to the parents but is also accountable to the selection committee.

Besides the assorted duties which the metapelet performs in the Children's House, she is an important educator. She teaches the children eating habits, cleanliness, and social attitudes, among other skills. She stays with a group of children for at least one year, although some metaplot continue with the same group for as long as six years. In the two kibbutzim to be described in this chapter, the metapelet usually remains with a group of children until they move to a new unit.

At age three to four the children are moved to another house, referred to as the "Kindergarten," where a number of toddler groups are combined into larger groups of fifteen to twenty children. At age seven, after having spent a year in a transitional class, the group enters grammar school. The children remain in grammar school until age twelve or thirteen, when they begin high school.

Prior to high school, the education of children is conducted in the children's unit of the children's own kibbutz. The high school, in contrast, may be located in any of the kibbutzim and is attended by children from other kibbutzim in the area.

At age eighteen, the young kibbutz members enter the military service for two and a half to three years. Afterward, a large number of the young people return to their kibbutzim. Their loyalty to the kibbutz has been attributed to the "feeling that it is home, because of the emotional ties to the landscape, the people, the worklife, and the social values of the kibbutz . . . [and to] the strong ties with the parents" [7:26].

STUDIES COMPARING KIBBUTZ AND FAMILY CARE

In a number of studies, the effect of group rearing upon the child's overall development has been explored using, for comparison, kibbutz children and children reared in the traditional middle-class family.

Gewirtz and Gewirtz found that in comparison with city mothers in Israel, the contacts of kibbutz mothers, in particular the physical contacts with their infants at two, four, six and eight months of age, are of longer duration [8:229-252]. They also found that more kibbutz babies are breast-fed than are city babies. Rabin compared children raised in the kibbutz with those raised in the city at four different age levels. He concluded that "intellectually the kibbutz children are at least as well-developed as non-kibbutz children and to some extent surpass the non-kibbutz children. . . . evidence concerning ego strength, emotional and over-all maturity favors the kibbutz child" [21:144].

Some studies have explored attitudes toward achievement among kibbutz as compared with those among city children. Rabin found that kibbutz children, unlike city children, value group achievement more highly than individual accomplishment [21:134]. In a detailed developmental investigation of the competitive attitudes in kibbutz and urban children, Shapira arrived at a similar conclusion. She found that competition tended to occur between groups of children in the kibbutz and between individuals with urban chilren. "A kibbutz child strives for his group to be better than groups in other kibbutzim. Within a particular group, however, the child's competitive feelings are thought to be restrained and his interaction with other members of the group to be mainly of a cooperative character" [23:30].

Among negative aspects reported of kibbutz upbringing is the tendency toward parental indulgence [7:261]. Bettelheim has commented on the lack of emotional depth in the parent-child relationship in the kibbutz as compared with a greater intimacy and intensity of affection in nuclear family upbringing [3:157]. However, Nagler, a psychologist at the Department for Special Education at the University of Haifa who has observed a number of families in the kibbutz and in the city, has found no difference between the kibbutz child and the urban child in the "capacity for deep emotions" in relationship to the parents [19:208; 20:311].

Let us try to put ourselves in the place of a child growing up in a kibbutz and then of one growing up in an urban, middle-class family.

The kibbutz child lives in the Children's House together with four or five other children. The children spend two and a half hours every day in the house of their parents (a simple one- or two-room structure) and their parents can visit them whenever they wish. (Usually the mother drops into the Children's House for half an hour or longer during the morning.) Each evening the child is brought back to the Children's House by the father or mother. Thus both mother and father enjoy the growing up and the love of their young child for a few undisturbed hours daily in the intimate atmosphere of their home. To a young kibbutz child, his parents are not "Do it" or "Don't do it" persons. They are primarily people who show him their affection and with whom the child feels close and at ease. His caretaker is the main "direction giver" and sometimes strict authority figure, who helps him to adhere to tasks and achieve goals, and from whom he learns many of his skills and the ways of his culture. In addition, the kibbutz children, even the very young ones, are decisively influenced by the affection and direction they receive from their peers.

In the Israeli city family, as in other urban, middle-class families, the mother's contact with her young child through the first years of his life is close and continuous. The city parents do most of the training and controlling, the punishing and the praising. Day by day the city child experiences a variety of parental affects—joy, anger, despair, and so forth. The child responds by manifesting a variety of feelings similar, to some extent, to those expressed by the parents. In contrast, the kibbutz child generally experiences a narrower range of parental emotions—usually more balanced and more positive. The mutual enjoyment of kibbutz child and parent at the child's afternoon visit has been likened to that of grandparents and grandchildren [4]. Many middle-class parents in city families enjoy their children as intensely as do the kibbutz parents, but they have to combine the roles of kibbutz parent and caretaker. They are concerned, in particular, with the child's intellectual accomplishments.

The peer group in the city nursery school is usually larger than that in the kibbutz, and for two or three years the children are generally in contact with their peers for only three hours daily. There is therefore less intense and prolonged peer influence on the city child's personality than on that of the kibbutz child who lives with a single small group throughout his school years.

Research Procedures

As stated earlier (Chapter 1), seven kibbutz and eight Israeli city families were studied. The particular kibbutz families were provided by the Institute for Research on Kibbutz Education, Oranim, Israel, and the city families by the Department of Psychology, Hebrew University, Jerusalem. The families were considered by professionals in these institutions to be representative of the kibbutz population and of the urban middle-class population, respectively. The fifteen families met the following requirements:

1. The child's four grandparents were of European origin.
2. The child was a boy, between three and three and three-quarters years old.
3. As far as could be assessed, the child was developing normally physically and mentally.
4. The child had one older siblling (this requirement was not fulfilled in one case).
5. The parent had completed twelve years of schooling.

Additional restrictions were that the kibbutz father and mother should have been born and raised in a kibbutz and that the mother and father of the city child should have lived in Israel for at least ten years. Since the study was carried out in 1970 the children were born in 1967, the year of the Six-Day War.

Four kibbutz families lived in the kibbutz we shall call Gan She'Arim, about eight miles outside Haifa. The three other kibbutz families lived in a nearby kibbutz. Both kibbutzim belong to the Artzi movement—one of the three major kibbutz movements and the most extreme in preserving the original collective and nonorthodox ideology. The two kibbutzim studied were founded approximately sixty years ago and each consists of about three hundred families. All city families involved in the study lived in Haifa.

The study was carried out from June to September 1970. Nurit Arbel and Mosche Hazan, two students at the University of Haifa, acted as observers and translators.

The parents and, in the kibbutz, the caretaker were interviewed with regard to their life histories and that of the child, as well as about certain childrearing practices. The metapelet was asked to rank each child in her group from "low" to "high" on each of the following characteristics:(1) attachment to peer group, (2) attachment to metapelet, and (3) stress tolerance.

Each adult (father, mother, and caretaker) was observed in interaction with the child in a series of MIM situations. In the kibbutz, the interaction sessions with the parents took place in the parents' house, and the ones with the caretaker, in the Children's House. The sessions with the city families took place in their home. Of the city children, only Yuval (Group A) was observed in nursery school. (Time did not permit making peer group observations on the other city children. Since the kibbutz children lived in the Children's House where the MIM sessions with the metapelet took place, they were also observed with their age mates.)

As was done in Chapter 2, the interactions will be reported separately for each MIM situation. The data to be used will consist of the transcribed and translated tape-recorded dialogues, the observational notes taken by the author and an assistant, and the additional types of information described above.

The Families

The fifteen families will be presented in three groups. Group A consists of the kibbutz child Aviv and the city child Yuval. Since the interaction in these two families was also filmed [18], it was possible to review their behavior repeatedly and in slow motion, making possible an even more detailed examination than in the case of the other two groups.

Group B consists of another five kibbutz and five city families. In many aspects the interactions in these families were similar to those in Aviv's and Yuval's families. Groups A and B will therefore be treated in combination when drawing conclusions.

In Group C, one kibbutz child (Eilon) and two city children (Zoor and Itai) will be presented. More frequently than the children in groups A and B, these children showed negative responses such as, for example, an unwillingness to participate in an activity.

A close look at the interaction patterns between these resistant children and their parents in both city and kibbutz families will provide additional insight into interaction patterns in groups A and B, i.e., where the affectionate interplay between parent and child was clearly expressed.

Thus interaction in the following groups of children will be studied as shown in Table 1.

Parent-Child Interactions

Interaction patterns in the following situations will be discussed:

1. Fantasy activity—hand puppets.
2. Organizing an environment—small figures of farmers, soldiers, animals, fences, etc.
3. Separation—the adult is told to leave for three minutes; upon returning, he or she is to take the child on lap.
4. Modeling and imitation—block building; the adult is instructed to arrange a set of blocks in a certain order, then to ask the child to duplicate the arrangement with the child's set of blocks.
5. Stress—puzzle.

As was the case in the discussion of the studies in Chapter 2, the above list constitutes only a selection from the original list of situations used in the

Table 1

Kibbutz Children	Group	City Children
Aviv	A	Yuval
Shemuel	B	Ezra
Yigael		Uzi
David		Dan
Dror		Yaakov
Zev		Amnon
Eilon	C	Zoor
		Itai

study. The situations included here seemed to discriminate most clearly between the kibbutz and city families.

Situations 1 and 2, because of their potential for shedding light on the adult's emphasis on affection or direction, were especially designed for the Israeli study, while situations 3 and 4 are essentially the same as those discussed in Chapter 2. Free block play, described in John's and Stephen's study, was omitted in the Israeli series in favor of the two new situations.

Fantasy Activity: Finger Puppets

The puppets (horse, rabbit, cat, mouse) were introduced for the purpose of observing how child and adult interact in a situation which has no other objective than to trigger imaginary play and allow child and adult to have fun, alone or with each other.

A child of three and a half can usually recognize and name a horse, rabbit, cat, and mouse, but in the unusual, incomplete form of finger puppets, the child does not readily pair them off or pit one against the other and therefore is not as likely to initiate fantasy play on his own. It is interesting to observe whether and how the adult begins to play the game, and hands the puppets to the child; how the adult handles the puppets; whether the child complies with or rejects the adult's suggestion; whether directions are given at all, or whether pure enjoyment and spontaneity are generated by the situation.

Group A

Aviv, the kibbutz child. Aviv's father drives a tractor and is also in charge of the motor vehicles in the kibbutz. Aviv's mother is a metapelet in the nursery for young infants. Aviv has a five-year-old sister who lives in another Children's House and also visits with the parents in the afternoon. Aviv has been in the Toddlers' House with the same metapelet, Dahlia, for two years.

Yuval, the city child. Yuval and his hard-of-hearing eight-year-old brother live with their family in an apartment in Haifa. Yuval goes to nursery school during the morning. In his school are about twenty-five children ranging in age from two and a half to five years.

Yuval's father is an engineer. Yuval's mother lectures to parents with children who have hearing difficulties. The parents did an excellent job in helping Yuval's brother adjust to his hearing defect. He is in a school grade corresponding to his age.

Yuval and his mother:

In performing the MIM, Yuval's mother shakes the puppets from the net. She tries to draw Yuval into the activity by taking various roles. She says, for example, "Here is a small mouse. Run after me, cat." Yuval seems somewhat reluctant to handle the puppets so she changes her story.

Yuval and his father:

Yuval's father empties the MIM bag. He asks Yuval how many animals there are, and Yuval counts them. Father initiates fantasy play and encourages Yuval to join in. Father suggests that Yuval's mouse should say hello to father's cat. Father asks what sounds the animals make, and Yuval imitates a horse and a cat. Father's rabbit says hello to Yuval's horse and asks for a carrot. Yuval responds readily.

Group B

The interactions in other city families resemble that in Yuval's family with regard to the parents' inclination to direct their children's fantasy. Their "direction giving" can be seen in the questions they ask and in the lead they provide, often through stories which they themselves invent.

Ezra's mother:	Let's see what the mouse tells the cat. Shalom, cat, where are you going?
Ezra:	Here.
Mother:	Shalom, Ezra. Meow, meow. Shalom, mouse. Aren't you afraid of the cat? I'll tell you a story. One day there was a rabbit who wanted to eat a carrot. He met the mule. Shalom, where is the mouse? He met the mouse. Shalom, why did you eat my carrot?

Of the three maternal figures involved in performing the tasks—the kibbutz mother, the metapelet, and the city mother—the city mother is most eager to arouse the child's fantasy and to engage him in her activity.

Ezra's father, after briefly suggesting that Ezra make up a story, tells one himself, assigning to Ezra his role in it.

Ezra's father:	Make up a story with the mouse and the cat. What does the mouse do to the cat? Does he always win?
Ezra:	Yes.
Father:	Let's say the cat is running after the mouse and all of a sudden the mouse is going under the horse and the horse is looking for him.
Ezra:	Yes.
Father:	"Now the cat will look for the mouse [joint laughter] coming from one side and going out the other side [joint laughter]. Now you know what?
Ezra:	Yes.
Father:	You'll be the horse and I'll be the mouse and cat. O.K.?
Ezra:	O.K. Shall I put two fingers in or one?
Father:	One.

The kibbutz parents are less eager to give directions than are the city parents. They leave more initiative to the child. They wait to see how the child reacts to the puppets before they provide cues for the child's fantasy. It is not at all unusual for a kibbutz parent to let the child lead:

Yigael's father: "How do you play this game? I see, you put your fingers in? What does your horse want from my rabbit?"

Yigael's mother: "Do you want us to play together?" Yigael smiles, does not handle puppets yet. Mother pats child. Yigael takes cat. Mother: "You want to be the cat? I'll be the mouse." Yigael's cat tries to catch mother's mouse. Joint laughter and joyful sounds.

Uzi's father:	What do you do with the puppets?
Uzi:	Like this, with your hand.
Father:	How are you going to call them?
Uzi:	Cat and rabbit.
Father:	Hello, children. They call me rabbit but I am a cat.
Uzi:	Now the mouse wants to dance, play with everyone. Birthday.
Father:	Who has a birthday today?
Uzi:	The cat.
Father:	Today is her birthday?
Uzi:	Now the mouse has a birthday.
[*Father sings. Uzi gasps, showing excitement.*]	
Uzi:	Today is birthday. Now the mule has a birthday.

It will be helpful for us occasionally to "zoom in" on an individual child who in some respects behaves differently from the other kibbutz or city children in groups A and B. One such child is the kibbutz child, David.

David is a thin, high-voiced boy, small for his age, who keeps to himself in his play group much of the time. He approaches adults who happen to come by and asks them questions. The metapelet ranks David among the children in her group as the most attached to her.

David's father is shy but spoke up defensively about participating in the session. He is the only kibbutz parent who asks about possible findings. He talks in an ironic fashion which might be an attempt to cover up some insecurity. The father is a technician in the assembly plant of the kibbutz. He shows David how to fix a mechanical toy David hands him during the session. When David does not understand the procedure, his father becomes impatient.

In his interview, David's father mentions that it is a particular advantage of kibbutz education that in the kibbutz the parents know with whom the child plays, and who is his particular friend, while in the city parents have no say about their children's friends. The following remarks by David reflect his image of his father as someone on whose directions he depends, whether they have been actually received or fantasied:

Yariv brings pails and Eli fills them with water. David says: "Father doesn't allow you to bring water." Another time, the metapelet asks David: "David, why do you splash mud all over the porch?" David: "Father told me to."

In his play group David seems intent on making up for feelings of dependency:

David: "I've built the tallest tower in the world." [a noisy airplane was passing by] "I'm not afraid of airplanes."

Unlike other kibbutz parents, but similar to the parents of the city child Yuval, David's father does not wait for his son's expression of his fantasy. More than other kibbutz fathers, he seems anxious to find out (or show off?) what his son knows about each animal. He directs both his son's intellectual and his fantasy activity.

Father:	What do you have? A mouse? And what is this? It's a horse, right?
David:	Right.
Father:	Who is running after whom?
David:	The cat.
Father:	After? You will be the cat. Put the cat on your finger and run for the mouse. Can you put it on your finger? I'll help you. Now we are ready to catch the mouse. Can you put it on? What is this? What animal is this?
David:	Horse.
Father:	Correct. And this?
David:	Rabbit.
Father:	How do you know? What does he have? What kind of ears?
David:	Don't know.
Father:	Big ears.

In contrast to David's father, David's mother does not question David but listens to him and is easily amused. He is able to lead and occasionally manipulate her.

In contrast to the kibbutz parents who tend to enjoy the puppet situation without taking the lead, the two metaplot typically arouse the child's interest by making the puppets move, by reminding the children of encounters with real mice or rabbits on their walk, etc., and by asking them questions about it. The metaplot try to interest the child in the puppets by saying, for example: "What is the horse doing? What is the mouse saying to the cat? Do you want to make up a story about the animals?" The metapelet rarely suggests to the children which scene they should enact. She rarely stages a plot for them. (As mentioned earlier, each metapelet was observed in interaction sessions with each child. The metaplot were also observed during routine activities in their groups of children.)

Each metapelet varies her direction perceptibly for each child. In her session with Dror, an outgoing, self-assured child, the metapelet, Dahlia, tends to participate in his activity. She tells Dror: "Oh, I'm afraid of the cat.

Where are you, horse? Can't you talk, horse?" Dror responds, similarly animated, with a series of neighing sounds. In her sessions with Aviv, who is gentler and less productive than Dror, Dahlia moves her fingers with the puppets to induce his initiative, but she abstains from taking part in the child's fantasy activity. Probably without being aware of it, the metapelet tunes in to each child's personality, much like the kind of mother who responds differently to each of her children.

Aviv's interaction with his father, similar to the one observed in other father-son pairs in the kibbutz, shows a mutual, vivid, and more exhilarated pleasure than does the interaction with the mother which is calmer. Aviv's intense joy in the interaction is noticeable when he succeeds in involving his father's fingers in the puppet play. The father's ability to "tune in" to Aviv's game would seem to foster the mutuality of affection giving and taking and the enjoyment of their interchange.

These observations are consistent with those of various writers who have pointed out that the kibbutz father is close to his young son. It has been argued that, since the traditional family and the patriarchal father role have been abandoned in the kibbutz, the most pronounced change is the attachment of young boys to their fathers. "The father is more of a close friend who plays with the child, takes him for a walk, and treats him gently, not the authoritative, fear-arousing figure [10:167-177].

Since the metapelet is the one who teaches skills and acceptable behavior, she needs to reinforce the children's self-control and, at times, to criticize them. Quite apart from the fact that the metapelet's feelings toward the children in her care, are, naturally not as strong as are those of the children's own parents, she has to be as impartial as possible and has to express both her affection and her negative feelings less openly and less intensely. The children tend to reflect the metapelet's attitudes in their interaction with her. Their affection toward her is of an even, nondemonstrative quality. In fact, both of the observers participating in this study described the children's behavior in interaction with the metaplot during the puppet task, and in the two other game situations, as much less "excited" than in the sessions with the parents.

Directing the child's fantasy by alerting him to the animals' properties, "monitoring" his production, asking questions, initiating a story, etc., are more often observed among city than among kibbutz parents. Watching the child play with minimal interference, giving free rein to his verbalized fantasy, and tolerating his silent interest in the figures, is more characteristic of kibbutz than of city parents. The attitudes of the city parents may be related to the obligation built into the role of parents-in-the-nuclear-family. (We have seen an exaggeration of direction giving in Stephen's family.) The city parents see themselves as solely responsible for their child's overall development, and for his intellectual growth in particular. The kibbutz parents, in contrast, are not the main educators of their children. Their child's intellectual accomplishment does not arouse their ambitions nor reflect upon their effort in developing the child's mental potential. Thus, a task which carries the possibility of fun for both parent and child tends to be carried out by kibbutz parents as a game. The puppet situation as such is apt to mobilize the affectionate feelings between parent and child: the incident where Aviv puts one puppet on each of his father's fingers instead of handling the puppets himself suggests his intimate bond with father.

The metapelet whose responsibilities include the fostering of the child's intellectual growth enlists, in this task, the child's participation by stimulating but not actively directing his fantasy. Thus she resembles the city parents only to a certain extent. In contrast to both city and kibbutz parents, the metapelet, as mentioned above, abstains from an intense, affectionate involvement with the child.

Group C

Two city families: Zoor and Itai, and their parents. Zoor was born the day before the outbreak of the 1967 war. (As mentioned earlier, all children in the sample were born during the year of the war. For Zoor's mother, although her delivery was without complications, its coincidence with the impending outbreak of war constituted a traumatic event.) During his newborn period, his mother worried about her husband being called to military duty. He was, in fact, drafted for defense duty after she returned from the hospital. Zoor's mother discontinued breast feeding after a few weeks because Zoor did not suck strongly enough and tended to fall asleep during nursing. When he was almost seven months old, he contracted a skin infection which lasted for a year. His mother describes this year as the worst time of her life. She blames the infection on herself. She was afraid even to wash or bathe the baby lest she would worsen his condition. Yet she felt obliged to minister to the child day and night. Even when recalling Zoor's illness, she speaks with notable anxiety, perhaps concealing some hostility.

Zoor's father spends little time with his son. He is a frustrated writer who, as an accountant, earns a meager livelihood for his family. Since he tries to obtain, in addition, occasional assignments from a newspaper, he is home at irregular hours. Zoor's mother considers herself a better planner than her husband. She is also the one who cuts down on family expenses by sewing some children's clothes herself and by doing minor repairs in the house. She apparently feels burdened by her various obligations. Her main worry, however, is that she cannot control Zoor's "stubbornness." He insists, she says, on staying up as late as his seven-year-old sister; he demands things in the store which his mother cannot afford; he plays with the electric cord although he has been spanked for doing it; he has difficulties going to sleep at night and sometimes stays awake until midnight.

Summing up her complaints, Zoor's mother says that both she and her husband are to blame since they have "spoiled" Zoor since babyhood. It seems likely that this mother's anxiety about her son originates in her past. This degree and kind of anxiety, related to unconscious, repressed hostility, has been said to characterize mothers of infants afflicted with eczema similar to that which Zoor had as a baby [24:509-514].

There are no children of Zoor's age in the neighborhood. His sister has no patience with Zoor and finds excuses for not having to play with him. Asked whether Zoor has a special corner in the apartment for his toys, etc., the mother responds that she does not see the need for it.

Zoor has not yet been enrolled in a nursery school although his parents consider entering him in the near future.

Presented with the MIM materials, Zoor does not touch the puppets in the presence of either of his parents. He is whiny, sucks his fingers, and refuses to participate. In his mother's session his repeated answer is: "I don't want." Zoor's mother responds to Zoor by saying: "You don't want to play with animals? Then what do you want?" She does not sound as if she expects an answer. She continues to urge him in different ways to "play with the puppets." Zoor remains passive. He looks away from the puppets with his fingers in his mouth.

Zoor's father responds to Zoor's initial refusal with indifference and is seemingly unconcerned: "You don't want to? You don't have to. You want to put it back?" The father is even less inclined than the mother to direct Zoor or to stimulate his fantasy.

Father: You don't know what this is?
Zoor: No.
Father: To everything you say no.
Zoor: Put it back.
Father: Put it back in the bag? O.K. we'll put it back.

It seems that the parents protect themselves against distress and irritation by trying to avoid too close a contact with Zoor (as perhaps they do with everyone else in their world). The father surrenders even earlier than the mother.

Itai's father is the rabbi of a small non-Orthodox congregation. He is friendly and talks in a matter-of-fact tone. He wears a skullcap (*yarmulka*) at home, not uncommon for Israeli men. Except for one evening in the week when the father has a commitment, he comes home at 4:00 and on Fridays at 2:00 P.M. He spends from one and a half to two hours every day with Itai and his five-year-old brother. Recently he started to read selections from the Bible to his sons. He also introduced them to certain principles of Jewish ethics, e.g., that one does not speak ill of an absent person. He believes that Itai understands it. Some Jewish rituals are already familiar to Itai. He tells his father in the interaction session that his block structure looks like Shabbat (Sabbath) candles.

Both parents are supportive but not overaffectionate to the child. Itai's mother is a warm, motherly person. She was born in Holland and, having escaped Nazi persecution with the help of relatives who were able to emigrate and to assist her in her emigration, she came to Israel in her late teens. Both her parents perished in a concentration camp.

Throughout the interaction session with his mother, Itai is sulking. He is still angry with his mother from earlier in the day when she did not let him wear a new jacket. The mother explains that in that particular instance she had made an effort to be firm. She has generally been too "soft," she says, too ready to give in. Her resoluteness is new to Itai and makes him angry. Here is the description of the puppet situation in the mother's presence:

Mother handles the puppets. Itai makes hitting gestures; his face serious. He sits immobile, arms on table, hands together. Mother smiles slightly, uneasily, A fleeting smile appears on Itai's face, too. He utters no word, does nothing. Mother motions to child to take one puppet. He shakes his head. Mother touches child's nose with puppet, playfully. Itai pushes puppet away, serious expression on his face.

In performing the MIM his father is both friendly and directive with Itai. Although Itai first refuses to touch the bag or the puppets, the father succeeds in interesting him in the activity.

Father gives the bag of puppets to the child. Itai does not touch it. Father tells him to see what he can do with that toy. Itai takes the puppets out and talks and smiles. Father asks Itai for the names of the puppets; Itai answers. Father does not put a puppet on his finger or on Itai's finger. He tells Itai how to do it. Itai puts two puppets on his fingers. He utters a joyful tone.

The obstinacy observed in Itai differs markedly from that observed in Zoor. It will be remembered that Itai's mother had forced herself not to give in to an unreasonable wish of Itai's. Thus, Itai's resistance, in contrast to Zoor's, is connected with a real event and does not seem to reflect an underlying conflict of long standing. Moreover, Itai must surely be aware that, simply by communicating with her again, he can, at any moment, regain his mother's habitual spontaneous affection. Zoor, in contrast, unless his parents are able to undergo inner changes themselves and admit to themselves some of their frustrations and anxieties, can hardly hope for their spontaneous affection and empathy.

Itai, in his interaction with his father, follows the father's directions which seem to be given patiently and without anxiety or without stifling the child's initiative.

It was proposed earlier that adequate affection would promote identification. Neither in the puppet nor in the following interaction situations does Zoor receive from his parents adequate affection or clear and encouraging direction. Nor is it possible to detect, in Zoor, behavior indicative of an incipient identification with one of his parents. Itai, on the other hand, whose parents convey their affectionate closeness with him and provide clear guidance, shows the beginning of identification with his father.

Except for Itai's negative reaction to his mother Itai could have been included in the B group. However, by grouping and comparing him with Zoor we are able to show how the different attitudes of the parents lead to prolonged resistance in the latter and to "pseudo"-resistance in the former.

Eilon, A kibbutz child. Eilon's family lived in two other kibbutzim before moving to Gan She'Arim when Eilon was two years old. One reason for the last move was that Eilon's mother did not get along with her mother-in-law. She says that her mother-in-law is headstrong, like herself. Eilon has a brother one year and three months old who is in the "Nursery."

In her previous kibbutz Eilon's mother had resented the close tie with her extended family, in spite of the fact that such ties are emphasized as important, both for the individual and for the social structure of the kibbutz [25:213-214]. In Gan She'Arim, she resents various obligations such as the long work hours. She keeps changing her work branch and has not yet found a satisfactory job.

Eilon's mother admits that she did not enjoy Eilon as a baby. He did not eat well, and he cried a lot. At the age of one and a half Eilon had a traumatic experience. He fell down a flight of stairs and had to have some stitches taken in his scalp. According to the mother's own account the accident was due to her negligence.

Eilon's mother seems tense and nervous. She speaks rapidly and is the only kibbutz parent to smoke during the session. The previous week Eilon's father had come back from military reserve duty. According to the mother, things get upset when her husband is around. She maintains that Eilon is "calmer" when his father is gone.

The metapelet reports, however, that Eilon has told her he likes playing with his father better than playing with his mother. He said: "Father is for play. Mother is to help and serve." The metapelet adds that Eilon was probably thinking of the extra treats his mother serves him when he visits his parents' house.

Eilon's father is the one who brings the boy back to the Children's House at night. Occasionally when Eilon insists, the father tucks him in and sits by his bed. The father admits he is "soft with Eilon but can't help it."

In his peer group Eilon shows some aggressive behavior and a tendency to tease other children. However, according to the metapelet, Eilon had been more obstinate and at times quite troublesome when he first joined her group at age two and a half. In her assessment of Eilon's "attachment to other children," the metapelet, Dahlia, ranks him highest. She qualifies her judgment, saying, "He needs the other children, especially when they reject him." She also ranks Eilon highest on "attachment to the metapelet."[9]

In the puppet situation with his mother, Eilon is uncooperative.

Mother tells Eilon: "Open it, put it on your finger." He handles one puppet briefly. She asks him for its name and he tells her. She repeats her request. He does not respond, does not touch any more puppets. She terminates the task, seemingly irritated.

The interaction between Eilon and his father proceeds as follows:

Eilon lines up the puppets on the table. He puts the cat on one finger and lets the father put the mouse on another finger. Father takes the rabbit for himself. He does not tell Eilon what to do. Father's rabbit approaches Eilon's mouse. Eilon pulls the puppet from his father's hands, teasing him, and throws it on the table. Eilon is quiet, leans with his face against father's arm. Father smiles.

Dahlia, in her session with Eilon, moves all the puppets to his side. When he has the horse on his finger, Dahlia says "Shalom" to the horse in a happy, loud voice. She helps him to slip on the mouse. He smiles at her when she says "Shalom" to his mouse. The interaction ends in the following manner:

He has the mouse and horse on his fingers; metapelet puts the cat on hers. He smiles. Smiles brighter now. Metapelet moves her cat to his mouse, says "Boo!" He puts horse down, keeps mouse, smiles brightly. They look at each other.

In addition to Eilon's passive resistance in interaction with his mother we shall presently see another defensive reaction of his toward his mother. The child-mother relationship might have been influenced, as was Zoor's, by certain incidents in the family history, in Eilon's case by the move from kibbutz to kibbutz. Moreover, the mother's guilt feelings and anxiety about Eilon's injury must have played a role in her relationship with Eilon. Like Zoor's mother who blamed herself severely for her son's illness, Eilon's mother experienced guilt feelings which may have adversely affected her mothering.

However, both Eilon and Zoor receive some affectionate support from their fathers. As briefly noticed earlier, Eilon's father is responsive to Eilon's need for protection. To some extent he fits the characterization of kibbutz fathers as being close to their young sons. When asked what he likes doing with his son the best, Eilon's father answers, bathing him and tucking him in at night (in the Children's House). Eilon's mother's answer to the question is, playing ball with Eilon—a less intimate activity than those mentioned by the father. Both Zoor's parents in answering the same question say that Zoor likes to play by himself and that they seldom play with him. Zoor's mother adds that Zoor imitates with his playthings her cooking and cleaning.

Itai's mother answers the question by: "singing" and "telling stories"; and Itai's father answers by: "building with blocks, dominoes, talking."

The answers of the three pairs of parents are thus consistent with the patterns of interaction with their children as observed so far.

Eilon's interaction with the metapelet is an example of a beneficial relationship with an adult outside of the family, available to the young kibbutz—but rarely to the city child. S. Nagler, an Israeli psychologist (cf. p. 189) who treats families from different kibbutzim, describes the metapelet as someone who loves the child without being as emotionally involved as the mother [19:208]. The interaction between Eilon and Dahlia shows that Dahlia is, indeed, inclined to relate to Eilon with affection but without being overinvolved emotionally. She also provides sufficient direction for Eilon to proceed with the task. It was pointed out earlier that the behavior of the metapelet varies from child to child. But she may also vary her approach to a particular child according to his emotional needs at the time. During the interaction session and also during routinely occurring situations in the Children's House, Dahlia sometimes conveys to Eilon her empathy and understanding and, at other times, provides firm guidance. In general, she seems aware of Eilon's need for a supportive and dependable adult. The emotional impact which Dahlia has on Eilon as well as his relationship with his father may satisfy Eilon's basic need to receive affection and enable him to give affection himself, as observed in the following situations.

Organizing an Environment: Small Figures

Small figures of farmers, soldiers, animals, trees, and fences are presented in a cardboard box. This task is less dependent on the free flow of the child's fantasy than is the puppet situation. While fantasy activity is by no means excluded, the task calls for a more systematic mode of proceeding. Although instructions are again omitted, the objects themselves elicit a purposeful activity by which real-life scenes and a particular environment are created and boundaries can be established through the placement of fences. Among other parental behaviors assumed to differentiate between the kibbutz and the city group were flexibility in allowing the child to proceed in this task versus giving specific directions, and the adult's concern with the child's orderly, meaningful organization of an environment. There could have been a certain bias in favor of the kibbutz children inherent in this task because of their greater familiarity with farm animals. Yet, the city children also recognized and named the animals and knew about their characteristic behavior and their sounds.

Group A
Aviv, the kibbutz child, and his mother.

Aviv first handles the tractor. (His father works a tractor in the field.) His mother asks what the tractor does, and he tells her. He sets up a fence for the animals as he has seen animals fenced in the kibbutz. Mother gives a little assistance. She also makes some verbal suggestions. Aviv feels free to spend some time rolling the tractor on his hand.

Aviv and his father.

Aviv puts up three fences for the horse, enlarges the enclosure. The horse and other animals are now inside. Father does not handle any figures. He watches the child quite seriously, his head moving with the child's movements. Father and child are calm. Child lets the tractor roll outside the fence, father places the rabbit under the tree. Aviv asks him why he puts it there. Father: "The rabbit likes to be under the tree." Aviv puts another animal where the trees are. Father: "What else do you want to add?" Aviv does not know. Father's and son's faces have a similar, content expression while they watch the scene.

Aviv and his metapelet, Dahlia.

The metapelet empties the box. Sometimes the metapelet allows Aviv to build his own world, but she often participates. Aviv responds quite readily. The metapelet guides Aviv by asking where he is going to put the horse; or where he is going to put the duck.

Yuval, the city child, and his mother.

Yuval moves the box to his side and says, his lips pouting, "*I* want to open it." His mother complies. She then takes some of the figures, saying: "I want to set it up over here." She tends to direct Yuval's fantasy, joining in the play and making suggestions, such as "Hide the soldier behind the trees," or "Make the rabbit run because he is very scared." Yuval tells his mother the rabbit cannot run because he has to eat.

Yuval places the soldiers on the edge of the scene, explaining that they have to keep guard. The mother acknowledges Yuval's resourcefulness. The scene now portrays their common existence under threat of war.

Yuval and his father.

The figures are spread out over the table. Yuval does not begin to set them up. Father: "First let's take the soldier." Father puts the soldier near Yuval and takes another soldier. Father: "Stand them up in a line." Yuval: "Here's a soldier." Father: "This is a soldier with a red cap. Now find an animal. Do you see a cow?"

Yuval and his father's hands are occupied with the figures, their hands cross. Father makes a rectangular enclosure of three fences. The soldiers stand outside by the fence. Yuval: "Here is the cow." Father: "And now where is the chicken? Yuval makes a rooster sound. Father puts the chicken near the duck. Father: "Where is the girl that feeds the chicken? Here, she feeds them." Father puts the girl near the chicken."

Father: "Now, where does the tree go?" Yuval puts the tree near a fence. Father praises him: "Good. This man should go here, he has to sweep the ground. Where shall we put the fences?" Yuval arranges two fences in a long line. Father: "Put the fences around the goose so it won't run away." Father arranges the fences perpendicularly. Father: "Now put a tree here. Good. Now give me the small rabbit." Yuval: "Where is the big rabbit? Shall I put the chicken here?"

Father: "Now I think the farmer will go to the girl who feeds the chickens." Child looks at what father does, moves over closer to father. He has stopped handling the figures.

In the session with his mother, Aviv first picks up the tractor and handles it for a longer period of time than any of the other objects. When Aviv's mother asks him what the tractor does, Aviv's answer shows that he is familiar with his father's occupation. Aviv's fascination with the tractor may also indicate his identification with this part of the father's life. On his afternoon visit to his parents Aviv often asks the father to walk with him to the fields where the father works.

As in the puppet situation, the stimulating role of Yuval's mother as well as Yuval's attempt to free himself from her constraints is again manifest. When he tries to hold onto the box, his mother briefly gives in to his wish for autonomy. Soon, however, she takes the lead by arranging the figures and directing Yuval's moves.

As she did in the puppet task, Aviv's mother makes only a few suggestions. She does not enter into Aviv's activities.

Both Aviv's and Yuval's fathers occasionally suggest how their sons should proceed. But Aviv's father more often leaves the initiative to Aviv and rarely handles a piece, while Yuval's father takes an active part in placing the figures.

The stimulation and assistance provided by Yuval's and other city parents in this and the previous task may have something to do with the parents' wish for the children's achievement. Individual achievement is more highly valued by city parents than by parents of the kibbutz [22:277-278].

Group B

As Yuval's parents had done, the other city parents give more actual assistance in this situation than do the kibbutz parents. Sixteen city parents begin by setting up the scene themselves. This occurs only twice in the kibbutz sessions, viz., in the sessions of Dror and Eilon with their mothers (see below). The city parents sometimes dramatize their production—e.g., "The soldier is watching so the wolves won't get to the cow." Occasionally the child is asked to add to the parents' scene: "Put all the animals inside the fence." The city children seem to get some satisfaction from watching their parents play like children. One boy asks his father to go on without him. Another tells his mother: "I don't know how to do it. *You* can play with it." Most kibbutz parents let their children set up the figures by themselves but make some vague suggestions, as for example, "Maybe you'd like to find another rabbit." However, the mother of Dror, an outgoing, self-assertive boy, sets up the scene by herself, although she must know that Dror is capable of doing it alone. She says in her interview that she sometimes can not refrain from doing things for her son as if he were still a baby. Other kibbutz parents encourage the child's autonomy more directly; "You fix them the way you want." "Let's see what you can do with the fence." One father underplays his own proficiency, saying: "How does one set it up? Show me."

David's father again gives more detailed directions to his son than do the other kibbutz fathers, e.g., to put all the animals inside the fence, to arrange the trees so that the animals could not get out. David responds to his father's request by saying: "I think it is a little too hard, isn't it, father?" Father: "Maybe."

As mentioned earlier, the playthings during this and the preceding tasks remind some parents, in all three groups, of incidents in the child's past. The kibbutz parents and metaplot recall experiences in their own kibbutz or in other kibbutzim they visit: "Don't you remember you saw a rabbit just like this one?" Both in the kibbutz and in the city the adults refer to stories they have read to the child: "Remember what the horse told the animals in the book?" The city parents remind their children of movies they had seen together, of a trip to the zoo, a scene on the street where a bus was loading people. The city children and their parents refer to the human figures as "man" and "girl" and "woman" while the kibbutz members frequently refer to them as "friends" (chaverim).

Both the kibbutz child, Aviv, and the city child, Yuval, place the three soldiers in a "guarding position." Similar responses to the soldier figures are made by other children of both the kibbutz and the city groups. Two statements about the soldier figures are relevant here: the remark by Eilon's mother to her son about the father coming home on leave (see below); and the statement by a father of the city group, explaining to his son his duty as a soldier:

Father:	Do you know what this is, Ezra?
Child:	What?
Father:	It's a soldier who is looking for mines. You see, this is what I do in the army.
Child:	When someone else finds mines, does he call you?
Father:	I discover the mines, not someone else. But if someone else does, yes, he calls me.

The reactions to the soldier figures in both kibbutz and city families bring into focus the body of common life experiences shared by city- and kibbutz-reared children. The threat of war and, since most fathers are soldiers in reserve, the danger to the father's life are apt to create similar fears and anxieties in children of both subcultures.

The kibbutz parents question their children more often about the names of the figures than do the city parents. That the kibbutz parents are interested in their children's verbal knowledge may be attributed to the high respect for knowledge in the kibbutz. Kibbutz members have been said to be insatiable in regard to knowledge. They are described as among the "most rewarding pupils to teach" [13:327]. The kibbutz parents may then welcome an opportunity to relish their child's verbal skill.

The metaplot participate more in this task than they do in the puppet situation, which calls for less foresight and planning and leaves more leeway to fantasy creations. In the puppet task, the metaplot may be avoiding intrusion into the children's creativity, which is highly respected in kibbutz society [13:327].

The metaplot occasionally tell the children more explicitly than do the kibbutz parents how to arrange the miniature environment. They may be reacting as they do in their daily contacts with the children when they give them directions as to how to use practical objects or how to fit pieces of playthings together and, on a conceptual plane, when they help them to connect their random thoughts.

The metaplot do not question the children about their knowledge of the animals, of which the metaplot are, probably, sure.

Only Zev, the youngest child in his kibbutz group, is asked by his metapelet for the names of some of the figures and what they are doing. The slow manner in which she questions him suggests that she wants him to understand what the figures represent.

The tendency of kibbutz children to refer to the human figures as *chaverim*, literally "friends," which is used in reference to all kibbutz members, signifies familiarity with a number of adults with whom they come in friendly contact throughout the day. According to our observations in the Children's House, adults typically express parental attitudes to children other than their own, and the children show also their intimacy with the adults.

Aviv's mother comes to visit him. While she holds him on her knee, Vedred and Cigal come and lean against her.

Vedred's grandmother comes into the yard and all the children crowd around her.

Yigael falls and cries. Vedred's mother happens to pass by the playground. She lifts Yigael up and kisses him.

When Gil's father leaves early at the social gathering on the Sabbath, Hadar's mother, who sits next to Gil, strokes his hair and comforts him.

Group C

In this situation, the city child, Zoor, again reacts negatively toward his mother. His mother talks about the figures while she arranges them, trying to interest Zoor: "Here is the small tree, here is another small tree, here is a girl, and here is a man. Here is a fence and here is a cow. What sound does the cow make?"

Zoor does not respond. She asks him to stand the cow up. Zoor answers: "I don't want." As she did earlier, the mother repeats his words. He pushes over the figures which his mother had set up. When she asks him to put things back in the box, he refuses to do so in a whiny tone, and sucks his finger.

In the session with his father, Zoor also refuses to play with the figures. However, a dialogue between father and child does develop. Father handles a toy car, one of the objects included in the box:

Father: You remember yesterday? There were tourists that we saw. What color was the bus of tourists that you wanted to see?
Child: Which one?
Father: The one we saw last night.
Child: The one in the street? Kind of red?
Father: Yes, this car looks like the bus with tourists.
Child: Here you go up and here you sit down.
Father: Right. Where does the driver sit?
Child: Up.

In his session with his mother, Itai—the other city child who responds negatively to his mother—looks briefly in the box, handles one figure a little, then pushes all the figures to his mother's side.

In his father's session, Itai does not set up the figures (although his father urges him to do so), but handles a few, smiling and obviously interested. Itai watches his father set up the scene. The father says: "I seem to enjoy it more than my son."

The climate of the interaction between Eilon and his mother is best conveyed by quoting their dialogue. (The observer's notes are in brackets.)

Mother: Try to make it stand up. [Child tries but does not succeed in making the gate stand up.] Never mind, take another one. Look at the animals.
Child: No, I want another one.
Mother: What's here?
Child: What is it?
Mother: It's a soldier. Do you remember when father came home on leave he had a gun in his hand? This soldier also has a gun.
Child: I want another soldier.
Mother: I can't find one. Here, take the farmers's wife who feeds the chicken.
Child: I want a drink.
Mother: What do you want?
Child: Juice. [Mother comes back with juice.] I want presents [motions to the other toys for the session]
Mother: What presents do you want? Here is the other soldier.
Child: What is this? [Mother sets up the figures, constructs a scene. The child has not handled any of the figures.]
Mother: Here is the horse, inside the gate.

Child:	Why?
Mother:	Because the horse likes to be inside the gate. What is this?
Child:	Another chicken.
Mother:	No, it's a goose. Now let's put all the animals inside the gate. The farmer girl gives them food to eat. Let's put her here. Here she comes to feed the animals. Now are you going to put the animals back into the box?
Child:	No, I don't want to.
Mother:	Yes, you are going to do this all by yourself. [Child does not move. Mother puts the objects into the box. Child has not touched any of them. Child sits away from mother.]

The following notes refer to Eilon's session with his father:

Eilon handles some figures. He asks for the rabbit. He wants certain figures, contradicts father. Wants the box to play with. He tries to join two fences and asks father to help him. They do it together. The father shows him how to stand the tree upright and Eilon succeeds, but he does not set up the scene. Father pats him. Eilon wants a drink and gets it. Father puts the figures away.

This is the interaction between the metapelet, Dahlia, and Eilon:

Child smiles when he sees the figures. Both smile. Child smiles while handling the gate. Metapelet does not touch any figures. Child sets up gate, takes tractor, talks in a high voice, sets up all figures by himself, shows her his scene. Metapelet asks him about the figures he did not use. He moves the tractor. He asks about soldier with goggles. She answers. He takes a tree, asks about a fence, "What's this?" He puts the deer outside the gate where the soldier stands. His movements slow down. He seems to think. Puts the goose near the milkmaid. Asks about the farmer. Rests his head on his hand. Seems to get tired.

As in the puppet situation, Zoor's mother does not succeed in changing Zoor's mood by verbally arousing him and making him participate. Zoor's father, in contrast, shows some empathy when he reminds Zoor of a recent, pleasurable outing. This recollection facilitates a scanty verbal exchange between father and son.

Itai's father, but not his mother, succeeds in interesting Itai in the toy figures. The father's childlike enjoyment of the play may create in Itai a new image of his father, different from that of a serious, demanding parent. Watching the father play with the figures may then be more gratifying for Itai than playing with the figures himself. We noticed a similar reaction in Aviv toward his father in the puppet situation. However, the handling of the puppets was initiated by Aviv and involved both father and son in close, affectionate contact.

In the present situation Eilon's mother is more controlling and strict than in the puppet situation, yet she easily yields to Eilon's requests. Hostility between mother and son, less tangible earlier, comes to the fore at the end of the task. Eilon's outspoken and demanding attitude reflects a different approach to his mother than the passivity we observed before. He reveals here more openly that he has a need for nurturing by his mother (he wants: "another soldier," "a drink," "presents"). On the other hand, he might also need to express his own will. Yet the mother does not encourage his initiative. She sets up the figures by herself. The nonaffectionate, somewhat brusque, dialogue differs from that in other parent-child pairs, especially the ones in the kibbutz. The mother's relationship with Eilon is probably aggravated by her general dissatisfaction with her life in the kibbutz. Unhappy in two other kibbutzim (including the one in which she grew up), she has not found a fulfilling existence in Gan She'Arim either.

While Eilon's mother has not been able to accept the restrictions of a kibbutz mother, Zoor's mother resents the responsibilities of a mother in the middle-class urban culture. Although their cultures differ strongly, they are similar in their relation to their child. The maternal feelings and intimacy with their children suffer because of their own conflicts and frustrations. Both mothers are unable to provide genuine, unconditional affection and adequate direction. Moreover, neither Eilon's nor Zoor's father is able to compensate, through his relationship with his son, for the lack of affectionate, intimate responses from the mothers.

Eilon, however, has the advantage of his relationship with his caretaker. It has been pointed out that in the kibbutz the metapelet serves a beneficial function in counteracting any deficiency of mothering through her influence on the child. Dahlia's interaction with Eilon in the above situation presents a vivid example of such "corrective emotional influence" [19:208, 215]. In his contact with Dahlia, Eilon appears as a different, stronger, happier, and more cooperative child than he does with his mother. In the above MIM situation, his organizing of the miniature environment is careful and productive. He is obviously affected by Dahlia's warm, understanding, and purposeful guidance.

One can infer from Eilon's interaction with Dahlia that he has begun to form an identification with her. He also retains his original identification with his parents, however, as his behavior toward each of them in the preceding situation indicates. The way in which he reflects each parent's attitudes suggests that he has incorporated characteristics of both parents.

Separation: The Adult Leaves the Room.

After leaving, the adult returns after three minutes and takes the child on his or her lap. As in our observations of Paul and Jerry (Chapter 2), this situation brings into sharper focus the quality of the emotional tie between parent and child. The responses to the separation are of particular significance in kibbutz families. The policy of separating children from their parents at night as well as providing communal child care during the day was initiated in the pioneer phase of the kibbutz movement in order to free mothers for the workloads of colonization which were to be equally shared by men and women. The first generation of settlers believed that marriage, family, and inequality of women were bourgeois residuals which would interfere with building a new, "free society." As one pioneer woman stated it:

We came here to work, conquer the new life and the country. I refused to learn the job of nurse because it would have removed me from the people with whom I wanted to build the country, to conquer it with my own hands [25:81].

In the next generation, which benefited from the settlers' successful adaptation to most severe conditions, the concern for the basic necessities gave way to a sense of "rootedness and permanence" [13:22]. From the 1920s on, the value of the family as an "emotional refuge for the individual" [15:33] again began to be recognized. Over the following decades, the idea of integrating the nuclear family into kibbutz society gained ground, and the arrangement by which small children sleep away from their parents in the Children's House became a focus of discussion. The issue is still debated among present kibbutz parents and educators. The large Artzi movement, to which both the kibbutzim studied here belong, favors the children's overnight stay in the Children's House for ideological reasons. The parents emphasized in their interviews that this arrangement makes it possible for the children to adapt to communal living and practice consideration within the group from an early age on. But, they also stressed that close family relationships are of crucial importance in the kibbutz.

Aviv's mother is particularly outspoken about the need for the mother's daily visits to the Children's House so as to be with her child at least for half an hour. In the intimate, but not intrusive, mother-child relationship she sees a protection against the pain of the daily separation. Her attitude may have something to do with her own developmental history. Her mother was among the first kibbutz women who seriously questioned the demand for equality of sexes built into the kibbutz system. These women recognized the importance of specific female roles, especially that of mother. Aviv's mother became even more convinced of the need for closeness of mother and child. This was evident in her intimate relationship with Aviv during her visits to the Children's House (see below).

From observing the parents' responses when leaving the Children's House in the evening, moments which include both tenderness and anxiety, one understands why some more individualistic kibbutzim are in favor of keeping the small child at home overnight and why they emphasize both the child's and the mother's need for physical and emotional closeness at the child's bedtime.

The task where the parent leaves the room was performed by kibbutz and city families as follows:

Group A
Aviv, the kibbutz child, and his mother.

The mother says quietly, "Wait just a minute. Mother will be back soon." As Aviv watches his mother walk away, his lips form the word "Ima" (mother). He calls her several times. Then Aviv begins to cry.

When his mother returns, Aviv calms down. But he begins to cry anew. Held close to her body, his crying increases. Aviv's mother tries to comfort him.

Aviv and his father.

Aviv's father leaves the room, walking erectly. Aviv pays little attention. Instead, he explores the various things he can do with the envelope left on the table. He pounds on it, tries to put his hand inside, flattens it with both hands, folds it and rolls it. When his father returns, they examine the envelope together.

Aviv and his metapelet, Dahlia.

The metapelet says, "Now wait for me. I'll come back soon. Wait here." Aviv's expression hardly changes. The only sign of tension is a slight pursing of his lips. When the metapelet returns, Aviv shows little emotion.

Yuval, the city child, and his mother.

Yuval's mother gets up and bends down to Yuval. She makes various excuses, but he says he doesn't want her to leave. When she does, Yuval looks after her longingly. Then he calls her and finally goes to find her. She seems relieved to be brought back.

Yuval and his father.

Yuval's father gets up, bends down, and talks to Yuval. When his father has left, Yuval seems to occupy himself with his thoughts and feelings. He rests his head on his palms, his elbows on the table. He talks to himself, scratches his ear, looks at father's chair, forms a circle with two fingers. Again, he rests his head on both hands. His tongue moves, he talks to himself, looks to the side, remains quiet.

Group B
The other kibbutz children did not respond to the mother leaving with prolonged crying as did Aviv. They did, however, show some signs of restlessness and irritation, including whining. Here are examples of their behavior:

When his mother leaves, David remains quiet for about a minute, sucking his finger. His mood changes and he throws an object down and steps on it.

When Yigael's mother gets up to leave, Yigael complains in a whining tone: "I don't want to sit here."

Zev shouts "No" when his mother gets up to leave. He grabs his mother's hand and holds it. The mother does not resist and stays.

Dror, physically strong and mentally advanced, reacts in a peculiar fashion when his mother announces that she will leave. He says loudly and somewhat aggressively: "Yes, mother, go!"

The city children rarely show discomposure to the extent observed in the kibbutz children. However, the city mothers tend to "buffer" their departure with lengthy explanations. The city children's emotional dependence on their mothers manifests itself in trying to talk their mothers into staying or asking her why and where she has to go. This sometimes leads to a lengthy argument of the following kind:

Mother: I'm going to look at something in the kitchen.
Child: I don't want you to.
Mother: I'm coming back soon. I'll buy you candy.
Child: I don't want candy.
Mother: Why? Oh, I have a coffee pot on the stove. It will burn.
Child: I don't want you to leave.
Mother: Then I'll just go out and see who is at the door and I'll come right back, O.K.?
Child: O.K.

One city child demands substitute gratification ("Give me more things to play"). Half of the city children and none of the kibbutz children go out to bring their mother back.

In a study by Eleanor Maccoby and S. Shirley Feldman on separation responses published in 1972, two-and-a-half-year-old kibbutz children were compared with U.S. children of the same age as to their behavior during their mothers' three-minute absence [16]. Among other findings, there was no significant difference between the kibbutz- and the city-reared children in the frequency of crying during the mother's absence [16:76]. This finding corresponds, on the whole, to the relative frequency of crying when alone as observed in our two groups. However, in contrast to our findings Maccoby and Feldman found no difference in the frequency of "upset" responses of any kind between kibbutz and city children in the mother's absence. It is possible that the discrepancy between the findings is due to the method applied here of paying attention not only to prearranged, but also to novel, unforeseen behavioral expressions, relevant to the behavior under study. Dror's reaction when the mother leaves is an example of such unforeseeable, yet relevant behavior.

On the occasion when the fathers leave the room, four of the eight city children, and only two of the seven kibbutz children, David and Yigael, feel free to terminate the separation themselves by bringing the father back.

David objects when his father tells him he is going to leave. In contrast to his upset behavior during his mother's absence, David is quiet after his father has left. He lowers his head to the table, utters sounds like "rrrr, prrrr," and becomes sleepy. Yigael, who objected when his mother left, remains calm when his father leaves the room. He makes "chirping" sounds, reclines on the chair, straightens out the cover of the couch next to him. Finally he, too, goes out to get his father.

For the city children, as for the kibbutz children, the separation from the father seems to be upsetting only when the child is under stress for other reasons. When this is not the case, the city children, after an initial period of discomfort, either terminate the separation on their own, or occupy themselves in some way—for example by making overtures to the observers. (The responses of the kibbutz children to the father's absence are described below.)

Most kibbutz children remain undisturbed by the separation from the metapelet, as illustrated by the following observations:

Dror: Stays quiet, his hands rest on the table.

Zev: Looks around, chews on a piece of string. Sits quietly, becomes dreamy.

Shemuel: Yawns, sits quietly, sleepy expression. Looks to window, no movement. Comes over, looks at the recorder, goes back sits quietly.

David: Lies on couch, finger in mouth, sleepy, slowly taps couch with heel.

Only one child, Yigael, follows his metapelet and tries to bring her back. But he returns by himself. However, the metapelet's way of preparing the child for the separation differs somewhat from the way the kibbutz and city parents introduce the task. The metapelet is more determined to enlist the child's cooperation than are the parents. This is illustrated by the mother's and the metapelet's contrasting approaches toward Zev.

Metapelet:	Zevy, I'm going out for a while and you will wait for me? Yes? Zevy, answer me. I'm going to leave.
Zev:	[Starts to whine, murmurs something.]
Metapelet:	I'll be back soon, okay? Answer me. [She repeats her question two more times until he nods in agreement. She goes out and he stays.]
Zev's mother:	Now, mother goes out and you'll stay here. Mother will go out and come back, O.K.?
Zev [*Loudly*]:	Nooooo. [He holds on to his mother (see above)].

The difference between the children's responses to separation from the mother and from the metapelet corresponds to the difference between both maternal figures as described by an expert on kibbutz education: "[the] difference in the child's relation to the two maternal images lies in the intensity of his emotional relationships. He is more intense to the mother for better or worse" [14:265].

One incidental observation points to a difference between the behavior of city children and that of kibbutz children toward the unfamiliar adult. Throughout the sessions the observers, in accord with their instructions, refrained from *initiating* any communication with the child, although they could respond briefly if the child addressed them. When the parent left the room, the city children often made a deliberate "social overture" to the observer. They would ask questions, hum, sing, clown, or in some manner try to elicit a response. In contrast, most kibbutz children abstained from social overtures; they waited quietly, moved around, "acted out" their momentary frustration, or occupied themselves with some activity, seemingly undisturbed by the observer. This difference between kibbutz and city children was also observed by Maccoby and Feldman, who reported a higher frequency of friendly interaction with "strangers" among the American middle class as compared with the kibbutz children in their study. They concluded that the American middle-class children (comparable to the Israeli city children in the present investigation) show less anxiety with strangers than do kibbutz children because they have more opportunity to meet strangers.

However, the city children's frequent approaches to the observer could have a quite opposite explanation. They could be seen as an attempt to counteract a certain anxiety with strangers, which would not be characteristic of kibbutz children. The following observation was made in a study on child care in Israel:

To the child in the conventional setting, most people, except those in his immediate family, are total strangers. The kibbutz infant, in contrast, becomes acquainted with many people other than family and caretakers, since they appear regularly in his surroundings [8:44].

Moreover, *chaverim* (friends) is often used by kibbutz children with reference to the adults they meet, whether they are members of the kibbutz or outsiders. Thus, the author and her assistant were also referred to by kibbutz children as *chaverim*.

A number of authors have emphasized the strong attachment of the young kibbutz child to his mother. They attribute it to the extensive time the mother spends with her infant during the first months of life as contrasted with the limitation on time spent together from later infancy on.[15:52, 61-62]. It has also been said that the fact that the metapelet, not the parents, makes the demands and imposes restrictions, strengthens the emotional tie to the parents [14:267-268]. The relationship between the kibbutz child and both parents has been described as reflecting "strong ties," and "depth of intimacy" [22:281].

The assumption that the kibbutz child, like the family-raised child, forms his most decisive emotional relationships with his parents is supported by clinical findings about the etiology of emotional disturbance in kibbutz children and family-reared children. Schmuel Nagler found that disturbed marital relations and adjustment difficulties of the parents were the major cause of the children's disturbance in both groups of children. [20:311].

Other investigators have concluded, on the contrary, that there is a lack of emotional depth in the kibbutz child's attachment to his parents as compared with that of the family-reared child. They argue that from an early age, the child forms affective ties, not only with his parents, but with other kibbutz members, in particular, with his peer group. The following conclusions have been drawn: In the kibbutz family, attachments and ambivalences are less intense than in the ordinary family situation" [21:208]. "Despite some exceptions [a kibbutz child's] emotional involvement with his parents and along with it his attachment, both positive and negative, is much less intense than that of the average middle-class American child" [3:125]. According to these authors, the limited time spent together by children and parents is not sufficient to form a strong affectionate bond, and in addition the emotional bond to the peer group contributes to a "diffusion of attachment" [21:143].

Our observations during the induced separation of mother and child are at variance with the view that the child's relationship with the parent is less intense in the kibbutz than in the city family. Instead, the children's behavior in the mother's absence reflected their strong attachment to the mother. Moreover, mutual expressions of affection and tenderness were also observed in mothers and children at the mothers' daily visit to the Children's House. Aviv and his mother, for example, reveal the closeness of their relationship on these occasions. When she visits the Children's House, Aviv's mother asks Aviv what he has done in the morning. He often suggests what they should do together, that she should read him a story or look at his drawings. At one of her visits, Aviv gets hold of a toy iron and "irons" his mother's skirt. Occasionally, mother visits Aviv in the middle of the day, before nap time, and tucks him in. Mother and child thus tend to create intimate, family-like situations within the group setting. Aviv's strong affectionate attachment to his mother is further indicated in the following episode:

Aviv cries because a child has taken a toy from him. His crying increases and he calls for his mother. The metapelet puts her hand on his shoulder and tells him to try to calm down. He becomes quieter, sits by the table and whispers "Ima" [mother].

It is relevant to mention, finally, that the close attachment of mothers to their children is emphasized by both kibbutz and city mothers. Yuval's mother comments about the importance of the mother to her young child as follows:"It is necessary that the mother is there when the child comes home from nursery school so that he can tell her all that has happened. The mother is the closest person to the child." And Aviv's mother says that the possibility of visiting her child whenever she wishes is most important to her.

Group C

Eilon reacts with indifference to the separation from his mother. He displays a "dreamy," seemingly relaxed mood. His behavior is in sharp contrast to the sadness or restlessness expressed by other kibbutz children when separated from their mothers. Expressions of indifference and apparent relaxation in this situation were also noticed in the group of emotionally disturbed boys in the Los Angeles study mentioned earlier. In both cases, these reactions may be due to conflicts in the parent-child relationship which, according to Nagler, affects kibbutz-reared and city-reared children similarly (see above).

When Eilon's father is leaving, Eilon shouts:"Good-bye, father." These words may be an attempt to counteract both his dependence on his father and the pain of separation, not too different from Dror's words "Mother, go!" mentioned earlier. Eilon's as well as Dror's utterances may express strength of attachment similar to the "Go away" game of a small child, attributed by Freud to an impulse to achieve mastery over the pain of separation [6:145-147]. It will be remembered that Eilon's father has assumed a maternal role in his relation toward Eilon. He tucks him in at night and, in Eilon's words, "Father is for play." Eilon, in turn, is receptive to the father's concern for him. That Eilon has a need to express affection is indicated by an episode in the Children's House when he gently and protectively stroked a dog which had strayed into the yard and brought it water, while the other children kept a cautious distance. However, Eilon does not express attachment to his peers, and at the time of the study has not been fully accepted as part of the group, let alone befriended by any of his peers.

The metapelet reads the instruction card aloud to Eilon and asks him, "O.K.?" He nods his consent. While she is gone, he remains sitting quietly, undisturbed, one hand resting on the table. When the metapelet returns, they smile at each other.

Zoor, the city child, is silent when his mother tells him she will go out and be back soon. But when she starts to get up, Zoor begins to whine. For the rest of her absence, he sits on the floor, with his head leaning against his mother's chair.

Zoor's father goes out without giving Zoor a reason for his absence. Zoor immediately follows his father and brings him back.

Itai's mother tells her son gently: "I'll be back soon. You sit here, O.K.?" Itai, who had been negative and sulky earlier, now starts to cry. He holds his mother's hand and, while sobbing, repeats, "No." He leaves after his mother. She tries to persuade him to return to the table, but he holds onto her hand and makes her come back to him.

Itai's father tells his son that he has to go out to look at the mailbox and will be back soon. Itai remains quietly in his chair for a while, looks at the bag of toys, and smiles. Then he goes out to get his father.

While Zoor, similar to Eilon, shows hardly any distress at separation from his mother, Itai needs to restore the contact with his mother immediately. Although he relies on his mother's continuing attachment, her retreating from him during his spell of obstinacy must seem like punishment and he needs reassurance of her love through her physical presence. Zoor, in contrast, has no expectation of affectionate support from his mother. He remains in his previous downcast state seeking substitute comfort from his mother's chair. Zoor and Itai terminate their fathers' absence themselves, but Zoor is the more eager to do so. Itai's father shares some of his interests and ideas with his son. He provides Itai with a reason for his absence. This may make it possible for Itai to delay his impulse to follow his father immediately. Zoor's father, on the other hand, communicates less openly with his son. Zoor is given no incentive to delay his wish to retrieve his father and to continue their play activities.

"Take Your Child on Your Lap"

After the three-minute separation, the adult is asked to take the child on his or her lap. The situation is designed to bring out other facets of attachment: the affective responses elicited by the physical closeness of parent and child; the child's willingness to comply; the ease with which the parent is holding the child; the readiness of child and parent to regress to earlier phases of interaction.

In this situation, mothers and fathers tend to caress the child at least once by stroking, kissing, administering a joking slap, and so on. Not infrequently the child will also touch the parent, affectionately either in response to the parent or on his own initiative.

Group A
The following descriptions begin after the required separation:

Aviv and his mother.

Holding Aviv close to her body, his mother tries to comfort Aviv, genuinely concerned, by putting her arm around him and bringing her head close to his. She says: "There was nothing to be afraid of." She holds him in a baby position. His head rests on her arm. "Mother went out for just a minute, isn't that right?" His tears dry while she strokes him. She then consoles him by giving him something to eat.

Aviv and his father.

Aviv looks at his father while he approaches. The father sits down very close to Aviv, takes Aviv on his lap. He adjusts Aviv's position and Aviv complies easily. Father and child look into the envelope (which contained the instruction card). Aviv puts his hand on his father's, looks at him; they look at each other.

Aviv and the metapelet.

When the metapelet holds Aviv he shows little emotion. He sits comfortably on her lap. She moves his chin so that they face each other, but Aviv turns his head back.

Yuval and his mother.

Yuval's mother seems relieved to be brought back by her son. Pouting, Yuval refuses to sit on her lap. Mother offers a reward: "Come and sit on my lap and I shall tell you what kind of helicopter I'll get you." This promise and the physical closeness seem to lead to affectionate responses between mother and child.

Yuval and his father.

Yuval looks at his father while he approaches. Father bends down right away while he is sitting down. Father asks Yuval what Yuval did while he was away and Yuval shows him how he sat. "You sat like this, so patiently? Good boy!" When on father's lap, Yuval puts his hand on his father's neck spontaneously. Father puts his arm around Yuval. They talk. Their heads are close to each other. Yuval smiles, pats his father's face.

Groups A and B

With one exception, the kibbutz children easily consent to being held by their mothers or their fathers. Mother and child, in particular, seem to enjoy the unexpected opportunity for closeness and it sometimes triggers spontaneous expressions of attachment. (In their day-by-day contacts with their young children, kibbutz parents tend to restrain to some extent their expressions of affection, probably in order to ease the stress of separation at the end of the day). In contrast, sitting on the mother's lap leads less often to affectionate exchange between city mothers and their children, possibly because they have more opportunities in the course of a day for affectionate contact.

Dahlia's behavior to Aviv when she holds him on her lap is typical of the impartial, empathetic, and unemotional demeanor of the metaplot in most situations. In our study the metaplot were only rarely observed to hug or kiss a child or express tenderness. Similarly, the children did not normally show a need to initiate affectionate contact with the metaplot. The following incidents may illustrate the emotional climate of Dahlia's relationship with the children:

Dahlia picks up Aviv who has hurt his foot. She asks him in a concerned voice how it happened, and pats him.

She holds Shemuel, who looks sad when his father has left in the evening.

She tells Vedred and her father, who have a hard time separating, "I shall help you to separate." Dahlia succeeds by talking sensitively to Vendred, enlisting her help in a common chore (putting the benches away).

These attitudes of the metapelet have been described by an Israeli authority on kibbutz education as follows:". . . The young girls and women distinguish themselves by greater empathy and warm understanding of the problems of children. They themselves have grown up in communal education, and their behavior toward the children is often more quiet and less tense than that of educators of the first generation."[1:288].

Group C

Eilon does not refuse to be taken on his mother's lap. The mother, while holding him, tells a story, illustrating it with finger movements. Eilon's expression becomes softer when lifted by the mother. He listens with interest to the mother's tale. The physical closeness with her seems to have "melted," temporarily, his negative reactions, and a primitive satisfaction from being held by the mother seems to break through.

Zoor, in contrast, shows no reaction to being held by his mother. He remains low-spirited as before. Nor does holding her child on her lap induce any gesture of affection or change in communication on the part of Zoor's mother. It is possible that her habitual lack of responsiveness and his inner tension inhibit Zoor from taking the opportunity to satisfy whatever need he may have for infantile gratification.

Itai lets his mother take him on her lap, his face still expressing resentment. While sitting on his mother's lap, he calls "father" and goes out to find him, thus attempting to gain from his father the pleasure he really desires from his mother.

Modeling and Imitation

As described earlier, this task requires the child to copy a block structure built by the adult. The major differences between this situation and the previous ones are: that a definite goal is set, and that adult and child are given identical play objects.

As we saw earlier, these features of block-building tend to indicate (1) the child's ease of imitating—depending, for example, on such factors as skill and motivation; (2) the parent's ways of modeling; (3) the parent's reactions to being imitated; and (4) since parent and child both "own" the same material, parental attitudes about achievement and competitive strivings in the child.

In urban, nonsocialist societies individual achievement is valued and, as a result, competition between individuals is approved. In the kibbutz culture, on the other hand, individual achievement is favored only when it benefits the community (although in recent years, this principle is said to be adhered to less rigorously than in the past). Competition may be fostered between kibbutzim or between different units within one kibbutz, but it is not encouraged between individuals. Indeed, abstaining from competition and from striving for individual goals are among the important principles of kibbutz education. In a fictional description of kibbutz life, one boy introduces a "greenhorn" from the city into the kibbutz, saying:"We don't have marks like 'good,' 'satisfactory,' 'unsatisfactory.' It's only in the city that you learn that way. . . . here we all like to learn because we know it is necessary"[12:67-70].

It has been stated that in the kibbutz, where parental pressure to achieve and parental concern with the child's success are at a minimum, a freer relationship prevails between child and parent. This relationship is believed to facilitate self-assertive behavior and self-confidence in the child, characteristics particularly valued by kibbutz parents and educators.

Group A
Aviv, the kibbutz child, and his mother.

In making his building, Aviv more often refers to his mother than he does to the model. She guides him calmly when he does not succeed. She is not impatient. Aviv moves his structure, which is quite unlike his mother's, over close to hers. She asks him smilingly, "Does that look like mine?" Aviv removes the block from the top of mother's building and puts it on his own.

Aviv and his father.

Aviv and his father coordinate their movements. While father watches Aviv build, Aviv checks his own progress carefully against his father's. Father smiles, and Aviv looks at him. Aviv remembers how the blocks should go and finishes first. Father appears amused at this.

Aviv and his metapelet.

The metapelet gives Aviv detailed instructions and praises each successful step. When Aviv makes an error, she points it out and he corrects it. She makes it possible for him to finish the task successfully.

Yuval, the city child, and his mother.

Yuval looks at mother's building and tries to copy it, but he does not succeed. While Yuval stoops down to retrieve a fallen block, his mother corrects and almost completes his structure. She asks, "Whose tower is higher, do you think?" Yuval says, "Yours." She says, "I think they are the same. Let's see." Yuval's mother slides her structure toward his. Yuval moves his away and she follows until the two structures meet.

Yuval and his father.

Yuval's father says, "Listen, Yuvali. You'll have to look carefully at what I do. Now, I'm standing this one up. No, don't build yet, just look. The last part is going to be hard. Have a good look, and now you build." At first Yuval reaches for his father's blocks.

While building, Yuval asks, "Like this?" and "Is this right?" Father points out a mistake and says, "Shall I help you? I'll help you just once. This goes here and this goes here. And now, you finish it by yourself."

At the moment when Yuval has almost copied his father's design, Yuval's structure begins to topple. Expressing his defeat by an outward and upward movement of his arms, he destroys it altogether.

Groups A and B

The playful, affectionate interchange between Aviv and his mother, their looking and smiling at each other, suggests that neither of them is concerned with Aviv's success at imitating mother's building. That Aviv moves his structure close to his mother's and adds one of her blocks to his building might signify his attachment to his mother. A slightly different version of this act has been observed in other children who move their building close to the model, remove their own highest block and add it to the top of the model. This sequence we have called "dedication gesture" (see also p. 103). It seems to express a wish for giving something of one's self to the adult. Aviv's movement seems to show his confidence that his mother wants to share with him what she has.

The dedication gesture in the block situation occurred most often between the kibbutz children and their parents (five out of fourteen sessions), less often between city children and their parents (three out of sixteen sessions), and only one in relation to a metapelet. The slightly higher incidence of this gesture in kibbutz as compared with city children may be due both to the intensity of attachment of child and parent in the kibbutz as discussed earlier, and to the communal emphasis on sharing (see below). Viewing intense attachment to parents as "underlying" the dedication gesture seems to be confirmed by the near absence of this behavior in the sessions with the metapelet.

Aviv accomplishes the building task in his father's presence by allying himself closely with his father and moving the blocks almost simultaneously with him. His father does not provide precise verbal instruction, nor does he praise Aviv, but their interaction is warm and friendly.

Yuval's interaction with his mother, in contrast, becomes a competitive game. In the city group, but not in the kibbutz group, a child occasionally tries to accumulate more than his share of blocks. The following excerpts illustrate this tendency: "Child takes some of mother's blocks. Does not want to let go. Mother firmly takes them away." "Child takes blocks from father." "Father tries to take blocks he needs from child. Child holds arms around his heap of blocks. Father: 'Give me some.' Child: 'No. They are mine.' "

The city parents tend to give their children detailed, systematic instructions right away, and to provide more frequent verbal and manual assistance during the procedure than do either the kibbutz parents or the metapelet. Only one kibbutz father (David's father) and one kibbutz mother (Dror's mother) introduce the task in a similar systematic fashion.

The father of the kibbutz child David, having previously expressed his ambition for his child's accomplishments, gives David somewhat anxiously detailed instructions as to how to proceed. David follows them and completes the task.

David does not imitate his mother's model. He builds his own structure instead and then adds one of his blocks to his mother's ("dedication gesture").

The mother of Dror, the strong, self-reliant kibbutz boy, changes from leaving the initiative to Dror ("Now you do whatever you feel like doing") to exerting control ("You didn't look carefully when I built. See whether you can do exactly what I do"). She applauds each of his successful moves.

Yet, in the father's session, Dror takes the lead from the very beginning. He distributes half of the blocks to his father, keeps the other half for himself, and provides his father with guidelines: "This must lie down, and this must lie down, and this must stand up." His father smilingly lets himself be led by his son.

Most kibbutz parents praise their child's structure regardless of whether or not he has imitated the parents' model correctly. Neither the city parents nor the metapelet praise the child if the imitation is incorrect.

The noncompetitive, nonthreatened attitudes of kibbutz parents and metapelet during the block-building task, as compared with the more tense, task-oriented behavior shown by the city parents, would seem to mirror in miniature form some major values in both subcultures. Both the metapelet and the kibbutz parents emphasize developing the child's sense of cooperation. The metapelet, Dahlia, says in her interview: "Most children are very close to each other. In certain cases, they help each other. They are mostly able to resolve a quarrel by themselves."

To Eilon, who occupies too much space in the wading pool, Dahlia says, "Eilon, you want the other children also to have fun in the wading pool, don't you?" This incident suggests that sharing is not always voluntary; as in other preschool groups, sharing is taught by adults and may give way to quarrels.

As illustrated in the following observation, cooperation can be developed to a considerable extent at the three- and four-year level: Dahlia gives Vedred a box with plastelline. Vedred brings it to the table. All of the children crowd around her, wanting some. Vedred distributes equal chunks to each child and to herself."[2]

Group C

Both Eilon's and Zoor's mothers are able to persuade their sons to try to imitate their model.

Eilon's mother makes Eilon comply by first praising him when he builds a structure of his own ("I didn't know you can build so well"), then encouraging him to imitate hers. Zoor's mother succeeds in making Zoor attempt to imitate by assuming a firm attitude. When he wants her blocks and tells her, "You took all the blocks away. So I take them all away from you," his mother resists, explaining to him, in a definitive tone of voice, what the instruction says. Zoor begins to imitate. But his cooperative mood lasts only a short time. Even while he is building, he responds to whatever suggestion his mother makes with "I don't want to." He gets whiny and does not complete the structure, nor does he want his blocks to be put away. Reinforced by his mother's praising and patting him, Eilon imitates her structure with just one error. As he builds he belittles his progress ("It's going to fall").

Eilon shows here a behavior markedly different from the negativism toward his mother which he displays in other interaction situations. He even moves his structure so that it is flush with his mother's and puts his highest block on her tower. The mother's initial confirmation of his right to build his own structure may account for the change in Eilon's mood, however transient it may be. Possibly gratified by his replicating her, the mother also responds more positively to Eilon in this situation than she does in others.

Eilon does not make the dedication gesture in his session with the metapelet, although he imitates the structure correctly.

In their sessions with their fathers, both Eilon and Zoor refuse to imitate the fathers' buildings and build their own structures. Zoor engages in the same competitive effort with his father as he does with his mother. His father, however, in contrast to his mother, lets him have all his (the father's) blocks as well as his own.

Stress

The difficult jigsaw puzzle described earlier (Chapter 2) elicits the parents' and the child's behavior under stress. But it also brings out attitudes about achievement, i.e., the emotional effort in achieving a goal. Thus the differences in attitudes between kibbutz and city families resembled those during the building task. The city child received more often help from both parents than did the kibbutz child. The kibbutz mothers assumed a more playful attitude than did the city mothers who showed, in their comments and facial expressions, anxiety about the child's moves. Here are a few comments made by kibbutz mothers about the jigsaw puzzle dog:

"If you don't finish the dog, he won't be able to eat the bone." "What's the dog's name?" "What do you want to call him?" "The dog is cold. So we have to put a piece next to him."

Both the city fathers and the metaplot tried to introduce the difficult task systematically. One metapelet was more successful than the other two metaplot in eliciting the children's interest and serious effort. She asked the child for his plan and, if necessary, alerted him to its difficulties. But she rarely took part in the task herself. The difference between her attitude and that of the other metapelet points once more to the role which the individuality of the metapelet might play in the child's development, even in an educational system so uniform as that of the kibbutz.

The differences observed between city and kibbutz parents both during the block building and in the puzzle task suggest that already at preschool age individual achievement is valued more highly by the former than by the latter.[3]

As in any culture or subculture, the specific attitudes toward individual accomplishment are built into the respective educational systems. Even early in life these attitudes affect the child's conception of human relationships. They are transmitted by the adult to the child through gestures, words, and spontaneous reactions like the competitive game initiated by Yuval's mother when she moves her block structure close to his, saying, "Which one is higher, do you think? Let's try." The laissez-faire attitude of Aviv's mother, in contrast, is transmitted to her son through her teasing and playfulness when she asks him about his imitation of her building, "Does this look like mine?"

Parental attitudes are further transmitted to children through the parents' preference for their leisure-time activities. When Aviv's father is asked what he likes to do when he and his son are together, he says, "Walking, swimming, driving a car." Yuval's father answers the same question by saying he likes to play dominoes or quartett with Yuval—both games that involve competition.

CONCLUSIONS

The observations of child-adult interactions in the kibbutz and in the city families have broadened our view on the identification process. It has become plausible that the child's identification with the parental culture is enhanced by the parents' perception of the child as a member of their culture. It is further likely that the kibbutz child, through frequent and intimate interactions with the metapelet, forms an additional, though less intense identification with an adult. Moreover, the observations of young kibbutz children in their peer group suggest that the kibbutz child develops strong identifications with his age mates.[4]

The city parents perceive their children (in accordance with their cultural norms) as inclined toward intellectual achievement and individual success and, perhaps, toward competitive effort. They further perceive them as dependent on parental direction and affection, and on parental protection even in situations of minor stress.

The kibbutz parents, on the other hand, transmit to their children their perception of them as not being particularly interested in intellectual matters, competition, and individual success. They also perceive their children as being independent to a considerable degree and as capable of coping with minor stress by themselves.

However, the most crucial difference between the city and the kibbutz parents' is reflected in their expectations of their children's solidarity with their wider group as compared with that to their family. Although both city and kibbutz parents expect their children to be close and loyal to their families, the city parents transmit to their children their pride in Israel as an urbanized society with a wide range of cultural, technical and educational possibilities and a variety of opportunities for an able and energetic young adult to succeed. The image of their child which the kibbutz parents convey to him is that of a responsible and contributing member of the kibbutz society, even at a young age. Since the metapelet has grown up in the kibbutz, and since she is chosen for her job by the education committee to which the parents also belong, her perception of the child as a loyal member of the kibbutz society closely resembles that of the parents.

The sense of solidarity with the group, rooted in childhood, remains an important part of the adult personality. This solidarity is demonstrated in reports of kibbutz members as soldiers and officers and as pioneers in frontier settlements. (The large proportion of war casualties among kibbutz members in the 1967 war has been explained by the fact that kibbutz soliders more frequently than others attempted to rescue comrades [2].)

It is obvious that group cohesion and group solidarity is heightened in a close community of small size, in a tranquil environment, and through a shared economy which virtually frees the individual from preoccupation with the fulfillment of basic needs. Yet, like the rural part of any society, the kibbutz buys its tranquility and predictability at the price of less stimulation and less diversity of interests.

In contrast, the abundance of stimulation and choices as well as the dehumanizing influence of the urban environment has often been held responsible for the tensions and conflicts, i.e., for the lack of solidarity between the frequently interacting and mutually dependent members of the nuclear family. At the same time, it must be realized that the isolation of the small urban family places the full responsibility for the young child's physical and emotional development on his parents. In the kibbutz, the young child's affectionate relationship is most intense with his parents while responsibility for direction giving and discipline is vested in the metapelet.

The kibbutz alternative, ideal as it might be, could not be duplicated in urban living. The physical rootedness, the sense of permanence, and the deep association with a particular social group and its history could not realistically be expected to develop in an urban setting. However, the assumption that the child's identification, resulting in the adult's self-confidence and maturity of character, could arise only from the close, affectionate mutuality of the nuclear family, will have to take into account the self-assuredness and maturity of the kibbutz-reared adult.

NOTES

[1] The information on kibbutz child rearing is partly derived from Shapira [23] and Gewirtz [8], and partly from A. Jarus et al. (Eds.), *Children and Families in Israel*. New York: Gordon and Breach, 1970.

[2] Apart from the adults' influence, a group of children who live in close contact with each other and are in the charge of competent caretakers seem to generate more mature social attitudes than is typical for other children of the same age. Anna Freud writes about six young children, Nazi victims, placed in an English foster home: "On walks they were concerned for each other's safety in traffic, looked after children who lagged behind, helped each other over ditches." [5:126]. A group of Headstart children who had just entered school behaved similarly: "On field trips, they stayed close to each other, took care of each other. They treated the retarded boy as if he were their responsibility; they comforted him, caressed him" [17:20].

[3] Results on standard exams which tapped motivation for individual achievement have shown that kibbutz pupils fall behind family-reared pupils. The difference has been attributed to the lower motivation toward scholastic achievement in the kibbutz as compared with the nonkibbutz group. It has been said that the kibbutz approves of a "pupil- and group-centered method of teaching, not overridden by skill training, not dominated by examinations" [22:275-76].

[4] That the kibbutz child patterns himself after the norms of behavior prevailing in his peer group was suggested, among other incidents, by the observation that one group of children in speaking of themselves used first names while another group of the same age, housed only a short distance away, used "I."

REFERENCES

1. Alon, M. The child and his family in the kibbutz: Second generation. In A. Jarus et al. (Eds.), *Children and Families in Israel*. New York: Gordon and Breach, 1970.
2. Bar Kama, G. Overview of kibbutz education. Lecture in the series: The Kibbutz (offered by the Council of Educational Development at UCLA, Spring quarter, 1971).
3. Bettelheim B. *The Children of the Dream*. New York: MacMillan, 1969.

4. Fraiberg, S. *Epilogue*, a 9-minute film in which Selma Fraiberg comments on the two films on Israeli kibbutz vs. family preschool education (Marschak, 1973).
5. Freud, A., and Dann, S. An experiment in group unbringing. In C. B. S. Tendler (Ed.), *Readings in Child Behavior and Development*. New York: Harcourt, Brace, 1964.
6. Freud, S. Beyond the pleasure principle. In John Rickman (Ed.), *The Works of Sigmund Freud*. New York: Doubleday, 1957.
7. Gerson, M. The child and his family in the kibbutz. In A. Jarus et al. (Eds.), *Children and Families in Israel*. New York: Gordon and Breach, 1970.
8. Gewirtz, H. B., and Gewirtz, J. L. Caretaking settings, background events and behavior differences in four Israeli child-rearing environments—some preliminary trends. In B. M. Foss (Ed.), *Determinants of Infant Behavior*, Vol. IV. London: Methuen, 1969.
9. Gewirtz, H. B. Child care facilities and the Israeli experience. In E. Grotberg (Ed.), *Day Care: Resources for Decisions*. Washington, D.C.: DHEW, Office of Planning, Research and Evaluation, 1971.
10. Golan, S. Collective education in the kibbutz. *Psychiatry*, **22**, 1959.
11. Kaffman, M. Adolescent rebellion in the kibbutz. *J. Amer. Acad. Child Psychiat.*, **17** (1), 1978.
12. Kritz, R. *Fresh Morning*. Tel Aviv: Pura Books, 1965.
13. Krook, D. Rationalism triumphant. In P. King and B. C. Parekh (Eds.), *Politics and Experience*. Boston: Cambridge University Press, 1968.
14. Levin, G. The child and his family in the kibbutz: Infancy and his early childhood. In A. Jarus et al. (Eds.), *Children and Families in Israel*. New York: Gordon and Breach, 1970.
15. Liegle, L. *Familie und Kollekiv im Kibbutz*. Weinheim: Beltz Verlag, 1971.
16. Maccoby, E., and Feldman, S. S. *Mother-Attachment and Stranger-Reactions in the Third Year of Life*. Monographs of the Society for Research in Child Development, 1972.
17. Marschak, M. *Teachers Evaluate the Progress of the Headstart Child*. Los Angeles: Economic and Youth Opportunities Agency, Training Dept., 1960.
18. _____. Design and narration of 2 films: (a) *Patterns of Parenting in Israel*; (b) *Two Climates of Childhood in Israel*. Observations of kibbutz-reared vs. city-reared young boys, in MIM situations and during a typical day in their lives. Completed in 1973. Distributor: New York University Film Library.
19. Nagler, S. Clinical observations on kibbutz children. *Israel Ann. Psychiat. Related Discipl.*, 1963.
20. _____. The child and his family in the kibbutz: Mental health. In A. Jarus et al. (Eds.), *Children and Families in Israel*. New York: Gordon and Breach, 1970.
21. Rabin, A. *Growing Up in the Kibbutz*. New York: Springer, 1965.
22. Segal, M. The child and his family in the school age kibbutz. In A. Jarus et al. (Eds.), *Children and Families in Israel*. New York: Gordon and Breach, 1970.
23. Shapira, A. Competition, cooperation, and conformity among city and kibbutz children in Israel. Ph.D. Thesis, Psychology Department, University of California, Los Angeles, 1970.
24. Spitz, R. A. The effect of personality disturbances in the mother on the well-being of her infant. In E. J. Anthony and T. Benedek (Eds.), *Parenthood, Its Psychology and Psychopathology*. Boston: Little, Brown and Co., 1970.
25. Tiger, L., and Shepher, J. *Women in the Kibbutz*. New York: Harcourt Brace Javonowich, 1975.

CHAPTER 5

Summary

Throughout this book the focus of our investigation has been the origin of youth movements. We have reached a number of conclusions. All of them, while tentative, have been supported by systematic observations, and appear to be promising conjectures for further study and further testing.

In Chapter 1 we have tried to link two youth movements—the American hippies and the German Wandervogel—to the social and historical context from which they emerged. This chapter contains definitions of and elaborations on the main concepts used, a description of the two movements, an overview of the literature on dissidence, and an introduction into the method applied for studying parent-child interaction.

By drawing a parallel between the hippie and the Wandervogel movements, we saw that both youth movements originated as a protest against the dominant urban society with its growing technology and bureaucracy, and its intense pursuit of material success. These trends of the industrial society, in an era of peace, were frequently interpreted as conflicting with the "natural," idealistic, irrational inclinations of youth. Yet, in each country only a relatively small segment of youth rejected the values sanctioned by the society at large, suggesting that, in addition to the widespread social and economic changes, specific early relationships within the family may also have contributed to the dissidence of youth movement members. This assumption was strengthened by an initial study comparing a group of previous Wandervogel members with a group of nonmembers. The members more often than the nonmembers told of frustrations they had encountered as children in their relationship with one or both parents. It would seem conceivable that these experiences resulted later in life in nonidentification with parental values and thus in nonidentification with the values accepted by society.

The attempt was made, in Chapter 2, therefore, to explore the early parent-child relationship in urban, middle-class families, paying particular attention to those parental attitudes which might or might not favor the child's identification with the parent. We considered, especially, the child's identification with the parents' moral values as influenced by parental attitudes toward the child's transgressions.

We have observed closely the interaction of two three-year-old boys with their parents. Through interviewing the mothers fifteen years later, we tried to relate the behavior of the parents in interaction with their children at three years of age to the development of the children's personalities. We found that the child who had been brought up with an overemphasis on affection and an insufficient concern with directions, as a young adult shows impulsiveness, immaturity of character, and a delay of identification with adult models. On the other hand, we saw that the child whose parents emphasized giving direction at the cost of showing affection developed into a young adult, frustrated at first because he could not meet his parents' excessive demands, is now beginning to pursue a goal and lifestyle of his own, yet continues to be dependent on his parents' recognition and proof of affection.

By studying the parent-child interactions and the interviews with the parents, we have come to see that the parental perception of the child's individuality plays a decisive role in determining the nature of the parent-child relationship. The degree to which this parental perception continues to influence the relationship was illustrated in a family in which the mother was observed in the hospital with her newborn child and, subsequently, in interaction with the same child at age three. The fact that, assigned identical tasks, entirely different interactions between this mother and her other child and between the father and both children were observed suggests that the parent's perception of each child influences the interaction differently. The life histories of these and other parents, furthermore, suggested that their perceptions of their children were influenced by own desires and frustrations. Among these parental desires appears to be a tendency for "self-replication," i.e., a wish that the child resemble the parent. How strongly, and which characteristics the parent wishes to be replicated, very likely has its effect on the parent's behavior to the child and this, in turn, could influence the child's identification. (See Figure 1, Chapter 2.)

In Chapter 3, having sharpened our vision of the parent's part in the parent-child interaction and the underlying relationship of parent and child, we once again looked at the childhood experiences of adults who radically abandoned their identification with their parents. The histories of the Wandervogel and of the commune movement having been sketched, the interviews with a previous Wandervogel and two members of a present commune were described and analyzed. Because of similar deprivations in their childhood, these persons appear to have become attracted to a counterculture movement. Most important among their felt deprivations was a lack of genuine, empathetic affection on the part of one or both parents. The deficiency of parental affection was felt to have inhibited the interviewees' ability for friendship and intimacy and their self-appreciation. All three persons recalled that their feelings of aloneness and their need for affection made them susceptible to the emotional security provided by the counterculture group.

Having described followers in each of the two counterculture groups, Chapter 3 goes on to present the life story and the value orientation of a leader in each of the two groups. From interviews both with the leaders and with the group members it became clear that, as the members abandoned their identification with their parents' values, they came to identify with group values and to take on aspects of the leaders' personalities.

Since both of the commune members in our investigation were mothers whose children lived with them in the commune, we rounded off our study of the commune by an overview of communal childrearing. Here we noticed a tendency to withhold direction and to show unrestrained affection. The commune members thus conveyed in the way they reared their children a nonidentification with their own parents' childrearing attitudes.

In Chapter 4 we turned to the adult-child relationship and the child's identification in the regulated child-care arrangements of the kibbutz. At the outset of Chapter 1, in describing the Wandervogel, we pointed out how the founders of the kibbutz, similar to the members of the German youth movement, rejected their parents' middle-class values and lifestyle. We further mentioned that the kibbutz has borrowed certain values such as equality, simplicity, and complete honesty in relationships from the German youth movement. Unlike the German youth movement whose values and lifestyle remained visions of a world to come, however, the founders applied the same values to the creation of the kibbutz society—a society which has survived with only minor modifications for three generations. It was suggested that this achievement of the Jewish youth flows from the strength of their idealism, the threat of persecution in their homeland and their association with Zionist and Zionist-socialist youth movements. The kibbutz is, in summary, an example of a youth movement which has been channeled into a reality-based, goal-oriented form of communal life. We began Chapter 4 by showing the educational schedules of the kibbutz. These schedules showed that, in contrast to the casual, noninterfering child care of the commune, planned education is a major objective of the kibbutz.

Having acquainted the reader with the major features of the kibbutz, we then described a series of parent-child interaction sessions in two kibbutzim. Interactions in a group of city parents and children in Israel were presented for purposes of comparison.

It could be seen that the kibbutz parents tended to watch their children performing the tasks with little interference and to enjoy the game aspects of the situations. The city parents, in contrast, seemed more inclined to direct the child and seemed more concerned with the child's achievement. Occasionally they even introduced a competitive incentive into the procedure. The kibbutz child-care worker (metapelet) was also observed in interaction with the children. She participated in the activities at a quieter pace than was characteristic of both groups of parents. Without taking an active part in the child's doings, she carefully watched him as he tried to master the task. She provided minimal directions, and then only if they seemed needed.

For the kibbutz child, as for the city child, the parents appeared to be the main source of affection. Expressions of affection by the metapelet were less intense than were those of the parents. The metapelet seemed intent on showing her affection equally to all the children in her care. We noticed that if a child is in need of mothering, however, the metapelet gives him special affectionate attention.

As for the development of identification in each of these two environments, it would appear that, from a very young age, the kibbutz child does not shape himself exclusively after his parents. He also turns to his close relationships with the metapelet and with the peer group as well as to other friendly and familiar members of the wider kibbutz society to provide him with varied models of identification. The child's sense of being a part of the community, the degree to which his childrearing is divided between his parents and his caretaker, and the autonomy granted to the adolescent, all have been said to minimize the motivation for youth rebellion.

During the period 1970-1975, however, signs of "storm and stress" and even of rebelliousness (e.g., the preference for up-to-date dancing instead of the folk dances and a taste for Western rock-and-roll music) were becoming evident, according to one recent study of the kibbutz [11:158-159]. Yet, the basic socialist values of the older generation and their clearly defined prohibitions (e.g., the ban on drugs) have never been questioned by the protesters. Since rather than refusing the young, certain concessions have been made to them, the new trends are beginning to lose their impact. An increase in family unity, moreover, is observed in this same report. On the other hand, books on therapy in traditional families show clearly that intergenerational conflicts are rarely settled flexibly and rationally. The emotional involvement of parents and children with each other tends to interfere with resolving conflicts constructively. If severe enough, such conflicts may make a young person susceptible to the language and goals of a youth rebellion.

However, as we have frequently pointed out, youth rebellion in Western countries tends not to be widespread. The majority of children in young adulthood do not drastically deviate from the parents' norms but by and large tend to perpetuate parental values.

What, then, are the unsettling circumstances which, in nuclear families, lead to the disruption of the identification process and to the discontinuity between generations? This question brings us full circle, back to the starting point of our inquiry. As discussed in Chapter 1, social, economic, and political changes, industrialization and urbanization, in particular, have been held to be responsible for changes in family life and in adult values. The youth movement, in these investigations, was interpreted mainly as representing a reaction against the lifestyle and values of the industrial, urban society.

In our investigation we have gone further and tried to uncover the incentives for youth protest by "microscopically" observing the process by which values are transmitted and identifications formed, both in individual families and in groups of families. The insights derived from our study suggest that this approach usefully complements the research and reflection on social change as a condition for youth rebellion.

Thus, in explaining youth rebellion, it appears important to pay attention to the quality of the parents' affection and direction.

What about a child not motivated to join a movement? What could have been his experiences in childhood? Ideally, we would picture him to have parents who would be clear about their own values and goals. Their directions to their child would be unambiguous and consistent, would take into account the child's maturity, and would respect his individual inclinations. Their affection would be genuine and unconditional and would enhance his disposition for following his parents' directions even at the cost of foregoing his infantile pleasures of the moment. A child brought up by this kind of parenting may form, for better or worse, particularly strong identifications with his parents. The nature of the parental affection and direction to which he had been exposed in childhood would make it seem unlikely that he would later be attracted to rebellion.

In the preceding pages we have frequently drawn attention to the critical importance of parental affection and direction and to their combined influence on the child's identification. Let us say in conclusion that we feel quite sure that, in the balance of parental direction and affection, it is parental affection which chiefly determines not only the child's propensity for identifying with the parent, but also the full development of his personality. It remains for future investigators to examine our claim. But the verse written two hundred years ago, implying affection and direction, touches a familiar chord:

Und doch vermoegen in der Welt, der tollen
Zwei Hebel viel auf's irdische Getriebe:

Sehr viel die Pflicht. Unendlich mehr die Liebe.
And yet in this world's maze and in man's turmoil
Two levers can accomplish much:
A great deal—Duty; infinitely more—Love.[1]

NOTE

[1] Written by Johann Peter Hebel (1760-1826), translated by Marianne Marsehak.

The Marschak Interaction Method (MIM) Abbreviated Form[1]

APPENDIX A

Introduction

USES

The MIM is used for three major purposes: (1) diagnosis and treatment, (2) teaching, and (3) research.

Clinically, the MIM is used both for the diagnosis and the treatment of individual children, parent-child pairs, and families.

1. *Diagnosis*. Child guidance centers use the MIM to help in understanding the origins of a child's particular emotional problem (e.g., fearfulness, low self-esteem, etc.).
2. *Treatment*. Child- or family-therapy centers use the MIM as a means for providing feedback to families and as a medium for direct intervention.

In conjunction with other teaching tools, MIM sessions demonstrate to the observing students some typical variations in parent-child relationships. Courses in child development use the MIM with children at different developmental levels to illustrate changes over time in the typical parent-child relationship (e.g., to make the point that, as the child grows older, interaction becomes a more cooperative endeavor). Courses in psychopathology and psychodiagnosis use the MIM to illustrate some aspects of normal versus abnormal personality development as related to parental influences (e.g., healthy vs. unhealthy attachment, alertness to the environment, or stress tolerance.)

By virtue of the structured, reproducible situations[2] of the MIM, the method constitutes a valuable research instrument. Subject pairs, differing in the variable to be explored, can be studied as to certain aspects of their interaction. For example, interaction can be compared between different parent-child pairs in the same family, between parent-child pairs in two cultural groups, and in families with a normal child versus families with a disturbed child.

Some ways of quantifying the observations of the interaction session will be discussed. However, the MIM procedures have not been standardized. It remains for future researchers to proceed toward establishing, for a given MIM situation and age level, standards of behavior to be expected of normal children and their parents in a particular culture and subculture.

THEORETICAL BASIS: DIMENSIONS OF INTERACTION

It is assumed that certain dimensions of the parent-child interaction influence the child's personality formation, that this influence begins soon after birth, and that it leaves traces in the child's adult personality. It is further assumed that behavioral expressions of these dimensions are amenable to observation and appraisal. The dimensions considered here are: Attachment, Direction, Imitation, Alertness, Stress Tolerance, and Playfulness.

The crippling effect of inadequate *attachment* has been most drastically demonstrated in institutionalized children as described by Provence and Lipton [1]. The infants' diminished *alertness*, i.e., their lack of interest in the environment, was attributed by the same authors to impersonal, infrequent mothering. The type of parental *direction*, e.g., severity versus leniency and consistency versus inconsistency of demands, has been shown [2] to affect the child's behavior in his peer group. That *imitation* is important for the development of identification is generally accepted by developmental psychologists. Throughout this book we have pointed out how the quality of the child's imitation depends on the behavior of the adult as model. How the parent can strengthen (or weaken) the child's *stress tolderance* has been discussed in detail in Chapter 2 (pp. 40-43; 74-77].

To these dimensions we have added the dimension of *playfulness*, which has received less attention from child development professionals than have the other dimensions. However, therapists at the Theraplay Institute in Chicago have been teaching playfulness to parents since 1968. In her forthcoming book on Theraplay [3] Dr. Ann Jernberg, clinical director of the institute, describes unhappy and handicapped children who have suffered from withholding of physical playfulness by their parents. By fulfilling this primitive need Theraplay therapists enhance the overall development of these children.

SOURCES AND SELECTION OF TASKS

Research studies have provided the design for several interaction tasks to be administered to infants at the neonatal level, i.e., for observations in the first few days after birth. A situation in which the adult attempts to elicit imitation of facial gestures in the newborn, for example, is derived from the research work on early imitation by Meltzoff and Moore [4]. Items to be administered to children age one month through the toddler level were selected from infant tests conducted on large samples of normal infants (e.g., the Gesell Developmental Schedules [5] and the Buehler-Hetzer [6] infant tests). Only those items were selected which could be expected to tap one of the above dimensions of behavior. While in their original form, these items were designed to tap the child's behavior only; when used as a task on the MIM, the quality of both the adult's and the child's behavior is assessed.

From the toddler level on, most (though not all) of the tasks were designed specifically for the MIM. (See List of MIM Situations, Preschool Level, Appendix B).

Six or seven well-selected tasks generally give an adequate picture at any one session.[3] In order to provide the best overall view of the parent-child relationship, the examiner should select at least one task from each of the five dimensions. The tasks vary as to the "purity" of the dimension tapped. Thus, *attachment* is most directly observable through tasks centering on feeding. It is less easily assessed through tasks like Pat-a-cake, which taps mainly *playfulness*. Having the adult leave is an example of a task which taps more than one dimension. The task elicits both *attachment* and the child's and the adult's *stress tolerance*. Similarly, "Dress-up" lends itself to exploring not only playfulness but also direction and attachment.

In the selection of tasks to be used and the sequence in which they are to be presented, gratifying tasks and entertaining materials should alternate with tedious or frustrating tasks and dull or difficult materials.

PROCEDURES

A Brief Overview

Parent and child together perform a series of tasks designed to reveal certain important aspects of their interaction.[4] The typical session requires thirty to forty minutes and covers six to seven items. The parent and child are encouraged to perform the tasks at their own pace. Insight into the various aspects of the child-parent relationship are arrived at through observation, ranging from the meticulous to the qualitative and intuitive.

Among the more systematic observational methods which have been devised, four are briefly described in this appendix. These are (1) a detailed step-by-step coding of specific nonverbal expressions and movements which is given in Appendix C; (2) a systematic method for observer rating of the seven theoretically important dimensions described above (see Appendix C); (3) a tape-recorded narrator's log; and (4) a descriptive system of behaviors chosen to be directly indicative of a high or low position of each of the six dimensions, at the preschool level. This is presented in some detail in Appendix D.

MIM situations have been designed for the newborn, one-month, four- to six-month, toddler, preschool, school-age, and adolescent levels.

Administration

The interaction sessions are conducted with the adult and child seated side by side, either at two small folding tables (see Chapter 2, p. 33) or at a table measuring about five by two and a half feet.[5] The adult sits to the right of the child if the child is right-handed and to the child's left if he is left-handed. At the early infant levels, the newborn or infant is lying, propped-up, or held in the lap of the adult.

Instructions for each task printed on numbered cards are given to the adult. Numbered envelopes contain the materials for some of the activities. A suitcase or carry-all bag containing these envelopes is placed next to the adult.

Types of Recording

The particular technique or techniques for recording to be selected will depend on the purpose for which the observations are made.

Coding of Nonverbal Behavior

The observer (or observers) sits behind a one-way viewing screen with a full view of the interaction between adult and child. (If an adjoining room with viewing screen is not available, the observations are made directly in the room in which the interaction takes place.)

The pad of paper on which the observations are recorded is divided into two columns corresponding to the two "territories" marked by a dividing line down the center of the interaction table. Half the page is titled "Adult," the other half, "Child." Under a new heading for each task the nonverbal behavior of parent and child is recorded in running notations (codes), using a specific key of symbols. These codes are presented in Appendix B. If the situation in which the MIM is employed does not permit the use of a tape recorder, the coders enter not only nonverbal behavior but relevant verbal expressions as well (see Appendix E, "Two Examples").

For reasons both of exactness and ease, the use of an event recorder may be preferred to coding "by hand." The Esterline Angus Event Recorder, for example, can be used for time-sequence recording of behaviors by simply depressing appropriate keys alone or in combination. Whatever the method used, the coder will record the elapsed time for each task. The frequency of each symbol recorded by a coder during a given task can then be converted into its frequency per minute.

The key to the symbols for entering nonverbal behavior is illustrated below. Whether a particular movement or facial expression is made by child or by adult is defined by the column, Child or Adult, in which the symbol is entered.

>	looks in the direction of
►	intense looking at
∪	smiles at
∪ ∪	both smile
⌇	frowns
⟶	moves toward
⟵	moves away from
BC	initiates body contact
BCr	responds to body contact

A segment of a protocol of nonverbal interaction might be as follows:

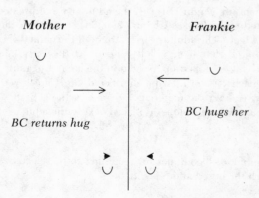

Mother	Frankie
∪	
	∪
⟵	
⟶	
BC returns hug	BC hugs her
►	◄
∪	∪

Two forms of the Key of Symbols have been developed (see Appendix B). One form has been used for a group of normal children and the other for a group of autistic, nonspeaking children with their parents. All children were three to four years old.

The symbol keys need not be used in their entirety. Professionals working with the MIM will select those which stand for aspects of behavior which may prove relevant to their particular purposes.

A remark on the coding of single events is in place here. In Chapter 1 we mentioned the shortcomings of trying to record a complex relationship item by item—gesture by gesture. The coding procedures and the Key of Symbols, as outlined above, suffer from the same shortcoming. However, two devices do, to some extent, remedy these limitations. One is the use of a "modifier"[6] which can be added to a single code. For example, to the code for "body contact" (BC) the observer can add a modifier, which will provide pertinent information about the observed behavior, such as: "incidental," "corrective," "clowning," "comforting," or "affectionate." The other device, used in the data analysis stage, consists of combining several single codes into an "aggregate." Thus the frequencies of the codes "looking at adult," "moving toward adult," "leaning on adult," "smiling at adult," could, for example, be combined into the aggregate "Attachment."

Tape Recording of Verbal and Vocal Expressions

Especially when the MIM is used for research purposes, the use of a tape recorder will be found to be very useful. In this way the full verbal record, as well as other vocal expressions, are available for later analysis.

Also, in addition to the recording of the adult-child pair, the tape recorders may be used to dictate an observer's log, i.e., a running commentary on the interaction by an observer. Previous research work employing such a log has shown that new and meaningful insights do occur during such a narration of intensely observed behavior. These observations have sometimes generated new hypotheses. If a two-channel (stereo) tape recorder is available, one channel can be used for recording the dialogue of the interacting pair and the other, with separate microphone, for recording the observer's log; otherwise, two tape recorders will be required. With a two-channel recorder, the two recordings can be played back simultaneously, a device which approximates the richness and immediacy of the original observations. Thereby a record of the verbal and non-verbal interaction is preserved. The recording allows making the data available to persons, researchers, for example, who were not present when the MIM session took place.

Finally, for research purposes, the typewritten transcripts of the dialogues and monologues of child and adult can be submitted to *content analysis*—a classification of words and phrases relevant to the topic under study.

Judging Procedures

The ways in which adult and child interact can be judged, according to certain dimensions, after a task or at the conclusion of a session. The dimensions to be selected will depend on the topic of the investigation. *Rating scales* devised to rate behavior on four of the MIM dimensions are presented in Appendix C.

Ranking a child or an adult relative to other subjects in a sample (with regard to each of the MIM dimensions), has also been applied, successfully, as a research technique. However, since ranking can be done only at the completion of a project after all subjects have been observed, it taxes the judges' memory and imposes particular limits on the size of the sample.

APPLICATIONS OF THE MIM

Clinical

The original material and data from subsequent analysis of the interaction sessions can be used for clinical assessment and intervention.

Assessment

The MIM has been used, for example, to provide additional information about austistic and retarded children considered for admission to the inpatient service of a clinic. (In one particular case a four-year-old boy's behavior with his mother and his father in the interaction sessions led the clinician to say, "There are indications of his ego being modifiable as he responded more adequately and was less tense with father than with mother.")

The MIM has been used to evaluate the progress of therapy. Interaction sessions before, during, and after therapy can produce important information about the changing nature of the parent-child relationship and about the ego resources of each as the relationship changes.

The MIM has also proved to be useful for assessing the goodness of fit between foster or adoptive parents and particular children. This approach has been especially valuable with older children.

Intervention

The MIM can be used to provide feedback to parents regarding their interactions with their children. Families attending the Theraplay Institute in Chicago, for example, are shown videotapes of their MIM sessions. This experience provides, not infrequently, new insights to the parents into their relationship with the child. Staff observers discuss their observations and impressions and then plan a program for the family.

In specific intervention sessions therapists help parents to "do it differently" either through role playing of parent-child scenarios or through guided repetitions of the parent's MIM sessions with their children.

Teaching

MIM sessions can be used for class demonstration in such fields as clinical psychology, anthropology, child development, pediatrics, nursing, and social work. The selection of parent-child pairs as well as of the dimensions and specific interaction situations will depend on the focus of the particular study program. The study of socialization, for example, can be made more realistic through the direct demonstration of direction giving and direction accepting in parent-child pairs with different age children. The study of cultural differences in the socialization process can be sharpened through the observation of parent-child pairs from different cultures as they engage in identical interaction tasks. (The tasks tapping Direction are again relevant here.)

Class demonstrations of MIM sessions have been offered to third-year medical students in a program in pediatrics and child psychiatry [7]. One goal of this program is to develop sensitivity in evaluating and treating the child patient who suffers from an emotional disturbance. Each child observed in interaction with a parent received therapeutic help from one of the students. Children seen with each of the two parents suffered from a variety of emotional difficulties (e.g., tantrums, bedwetting, destructiveness and loss of appetite [anorexia]). Only four interaction tasks were selected for each session. These tasks were chosen so as to focus on aspects of the parent-child relationship which might be contributing to the child's difficulty. Occasionally, the addition of a specially designed situation elucidated a particular conflict and the parent's way of handling it.

It has been found that the effectiveness of the MIM demonstrations as a teaching device is heightened when students are encouraged to form a judgment of the child's and the adult's behaviors through use of the *rating scale* discussed above. The scale is reproduced in Appendix D.

The instructors also would do well to complete the scale themselves. At a follow-up class the students' evaluations can then be discussed and compared with those of the instructors.

Research

The MIM has some obvious research applications. Among these are studies of parent-child relationships in different social classes, ethnic groups, and cultural groups. Also families with a physically handicapped child can be compared with families with a normal child.

Research based on the MIM will preferably be carried out by teams of two coders and judges. This will help to minimize subjective biases and inconsistencies not entirely avoidable in the case of a single observer.

Some practice in coding and judging is advisable prior to carrying out a research study. The skill of coding is best acquired by viewing and coding interaction behavior together with a person experienced in coding. Videotaped sessions are particularly useful for training purposes since they can be replayed, segment by segment, and differences in coding can be discussed and reduced.

Because of the small size of most of the samples studied by the MIM, the reliability tests for the two research workers will usually be of the nonparametric kind, such as the rank sum test.[7] Rank correlations between relative frequencies of observed occurrences can be used to test the degree of agreement between:

1. Two coders of single characteristics (e.g., "child initiates game," "child clowns") or of aggregates[8] of single characteristics ("child playful" or "child spontaneous").
2. Two content analysts analyzing the dialogues of the same interaction session.
3. Two analyses of the same verbal record performed by one analyst at the beginning and at the end of an interval of two or three weeks ("individual consistency").

The rank correlation method can also be used to test the degree of agreement between:

1. Ratings, on a 1 to 6 or on a 1 to 4 point scale assigned by each of two judges, after each session, to each of the parental and each of the child's dimensions (e.g., attachment).
2. Rankings of all subjects in a group with regard to some of the dimensions by each of the two judges after completion of all sessions.

The rank correlations can be computed separately for each of the subject groupy to be compared, e.g., normal child with mother, father; handicapped child with mother, father. In each study it will be decided which degree of agreement between coders, between content analysts, and between judges is needed for a characteristic to be included for further analysis.

While the preceding brief remarks indicate that the MIM can be a basic research tool, it can also serve as a useful supplement to more traditional instruments such as checklists, questionnaires, etc. In general, any research concerned with the behavior and/or attitudes of parents toward their children (and, indeed, the children toward their parents) can gain in depth and profundity through an analysis of controlled and repeatable parent-child interaction sessions.

It is evident from the foregoing that the Marschak Interaction Method is not a "test" in the traditional sense of the word. It is a method for gaining an understanding of a particular adult-child relationship. The understandings arrived at depend on sensitivity, experience, and common sense, and, in the case of psychopathology, on clinical insight. Only with intensive training of coders and judges can consistently reliable results be expected. However, even without intensive training it is possible for a sensitive observer to see that one parent is more nurturing or more demanding of correct performance than another. It is also possible to say that a parent is not as accepting or as demanding as a particular child needs him or her to be. Similar judgments may be made about the child in relation to the parent. It is also possible to extrapolate from the MIM situations and make the judgment that we are seeing typical aspects of a relationship and not just situation-specific aspects. But, until such time as MIM responses are codified and standardized, it will *not* be possible to say that this or that parent or child or parent-child pair falls into any particular score range.

A word seems appropriate about the temptation to evaluate MIM performance in intelligence terms (typically expected by parents and almost second nature for many mental health and education professionals). Even though it must be assumed that, particularly at the extremes, a child's intelligence will have an effect upon the behavioral style of the parent, the MIM is not designed to determine a child's intellectual strength or weakness, and it would be inappropriate to use it as a test of intelligence.

NOTES

[1] © Copyright 1960. A kit has been designed which includes directions and materials for these seven stages. For complete directions and information regarding the Kit for the Marschak Interaction Method, as well as the video tape series "Lessons in MIM Observations," contact: The Theraplay Institute, 333 N. Michigan, Chicago, Illinois 60601.

[2] The terms "situation" and "task" will be used interchangeably.

³ Two films have been produced which illustrate the interaction behavior during two sessions of MIM situations: *Nursery School Child-Mother Interaction* and *Patterns of Parenting in Israel*, distributed by New York University Film Library. (See Chapter 1, References 23 and 26.)

⁴ Although it is not discussed in the text and is neither considered necessary nor always workable, the MIM occasionally lends itself to the observation of both parents and/or of more than one sibling at a time.

⁵ The "interaction table" is divided down the center with a strip of masking tape to facilitate coding the movements within and outside each subject's "territory."

⁶ Either another code from the Key of Symbols or a specific code may serve as modifier.

⁷ Dr. Ann Jernberg contributed substantially to this most recent version of the MIM. She designed a number of tasks for the preschool and subsequent levels which are successfully used at the Theraplay Institute and other institutions.

⁸ The aggregates formed through combining single codes may or may not be the same as the "dimensions" of behavior to be assessed through rating or ranking.

REFERENCES

1. Provence, S., and Lipton, R. C. *Infants in Institutions*. New York: International Universities Press, 1962.
2. Baumrind, D. Childcare practices anteceding three patterns of preschool behavior. *Genet. Psychol. Monogr.*, **75**, 1967.
3. Jernberg, A. M., *Theraplay: A New Treatment Using Structured Play for Problem Children and Their Families*. San Francisco: Jossey-Bass, in press.
4. Meltzoff, A. N., and Moore, M. K. Imitation of facial and manual gestures by human neonates. *Science*, **198** (no. 4312), 1977.
5. Gesell, A., and Amatruda, C. S. *Developmental Diagnosis*. New York: Hoeber, 1941.
6. Buehler, C., and Hetzer, H. *Kleinkindertests*. Munich: Johann Ambrosius Barth, 1961.
7. Marschak, M., and Call, J. D. Observing the disturbed child and his parent: Class demonstrations for medical students. *J. Amer. Acad. Child Psychiat.* **5** (4), 1966.
8. Dixon, V. J., and Massey, F. J. *Introduction to Statistical Analysis*. New York, McGraw-Hill, 1957 (p. 468, Table a-30a).

APPENDIX B

Key of Symbols for Nonverbal Behavior

LIST 1: CODES FOR NORMAL CHILDREN

		Parent	Child
1	child looks at parent		<
2	parent looks at child	>	
3	intense looking at parent		◀
4	intense looking at child	▶	
5	child and parent look at each other	✕	
6	child watches parent work		HP
7	parent watches child work	HC	
8	child looks at parent in mirror[1]		Ⓒ< *(circled <)*
9	parent looks at child in mirror	Ⓞ> *(circled >)*	
10	child moves toward parent		⟵
11	parent moves toward child	⟶	
12	child and parent move toward one another	⟶	⟵
13	child sitting near or leaning on parent, or sitting on parent's lap		Ⓟ
14	parent puts arm around child	Ⓒ	
15	child initiates body contact		BC
16	parent initiates body contact	BC	

246

		Parent	Child
17	child responds to body contact		BCr
18	parent responds to body contact	BCr	
19	mutual, affectionate body contact	B	C
20	parent directs child through body contact	Bd	
21	child moves away from parent		⟶
22	parent moves away from child	⟵	
23	child smiles		∪
24	parent smiles	∪	
25	child and parent smile	∪	∪
26	child smiles at parent		∪P
27	parent smiles at child	∪C	
28	child and parent smile at each other with affection	∪⌐∪	
29	child kisses parent		K
30	parent kisses child	K	
31	child and parent smile at each other without affection	∪⫽∪	
32	child smiles inappropriately (mask-like, grimacing, etc.)		⩗
33	parent smiles inappropriately	⩗	
34	child laughs		L
35	parent laughs	L	
36	child laughs inappropriately		Ⱡ
37	parent laughs inappropriately	Ⱡ	
38	child, self-assertion		sa
39	child serious face		∩
40	parent serious face	∩	
41	child and parent serious face	∩	∩
42	child frowns		∿∿∿
43	parent frowns	∿∿∿	
44	both frown	∿∿∿	∿∿∿
45	child bored		— —
46	parent bored	— —	
47	child excited		↑

	Parent	Child
48 child happy		+
49 parent happy	+	
50 child unhappy		−
51 parent unhappy	−	
52 child hostile		h
53 parent hostile	h	
54 child stares		I
55 parent stares	I	
56 child outside interest		out
57 child touches own body		b
58 parent touches own body	b	
59 child puts finger in mouth		⊕
60 child puts object in mouth		⊖
61 child touches, manipulates parent's material		T
62 parent touches, manipulates child's material	T	
63 child drops material		↓
64 child pounds table		⊥
65 child stands up		♀
66 parent stands up	♀	
67 child initiates game		g
68 parent initiates game	g	
69 child clowning		ℓ
70 parent clowning	ℓ	
71 child imitates parent vocally		vi
72 child imitates parent's facial expression		fi
73 child imitates parent's movements		mi
74 parent imitates child	i	
75 child anxious, tense		‖
76 parent anxious, tense	‖	
77 child whines		W
78 child cries		C
79 child shrieks		S

	Parent	Child
80 child looks at mirror[1]		◯
81 parent looks at mirror	◯	
82 child gesticulates at mirror		⌀
83 child grimaces at mirror		⊖
84 child's behavior out of context, inappropriate		✕

LIST 2:
CODES FOR NONVERBAL AUTISTIC CHILDREN[2]
(may be used as needed for normal group)

		Parent	Child
1	rocking		ro
2	undulating yell		y
3	jumping		j
4	running		r
5	running from parent		r⟶
6	sitting on floor		⊥
7	lying down		—◯
8	biting objects		⊙
9	isolated		□
10	peculiar movement of fingers		f
11	vocalization		vo
12	pounding material or object		H
13	grimacing at parent		⤺P
14	striking or pounding own body		b⟵
15	"twirling" or spinning object		tw
16	stamping		st
17	biting lips		↓
18	child throws object (deliberately)		thr
19	scratching objects		Sctt
20	"flying" movement of arms		fl

NOTES

[1] The one-way viewing screen appears as a mirror in the adjoining room in which the interaction takes place.

[2] Most codes of List 1 are also applicable for nonspeaking children.

Judging Procedures— Observer's Form[1]

In your evaluation, place child in normal range of your sample. Circle the number you choose.

1. very low	4. moderately high
2. low	5. high
3. moderately low	6. very high
	0. no evidence

PARENTAL BEHAVIOR

A. Affective responses to child

    1. Genuine warmth (attachment)   1 2 3 4 5 6 0

    2. Deliberate, artificial way of showing affection   1 2 3 4 5 6 0

    3. "Lost" in child, absorbed by loving feelings   1 2 3 4 5 6 0

    4. Negative feelings (irritation, hostility)   1 2 3 4 5 6 0

B. Direction

    1. Appropriate helping pattern (gaining child's cooperation without undue demands or controls)   1 2 3 4 5 6 0

    2. Aspiration for child's achievement   1 2 3 4 5 6 0

3. Attempts to curb, influence, evaluate, criticize, setting rules, restricting   1   2   3   4   5   6   0

4. Clarity (parent explains, conveys directions clearly, models distinctly in imitation tasks)   1   2   3   4   5   6   0

5. Consistency (persistent adherence to a particular course of action)   1   2   3   4   5   6   0

6. Sureness of own wants and acts   1   2   3   4   5   6   0

C. Playfulness

1. Spontaneity (initiating activities or gestures enjoyed by the child but not prescribed by the task)   1   2   3   4   5   6   0

2. Imagination shared with child   1   2   3   4   5   6   0

3. Humor, adapted to child's sense of humor   1   2   3   4   5   6   0

D. Stress tolerance

1. Aware of stressful situations as potentially disturbing for child   1   2   3   4   5   6   0

2. Adequate handling of stress situation (neither overprotective nor indifferent), trying to strengthen child's stress tolerance   1   2   3   4   5   6   0

CHILD'S BEHAVIOR

A. Affective responses to parent

1. Genuine warmth (attachment)   1   2   3   4   5   6   0

2. Deliberate, artificial way of showing affection   1   2   3   4   5   6   0

3. Negative feelings (irritation, hostility)   1   2   3   4   5   6   0

B. Child's quest for parent's direction

1. Child asks for and accepts direction or help when it is needed   1   2   3   4   5   6   0

2. Child asks parent to "tell how . . .," help, or take over when it is not needed   1   2   3   4   5   6   0

3. Child leads and directs task   1   2   3   4   5   6   0

4. Child pouts in order to get his way   1   2   3   4   5   6   0

5. Child succeeds by above methods or   1   2   3   4   5   6   0
   others (parent swayed by child)

C. Playfulness

1. Spontaneity (initiating fun activities or   1   2   3   4   5   6   0
   playful gestures)

2. Imagination (fantasy activity)   1   2   3   4   5   6   0

3. Sense of humor   1   2   3   4   5   6   0

D. Stress tolerance

1. Deals with stressful situation adaptively;   1   2   3   4   5   6   0
   responds positively to parent's attempt at
   strengthening his resilience

NOTE

[1] To be used for clinical, classroom, and research purposes. Only four dimensions are presented here; scales for other dimensions (e.g., Imitation, Alertness) can be constructed from the lists of "Contrasting Behaviors" (see Appendix D).

APPENDIX D

Lists for Describing Behaviors

The following illustrates the MIM as it is applied to one developmental level (preschool). A number of "tasks" or "situations" are presented to tap each of the six dimensions. For each task the material needed and the procedure to be carried out are briefly described. This is followed by examples of behavior which can be expected of adult and child in response to the particular task's demands.

The behaviors are divided into two groups. Behaviors in group A and B are indicative, respectively, of high and low values on the dimension to be studied in that task. In the separation task ("Parent Leaves the Room"), for example, the parent who is "close and empathetic" ("I know how you hate this but I'll be back") shows a higher attachment value than does the parent who is "distant and unempathetic" ("Bet you can't wait for me to get out of here").

The General List for Describing Behaviors—All Tasks is to be used, whenever appropriate, for analyzing behavior on *each of the tasks* at the preschool level. In addition to these "general lists" *Task-Specific Lists* are provided. They are to be consulted when analyzing a particular task. However, for some of the tasks the General lists alone seem sufficient. The lists are arranged in groups A and B.

Neither group A nor B is meant to provide a "profile" of a given individual. They represent, instead, single behavior characteristics. Moreover, the lists are to serve merely as guidelines to the observer. They are not exhaustive. There may occur many behaviors which will fall in neither classification. Moreover, no individual will consistently exhibit only one type of behavior. Both A and B types of behavior may, occasionally, be seen in the same individual during a given interaction situation.

GENERAL LISTS FOR DESCRIBING BEHAVIORS—ALL TASKS

Adult	A	B
	Active	Withdrawn
	Attentive	Bored
	Captivating	Boring

254

Helpful	Not helpful
Help, explanation appropriate to this level	Help, explanation beyond this level; explanation above this level
Engaged	Aloof
Imaginative	Unimaginative
Spontaneous	Constricted, task-bound, reality-bound
Joyful	Serious
"In tune" with child	Not "in tune" with child
Personal tone	Impersonal tone
Playful	"Teaching"
Responsive to an adequate degree	Overresponsive, underresponsive
Stimulating, lively	Dull
Tolerant of child's failure	Intolerant of child's failure
Trusting	Fearful

Child	A	B
	Active	Withdrawn
	Attentive	Bored
	Calm	Restless, fidgety
	Cooperative	Uncooperative, resistant
	Enjoying	Pained, strained
	Excited	Dull, unmoved
	Humorous	Serious
	Imaginative	Unimaginative
	Personal	Impersonal
	Relaxed	Tense
	Spontaneous	Constrained
	Trusting	Fearful
	Wishes more of the same	Glad it's over with

LISTS FOR DESCRIBING TASK-SPECIFIC BEHAVIOR (PRESCHOOL)

Attachment

Feeding

Material: 1 carrot, paring knife, 1 small bowl, and 1 spoon

Procedure: Adult prepares a "meal" for child

Adult:	A	B
Food Preparation	Shows confidence in child's cooperation	Seems uncertain or anxious about child's cooperation
	Explains, comments on task	Silent

	Keeps in friendly (visual and/or verbal) contact with child	Initiates infrequent and mostly impersonal contact with child
	Includes child in preparation	
	Suggests child should "help"	
	Offers food in a friendly manner	Offers food in "no-nonsense" and/or constraining manner
	Offers food with humor	
Child Eats	Shows happy, peaceful relaxed expression	Shows anxiety
	Uncritically corrects child's eating habits	Nags, coaxes, criticizes child's eating habits
	Enjoys watching child eat	Shows disinterest in child's eating
	Lets child eat at his own speed and/or in his own way (within reasonable limits)	Imposes unreasonable restrictions on child's speed and way of eating
After Meal	Expresses affection by petting or hugging	Terminates task stiffly, impersonally
	Smiles at child, elicits child's smile	Shows serious expression

Child:	A	B
Food Preparation	"Helps" with preparing food	Passive while food prepared
	Interested in adult's doings, communicates with adult	Withdraws
	Follows adult's preparation with animated expression	Conveys hostility by facial expression or words, criticizes adult's doings
	Teasingly, playfully refuses to eat	Angrily, defiantly refuses to eat
Child Eats	Accepts food eagerly, with "gusto"	Tense, restless while eating, "picky"
	Wants adult to share meal	
	"Feeds" adult	
	Playfully wants to be fed, baby-fashion	Aggressively demands to be fed
After Meal	Visually and/or verbally contacts adult	Remote
	Smiles at adult	Seriously looks at adult
	Relaxed, animated	Tense, dull

Bandaid

Material: Container of small bandaids (multicolored, if possible)

Procedure: Adult takes bandaid out of box and asks child, "Where on you shall I put it (them)?"

Adult:	A	B
	Imaginative ("Here comes the ambulance . . . wheeee . . .")	Reality-bound ("What do you mean, 'put it there'? There's no sore there!")
	Sharing (e.g., makes beautiful ring out of bandaid, then lovingly places it on child's finger)	Withholding (e.g., formal placing of bandaid)

Child:	A	B
	Trusting	Fearful (of hurt)
	Accepting	Rejecting
	Calm	Anxious

Hair Combing

Material: 2 combs

Procedure: Adult and child "comb each other's hair"

Adult:	A	B
	Emphasis not on grooming	Emphasis on grooming
	Soothing	Pained
	Kind	Harsh
	Stroking included	No stroking
	Prolonged	Abrupt
	Fluid	Jerky
	Relaxed	Perfectionistic
	Tolerant of child's "failure" in combing adult	Intolerant of child's "failure"
	Allows child to experiment with hairdo	Forbids child to experiment with hairdo

Child:		
	Familiar, intimate	Estranged
	Experimenting	Constricting, timid

Baby Memories

Material: None

Procedure: Adult tells child the story, beginning, "When you were a little baby . . ."

Adult:	A	B
	Detailed ("And I used to sing a little song to you. Do you remember how it went? It went like this . . .")	Sparse ("When you were a little baby you cried.")
	Warm	Cold
	With physical contact ("And I held you on my lap like this . . . and rocked you this way . . . and picked you up on my shoulders when you had to burp, like this . . .")	No physical contact
	Tender	Harsh
	Soft voice	Brusque voice
	Reliving is apparent	Reliving not evident
	Content is positive ("You were the sweetest little baby!")	Content is negative ("You were fussy")
	Content involves closeness ("Remember what fun we had when you were a baby?")	Content reveals distance ("Boy, I'm glad I don't have to go through *that* with you anymore!")
Child:		
	Calm	Tense, restless
	Responsive	Uninterested
	Wakeful	Sleepy
	Eager	Avoiding
	Accepting	Rejecting

Lotioning

Material: 2 small bottles of baby lotion

Procedure: Adult and child each take one bottle. Adult and child apply lotion to one another.

Adult:	A	B
	Enjoying (Really gets into it: "This is fun!")	Disgust (Minimal participation with lotion: "Yuk!"; or no involvement, refusal)

Engaged (Highly involved—lotion may get on both of them—much chatter)	Aloof (Task completed at arm's length and/or in silence
Sensuous ("This feels good")	Intellectual
Slow (Task takes long time to complete)	Fast (Task completed instantly)
Loving (Kisses, strokes)	Task-oriented (Activity strictly task-limited)
Large skin area covered (Whole child)	Small skin area covered (e.g., size of one finger print)
Cheerful (Light, playful; "Whee . . . look at these great designs we can make on you!")	Sober (Measured, serious; "Now we must do it this way.")

Child:

Familiar, intimate	Estranged
Experimenting	Constricted
Messy	Finicky

Powdering

Material: Small container of baby powder

Procedure: Adult puts powder on child

Adult: *A*	*B*
Enjoying (Really gets into it, "This is fun!")	Disgust (Minimal participation with powder . . . "Yuk!"; or no involvement, refusal)
Engaged (Highly involved—powder may be on both of them—much chatter)	Aloof (Task completed at arm's length and/or in silence)
Sensuous ("This feels good")	Intellectual
Slow (Task takes long time to complete)	Fast (Task completed instantly)
Loving (Kisses, strokes)	Task-oriented (Activity strictly task-limited)
Large skin area covered (Whole child)	Small skin area covered (e.g., size of one finger print)
Intimate area powdered (Toes, feet, tummy, face)	Impersonal area powdered (Back of hand, knee, arm)
Generous amount of powder (Handful[s])	Skimpy amount of powder (Few grains used, area carefully circumscribed)
Disregarding mess (All over everything)	Finicky

Human being (Great empathy with person being powdered)	Inanimate object (Powdering a piece of furniture would be no different)
Positive experience (Powder used in loving, friendly, esteem-enhancing manner)	Negative experience (Powder used in anger, punitively, or in demeaning manner)
Cheerful (Light, playful; "Whee . . . look at these great designs we can make on you!")	Sober (Measured, serious; "Now we must do it this way")

Child:

Sensuous	Indifferent
Cheerful	Stolid or sad
Vocal	Silent

Lap

Material: None

Procedure: Adult takes child on lap, talks and plays with child

Adult: A	B
Positions child comfortably	Positions child uncomfortably
Vocalizes pleasantly	Vocalizes unpleasantly or not at all
Affectionate	Distant
Calm, placid	Anxious
Appropriate degree of restraining	Letting go or clinging

Child:

Close to adult	Arching away
Relaxed	Stiff or tense
Calm	Overactive, fidgety, jumpy
Participating	Not participating

Singing

Material: None

Procedure: Adult sings a lullabye to child

Adult: A	B

Tender facial expression	Facial expression lacking feeling
Tender manner	Harsh manner
Tone and rhythm adapted to child	Tone and rhythm not adapted to child
Delighted	Irritated
Eye contact	Eye contact avoided
Appropriate body contact (e.g., personal, intimate, warm, cuddling, rhythmical, etc.)	Inappropriate body contact (e.g., impersonal, distant, cold, mechanical, awkward, jerky, etc.)

Child:

Close	Distant
Snuggling	Aloof
Soothed	Pained

"This little piggy"[1]

Material: None

Procedure: Adult removes child's sock from one foot then plays on child's toes, "This little piggy went to market . . . this little piggy stayed home . . ."

Adult:	*A*	*B*
	Affectionate	Cold, remote
	Rewarding (e.g., "Yum, yum . . . what yummy toes you have!")	Punishing (e.g., "Yuk! These stink. I don't want to have anything to do with stinking feet.")
	Imaginative (e.g., "This little piggy named Johnny went down to the A & P to buy some . . . let's see . . .what do you especially like? . . . to buy some . . . oh yea . . . some poptarts . . .")	Task-bound (e.g., "This little piggy . . . and this little . . . that makes only four. But there are five toes. Something is wrong. I'll have to count again.")

M & Ms

Material: Envelope, containing handful of chocolate (*not* peanut) M & Ms

Procedure: Adult and child feed M & Ms to each other

Adult:	*A*	*B*
	Alive	Flat
	Giving	Withholding
	Imaginative (e.g., "First let's make a face on your tummy with them")	Constricted (e.g., "M & Ms are chocolate-covered candy")

Child:

Active	Passive
Giving	Withholding

Leave[2]

Material: None

Procedure: Adult leaves room without child, for three minutes

Adult:	*A*	*B*
	Close and empathetic ("I know how you hate it when I do this but I'll be back")	Distant and unempathetic ("Bet you can't wait for me to get out of here")
	Imaginative ("I'm going to go out and find you some extra yummy thing to suck")	Constricted ("It says here I must leave")
	Appropriate length of absence	Absence unduly long or unduly short
	Comfortable, relaxed	Anxious, tense
	Tolerates child's "failure" to stay	Intolerant of child's "failure" to stay

Child:		
	Aware of adult's departure	Unaware of adult's departure
	Untroubled	Tense
	Alert	Withdrawn
	Forgiving	Enraged
	Calm	Overactive
	Creative	Numb, "Frozen"

Alertness
Textures

Material: Three 8½" x 11" cardboard pages. Each page contains three swatches of different textures (some rough, some smooth, some soft, some hard, etc.)

Procedure: Adult asks child, "Which is rougher?" "Which is harder?" "Which is bumpier?"

Adult:	*A*	*B*
	Questions clearly enunciated	Questions hard to grasp
	Questions carefully elaborated to meet child's capacity	Questions eleborated beyond or below child's capacity

Similar-Different

Material: Pattern Book I. Four 8½″ x 11″ cardboard pages of three patterns (2″ x 2″ each). Two patterns are similar. One is different. Placement with respect to one another varies from page to page.

Procedure: Adult turns pages of pattern book asking child, "Which two are alike?" "Which is different?"

Reading

Material: Book of children's verses

Procedure: Adult reads to child

Adult:	A	B
	Chooses appropriate rhyme	Chooses inappropriate rhyme
	Attempts to make rhyme interesting to child	Does not attempt to make rhyme interesting to child
	Prefers body contact (e.g., holds child on lap)	Minimum body contact
	Musical voice	Dull voice
	Goes beyond limits of rhyme	Confined to rhyme
	Gives consideration to child's ability to comprehend	Reads in such a way that child is likely not to comprehend
Child:		
	Enjoying body contact	Disliking body contact
	Interested in illustrations	Uninterested in illustrations

Flash Cards III

Material: Nine cards showing action pictures of children in different feeling states (e.g., angry, frightened, happy, etc.)

Procedure: Adult shows cards to child one at a time, saying, "What can you tell me about that little girl/boy?"

Adult:	A	B
	Facilitates child's awareness	Impedes child's awareness or is indifferent to it
	Holds cards appropriately for child's position and eye level	Holds cards inappropriately
	Expectations of child's ability are realistic	Expectations of child's ability are unrealistic
Child:		
	Recognizes some feeling states	Generally fails to recognize feeling states

Mirror

Material: One large mirror, 10″ x 15″ or larger

Procedure: Show child his reflection in mirror

Adult:	A	B
	Facilitates child's recognizing reflection	Hinders child's recognizing reflection
	Holds mirror appropriately for child's position and eye level	Holds mirror inappropriately
	Expectations of child's ability are realistic	Expectations of child's ability are unrealistic
Child:		
	Smiling	Nonreacting
	Vocalizing	Silent
	Involved with reflection	Avoids glancing at reflection

"Where Is Kitty?"

Material: Three small pasteboard boxes and a small toy cat

Procedure: Lining up the three small boxes, adult hides cat under one box, then, taking child's hands in his/her own, counts to ten and says, "Where is the kitty?"

Adult:	A	B
	Counts at appropriate speed	Counts too fast or too slow
	Encouraging ("I'll bet you can find it")	Discouraging ("I'll bet you won't do this right")
	Expectations of child are realistic	Expectations of child are unrealistic
Child:		
	Appropriate response to question	Inappropriate response to question
	Attentive	Distracted
	Curious	Indifferent

Direction
Doll Caretaking

Material: One rubber doll with moveable limbs, one small wooden doll bed, one doll's cup, and one doll's handkerchief

Procedure: Adult asks child to (a) blow Dolly's nose, (b) give Dolly a drink, (c) put Dolly to bed, and (d) talk to Dolly

Adult:	A	B
	Appropriate kind and degree of guiding, limiting, setting expectations, etc. (e.g., "Here, I can see you're having some trouble making her legs bend. Let's see if I can help you . . .")	Inappropriate kind and degree of guiding, limiting, setting expectations, etc. (e.g., "*I'm* going to do it" or "That's *your* thing to do. I can't help you. You'll have to figure it out.")
	Tolerant (may be empathetic) at failure	Intolerant (may be antagonistic) at failure
Child:		
	Appropriate response to direction	Inappropriate response to direction:
	Attentive to direction	(A) Inattentive to requests
	Tries to follow requests	(B) Rejects requests ("No, all by myself," "*I* can do it!")
		(C) Demands that adult should take over ("I *can't!*" "*You* do it")
	Uses imagination	Uses minimal imagination

Reading[3]

Material: Book of children's verses

Procedure: Adult reads to child, asks child to repeat phrase by phrase, line by line

Adult:	A	B
	Chooses appropriate rhyme	Chooses inappropriate rhyme
	Body contact (e.g., holds child on lap)	Minimum body contact
	Eye contact	Minimum eye contact
	Musical voice	Dull voice
	Waits for child to repeat	Impatient, does not wait till child is ready to respond
	In reading, gives consideration to child's ability to comprehend	Reads in such a way that child is likely not to comprehend

Child:

Cooperative	Resistant
After completion, comments, asks questions	After completion, silent
Desiring more rhymes	Glad rhyme is ended

Teach

Material: None

Procedure: Adult teaches child something he or she doesn't know

Adult:	A	B
	Productive	Unproductive (cannot think of something to teach)
	Enjoying	Disliking
	Lively	Dull
	Chooses simple task	Chooses complex task
	Task age appropriate	Task appropriate to older or younger children

Musical Instrument III

Material: Xylophone and two sticks

Procedure: Adult composes a quick tune on xylophone with sticks, then tells child to compose a tune

Adult:	A	B
	Appropriate kind and degree of limiting, setting of expectations, guiding and allowing for child's initiative ("That's how one makes a tune. Now you make one you like")	Inappropriate kind and degree of guiding, limiting, setting of expectations, etc. ("That sounded too jumpy. Do it over till you get it right"; "I'll teach you a real nice piece"; "You go ahead. I don't need to show you")

Child:		
	Attentive to directions. Tries to follows adult's procedure, then invents his/her own	Inattentive to direction. Rejects being shown ("I don't need help" or "I can do it alone!")
		Demands that adult should go on playing ("You got to do it for me")

Whispered Instructions

Material: None

Procedure: Out of child's line of vision, adult whispers one simple instruction for child to carry out

Adult:	*A*	*B*
	Clear communication	Unclear communication
	Realistic expectations	Expectations too high or too low
	Rewarding	Punishing
Child:		
	Cooperative	Uncooperative (resistant)
	Attempts to carry out assigned task	Does not attempt to carry out task
	Sticks to task till completed	Begins task, dawdles, does not complete

Familiar game[4]

Material: None

Procedure: Adult plays game with child which both know

Child:	*A*	*B*
	Anticipates directions	Does not anticipate directions
	Attempts to participate	No attempt to participate
	Participates in a friendly way	Participates in a forced manner
	Gets excited	Lethargic

Obeying Simple Commands[5]

Material: One chair, one pencil, one box, one door that can be opened and/or closed by child (all put in place before session begins)

Procedure: Adult gives child three instructions, not allowing child to carry them out until the whole set has been repeated twice

Adult:	*A*	*B*
	Appropriate kind and degree of guiding, limiting, setting expectations, etc.	Inappropriate kind and degree of guiding, limiting, setting of expectations, etc.
	Directions clearly given	Lack of clarity of directions
	Directions firmly given	Lack of firmness of directions
	Attentive to child's effort	Indifferent to child's effort
	Enforces child's success by acknowledgement	Unresponsive to child's success

Child:

Attentive	Inattentive
Eager to please	Indifferent to adult
Friendly response to direction	Negative response to direction
Attempts to carry out assigned tasks	Does not attempt to carry out assigned tasks

Playfulness
Bunting

Material: None

Procedure: Adult and child "bunt" foreheads together

Adult:	A	B
	Patient in helping child approach him/her	Impatient in showing child how
	Concerned that child should do what he/she does	Indifferent to whether or not child replicates what adult does
	Movement attuned to child	Not attuned to child's movement
	Cheerful	
	Much physical contact	Gloomy
	Eye contact	Little physical contact
	Goes beyond the task (playfully)	Minimal eye contact
	Careful	Task-limited
		Careless

Child:

Happily tries to approach adult	Remains passive, motionless
Tries to "copy" adult	Makes no effort to copy adult
Laughing	Crying
Encouraging adult	Discouraging adult
Body relaxed	Body tense

M&Ms

Material: Envelope containing handful of chocolate (*not* peanut) M&Ms

Procedure: Adult and child feed M&Ms to each other

Adult:	A	B
	Imaginative ("Here's a cream puff . . . and a chocolate ice cream cone . . . and popcorn . . .")	Reality bound ("M&Ms are chocolate-covered candy")
	Alive	Flat

Imaginative ("First let's make your face with the M&Ms")	Sober (Impersonal)
Giving	Withholding

Child:

Joyful	Serious
Trusting	Apprehensive
Moving	Stiff

Squeaky Animals

Material: 2 small squeaky animals

Procedure: Adult and child each takes one squeaky animal. Have squeaky animals "play" together

Adult:	A	B
	Pleasurable animal play (". . . and a little kiss on your nose, and a little tail wag here behind your ear . . . and now I'm going to go hopping up your chest and onto your shoulder, hop . . . hop . . . hop")	Animal play used to express unresolved conflict (". . . and here I come to bite you for all the times you were so mean to me")
	Free	Constricted
	Light, graceful (see above)	Heavy ("What are these dogs made of? Rubber. That's right. Now how do you spell rubber?"

Child:

	Trusting	Fearful, resistant, unsure
	Happy, animated, turned-on	Listless

Piggyback ride

Material: None

Procedure: Adult gives child a piggyback ride

Adult:	A	B
	Great participation	Refusal to participate
	Pleasure-focused	Task-focused
	Varying ("Now you give *me* a ride")	Programmed ("No. That's not how we do it")

Whimsical ("Ready for the takeoff? Vroom!")	Serious (Your legs have to be on my shoulders just like this")
Unlimited ("Let's do that some more, shall we?")	Limited ("Only around the room two times. No more")

Child:

Trusting	Fearful
Wanting to prolong	Wanting to discontinue
Calm	Restless, jittery
Happy	Sad or cheerless or discontented

Hats

Material: Box of dress-up hats, all kinds, for all ages, and for both sexes

Procedure: Adult and child dress each other up with hats

Adult: A	B
Joyful	Serious
Rewarding (e.g., "You look so pretty in this hat")	Punitive (e.g., "That hat makes you look even uglier than the other hats do")
Personal (e.g., "Red's always been your greatest color")	Impersonal (e.g., "Pink hats are for girls")
Slow	Fast
"In tune" with child (e.g., "Come and let me show you in the mirror")	Not "in tune" with child (e.g., has no awareness that child cannot see hats and/or is bored)
Cooperating, sharing, exchanging	Dictatorial
Treats child as human being	Treats child as inanimate object
Positive experience ("Now I can really see those lovely eyes!")	Negative experience ("That hat makes you look even fatter")
Free use of fantasy ("This is my fly-away hat . . . look at me fly")	Reality-Bound ("Now you can see that's *two* hats. Put only *one* on")
Sex roles fluid ("Hello, Mr. Milkman [to girl]")	Sex roles limited ("That's no hat for a boy")
Imaginative ("A green dress just made for butterflies in the springtime")	Dry, pedantic ("A green hat for your green dress")
Age fluid ("How's my leetle baby?)	Age limited ("That's a silly hat for a big kid like you")

Child:

Animated	Disinterested
Engaged	Withdrawn
Spontaneous	Constricted
Imaginative	Unimaginative

Pat-a-cake

Material: None

Procedure: Adult plays "Pat-a-cake" with child

Adult: A   B

A	B
Enjoying	Disgusted
Cheerful	Sober
Loose	Neat (Pat-a-cake is carefully circumscribed and punctuated)
All of palms and fingers touch child's	Gingerly touches child's hands
Involved (responsive to child)	Adult does "his/her own thing"
Treats child as human being	Treats child as inanimate object
Imaginative ("Patty cake, patty cake . . . French Pastry Man . . . and put it in the microwave oven for my hungry pal Robert and me")	Reality bound ("That's not a 'B'. This is a 'B' ")
Lively tone of voice, manner	Flat tone of voice, manner, monotonous recitation
Joint undertaking	One-way endeavor

Child:

Complying	Resisting
Palm and all fingers touch adult's	Gingerly touching adult's hands

---

Peek-A-Boo

Material: None

Procedure: Adult plays peek-a-boo with child

Adult: A   B

A	B
Enjoying	Disgusted
Frivolous	Sober
Slow	Fast

Joint undertaking (Alternately or simultaneously hides own and child's face)	Isolating (hides own face only)
Loose (Peek-a-boo is played all over room and in all positions)	Pedantic (Peek-a-boo is carefully circumscribed and punctuated)
Intimate	Impersonal
Treats child as human being	Treats child as inanimate object
Turned-on	Disinterested
Alive (musical tone of voice, lively manner)	Flat (flat tone of voice, manner)
Fantasy	Reality bound
Expansive	Constricted
Age fluid	Age limited
Boisterous	Silent
Much physical contact	Little physical contact
Repeated eye contact	Eye contact rare
Extends game beyond task requirement	Task-limited

Child:

Trusting	Apprehensive
Enthusiastic	Flat
Active	Resisting
Encouraging adult	Discouraging adult
Body relaxed	Body tense

Tickling

Material: None

Procedure: Adult gently tickles child

Adult: A	B
Heeds request for gentleness	Tickling becomes rough
Kind, loving expression	Displays aggressive quality of game

Child:

Complaint	Resistant
Joyful	Serious
Trusting	Frightened

Singing

Material: None

Procedure: Adult and child sing a song together

Adult:	A	B
	Pleasure-focused	Task-focused
	Whimsical	Reality-bound
	Humorous ("Pop Goes the Weasel")	Serious ("Now I Lay Me Down to Sleep")
	Varied	Predictable, pedantic
	Enjoying ("Isn't this fun?")	Suffering ("I hate to sing")
	Refers to child ("My Jane's the sweetest cupcake; / There's icing on her knee, / And every time I sniff her (sniff, sniff) / I'm a lucky honey bee")	Impersonal ("Hi diddle diddle, the cat and the fiddle, the cow jumped over the moon . . .")
	Tender manner	Harsh manner
	Empathetic to child's voice	Unempathetic to child's voice
	Delighted	Irritated
	Facial expression appropriate	Facial expression inappropriate
	Repeated eye contact	Eye contact rare
	Appropriate body contact (e.g., personal, intimate, warm, cuddling, rhythmical, etc.)	Inappropriate body contact (e.g., impersonal, distant, cold, mechanical, awkward, jerky, etc.)

Child:		
	Close	Distant
	Snuggling	Aloof
	Soothed	Pained
	Active	Passive, withdrawn
	Compliant	Apprehensive

Familiar Game[6]

Material: None

Procedure: Adult plays game with child which both know

Adult:	A	B
	Cheerful	Serious
	Imaginative	Unimaginative
	Good natured	Irritable
	Casual	Intense

Child:

Joyful	Low mood
Trusting	Apprehensive
Vocal	Silent
Body moving	Body still
Amused	Sullen
Gets excited	Lethargic
Awake	Dazed

"This Little Piggy"[7]

Material: None

Procedure: Adult plays "This Little Piggy Went to Market" on child's toes (one foot)

Adult: A	B
Sensitive to child's mood	Insensitive to child's mood
Kind	Rough
Imaginative	Rigid, pedantic

Child:

Compliant	Objecting
Joyful	Serious
Trusting	Apprehensive
Moving	Stiff
Vocal	Silent

Bouncing

Material: None

Procedure: Adult bounces child on adult's knees

Adult: A	B
Positions child skillfully	Positions child awkwardly
Expectations of child are appropriate	Expectations of child are inappropriate
Careful	Careless
Cheerful	Serious
Appropriate persevering	Inappropriate persevering (Too much or gives up)

Child:

Eager	Dispirited
Goodnatured	Cranky
Trusting	Anxious
Self-confident	Showing self-doubt

Imitation
Hand Washing

Material: 2 packages of premoistened paper towelettes

Procedure: Adult gives one package to child, keeps one for him/herself. Removes towelette from package and begins to "wash" own hands with it, first both hands, then concentrates on one. Adult says, "I wash *my* hands *this* way. Try to wash yours like I do"

Adult:	A	B
	Patient in helping child to imitate	Impatient in helping child to imitate
	Nonverbal modeling clear, consistent	Nonverbal modeling confusing, inconsistent
	Verbal explanations clear, understandable ("See how I first do both hands and then only one")	Verbal explanations "adult," not easily understandable
	Makes sure that child knows what is expected	Does not pay attention to whether child understands what is expected
	Concerned with child's attempts at imitation	Indifferent to child's attempts at imitation
	Tolerates or encourages occasional deviation ("Now that's another way to do it")	Firmly discourages any deviation from the adult's activity

Child:		
	Readily attempts to imitate	Attempts to imitate after considerable delay
	Imitates	Does not imitate
	Responsive to adult's help (suggestions)	Disregards adult's help (suggestions)
	At ease when deviating from adult's model	Anxious when deviating from adult's model
	Happy at successful imitation	Indifferent to successful imitation
	Calm, composed at failure	Irritated, complaining, aggressive at failure

Doll, Imitates Adult's Caretaking

Material: 1 small doll with flexible limbs, bottle, washcloth

Procedure: Adult takes care of doll in a variety of ways (e.g., feeding, washing), then hands doll to child saying, "Now *you* do the same things for Dolly"

Adult:	A	B
	Patient in helping child copy him/her	Impatient in showing child how, making child understand
	Concerned that child should do what he/she does	Indifferent to whether or not child replicates
	"In tune" with child's ability to handle the doll	Not "in tune" with child's ability to handle the doll
	Responsive to emotional aspect of caretaking (seen for instance in holding, smiling at doll)	Unresponsive to emotional aspect of caretaking

Child:		
	Follows movement of adult with eyes.	Eyes do not follow adult's movements
	Attempts to imitate	No *attempts* to imitate
	Responsive to emotional aspects of caretaking	Unresponsive to emotional aspects of caretaking

"I Like This One . . ."

Material: Pattern Book. Loose-leaf binder of nine legal-size cardboard pages. On each page there are three abstract designs. Two designs resemble each other in form or color. The third is entirely different. (Placement of the two similar and the different patterns varies from page to page.)

Procedure: Adult turns pages of book pointing to one design on each page and says, "I like *this* one. Which one do *you* like?"

Adult:	A	B
	Preference stated clearly but not suggestively	Preference stressed suggestively
	Interested in child's choices	Indifferent to child's choices
	Allows or encourages deviation ("Yes, that *is* nice")	Covertly or overtly encourages imitative choices ("I think mine is the prettiest")
	Friendly, accepts either high or low proportion of child's imitative choices	Greatly pleased with high proportion of child's imitative choices

Child:

Chooses most but not all patterns chosen by adult	Chooses only patterns chosen by adult, chooses no pattern chosen by adult
Interested in adult's choices	Indifferent to adult's choices

Tower

Material: Building blocks

Procedure: Adult copies design from model in Card A, then says to child, "Can you build one like mine?"

Adult: A	B
Facilitates child's imitation if needed ("See how I put the big one on the bottom . . . like *this*")	Provides no assistance although help is needed
Encourages child's own completion of the task	Helps child too early and/or too much
Allows (or encourages) deviation (e.g., "That's different . . . but it's beautiful")	Intolerant of (irritated about) child's deviation ("Can't you do it right?")

Child:	
Makes serious effort to copy adult's model	Does not attempt to copy adult's model
Accepts, asks for adult's help when help is needed	Accepts, asks for adult's help when help is not needed
Happy at completed imitation	Indifferent to completed imitation
Adds blocks from own to adult's structure	Adds blocks from adult's to own structure
Moves completed structure to adult's side	Keeps structure on own side

Vocalization I

Material: Card listing basic sounds

Procedure: Adult models sounds on card one at a time and asks child to repeat the sound

Adult: A	B
Patient in helping child	Impatient in helping child
Adapts to child's ability to hear (perceive) sounds	Pronounces sounds too fast, pronounces sounds too softly

Joyful, game-like intonation	Serious or abrupt intonation
Tolerant of child's deviation	Intolerant of child's deviation

Stress Tolerance
Leave[8]

Material: None

Procedure: Adult leaves room without child for three minutes

Adult:

A	B
Preparation (e.g., "Johnny, I'm going to step out of the room for a few minutes. While I'm gone you can play with my key chain or do whatever you like")	Preparation (*no* preparation or superfluous amount of preparation, e.g., "I'm afraid I have to leave you. I don't want to but on this card they're making me. But I guess I don't really have to if you don't want me to . . .")
Tender gesture or words	
Departure (e.g., "Bye bye," "I'll be back," "See you in three minutes")	Departure (Abrupt leaving, e.g., "You *sure* you're going to be all right now? Tell Mommy if you don't think you *will* be . . .")
Alive	Flat
Comfortable, relaxed	Anxious, tense
Tolerates child's "failure" (i.e., following adult)	Intolerant of child's "failure"
Return (Three minutes later) (Rewarding: "Oh, I can see you turned yourself around while I was gone. How did you do that? Show *me* that trick")	Return (Under three minutes, over three minutes) (Punitive: "What bad thing did you do now?") (Symbiotic: "Tell Mommy how much you missed her;" or, "Tell Mommy everything you did while she was gone")

Child:

Aware of adult's departure	Unaware of adult's departure
Remains in room and occupies self ("Thinks," talks to self, explores)	Runs after parent, cries
Alert	Withdrawn or "trance" state
Forgiving	Enraged, shows aggression
Calm	Overactive, restless

Hampered Movement

Material: One large-size bandana

Procedure: Adult joins one leg of his/hers to one leg of child by means of bandana, then tells child, "Now take me for a walk"

Adult: A   B

　　　　Careful   Careless
　　　　Supportive   Destructive, inhibiting
　　　　Stops when appropriate   Prolongs unduly or stops too
　　　　　　　　　　　　　　　　　　　　　　　　　　　soon

Child:

　　　　Confident   Bewildered
　　　　Happy   Unhappy
　　　　Patient   Impatient
　　　　Forgiving   Angry
　　　　Persevering   Giving up
　　　　Trusting   Apprehensive
　　　　Calm   Irritated

Unattainable Candies

Material: One small, plastic, "child-proof" medicine bottle containing tiny, brightly colored candies

Procedure: Adult places candy-filled unopenable bottle in front of child, saying, "If you can get it open you may have some"

Adult: A   B

　　　　Supportive   Destructive
　　　　Rewarding   Punishing
　　　　Stops when appropriate   Prolongs unduly or stops too
　　　　　　　　　　　　　　　　　　　　　　　　　　　soon

Child:

　　　　Confident   Bewildered
　　　　Happy   Sad
　　　　Forgiving   Angry
　　　　Persevering   Giving up
　　　　Trusting   Apprehensive
　　　　Calm   Irritated

Puzzle I

Material: Six-piece wooden puzzle (somewhat too complex for this age level)

Procedure: Adult removes puzzle pieces and frame from envelope

Adult:	A	B
	"In tune" with child	Not "in tune" with child
	Stops when appropriate	Prolongs unduly or stops too soon
	Provides help where appropriate (e.g., "Maybe it'll help you if you know that all the red pieces go down here and all the blue up there . . .")	Provides inappropriate help (e.g., assists too early or fails to assist at all: "Here, I'll do it, you can watch"; "You'll just have to learn to figure things out for yourself more")

Child:		
	Confident	Bewildered
	Happy	Unhappy
	Forgiving	Angry
	Persevering	Giving up
	Trusting	Apprehensive
	Calm	Irritated

Jack-in-the-Box I

Material: Small Jack-in-the-box. *Note:* Box should be of the kind which cannot be easily opened

Procedure: Adult opens box to allow Jack to pop up, then closes box in such a way that child cannot open it

Adult:	A	B
	Supportive	Destructive
	Rewarding	Punishing
	Stops when appropriate	Prolongs unduly or stops too soon

Child:		
	Confident	Bewildered
	Happy	Unhappy
	Forgiving	Angry
	Persevering	Giving up too soon
	Trusting	Apprehensive
	Calm	Irritated

NOTES

[1] For this task no task-specific behaviors for the child are listed. If task-specific behaviors are not listed for child and/or adult, the General Lists of Describing Behavior should be consulted. This task reveals also Playfulness.

[2] Reveals also Stress Tolerance.

[3] Reveals also Imitation.

[4] Reveals also Playfulness.

[5] Adapted from the Stanford-Binet Intelligence Scale, Form L-M, Level II-6 (age 2 years, 6 months). Boston: Houghton Mifflin, 1960.

[6] Reveals also Direction.

[7] Reveals also Attachment.

[8] Reveals also Attachment.

Two Examples
Illustrating The MIM Method

(From the files of the Theraplay Institute, Chicago)

The method was applied by one observer in recording and analyzing the interaction of two mother-child pairs.

DIMENSION: Playfulness
TASK: Dogs ("Make the two dogs play together")
MATERIAL: Instruction card in envelope and two toy dogs

CASE 1
Duration: 1 min. 25 sec.

MOTHER		MARIA
It says here we're supposed to make the two dogs play together . . .	<	
	<	*(Snatches envelope)* Here, let me see!
(Struggles for envelope and retrieves it)	⟶ ⟵ ⟶	
Here, here is your dog	⟶ ∪	

                                                        (*Takes it and squeaks it*)

and here is mine
(*pursues child's dog with
her's*)

Now . . . make yours
jump like this . . .   (*examines dog*)

What kind of dog would
you say this is?   (*ignores question*)

                                   (*vigorously jumps dog at*
                BC   *mother's dog*)

MOTHER   MARIA

What kind?

Tell me what kind of   I don't know
dog this is Maria

Sure you know

Remember your *Dogs of*   Huh?
the World book?

Well then count how
many spots on him

                                   (*Jumps off chair and*
                                   hops around room with dog
                                   . . .

                                   finally setting it on
                                   mother's shoulder)
                BC

Oh. Now you're just
being silly, Maria

(*Brushes her dog and
her hand away*)

                                 Mom?
                BC

Shh! Maria. We're
playing now   BC

CASE 2
Duration: 1 min. 30 sec.

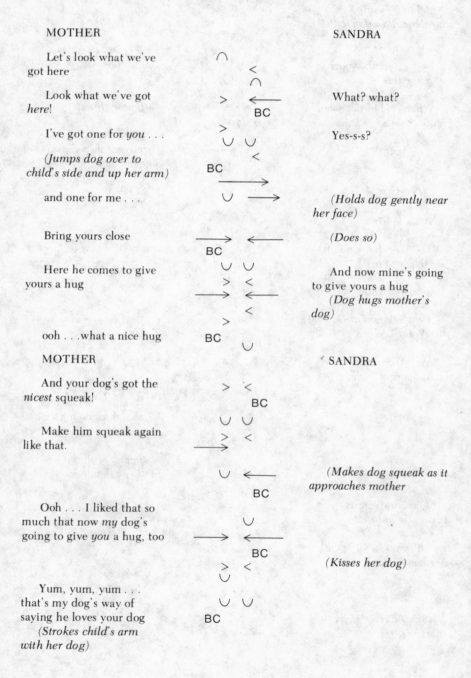

MOTHER

Let's look what we've got here

Look what we've got *here!*

I've got one for *you* . . .

(Jumps dog over to child's side and up her arm)

and one for me . . .

Bring yours close

Here he comes to give yours a hug

ooh . . . what a nice hug

MOTHER

And your dog's got the *nicest* squeak!

Make him squeak again like that.

Ooh . . . I liked that so much that now *my* dog's going to give *you* a hug, too

Yum, yum, yum . . . that's my dog's way of saying he loves your dog
(Strokes child's arm with her dog)

SANDRA

What? what?

Yes-s-s?

(Holds dog gently near her face)

(Does so)

And now mine's going to give yours a hug
(Dog hugs mother's dog)

SANDRA

(Makes dog squeak as it approaches mother

(Kisses her dog)

A COMPARISON OF THE TWO CASES
—ONE TASK NONVERBAL INTERACTIONS[1]

Case 1 (1 min. 25 sec.)   Case 2 (1 min. 30 sec.)

POSITIVE BEHAVIORS

3	Child moves toward mother	3
2	Mother moves toward child	3
0	Mother and child move toward each other	2
2	Child looks at mother	3
3	Mother looks at child	3
1	Mother and child look at each other	4
2	Child smiles at mother	3
1	Mother smiles at child	3
0	Mother and child smile at each other	3
3	Child initiates body contact	4
1	Mother initiates body contact	4
Total 18		35

NEGATIVE BEHAVIORS

3	Child serious face	1
5	Mother serious face	1
3	Mother frowns at child	0
2	Child frowns at mother	0
6	Mother moves away from child	0
2	Child moves away from mother	1
Total 21		3

CASE 1. DOGS

Even on a task as highly playful as this one, this mother manages to be the school teacher. When she is not questioning Maria's intellect (e.g., "What kind of dog would you say this is?" "What kind?" "Tell me what kind of dog this is, Maria." "Sure you know." "Remember, your *Dogs of the World* book?" etc.), she is directing her actions (e.g., ". . . Now make yours jump like this," ". . . count how many spots on him"). Perhaps motivated by her own stance of "good girl" conformity (e.g., "It says here we're supposed to . . . ") she allows Maria little pleasure or spontaneity (e.g., "Oh, now you're just being silly, Maria," "Shh Maria, we're playing now"). Even her nonverbal behavior is heavy-handed and disapproving. There is little warmth in the interaction. The signs of positive behaviors are offset by signs of negative behaviors.

As though having momentarily forgotten with whom she is dealing, Maria reacts to this new playful task with initial eagerness ("Here, let me see"), then lapses into helplessness punctuated by occasional hostile or demanding outbursts (ignores mother's question, jumps at mother's dog, "I don't know," "Huh?", jumps off chair and places dog on mother's shoulder).

Even nonverbally it is Maria who has to initiate what little playful contact there is (moving toward, smiling at, imitating body contact eight times compared to the mother displaying these behaviors four times).

Interactions with one another and incidents of play are minimal. The perception each has of the other is doomed to imperil their relationship—the mother's in having a child who is too playful and not enough of a "student"; the child in having an overdirecting, play-withholding mother. Their reciprocal, nonverbal interactions elaborate the story: mother and child approach each other, no times; mother and child look at each other, once; and mother and child smile at each other, never.

In summary, the disappointment and bitterness already present between this mother and her preschool child could easily develop into open hostility—repressive efforts from the parent, who encounters obstinacy of the child. Long before adolescence there may be troubled times between them. Prompt intervention, directed to making their lives together more enjoyable, should reduce excessive strains between them later.

CASE 2. DOGS

Presented with the opportunity to do so, this mother and her daughter *play*. Physically, vigorously, affectionately, and imaginatively, they engage each other in activities which both of them find pleasurable. There is nothing distant, intellectual, ambitious, or competitive about them. There are no pretentions; and love (and playfulness) are not conditional upon conformity or performance. What could pertain only to the dogs is specifically directed to one another (e.g., "Here he comes for a hug," "Ooh, what a nice hug," "Now my dog's going to give *you* a hug too," etc.)

Not only is their interaction playful and loving verbally (mother's in particular)—but nonverbally as well. Thus Sandra and her mother move toward, look at, smile at, and touch each other a total of seventeen times (as compared with Maria and her mother who do so only five times in an approximately equal length of time). By the same token, although Maria and her mother frown at, and move away, from one another a total of thirteen times, Sandra and her mother do so only once.

Judging from their interaction on this one task it can safely be assumed that, beyond her present level of performance, little is expected of Sandra. This is not to say that her mother discourages her progress, only that she feels most comfortable and competent as mother in a climate of mutual affection. For now, this much intimacy meets the needs of both. Later on, however, when Sandra moves toward autonomy some real struggles may develop. With this eventuality in mind, it may be helpful if, just to "take the heat off," mother were to find herself some outside interests—a possibility she had not yet considered.

NOTE

[1] Modifiers which would have further characterized the observed behavior were not recorded. Thus all incidents of "looking at" and "body contact" were computed as Positive Behaviors although the behavior may have had negative undertones.

Subject Index

Adolescence:
  identification changing in, 16-17
  "omnipotentiality" of, 106
  parent's death in, 59
  (*See also* Youth movements)
Affection, parental, 25-27
  and identification of child, 28, 159-160, 200-201, 233
  impermanence of, 180
  to newborn, 26

Childrearing:
  in communes, 164-179
  family care compared with kibbutz care, 188-225
  in kibbutz, 187-190
  (*See also* Parent-child interaction)
Communes, 131
  adult personality characteristics in, 179-182
  apocalyptic views in, 149
  child autonomy in, 165-166
  childbirth in, 172-173
  children's characteristics in, 166-167, 178-179
  childrearing in, 164-179
  compared with communities, 132-134
  compared with nuclear family, 182
  compared with Wandervogel, 5, 6
  direction, parental, 25-28
  Farm, The, 147-148, 167
  Findhorn, 149
  Haven, 134-136
  Heathcote, 135
  identification in, 157, 179
  identification reversal reinforced, 163

impermanence of affection, 180
leaders' characteristics, 135, 146, 154-159
life history of two members, 136-146
motives for joining, 134, 149-151
New Age, 157
number of, 134
personality changes occurring in, 151-152
Pharos, 146-149
rejection of commitments, 153
rituals in, 173
Rockridge, 179
self-development, 151-152
"space", 152
stability of group characteristics, 181
Twin Oaks, 134, 147, 149, 172
Types of, 134-135, 147-148, 182
Values in, 147-149
Yeah God, 167, 172
(*See also* Youth movement; *Wandervogel*)
Counterculture, 8
  characteristics of persons belonging to, 178-182
  concept of "space" in, 136, 152, 162, 163
  identification in members of, 154, 157
  (*See also* Communes; Youth movement; Wandervogel)

Dedication gesture, 222-223
Direction, parental, 20, 25
  and identification of child, 27-28, 160-162, 233
  in infancy, 27
  at school age, 27

Dissidence, 1, 8
   in "alienated" students, 10, 11
   in hippie movement, 11-12
   in Wandervogel movement, 9-9
   studies on, 8-12
   transitory in kibbutz, 232
   (*See also* Identification reversal)

Family, in kibbutz vs. city, 190, 226
   value of nuclear family for child, 182
Father,
   authoritarian, 9, 115-117
   changing role of, 79
Fischer, Karl, 3-4, 121

German youth movement (*see* Wan-
      dervogel)

Hoffmann, Hermann, 2-3, 121

Identification, 1
   in adolescence, 16-17
   changed parental social roles and,
      79-80
   with commune leader, 62
   with commune members, 179
   in counterculture, 154, 162
   durability of, in counterculture, 157
   and "healthy omnipotentiality", 106
   imitation distinguished from, 1, 14
   imitation, relevant to, 12-16
   parent authority and, 37-38
   parent characteristics affecting, 159,
      (Fig. 1)
   with parent ego, 87
   with parent humor, 72
   with parent superego, 87
   parent-child interaction and,
      (Fig. 1), 225-226
   parent's perception of child and, 63-
      64, 69, 86, 226
   with peer group in kibbutz, 227
      (Note 4), 232
   with Wandervogel leader, 120, 121,
      129
with Wandervogel members, 129-130
   (*See also* Affection, parental and Di-
      rection, parental)
Identification reversal 1-2
   in commune members, 159-161
   in nuclear family, 54-55
   and persistence of early identifica-
      tions, 153-154

in youth movement members, 129,
      154
   (*See also* Dissidence)
Imitation, 1
   in early childhood, 13-14
   identification distinguished from, 1,
      14
   MIM in study of imitation, 35-38,
      73-74, 220-224
   motivation for, 13-14
   parental characteristics affecting, 20
   parent's perception of child and, 73-
      74
   role in identification, 12-16
   (*See also* Identification)
Interaction, 2

Kibbutz, 187
   childrearing in, 187-189
   competition within, 221
   family care compared to, 188-225
   mother-child attachment in, 215-217
   metapelet (caretaker) in, 187-188
      attitudes of, 220
      compared with mother, 215-216
      role of, 187-190
      parent-child relationship in, 189-
         190, 221
      parent-child separation in, 210-211

Leaders:
   charisma, 156-157
   in commune, 135, 154-158, 163-164
   in Wandervogel, 120-123, 129, 163-
      164

Marschak Interaction Method (MIM),
      19-20
   applications of,
      diagnosis and treatment, 237, 242
      research, 243, 244
      teaching, 242, 243
   interaction situations eliciting:
      attachment, 218-220, 255-262
      choice making, 71-73
      fantasy activity, 193-203
      individual activity of parent and
         child, 33-35, 68-70
      modeling and imitation, 35-38, 73-
         74, 220-224, 275-278
      organizing an environment with
         play things, 203-210
      moral judgement, 90, 93-105

responses to separation, 81-86, 212-218

responses to stress, 4-43, 224-225

procedures:

administration, 239

coding of non-verbal behavior, 240-241

judging procedures, 241

lists for describing behavior, 254-280

symbols for recording non-verbal behavior, 246-249

tape-recording of verbal and vocal expressions, 241

Morality:

development of, 87-90

parental attitudes and child's, 87-106

Oedipal conflict, "dilution of", in kibbutz, 108

Oedipal phase and identification, 15-16, 37-38

Parent-child interaction:

and stress tolerance, 40-41, 74-77, 224-225

and Wandervogel, 112-113

(*See also* Affection, parental; Direction, parental)

Parent's perception of child:

and identification, 83, 84

and parent's response to separation, 82-83

Self-replicating tendency, 36, 141, 177

Separation:

adverse effects of long-time, 80

animal studies on, 81

in Kibbutz, 210-211

MIM in study of, 81-86, 212-218

Stress, 40

MIM in study of, 40-43, 74-77, 224-225

parents' perception of child and child's tolerance of, 74-77

Student activists, father-son relationships and, 10

Superego:

development of, 87-90, 97

identification with parental, 87

Wandervogel, 2

anti-semitism in, 5-6

Blau-Weiss, 6-7

comparison with present-day youth movements, 4-6, 130, 166

dissidence in members of, 166

interviews with previous members, 112-113

Hesse, 5

hippies compared with, 4-6

historical basis for, 2-6, 107

identification in members of, 17, 128-131

leaders in, 5, 121-123

life history of member of, 113-127

Meissner resolutions, 4, 130

parents' attitudes toward, 166, 183 (Note 3)

personality changes occurring in, 128-131, 151-152

underground, anti-Nazi activities by previous members of, 6, 108 (note 4), 184 (note 8)

values, 130

(*See also* Communes; Youth movements)

Youth movements:

father-son relationship and origin of, 10

German (*see* Wandervogel)

Jewish, 6-7

and kibbutz, 7

psychoanalytic view of, 106

sociological view of, 107

traces in adult personality of, 181

(*See also* Communes; *Wandervogel*)

Author Index

Ainsworth, M.D., 81, 82
Becker, G., 121
Berger, B. M., 165, 179
Bettelheim, B., 189
Bowlby, J., 80
Buber-Neumann, M., 118, 124, 125, 146
Call, J. D., 20
Dagdale, R., 55
Deutsch, H., 157
Dilloo, R., 181
Dwight, J. S., 132
Erikson, E.,, 38, 94, 115
Feldman, S. S., 213, 215
Feuer, L. S., 10
Flacks, R., 10, 12
Fourier, 131-132
Freud, A., 40, 97-98, 106-107, 131, 157, 180
Freud, S., 2, 40, 217
Gewirtz, H. B., 189
Gewirtz, J. L., 189
Ginsberg, A., 11
Goldfarb, W., 80
Gorer, G., 38
Haas, K., 181-182
Haley, J., 12
Harlow, F., 81
Hauptmann, G., 4
Hawthorne, N., 132, 133
Hesse, H., 5, 120
Hoffman, M. L., 89
Hurd, G., 181
Kanter, R., 134, 147-148, 153, 156-157

Keniston, K., 8, 10-11, 179-180
Kerouac, J., 11
Kohlberg, L., 88
Kohut, H., 48
Laqueur, W., 6
Lewin, K., 17
Lippit, R., 17
Lorenz, K., 26
Luetkens, Ch., 8-10
Maccoby, E., 213, 215
Mannheim, K., 107
Marschak, M., 19
Mead, M., 38, 72, 78
Mussen, P. H., 89
Nagler, S., 189, 203, 216, 217
Noyes, J. H., 157
Owen, 131-132
Paetel, K. O., 129
Piaget, J., 1-2, 13, 87-91, 93, 96, 98
Pumpian-Mindlin, E., 106-107
Rabin, A., 189
Rapp, G., 131, 157
Redfield, R., 8
Reich, W., 158
Schaefer, E. S., 18-19
Shapira, A., 189
Spitz, R. A., 80
Steiner, R., 127
Toffler, A., 182
Veysey, L., 151, 157, 179
Weber, M., 4, 8, 156
White, R. K., 17
Wyneken, G., 4